ENTERED APR 2 5 2001

The Rhetoric of
First Lady
Hillary Rodham Clinton

**Recent Titles in the
Praeger Series in Political Communication**
Robert E. Denton, Jr., General Editor

World Opinion and the Emerging International Order
Frank Louis Rusciano, with Roberta Fiske-Rusciano, Bosah Ebo, Sigfredo Hernandez, and John Crothers Pollock

Seeing Spots: A Functional Analysis of Presidential Television Advertisements, 1952–1996
William L. Benoit

Political Campaign Communication: Principles and Practices, Fourth Edition
Judith S. Trent and Robert V. Friedenberg

Losing Our Democratic Spirit: Congressional Deliberation and the Dictatorship of Propaganda
Bill Granstaff

Communication Patterns in the Presidential Primaries: A Twentieth-Century Perspective
Kathleen E. Kendall

With Malice Toward All?: The Media and Public Confidence in Democratic Institutions
Patricia Moy and Michael Pfau

Making "Pictures in Our Heads": Government Advertising in Canada
Jonathan W. Rose

Videostyle in Presidential Campaigns: Style and Content of Televised Political Advertising
Lynda L. Kaid

Political Communication Ethics: An Oxymoron?
Robert E. Denton, Jr., editor

Navigating Boundaries: The Rhetoric of Women Governors
Brenda DeVore Marshall and Molly A. Mayhead, editors

Talk of Power, Power of Talk: The 1994 Health Care Reform Debate and Beyond
Michael W. Shelton

When Congress Debates: A Bakhtinian Paradigm
Theodore F. Sheckels

The Rhetoric of First Lady Hillary Rodham Clinton

Crisis Management Discourse

Colleen Elizabeth Kelley

Praeger Series in Political Communication

Westport, Connecticut
London

Library of Congress Cataloging-in-Publication Data

Kelley, Colleen (Colleen E.)
    The rhetoric of First Lady Hillary Rodham Clinton : crisis management discourse / Colleen Elizabeth Kelley.
      p. cm.—(Praeger series in political communication, ISSN 1062–5623)
    Includes bibliographical references and index.
    ISBN 0–275–96695–X (alk. paper)
    1. Clinton, Hillary Rodham—Language. 2. Presidents' spouses—United States—Language—History—20th century. 3. Rhetoric—Political aspects—United States—History—20th century. 4. United States—Politics and government—1993– 5. Communication in politics—United States—History—20th century. 6. Crisis management in government—United States—History—20th century. 7. Clinton, Hillary Rodham—Relations with journalists. 8. Press and politics—United States—History—20th century. I. Title. II. Series.
E887.C55K45   2001
973.929′092—dc21   00–042775

British Library Cataloguing in Publication Data is available.

Copyright © 2001 by Colleen Elizabeth Kelley

All rights reserved. No portion of this book may be reproduced, by any process or technique, without the express written consent of the publisher.

Library of Congress Catalog Card Number: 00–042775
ISBN: 0–275–96695–X
ISSN: 1062–5623

First published in 2001

Praeger Publishers, 88 Post Road West, Westport, CT 06881
An imprint of Greenwood Publishing Group, Inc.
www.praeger.com

Printed in the United States of America

The paper used in this book complies with the
Permanent Paper Standard issued by the National
Information Standards Organization (Z39.48–1984).

10 9 8 7 6 5 4 3 2 1

Copyright Acknowledgment

The author and publisher gratefully acknowledge permission to use the following material:

Excerpts from L.J. Sabato (1991). *Feeding frenzy: How attack journalism has transformed American politics*. New York: Free Press.

To my parents
Arthur Thomas Kelley and Jacqueline Gwenith Kelley
and to my son
John-Daniel Kelley

Contents

Series Foreword *by Robert E. Denton, Jr.*		ix
Acknowledgments		xiii
Introduction		xv
1.	The Historical First Lady	1
2.	Politics and Mediated Realities	25
3.	Mitigating Factors in Press Mediation	65
4.	Crisis Management Rhetoric	95
5.	Crisis Management Styles of First Couples	119
6.	Mini-Scandals to Whitewater: The Early Crisis Management Discourse of Hillary Rodham Clinton	151
7.	Travelgate to Impeachment: The Later Crisis Management Discourse of Hillary Rodham Clinton	181
8.	The Rhetorical Evolution of Hillary Rodham Clinton	217

9.	Rhetorical Strategies of Hillary Rodham Clinton	243
Conclusion		281
Bibliography		285
Index		299

Series Foreword

Those of us from the discipline of communication studies have long believed that communication is prior to all other fields of inquiry. In several other forums I have argued that the essence of politics is "talk" or human interaction.[1] Such interaction may be formal or informal, verbal or nonverbal, public or private, but it is always persuasive, forcing us consciously or subconsciously to interpret, to evaluate, and to act. Communication is the vehicle for human action.

From this perspective, it is not surprising that Aristotle recognized the natural kinship of politics and communication in his writings *Politics* and *Rhetoric*. In the former, he established that humans are "political beings, [who] alone of the animals [are] furnished with the faculty of language."[2] In the latter, he began his systematic analysis of discourse by proclaiming that "rhetorical study, in its strict sense, is concerned with the modes of persuasion."[3] Thus, it was recognized over twenty-three hundred years ago that politics and communication go hand in hand because they are essential parts of human nature.

In 1981, Dan Nimmo and Keith Sanders proclaimed that political communication was an emerging field.[4] Although its origin, as noted, dates back centuries, a "self-consciously cross-disciplinary" focus began in the late 1950s. Thousands of books and articles later, colleges and universities offer a variety of graduate and undergraduate coursework in the area in such diverse departments as communication, mass communication, journalism, political science, and sociology.[5] In Nimmo and Sanders's early assessment, the "key areas of inquiry" included rhetorical analysis, propaganda analysis, attitude change studies, voting studies, government and the news media, functional and systems analyses, technological changes, media technologies, campaign techniques, and research techniques.[6] In a survey of the state of the field in 1983, the same authors and Lynda Kaid found additional, more specific areas of concerns such as the presidency, political polls, public opinion, debates, and advertising.[7] Since the first study, they have also noted a shift away from the rather behavioral approach.

A decade later, Dan Nimmo and David Swanson argued that "political communication has developed some identity as a more or less distinct domain of scholarly work."[8] The scope and concerns of the area have further expanded to include critical theories and cultural studies. Although there is no precise definition, method, or disciplinary home of the area of inquiry, its primary domain comprises the role, processes, and effects of communication within the context of politics broadly defined.

In 1985, the editors of *Political Communication Yearbook: 1984* noted that "more things are happening in the study, teaching, and practice of political communication than can be captured within the space limitations of the relatively few publications available."[9] In addition, they argued that the backgrounds of "those involved in the field [are] so varied and pluralist in outlook and approach, ... it [is] a mistake to adhere slavishly to any set format in shaping the content."[10] More recently, Swanson and Nimmo have called for "ways of overcoming the unhappy consequences of fragmentation within a framework that respects, encourages, and benefits from diverse scholarly commitments, agendas, and approaches."[11]

In agreement with these assessments of the area and with gentle encouragement, in 1988 Praeger established the series entitled "Praeger Series in Political Communication." The series is open to all qualitative and quantitative methodologies as well as contemporary and historical studies. The key to characterizing the studies in the series is the focus on communication variables or activities within a political context or dimension. As of this writing, over seventy volumes have been published and numerous impressive works are forthcoming. Scholars from the disciplines of communication, history, journalism, political science, and sociology have participated in the series.

I am, without shame or modesty, a fan of the series. The joy of serving as its editor is in participating in the dialogue of the field of political communication and in reading the contributors' works. I invite you to join me.

Robert E. Denton, Jr.

NOTES

1. See Robert E. Denton, Jr., *The Symbolic Dimensions of the American Presidency* (Prospect Heights, IL: Waveland Press, 1982); Robert E. Denton, Jr., and Gary Woodward, *Political Communication in America* (New York: Praeger, 1985; 2d ed., 1990); Robert E. Denton, Jr., and Dan Hahn. *Presidential Communication* (New York: Praeger, 1986); and Robert E. Denton Jr., *The Primetime Presidency of Ronald Reagan* (New York: Praeger, 1988).

2. Aristotle, *The Politics of Aristotle*, trans. Ernest Barker (New York: Oxford University Press, 1970), p. 5.

3. Aristotle, *Rhetoric*, trans. W. Rhys Roberts (New York: The Modern Library, 1954), p. 22.

4. Dan Nimmo and Keith Sanders, "Introduction: The Emergence of Political Communication as a Field," in *Handbook of Political Communication*, eds. Dan Nimmo and Keith Sanders (Beverly Hills, CA: Sage, 1981), pp. 11–36.

5. Ibid., p. 15.

6. Ibid., pp. 17–27.

7. Keith Sanders, Lynda Kaid, and Dan Nimmo, eds. *Political Communication Yearbook: 1984* (Carbondale, IL: Southern Illinois University: 1985), pp. 283–308.

8. Dan Nimmo and David Swanson, "The Field of Political Communication: Beyond the Voter Persuasion Paradigm," in *New Directions in Political Communication*, eds. David Swanson and Dan Nimmo (Beverly Hills, CA: Sage, 1990), p. 8.

9. Sanders, Kaid, and Nimmo, *Political Communication Yearbook: 1984*, p. xiv.

10. Ibid.

11. Nimmo and Swanson, "The Field of Political Communication," p. 11.

Acknowledgments

As with any rhetorical act, this book took shape as a discursive response to what I suspected was at best an understated, if not misrepresented or misunderstood, framing of the role that Hillary Rodham Clinton enacted as First Lady during her husband's tenure as president. To that end, I have worked with a distinct yet decidedly diverse audience of readers in mind—those even tangentially interested in my subject who are also willing and able to continue talking about any of the issues discussed herein. I have also worked within the constraints of the situation, not the least of which included its scope as well as the volatility of its chief rhetorical players. Finally, I have worked within my own situational constraints, meaning that I have been living my life as well as writing this book. On occasion, this has been no small feat.

I wish to acknowledge three individuals in particular who facilitated that feat. Trinette Zawadzki has been a cohort for sometime and a friend for even longer. As both, she has been invaluable to me during the writing of this book and I cannot thank her enough. I am also indebted to Michael Miller, whose friendship and professional expertise were instrumental in moving the project ahead while keeping my head on straight as well. Thirdly, I wish to thank Clare Howell for the generosity she evidenced while skillfully indexing my book.

Finally, I want to acknowledge my family and friends who always were interested in what I was doing, my son in particular for keeping Mom grounded, even on tough writing days, with unconditional love.

Introduction

That American presidents have been known to participate in improper relationships with women who were not their wives or tell lies to the American public or engage in other forms of scandalous behavior is nothing new. James Garfield, Grover Cleveland, Woodrow Wilson, Warren G. Harding, Franklin D. Roosevelt, Dwight D. Eisenhower, John F. Kennedy, Lyndon Johnson, and Richard Nixon are only some of the U.S. presidents who were all embroiled in scandal, at one time or another. That American presidents' wives have more often than not been known to stand by their men before, during, and after such crises is also nothing new. Lucretia Garfield, Frances Cleveland, Edith Wilson, Florence Harding, Eleanor Roosevelt, Mamie Eisenhower, Jacqueline Kennedy, Claudia "Lady Bird" Johnson, and Patricia Nixon all played various roles in managing their husbands' scandals.

Sabato (1998) identifies dozens of occasions in the past four decades when the news media have engaged in a feeding frenzy and "gone after a wounded politician like sharks." He continues "The wounds may be self-inflicted, and the politicians may richly deserve their fates, but it is the journalists who take center stage, creating the news as much as reporting it, altering both the layout of the political landscape and the contours of our government" (p. 1). Worland (1998) argues that what separates modern scandals from those in the past is the element of publicity or media coverage. With few exceptions, past presidential scandals always came out after the fact because the "press in those days honored the privacy of the White House. It was a different era" (p. 6). Hahn (1998) believes that contemporary Americans utilize the media as an "arbiter of thought," which creates a "monopolization of meaning" by the media (p. 251). The images Americans have of politics are rarely the products of direct involvement. They are, instead, perceptions focused and filtered by mass communication as well as from their personal and group contacts.

Gould (1996d) argues that Americans are ambivalent about presidential wives. The public expects the First Lady to fulfill a multitude of roles flawlessly and criticizes any departure from perceived standards. At the same time the criteria for success as a First Lady constantly change as the public's view of women evolves.

Like Richard Nixon, Bill Clinton was capable of bringing out the worst in people, and like Nixon, people had few illusions about Clinton's "character"—most Americans, after all, met him, via the mass media, defending himself against adultery charges. Many ignored that and hired him for his expected competence on certain issues (Reeves, 1996) as well as the image of him they saw reflected in his wife, Hillary Rodham Clinton.

First Lady Hillary Rodham Clinton's rhetorical management of the media during the investigation of several political crises during her husband's administration is the subject of this book. It is a significant area in which to conduct research because the role of the American First Lady goes far beyond its stereotypical conception as First Hostess or even First Wife. Historical precedent has essentially guaranteed that any twentieth-century First Lady would certainly be called on to serve as more than an appendage on the president's arm. She is a political institution and a powerful ally as well as a presidential partner. Although hers is an unpaid job defined by her interests and ambitions, "more than any individual besides the president himself, the First Lady has the power to set the tone of an administration and even influence the course of history" (Martin, 1998).

American First Ladies have always been not only personally and strategically important to presidents, but, arguably in varying degrees, politically important to the nation. Initially, First Ladies were among the few women who had a substantial influence on American politics because they were married to presidents. During the twentieth century, with the egregiously slow and occasionally controversial transformation of women into politicians, First Ladies have redefined their roles and expanded their power bases to become political animals in their own right. This is a significant point; even in the late twentieth century, American women accounted for only 20 percent of elected officials in the United States while constituting 51 percent of the population (Ciabattari, 1998).

In addition every First Lady has also served as a metaphor for her generation of women. Each has mirrored the status of American women of her time, symbolizing the "new" or "modern" woman of her era, while simultaneously shaping expectations of what future women might do and become (Caroli, 1995). One critic writes, "Nancy Reagan and Barbara Bush were typical of their time, but that time has gone. Pretending that Hillary Clinton is an aberration rather than the beginning of a permanent generational trend will be politically impossible to sustain" (Means, 1995, p. 2). Terry (1998) argues that Hillary Rodham Clinton has taken the activist precedent set by Eleanor Roosevelt and carried it even further and that the "remarkable trajectory of Mrs. Clinton's six years in Washington" continues to be "history in the making" (p. 1). Historian Kitty Sklar believes that Hillary Rodham Clinton is an important historical figure and suggests she will make more important things possible for spouses of presidents who follow her (Terry, 1998). An examination of Hillary Rodham Clinton's rhetorical responses to mediated versions of crises in the Clinton administration and of her First Ladyship as well as her role as "mother, wife, woman" is therefore an important contribution to both political communication and feminist scholarship.

The historical American First Lady as well as the political and social significance of the women who have enacted that role is initially discussed in *The Rhetoric of First Lady Hillary Rodham Clinton: Crisis Management Discourse*. Segments next examine the political press as well as mediated realities, including those directly influential in the Clinton administrations. The mediated realities many Americans have of politics in general and of the presidency—including the First Lady—in particular are also significant. The text then explains and justifies the importance of rhetorically studying these mediated realities and the responses to them. The crisis management styles of selected First Ladies prior to Hillary Rodham Clinton, including Florence Harding and Eleanor Roosevelt, are also examined, as are Hillary Rodham Clinton's responses to the mediated images of crises during her husband's tenure as president, including health care, the firings in the White House travel office, Whitewater, and the allegations of sexual misconduct. In addition, specific discursive strategies and rhetorical devices Mrs. Clinton employed in her attempts to re-form, redirect, and control mediated images of her husband's presidency are detailed.

The project is grounded in Kenneth Burke's rhetorical framework of language as a symbolic means of "inducing cooperation in beings that by nature respond to symbols" (1969b, p. 43). The cooperation (or persuasion) occurs when one person is able to identify with another through "talking his language by speech, gesture, tonality, order, image, attitude, idea" (p. 5). While a rhetorical perspective assumes that symbols present a source's view of reality (Cooper, 1989), a rhetorical analysis examines how these symbols are put together to achieve identification between a source and a receiver. Identification produces an ideology, a coherent worldview that allows interpretation of events, justifies power, and guides action. This "commonsense" ideology, rhetorically created, provides its participants with criteria for determining "good," "bad," "right," and "wrong." Such an ideology also provides a discursive defense for the beliefs, values, and myths accepted by members of the rhetorical community sharing this vision. Those not identifying with the vision may find fault with it, but those immersed in the ideology will likely accept it as an accurate representation of the way the world works, at least as rhetorically framed by the speaker (Cooper, 1989).

As Muir and Benitez (1996) observe, identification is one of the rhetorical strategies employed by Hillary Rodham Clinton, with varying degrees of success, during the early stages of her First Ladyship as a way to reach American audiences. This book tracks the First Lady's use of identification—as well as other rhetorical strategies—as a counter to or instrument of clarification for the mass-mediated realities produced during the scandals in both Clinton administrations. A critical portion of the text includes an analysis of her rhetorical evolution as the scandals played out. The book concludes with speculation regarding both the degree of success of the First Lady's efforts as well as the implications of these efforts for political communication and future First Partners.

Hillary Rodham Clinton has continued the historical trend of pushing the parameters of her role as First Lady and making the position uniquely her own. Yet the defining characteristic of her enactment of this role is the rhetorical merging of the traditional wife's role with that of a savvy politician, skilled in the discursive management of crisis situations. This book is dedicated to exploring the singular and successful rhetorical persona of the last First Lady of the twentieth century.

Chapter One

The Historical First Lady

[The First Lady is] a partner who represents for all of us a view of who her husband is, as well as a symbol of women's concerns and interests at a particular time. (Hillary Clinton quoted in Osborne, 1997, p. 103)

EVOLUTION OF THE ROLE

This chapter examines where Hillary Rodham Clinton belongs in the roster of presidential spouses who have preceded her. It begins with some observations about First Ladies, followed by an initial examination of Mrs. Clinton's tenure as First Lady, and concludes with some thoughts regarding the future of both Hillary Clinton and the role of First Lady.

The role of the president's wife has responded to changes in the nation's highest office itself and the social demands on women. Between 1789 and 1861, First Ladies were mostly private personages, with Dolley Madison as the notable exception and Julia Tyler a brief portent of fame to come. With the advent of Mary Todd Lincoln and her notoriety during the Civil War, the possibility of intense newspaper attention to First Ladies became a reality. None of Mary Todd Lincoln's late-nineteenth-century successors equaled her celebrity, although the coverage devoted to Lucy Webb Hayes and Frances Folsom Cleveland indicated a mounting degree of popular interest in the White House and its families.

During the early twentieth century, First Ladies slowly acquired a true institutional apparatus to help with meeting the mounting demands on their time. Isabelle "Belle" Hagner represented the first social secretary to a First

Lady in the modern sense when Edith Kermit Roosevelt employed her in 1902. During Mrs. Roosevelt's tenure, the role of the president's wife began to become that of social arbiter of good taste and leader of feminine fashion. Illness prevented Helen Herron Taft and Ellen Bolling Wilson from building on Edith Roosevelt's legacy before World War I.

Edith Wilson became a negative role model in her performance after President Woodrow Wilson became seriously ill in 1919. The consensus was that she had overstepped the implied limits of her position when she screened correspondence and visitors to her sick husband. Her example served as a powerful cautionary lesson against First Lady activism (Gould, 1996d).

The major innovations in what a First Lady could do came with the twelve-year tenure of Eleanor Roosevelt. Her press conferences, daily newspaper column, and extensive travels made her a national personality in a way that no previous First Lady had achieved. While some of the changes she made in the institution, such as regular press conferences, did not endure, her example as an activist role model gave her successors a precedent to invoke when they wished to pursue a cause or a campaign (Gould, 1996d). Beasley (1987) believes that Eleanor Roosevelt and the press engaged in a "symbiotic process of image making" (p. 5). As a daughter, wife, and mother in a "period of shifting social roles for women," Eleanor Roosevelt relied on the media to make herself into a role model for others by combining traditional aspects of a woman's role with the requirements of changing times. As the niece of one president, Theodore Roosevelt, and the wife of another, Franklin D. Roosevelt, she inhabited a world of political power that depended increasingly on the media. Following Theodore Roosevelt's enactment of the presidency as a "bully pulpit," relying on newspapers to mobilize public opinion, Franklin Roosevelt transformed it into a channel of intimate communication, speaking directly to the electorate by radio fireside talks.

Mrs. Roosevelt combined all the forms of media available to her to voice her opinions, unprecedented behavior for a nation unaccustomed to listening to a woman speak from a White House platform (Beasley, 1987). Rejecting the pattern set by her predecessors, Eleanor Roosevelt became the first president's wife to use her position as First Lady openly to seek media access, turn that access to her own advantage, and in the process break down barriers that had imprisoned her predecessors. She became the first president's wife to hold press conferences, write a syndicated newspaper column, send articles to popular magazines, earn money as a lecturer, and be a radio commentator. In Beasley's (1987) opinion, Eleanor Roosevelt was able to use her role as First Lady to "inspire the public with a message that reinforced traditional values at the same time that it enlarged them" (p. 81). As a First Lady functioning in a position of symbolic importance, she presented via the media spotlight her own idea of an appropriate role for a woman and transformed herself from a "potential victim into a renowned world figure" by fulfilling her personal needs while enacting the role of president's wife. For example, she used her column, "My Day," as a public means of personal accounting, which meant it "assumed an unusual importance" (Beasley, 1987, p. 130). Beasley speculates that the column—and other atypical "First Lady behaviors"—may have come into existence because Eleanor Roosevelt "wanted to match her husband's accounting to the public, as chief executive, with a parallel explanation of her performance as the chief executive's wife, subconsciously trying to make her role somewhat comparable to his" (pp. 89–90).

By 1939, Mrs. Roosevelt had mastered the techniques of media manipulation and learned to "give herself latitude for shifts of position when speaking for publication." She could do this because, as the wife of a public official, she was not held to any particular standard (Beasley, 1987, pp. 130–131). For example, after leaving the Civil Defense Office in 1942 under some criticism, she cast herself in the role of a traditional wife, noting that she would "list myself as a housewife—with some experience in writing a column and in speaking—and that's all" (quoted in Beasley, 1987, p. 150).

Beasley (1987) argues that when Eleanor Roosevelt chose to draw attention to herself and issues about which she cared, she also focused attention on the process of communication and "legitimized its use by other women" (p. 186). In addition, she "made it respectable for respectable women to participate in the man's world of public controversy" and "used the media as a vehicle for self-assertion in her life, much of which was a struggle between the Victorian idea of womanly subordination and the modern concept of self-actualization." She never surrendered the image of conventional femininity and in emphasizing "old-fashioned, family-centered values, Mrs. Roosevelt shielded herself with the Victorian ideal of womanhood while she pushed forward to claim a place in the modern world. It was a place she claimed on behalf of other women as well as herself" (p. 190).

Bess Truman and Mamie Eisenhower represented a return to the more traditional model of the First Lady as the helpmate, out of the public eye. Jacqueline Kennedy infused the institution with glamour and celebrity and aroused popular interest in the First Lady, even if her own accomplishments were limited. With the growing influence of television, the First Lady became a focus for media attention.

During the three decades since Jacqueline Kennedy, a growing emphasis on activism has marked the role of First Lady. Lady Bird Johnson identified herself with the environment and beautification. Her use of staff, involvement with conservation legislation, and advocacy of environmental causes set a precedent for her Democratic successors. Patricia Nixon was less visible in her public role but was as "involved in serious causes as her husband's conservative administration would allow her to be" (Gould, 1996d, p. xvii).

Betty Ford campaigned for the equal rights amendment. Although her husband's term was brief and she had her own problems with chemical dependencies, Mrs. Ford pushed the boundaries of the First Ladyship in many ways. Rosalynn Carter attempted to forge a public partnership with her husband, a strategy that produced a public backlash and cemented the traditional ideas regarding the proper behavior for the wife of a president. And faced with public outcry against her "opulent" lifestyle during her first two years, Nancy Reagan turned to a "Just Say No" campaign against drugs to link her tenure as First Lady to a cause. During the second Reagan term, her influence on the presidency evoked memories of Edith Wilson and similar male criticism of her First Lady enactment (Gould, 1996d). Conversely, Barbara Bush was popular as First Lady during all four years of George Bush's presidency, often outpacing him in the polls. Her endorsement of literacy never attracted any serious criticism, and she also benefited from following Nancy Reagan's controversial First Ladyship.

Gould (1996d) argues that Hillary Rodham Clinton's experience highlights the conflicting expectations Americans still have about the wife of an American president. For some, she is an inspiring role model; for others, a "figure of such evil intentions as to render her almost devilish in character" (p. xviii). In November 1996, Hillary Clinton said, partly in jest, that the only way a president's wife could escape from politics was "to totally withdraw and perhaps put a bag over your head, or somehow make it clear that you have no opinions and no ideas about anything—and never express them, publicly or privately." She also commented that while "there is something about the position" of First Lady "which raises in Americans' minds concerns about hidden power, about influence behind the scenes, about unaccountability," she believed "the answer is to just be who you are"(quoted in Kurtz, 1998, p. 79). Mrs. Clinton has argued that although "almost without exception" every First Lady beginning with Martha Washington "was criticized for something by somebody," every president's wife "has defined the role in a way that is true to herself, how she can help her husband, take care of her family, make her contribution to our nation" (quoted in Osborne, 1997, p. 105–107).

EXPANSION OF PUBLIC SPACE AND VOICE

Some have argued that there should be no "First Lady" title. Former *New York Times* political correspondent Richard Reeves suggested in 1996 that Hillary Clinton should have the "zone of privacy" she had talked about: "She has never been elected to anything and you do not have to be a sworn political opponent of the Clintons to be uneasy about the idea of secret power at the highest levels without any public accountability. Unlike every other person around the president, she cannot be fired, ignored, impeached, or defeated in election" (pp. 92–93).

A *New York Times* columnist wrote after the 1993 inauguration that Hillary Rodham Clinton's apparently revolutionary take on being First Lady was indeed a "logical" progression in the evolution of a society where women are "partners and co-workers, not simply homemakers." In addition, since Mrs. Clinton was "clearly as much a running mate" for her husband as was Vice President Al Gore, how could "anyone doubt that she would play a policy role" in the Clinton administration (quoted in Brock, 1996, p. 328)?

For all his long and distinguished career, Edmund Muskie will probably be best remembered as the presidential candidate who wept in public because of some squalid attacks made on his wife's character. At the time, former British Prime Minister Harold Macmillan expressed disdain for this performance. Asked by his secretary how he would have reacted if someone had said his wife was nothing but an old drunk, he replied, "I would have said, 'Ah, but you should have seen her mother'" (Reno, 1996).

Reno believes that Americans have a problem with presidents' wives, arguing that "unless they behave like insipid, unopinionated cows, we persist in characterizing them as meddlers, dragon ladies and ambitious harridans." This is nothing new. A recent editorial regarding Hillary Clinton's Israeli/Palestinian statements argues, "Isn't it enough to have a president who can't keep his fly zipped? Must we suffer the further indignity of a first lady who can't keep her mouth shut—who absent the semblance of a mandate, is driven to policy-making?" (Feder, 1998).

In two centuries, the role of the American First Lady has evolved from ceremonial backdrop to, in some cases, legendary world figure (Caroli, 1995). Americans have always had such legends in their immigrant heritages, from Spain's Isabella and her funding of Columbus to France's Margaret, who left court to travel alongside Louis IX in the seventh crusade, to Swedish linguist, athlete, and queen Christiana, to African matriarchal tribes, to the Iroquois nations with families living in squaws' long houses, to England's Elizabeth II, more powerful than most kings (Anthony,

1990–1991, 1:32). The American colonies had already experienced such women as the wife of a member of the Continental Congress who hoped democracy would give all women rights and warned, "If particular care and attention is not paid to the ladies, we are determined to ferment a rebellion, and will not hold ourselves bound by any laws in which we have no voice or representation," and who, as the American Revolution continued, warned, "If our men are all drawn off and we should be attacked, you will find a race of Amazons in America." These are the words of Abigail Adams, who in 1797 became the nation's second First Lady (quoted in Anthony, 1990–1991, 1:32–33).

Hillary Clinton, who might have uttered similar words had she been an eighteenth-century president's wife, inherited the "First Lady" label from a eulogy for Dolley Madison delivered by President Zachary Taylor. It was in 1849, four decades after her tenure as the wife of President James Madison, that "presidentress" (Caroli, 1995, pp. xv-xvi) and other labels such as "The Lady," "President's Lady," and "Mrs. President" fell to the new title introduced by Taylor when he said of Mrs. Madison: "She will never be forgotten, because she was truly our First Lady for a half-century (Anthony, 1990–1991, 1:147).

Mrs. Clinton and her husband have received steady criticism for presenting themselves in a way some believe to be unprecedented for a president and his spouse: as political as well as marital partners. In truth, this is not a new phenomenon. When John Adams was elected to serve in the First Continental Congress in 1774, Abigail Adams was welcomed as his adviser on government structure and world economics. She received classified information from him in Paris in 1778 and by his 1797 presidency thought herself as more of a "copresident" than "Lady," encouraged by her husband who referenced his wife as "my dearest Partner . . . my . . . wisest friend in this world" and who said "I think you shine as a Stateswoman" (quoted in Anthony, 1990–1991, pp. 60–61). The Madisons' partnership was not in doubt when one observer of the "Second First Couple" wrote that Dolley Madison was "fully capable of entering into her husband's occupations as he; and there is little doubt that he owed much to her intellectual companionship" (cited in Anthony, 1990–1991, 1:103–104). Mary Todd and Abraham Lincoln's relationship was based on equality and, often, political disagreement. It has been argued that she was the "moving undertow of their mutual ambitions" (Anthony, 1990–1991, pp. 176–177). And early in the twentieth century, Nellie Taft received a note from her husband, William, addressed, "Memorandum for Mrs. Taft—the real President from the nominal President" (Anthony, 1990–1991, 1:315). Although usually limiting her opinions to the privacy of family and also focused on her ceremonial role as "first hostess," Mrs. Taft perceived her role as a copresident and political partner to Taft, saying, "I had always had the satisfaction of knowing almost as much as he about the politics and intricacies of any situation in which he found himself" (quoted in Anthony, 1990–1991, 1:318–319).

Equal power was also a goal for Edith Galt when, after the 1914 death of Ellen Wilson, she "burst forth on politics . . . bitten with the intrigue of love [of Woodrow Wilson] and political power . . . secure in her vision of becoming a partner in the presidency" (Anthony, 1990–1991, 1:352–353). And when one talks of partnerships and power relations between husbands and wives in the presidency, Eleanor Roosevelt, who "worked politics for herself as well as the president" (Anthony, 1990–1991, 1:464), stands tall. Arguing that the "ideal type of modern wife" was a partner, before mother or homemaker, she became FDR's eyes and ears after polio struck him down (Anthony, 1990–1991, 1:450). And it has been argued that Nancy Reagan elevated the job of First Lady to a kind of "Associate Presidency" (Caroli, 1995, pp. xviii).

Simonton (1996) concludes that even the most casual reading of history reveals that women are underrepresented in history. Nowhere has the proportion of women among luminaries come anywhere close to the 50 percent that might be expected from population ratios. For example, females represent only about 3 percent of all historical figures in Western civilization. In some areas, the percentage of women shrinks even lower. Only about 1 percent of the notable contributors to science and technology are female, and the proportion of women among eminent classical composers is essentially zero. There are a few domains where women have better odds of making history, such as creative writing; examples are Lady Murasaki and Virginia Woolf. Even so, only one out of ten famous authors is female, which remains one-fifth the anticipated expectancy.

Although there have been numerous distinguished female political figures, including Elizabeth I of England, Maria Theresa of Austria, and Catherine the Great of Russia, even in this area, women constitute fewer than half of the notables.

Why? The early biological interpretations of women having less innate talent than men has generally become more untenable as the presumed contrasts of nature are discovered to be more and more changeable results of nurture. There is also the argument that these disproportions may only reflect the effects of male-dominated societies. As a result, gifted women were and often still are neither encouraged to develop their talents nor granted recognition for what they managed to accomplish despite limitations of all kinds. There is empirical evidence to support this notion that biased gender role expectations, sexist ideologies, and strongly male-oriented cultures can stifle female attainments. The confining of women to motherhood as a sole "career" and its accompanying focus on domestic skills such as cooking and home crafts, as well as other gender-typed endeavors, results in women often being allowed little latitude for achieving greatness in the sorts of activities that would be historically recorded. As a result, the annals of history overflow with male names.

However, this is not the whole story. Talented women have created alternative routes, typified by the role of First Lady, which allows them to negotiate between home and history. Such an individual might become "the woman behind the man" and attain some personal fulfillment by facilitating the ambitions of her husband, or she might achieve more lasting acclaim by linking her fate to the "right man." In such cases, a wife might make direct contributions to her husband's success as a collaborator in his career and so become a genuine "woman behind the man" phenomenon, as Lady Bird Johnson and Jacqueline Kennedy Onassis were. Such an association may also give a woman access to resources or roles she might not otherwise enjoy which she can then translate into her own personal achievement, as Eleanor Roosevelt did.

It could also be that the woman's primary function in such a relationship is to "bask in reflected glory" and maintain a comfortable, stable, quiet home environment where her husband may rise to fame without domestic or family distractions. For example, the "celebrity status" of First Ladies such as Bess Truman and Mamie Eisenhower and Barbara Bush came indirectly from their roles as mothers and enablers, from performing tasks expected of them according to more traditional gender roles.

A final consideration is that the two halves of the presidential couple may share common attributes as a consequence of "assortative mating," or the principle of "birds of a feather flocking together." In other words, couples may match on certain traits that contribute separately to their respective reputations, such as intelligence. As a result, some women may enjoy reputations that closely parallel those of their husbands because both share common assets that contribute independently to their respective reputations. This may be the case for Hillary Rodham Clinton.

Much of the controversy surrounding Mrs. Clinton originates from what Caroli (1995) labels a "First Lady Paradox" (p. xx): she must be "modern" but not "push too far"; her short-comings are maligned, her strengths dismissed. She must contribute but not meddle; be progressive but not radical; political but social; loyal but not blind; international but American. She must be a partner but an individual. She must be a lady but a woman (Anthony, 1990–1991, 2:450).

One of the major components of this paradox is the power of the First Lady. Because of the marital partnership, she possesses what some consider to be more latent power over the president than the business partnership of the vice presidency. She becomes an unknown quantity, a "wild card of the executive branch," and possibly the most powerful unappointed post in the federal government (Anthony, 1990–1991, p. 449). Eleanor Roosevelt and Bess Truman were called among the "most powerful people in Washington" during their husbands' administrations. Betty Ford said she resorted to "pillow talk" to convince her husband of her point of view, which President Ford has said carried weight on some controversial issues, including the pardon of Richard Nixon (quoted in Caroli, 1995). She is accountable to no one and everyone—a paradoxical person in a paradoxical position grounded in power with powerful expectations.

Abigail Adams believed public life "requires courage and firmness, wisdom with temperance, patience and forebearance to stand in such a conspicuous, such an elevated position." She said, "I expect to be vilified and abused with my whole family when I come into this situation" and when a friend called the [first]ladyship "splendid misery," Abigail Adams admitted, "She was not far from the truth" (quoted in Anthony, 1990–1991, 1:60).

Image has also been influential in the public perception of First Ladies, particularly since their role is not constitutionally defined. Blumenfeld (1996) suggests that "Americans want to see an idealized woman at the president's side, combining the grace of Jackie Kennedy, the nurturing of Barbara Bush and the talent for making her man look good" (p. 6). Eleanor Roosevelt, after three terms of an unprecedented First Ladyship, "wearily admitted, "sometimes I feel like I am dressing the Washington Monument" (quoted in Anthony, 1990–1991, 1:506).

Ultimately, with little public debate and no constitutional grounding, the role of First Wife has evolved into one of great power. The president is the only public official elected by every citizen of the United States; the First Lady is selected by no one other than her husband. His position is defined by the Constitution, hers by marriage and her own interests and ambitions. Yet she has as much, and at times perhaps more, power to set the tone of an administration and perhaps influence the course of history (Martin, 1998).

Some spouses of American presidents chose not to use their position as much as others. Although well educated and articulate, Grover Cleveland's wife, "Frances/Frankie," agreed with her husband's claim that "a woman should not bother her head about political parties and public questions, and that she should be content to rule in the domain of the house" (Anthony, 1990–1991, 1:262). From the onset of her husband's presidency, Grace Coolidge argued that "being the President's wife isn't going to make me think less about the domestic duties I've always loved" (quoted in Anthony, 1990–1991, 1:398). Mrs. Coolidge once remarked, "I know nothing of the conducting of affairs in the Executive Offices.... Considering they lay outside of my province [and] if I had manifested any particular interest, I feel sure that I should have been properly put in my place" (quoted in Anthony, 1990–1991, 1:400). Ellen Wilson focused public attention on art. Although she was influential in some of Woodrow's political decisions, she seemed uninterested in pursuing any kind of a co-presidency.

Conversely, Harry Truman was frustrated by First Lady Bess's refusal to play a public role. She once snapped, "I am not the one elected. I have nothing to say in public" (quoted in Anthony, 1990–1991, p. 527). The relationship of female journalists to President Truman was conditioned initially by Mrs. Truman's decision to discontinue the occasional meetings with female reporters begun by Eleanor Roosevelt. Although Bess Truman's secretaries provided weekly information about activities scheduled on the First Lady's social calendar, Mrs. Truman maintained a low profile in deference to her own desires and because of her belief that a president's wife should not play a public role in the policies of her husband's administration (Mitchell, 1998).

Bess Truman essentially believed in saying nothing to the press. She effectively distanced herself from an inquiring press by delegating her social secretary, Edith Helm, and her personal secretary, Reathel Odum, for weekly meetings with female reporters accredited to the White House. When she met with the press at the beginning of the Truman administration to explain that she would not personally hold news conferences, a reporter remonstrated, "'But Mrs. Truman, how are we ever going to get to know you?' to which Mrs. Truman replied 'You don't need to know me. I'm only the president's wife and the mother of his daughter.' ... Bess Truman instructed Odum to 'Keep on smiling and tell *them* nothing'" (quoted in Mitchell, 1998, p. 195). In the 1950s, Mamie Eisenhower was proud to say, "Ike runs the country, I turn the porkchops" (quoted in Anthony, 1990–1991, 1:563), and Barbara Bush argued, "I have priorities—George and the children and grandchildren—and all else falls into place" (quoted in Anthony, 1990–1991, 2:440). Nancy Davis made only two more films after her 1952 marriage to Ronald Reagan, insisting, "I had no desire to continue as an actress once I became a wife.... I had seen too many marriages fall apart when the wife continued her career" (quoted in Anthony, 1990–1991, 2:544).

While their husbands campaigned and debated, Jackie Kennedy and Pat Nixon were the focus of a press fashion war regarding how much they spent on clothes (Anthony, 1990–1991). Early in her career, as the wife of the 1960 Democratic candidate for president, Jackie Kennedy refused to "express any views that were not my husband's" (quoted in Anthony, 1990–1991, 1:592). Although she provided input for speeches and created political allies, Jackie Kennedy's First Ladyship was primarily one of a well-educated but traditional wife keeping a house (albeit the White House).

One of the major sources of both praise for and blame of Hillary Rodham Clinton was her husband's decision to appoint his wife as the head of his drive to reform health care, a central goal of Clinton's early presidency (Caroli, 1995). Although some thought this situation unique, it was not. Despite the preference of some First Ladies for traditional roles, presidential wives have rarely been only "hand wavers and shakers" (Anthony, 1990–1991, 1:8). All American First Ladies have served in some capacity as advisers to their presidential husbands. Some were highly and visibly connected to presidential power such as Abigail Adams, Eleanor Roosevelt, and Hillary Clinton. Others maintained low but still influential levels of involvement, such as Eliza Johnson, who was an influence in Andrew Johnson's Reconstruction policy and his 1865 Proclamation of Amnesty, a pardon to nonleaders of the Confederacy who would take an oath of Union loyalty (Anthony, 1990–1991).

John Adams's political foes were alarmed at his wife's power. She often served as his representative at official government events and once wrote to him about an occasion that "I acted as your proxy" (quoted in Anthony, 1990–1991, 1:62). One of Adams's critics observed that "the President would not dare to make a nomination without her approbation" (quoted in Anthony, 1990–1991, p. 63). Dolley Madison laid the foundation for her power when she served as a surrogate "presidentress" for the widowed Thomas Jefferson between 1801 and 1809. She solidified her role during her husband's two terms (Caroli, 1995), assuming some responsibility in the administration of the executive branch when Madison became ill in 1813 (Anthony, 1990) and regularly led a procession of women to House debates.

And Sarah Polk was influential in her husband's declaration to gain southwestern territory—the "manifest destiny" believed by both to be part of God's plan for America as a chosen land (Anthony, 1990–1991). In the mid-1800s, Julia Tyler made her husband's ambition hers—and ultimately Texas's statehood was attributed to her as much as to President Tyler (Anthony, 1990). Abigail Fillmore's most important, but ultimately ignored, advice was that President Millard Fillmore not sign the fugitive slave bill that would enable slave owners to reclaim their runaway slaves (Anthony, 1990–1991). Mary Todd Lincoln, upon her husband's victory, boasted that she would help him choose his cabinet—not an exaggeration. As a result of his confiding military secrets to her, she wrote that the president should "put a fighting General in the place of McClellan" (quoted in Anthony, 1990–1991, p. 168).

Julia Grant influenced cabinet dismissals and Supreme Court appointments during her husband's presidency, and James was regularly consulted by his "politically astute" wife, Lucretia "Crete" Garfield (Anthony, 1990–1991). After Woodrow Wilson's stroke in 1918, critics warned against his wife's "petticoat government" and "the Mrs. Wilson regency," complaining that "Mrs. Wilson is President!" (Anthony, 1990–1991, 1:375). Others acknowledged her power by saying that Edith Wilson proved herself "the finest argument for suffrage" (Anthony, 1990–1991, 2:379). A reporter noted in 1923 that Florence Harding was "the first of all the wives of our presidents who takes an actual hand in politics and is just as intense and enthusiastic in the game as if she were herself a candidate for re-election" (Kates, 1998). And in 1985, three people were said to be in control of the White House during Ronald Reagan's convalescence: the president, his chief of staff, and Nancy Reagan (Caroli, 1995).

The argument has been made that as Woodrow Wilson "freely admitted" (Anthony, 1990–1991, 2:448), most presidents' ability to govern depends on their social and political partnerships with their spouses. Anthony (1990–1991) asks, "Where would William Howard Taft, Lyndon Johnson, John Adams, Jimmy Carter, Warren Harding, Ulysses S. Grant, or Ronald Reagan have been without Nellie, Bird, Dearest Friend, Rosie, the Duchess, Mrs. G and Mommy, respectively?" (2:448).

What accounts for the power evolution of First Lady as initially acted by Martha Washington and currently performed by Hillary Rodham Clinton? First, there is the Constitution. The nature of the U.S. presidency, as configured in the 1787 Constitutional Convention, included two tasks usually performed by separate individuals in other governments: head of state for ceremonial occasions and head of government for legislation decisions. The American president often sent substitutes on ceremonial occasions, most often the presidential wife. Martha Washington began what became a tradition when she attended a church service while her husband was ill. Nearly two hundred years later, Nancy Reagan left her husband's hospital room to announce that she was "the president's stand-in" (quoted in Caroli, 1995, pp. xviii-xix).

The election process also pushes presidential wives into the spotlight. Although it was considered inappropriate for women to campaign openly until well into the twentieth century, the groundwork was laid much earlier. Although her participation in the 1993 inaugural festivities mirrored that of the most traditional First Ladies, Hillary Clinton soon made headlines by taking an office in the West Wing of the White House. This was an unprecedented power move; even her most outspoken predecessors had seemed content with space in the East Wing, the traditional place for presidential spouses (Caroli, 1995).

While her appointment as head of health care reform in her husband's administration was not the first powerful position for a First Lady, it was far beyond any previous task allowed for or taken on by the wife of a president. Her commission promised proposals for changes far more expansive and influential than the reforms in Rosalynn Carter's mental health care program, Lady Bird Johnson's beautification plan, Barbara Bush's literacy campaign, and Nancy Reagan's "Just say no" media blitz. And her health care reform package proved a lightning rod for intensified scrutiny about her enactment of First Lady. For example, physicians, who sought to participate in hearings of her commission, were barred because the hearings were made up only of "government officials." Their argument was that Hillary Clinton was not a government official; therefore as long as she chaired the hearings, they should be open to the public, including them. A district federal court agreed, but the decision was reversed on appeal because there existed "a longstanding tradition of public service by First Ladies who have acted as advisors and personal representatives of their husbands" (Caroli, 1995, p. 304). This is another example of the paradox of the American First Lady: the tradition of the First Spouse is used to justify a First Spouse behaving in a most untraditional manner. This paradox was evident during the 1992 primaries and again in 1996, when reporters were in a quandary as to whether to single out Hillary Clinton's hair or her record on issues (Caroli, 1995).

First Ladies have never lacked detractors. The press has always dogged them, sometimes spinning positively, as they did with Julia Tyler, but more often harassing "maliciously," as they did with Mary Todd Lincoln (Anthony, 1990–1991, 1:213). In the 1860s, Mary Lincoln was called "extravagant" (Caroli, 1995, p. xxi), considered a traitor by the South, and mistrusted by the North (Anthony, 1990–1991). She was chastised during the 1864 presidential campaign for everything from being enormously in debt to getting drunk with Russian sailors on a New York yacht (the latter a lie, the former a truth) (Anthony, 1990–1991).

Dolley Madison was thought "too casual" for 1810; Margaret Taylor "coarse" in 1849; Elizabeth Monroe too "elite" for 1817; Harriet Lane overly "gay" as President Buchanan's hostess in 1858; Martha Washington "too old" in the 1790s and Julia Tyler "too young" in the 1840s. Edith Wilson was guilty of running her "petticoat government." Florence Harding ran "rough shod" over her husband's career in the 1920s. Eleanor Roosevelt put words in FDR's mouth in the 1940s. Nancy Reagan got "people fired" in the 1980s. And Hillary Clinton made her husband "look like a wimp" (Caroli, 1995, p. xxi).

Dolley Madison was regularly criticized by the early-nineteenth-century press for her clothing (she "loads herself with finery and dresses without any taste"), her informality (it was "without distinction either in manners or appearance"), and her figure (she was "fat, forty, but not fair"). Julia Tyler made scandalous history in 1845 by "hiring" a press agent, and immediately upon the 1877 inauguration of Rutherford as president, Lucy Hayes was targeted by the women correspondents, who by this time covered the president's wife regularly. One editorial criticized that although "everyone praises the way Mrs. Hayes plasters down her hair and enthuses over her dresses . . . in 90 days she will be picked to minute shreds" (Anthony, 1990–1991, 2:96, 129, 225–226).

Playing to the First Wife paradox, the media condemned Mamie Eisenhower in the 1950s for being "perfectly satisfied to be known as a housewife" and criticized her for her inactivism rather than overinvolvement with the presidency (Anthony, 1990–1991, 2:557). And what better illustration of this paradox than this First Lady whom the media now insist is "the wronged woman, still standing by her man" but only a relatively short time ago was "the feminist who had wronged her man by refusing to stand by him?"

Initially, Hillary Clinton was supposed to "completely rewrite the job of First Lady," become "First Partner" to Bill Clinton, and break new ground—a sort of "presidential super spouse" (Caroli, 1995, p. 288). What happened after the initial honeymoon of First Ladyhood was not unlike what happened to many of her predecessors. One essay critical of Mrs. Clinton presents a shopping list of "where she went wrong." Perhaps her biggest blunder in attempting to partner the president politically was her handling of health care reform and other big issues such as the budget. It may have just been a "bad idea," or it might have turned out differently if she had done a better job (Harris and Devroy, 1996, p. 7) or not demonstrated so "much control" (Muir and Benitez, 1996, p. 154). Her reluctance to disclose information about the First Couple's Arkansas investments in the 1980s produced questions not only about Mrs. Clinton but about the couple's integrity (Harris and Devroy, 1996, p. 7). Reporters frequently spun "Whitewater" into "Watergate," the first obvious connecting of the Clintons with the almost impeached and forever infamous Nixons (Caroli, 1995, p. 306).

Whitewater symbolized the first time in U.S. history that a First Lady had been interrogated about subjects she discussed with her husband. This was not a question of meddling in talk between a wife and her husband, albeit a

First Wife and a First Husband. It was about substantive matters dealing with money and power (Caroli, 1995)—his and hers.

Other flashpoints of criticism surrounding Hillary Rodham Clinton include her role in the firing of the White House travel office staff and the role she played in selecting the first two candidates for attorney general as well as in the appointment of now-resigned White House counsel Bernard Nussbaum. There are the former members of her Rose Law Firm who experienced various misfortunes after joining the Clinton administration: White House deputy counsel Vincent Foster's suicide, former associate attorney general Webster L. Hubbell's fate after admitting to fraudulent billing practices at the firm in Arkansas, and former White House associate counsel William Kennedy II's problems after he failed to disclose that he had not paid taxes on the family nanny (Harris and Devroy, 1996).

Hillary Clinton has been criticized for her syndicated newspaper column, which began in more than 100 newspapers and magazines worldwide in 1995 (Purdum, 1995). That the column addressed topics ranging from personal issues like motherhood and breast-feeding to public policy concerns prompted Dowd (1995a) to argue there is a "duality Picasso would appreciate" when one observes the First Lady writing "in her daily column about feeding Socks and being an anxious Mom while Congressional hearings investigate a Whitewater." There is also the criticism of her handling of the publicity of her book *It Takes a Village*, with one skeptic observing that every time she walked from a car into a building, Hillary Rodham Clinton carried "something in her hand . . . a copy of her book" (Greene, 1996).

It has been argued that Hillary Clinton's major problem is her failure to acknowledge the tensions and problems caused initially within her husband's administration by the "two for one" deal: "when the boss's wife is also a boss, aides are even more afraid to say 'I don't think this works'" (Dowd, 1995b). Brant and Thomas (1996) suggest that Mrs. Clinton has "backed away from hard ball" and "become more circumspect" (p. 24). She does not show up at formal White House work sessions as much as she did early in her husband's presidency and uses the traditional formal Office of the First Lady and its staff to carry out an agenda of travel and policy projects (Harris and Devroy, 1996, p. 7).

After the failed health care plan, Shogren (1998) believes Mrs. Clinton has linked herself to more traditional First Lady "women and children" issues and undergone a "remarkable transformation" from a "threatening ideologue on the liberal fringe to an appealing advocate for centrist family-friendly politics." She has "taken a page" from her husband's political manual, focused on "more palatable" issues, and has "won many converts from the political center" by focusing more on "pragmatic progress and incremental goals." This strategy is evident when tracking her First Wife activities since 1996, which have included an eight-day tour of Europe—"shoulder-to-shoulder" with her sixteen-year-old daughter—that was a mix of diplomacy, politics, and sightseeing when she became the first presidential spouse since Eleanor Roosevelt to address troops in a hostile area, Bosnia (Fournier, 1996).

Still, it is more likely that Hillary Clinton's "hairstyles have changed more than her agenda" in the past few years (Brant and Thomas, 1996, p. 22). She has remained a "tough, shrewd lawyer and political advisor" to her husband's administration (Marcus, 1998) and has taken on congressional opponents as "reckless" partisans (Harris and Devroy, 1996, p. 6). As President Clinton faced a congressional investigation into the possibility of impeachment, his wife, in the "most wrenching of ironies," became the most viable and persuasive spokesperson for his policies (Lavelle and Barnes, 1998, p. 16).

It is interesting to consider the different perceptions of Hillary Rodham Clinton and Elizabeth Dole in Campaign '96. If Bob Dole and Bill Clinton offered competing ideas of America, their wives offered "clashing visions of womanhood" in 1996. Presidential candidate Bob Dole went out of his way in 1996 to reassure voters that in his administration, "Elizabeth won't be in charge of health care." Reno (1996) noted that Dole talked as if his wife was learning disabled and asked, "Why shouldn't she have been in charge of health care? The woman had served in two cabinet posts, transportation and labor, under two presidents, and as president of the Red Cross, probably knew more about health care than she did about transportation or labor."

Still, Dole's handlers thought it the smart thing for him to say. What would have been wrong with her serving as secretary of health and human services? John Kennedy made his brother attorney general. But Elizabeth Dole is a woman and was being set up for the Dole handlers' image of what they thought Americans wanted in their next First Lady. "God forbid" a First Lady should have an opinion "more provocative than Martha Stewart's rules for place settings" (Reno, 1996). The price Mrs. Clinton paid for forgetting this early in her First Lady career was substantial.

The contrast between Hillary Clinton and Elizabeth Dole was much subtler than in 1992, when Mrs. Clinton, working mother, was matched against Barbara Bush, "America's grandma." In 1996, both Mrs. Dole and Clinton "adorned themselves with power but wore it differently." If Hillary was "a Lady Macbeth, Elizabeth was Cinderella" (Kathleen Hall Jamieson quoted in Blumenfeld, 1996, p. 6). One poll at the time noted that three times as many Americans liked Elizabeth Dole as disliked her, while Hillary Clinton's fans barely outnumbered her critics. One analyst explained the discrepancy: "It's the 'don't ask, don't tell' policy about First Ladies—just don't put it in our face."

The question became, "Whom would you rather have as your mother: Elizabeth Dole or Hillary Clinton?... The soft nurturing quality is perhaps more important [for a First Lady] than 'Jackie chic.'" One observer quipped: "Look at Barbara Bush, the much adored president's wife: She had a bosom built to burp a nation," and continued, "Folks elect a president, not a first lady, and the most a spouse can do is serve as character witness. People want a first lady who improves her man by association.... If Hillary hardens Bill, Elizabeth brightens Bob.... Hillary is a bad cop, Elizabeth is good cop . . . but peel back the myths, images and political beliefs, and you'll find that the two women are more alike than different." Ultimately questions were raised about Elizabeth Dole's finances, and though her approach to the First Ladyship was relatively "safe" compared with Hillary Clinton's, it still broke from the traditional "first lady formula" of staying out of politics, promoting do-good projects and smiling and patting the air" (Blumenfeld, 1996, p. 7).

There is one ongoing crisis that has dominated Hillary Rodham and Bill Clinton's public and private lives for years. In keeping with a long-established pattern, Mrs. Clinton moves to resolve questions, responding as she has again and again in times of personal and political crisis by doing whatever is required for the survival of the tumultuous and resilient partnership of Clinton and Clinton. In 1998, she found herself back in a role that would be one of the most painful for many wives but was perhaps the most valuable she could enact for her husband as First Lady: standing by her man after his admission of marital infidelity. She has had to deal with allegations about her husband's unfaithfulness for twenty-five years and has been the singularly essential figure in each recovery he has made in the repetitive cycle of loss and recovery that defines his political career.

She helped Bill Clinton extricate himself from allegations of marital infidelity when he was governor of Arkansas and sat at his side in the *60 Minutes* interview when he admitted to "causing pain in my marriage." What allegedly had happened regarding Gennifer Flowers, she said then, was between her and her husband, and if she could deal with it, that was all that mattered. "If that's not enough for people," she said, "then heck, don't vote for him" (quoted in Maraniss, 1998). In explaining how and why she maintains a relationship with Bill Clinton, Mrs. Clinton insists that "the only people who count in any marriage are the two that are in it. We know everything there is to know about each other, and we understand and accept and love each other.... I probably know him better than anybody alive in the world, so I hope that I'd be his best defender" (quoted in "Excerpts of Mrs. Clinton's," 1998).

Where once she was scolded for promising *not* to stand by "her man," she now is chastised by some for doing just that. Emery (1998) insisted "whatever becomes of the Clinton presidency, it is certain that Hillary Rodham Clinton the icon is dead. Instead of praising her brains, people now wonder at how she has chosen to use them." Instead of looking up to her co-equal, power-shared marriage, it is now a "sick" or a "repugnant relationship," "stupefyingly weird" and even "creepy." Hillary Clinton is First Lady turned First Enabler and First Victim who is "disturbingly complicit in her husband's excesses" (Emery, 1998). A *Washington Times* reporter complained that she was "willing to adopt any role—tough advocate, abused wife, helpless little woman, political strategist, shrew-in-chief—to keep her husband in office" (Pruden, 1998). Wills (1997) suggests that Bill Clinton's history of seduction includes seducing "his own wife—away from her principles." Another observer argues that Bill Clinton did not betray his wife with the Lewinsky affair, but when he made "his presidency and their time in the White House, things for which she also worked her whole life, worthless for the sake of trivial sexual indulgence" (Phyllis Rose quoted in Horn, 1998).

While Marcus (1998) speculates that the First Lady stood by Bill Clinton out of love and her "strong religious faith," others argued that her behavior was more complex. The key to understanding her support, they say, is in the original nature of the relationship she has shared with Clinton since they began dating at Yale in 1970. At that time they shared a passion for "politics, policy, power, books and ideas," believed they could "attain heights together they might not reach separately," and were both cognizant of Clinton's reputation as a "ladies' man" (Wills, 1997).

Initially, Hillary Rodham Clinton argued that a "vast right-wing conspiracy" was attempting to bring her husband's presidency down through accusing him of marital infidelity with Monica Lewinsky. She had gone to the media to defend her husband, blame his accusers, and declare that she believed his denials (Hall and Lee, 1998). At one point, she even argued, "I think a lot of this is prejudice against our state" and "they wouldn't do this if we were from some other state" (quoted in Alvarez, 1998, p. 2). Hillary Clinton's rhetorical management did take the public's eye off the central issue of what the real relationship was between the president and former White House intern and whether he lied about it and tried to get Lewinsky to lie as well (Wills, 1997).

One conclusion of Simonton's (1996) research is especially relevant to an examination of Hillary Rodham and Bill Clinton's partnership: men who are high in the need for achievement link up with women who are noted as campaigners and leaders in causes, have significant accomplishments, and are better educated. Conversely, men who are high in the need for power are joined by women who are most likely to make substantial improvement in the White House and thereby contribute to presidential image and prestige. "Achievement" and "power" could certainly describe Bill Clinton, while "accomplished" and "educated" might be descriptors for Hillary Rodham Clinton. One British writer quipped that "for years now, Hillary Rodham Clinton has been the target of suspicions that she is cleverer than her husband" (Smith, 1998, p. T002). Considering the public's generally pro-Clinton reaction to the most recent "image and prestige" crisis surrounding the Lewinsky scandal, the partnership seems to be paying off.

In spite of, or perhaps even because of, Bill Clinton's public admission that he lied about his relationship with Lewinsky, Hillary Rodham Clinton continued her decades-old support of her husband. Many Americans seemed to take their cue from Mrs. Clinton about how to view the Clinton presidency in the light of the president's admissions: "If she can deal with her husband's infidelity, the reasoning goes, why should it bother me?" Hall and Page (1998) suggest that his wife's "rock solid support" could do as much for her husband's public image as any of his efforts during this most perilous period of his presidency. One American University political scientist believed that if Hillary Clinton "were to falter, it would be the end of Bill Clinton (Allan Lichtman quoted in Hall and Page, 1998, p. 1A). Walsh (1998) believes that after the president's statement that he misled his wife and the country about his relationship with Lewinsky, Hillary Clinton knew she could no longer "command a moral high ground" on her husband's behalf as she did prior to his admission. Since the president's admission of infidelity in August 1998, among the strategies Hillary Rodham Clinton used in the rhetorical management of the crisis was ignoring it while continuing to focus on issues and making no allusion to the president's personal behavior or to Kenneth Starr's release of print and video testimony. During a Democratic fund raiser in September 1998 she said, "I'm very proud of the person I'm privileged to introduce. I'm proud of his leadership. I'm proud of his commitment. I'm proud of what he gives our country—and all of us every day—by his commitment. And I'm proud to introduce my husband and our president" (quoted in Sobieraj, 1998) .

Like her predecessors Florence Harding, Eleanor Roosevelt, Mamie Eisenhower, Jackie Kennedy, and Lady Bird Johnson, who never publicly admitted their husbands' affairs (Martin, 1998), Hillary Rodham Clinton became the "silent woman," confirming that "she would need more than a new hairstyle to get opinion on her side" (Smith, 1998, p. T002). Historian Carl Anthony suggests, "There's something called institutional dignity that comes with living in the White House, and Hillary Clinton seems quite aware of it. She is not going to be railroaded by anyone to emotionally forgive her husband in a public speech. Instead, she'll do what she's doing: maintain her dignity" (quoted in Connolly, 1998, p. 1D).

Adair (1998) argues that the Clinton sex scandals changed the country for the better and asked, "How can we after this, go on with our idealistic but unworkable requirement that our presidents be flawless? We are growing up. We are becoming a people capable of living comfortably with contradictions. A people who can realize that men with great shortcomings may be capable of great things." Perhaps Hillary Rodham Clinton has always seen her husband in this way. This may also be why this woman of independent means and mind may be making her chief contribution to her husband's administration through steadfastly standing her ground as William Jefferson Clinton's First Lady.

Although the scandals in the Clinton presidency are not without precedent, there is one substantial difference between the crises overhanging the Clintons and those that entangled other administrations: publicity. Except for a paternity case during Grover Cleveland's presidency, Worland (1998) reports that scandals surrounding the presidents' "intimate" lives have always "come out after the fact." Leonard (1998) suggests that some Americans fear a "sexual McCarthyism" has developed over the past two decades as politicians, through the media, continue to polarize the country over issues arising from private behavior. According to Horn (1998), there is a belief that even for elected officials, "there are things no one else has the right to reveal about you." However, the press no longer honors the privacy of the White House as it did in the pre-Watergate era (Worland, 1998). The establishment of the office of independent counsel in 1978 has positioned special prosecutors as "semipermanent agents of the attack culture" who regularly use tactics that would have raised objections a few years ago but are now accepted as routine. One *U.S. News and World Report* writer believes the courts are partly responsible for one of those tactics, "blurring the line between what is public and what is private by casually rummaging through people's sex lives. That's why the Paula Jones case, which should never have been brought, led to the Lewinsky scandal" (Leo, 1998).

Historian Betty Caroli believes that Hillary Clinton and the First Lady whom she has often referenced as her role model, Eleanor Roosevelt, have much in common: strong views of their own, a public "hotly divided over their strengths and failures, and husbands known to stray." Caroli suggests that if, as she has admitted in the past, Mrs. Clinton seeks solace in imaginary conversations with Mrs. Roosevelt, the latter may be "counseling caution and a cheerful" front for the former. Caroli goes on to recall that Mrs.

Roosevelt did not have to face public questioning, as Mamie Eisenhower did in 1954. If Hillary Clinton "could escape as unscathed as Mamie Eisenhower," Caroli suggests, then perhaps the current First Lady might be willing to engage the press more often. Then Mrs. Roosevelt might point out the example of Ellen Wilson, who lived in the White House for about a year and one half before she died in 1914 and who, when rumors circulated about Woodrow Wilson and another woman, Mary Peck, invited Ms. Peck into the White House, "treating her as a family friend." Caroli concludes:

Eleanor Roosevelt would be shocked at the very different circumstances in which first lady Clinton is required to operate. Franklin Roosevelt's infidelity was treated as a family matter, known only to relatives and close associates but not to the public at large until after both he and his wife were dead. . . . [She] never had to face the prospect of newspaper articles and TV talk shows delineating just exactly what her husband did with any other woman. Nor was the prospect of impeachment or resignation ever connected to his personal liaisons or to his efforts to conceal them. (1998)

Irrespective of whether one believes these assertions regarding these situations, the fact remains that essentially any aspect of an elected official's life, public or private, is fair game for political, and thus media, exploitation in the 1990s. This blurring of parameters is unique to the late twentieth century.

First Ladies have always reflected—sometimes "uncannily, marvelously mirrored" (Anthony, 1990, p. 9)—the status of American women of their time while simultaneously shaping expectations of what women could, in their respective times, "properly do" (Caroli, 1995, p. xxi). Simonton (1996) suggests that American First Ladies have become progressively better educated and actively involved in the world of politics, mirroring the general improvement in the status of American women, from the days when they could neither vote nor own property, to the days of various degrees of political and social equity. Just like the women before her, Hillary Rodham Clinton symbolizes cultural change and its corollary, cultural conflict. As such, she joins other American First Ladies as "the courtyard walls upon which these anxieties are scrawled" (Blumenfeld, 1996, p. 7).

Trends dictate the era that is "uniquely paralleled" by the woman in the White House at any moment in history. This is what allowed Rosalynn Carter to discuss her attendance at cabinet meetings in the 1970s, while Nellie Taft at the beginning of this century attended her husband's conferences almost secretly (Anthony, 1990–1991, 2:449–450).

Personality, political ambition, and one's role in a marriage also merge with the zeitgeist of a presidential wife's era to produce her unique enactment of the First Lady's role. Each of the women who has shaped the two hundred-year-old American First Ladyship has worked within the parameters of her time and place and within the "confines imposed by the special constraints of a political marriage" (Caroli, 1995, p. xxi). This may account in part for Hillary Clinton's retreat to the tradition of "standing by your man" during all of her husband's political crises. This also explains why Abigail Adams could become enmeshed in the question of war with France in the Federal era, why Grace Coolidge learned about the Kellogg-Briand Pact only through reading newspapers, and why Florence Harding met happily with the press in the 1920s, but a quarter of a century later, Bess Truman would not (Anthony, 1990–1991, 2:449–450).

These factors call into question pigeon-holing a woman into some arbitrarily defined First Lady ideal and, in particular, comparing these women across generations, if not centuries, except in the broadest sense. How can one compare a Mary Todd Lincoln, whose mental health was probably affected by diabetes of which mid-nineteenth-century medicine was unaware, to a Betty Ford who lived in a time when physicians could operate on cancer and psychologists could begin to grasp alcohol addiction. And is it fair to compare the university-educated Lady Bird Johnson with Julia Tyler for whom a formal education was "deemed socially improper" (Anthony, 1990–1991, 2:10)?

This generational gap was evident between Barbara Bush and Hillary Clinton in many ways. Barbara Bush, born in 1925, and Hillary Clinton, born in 1947, grew up in and envisioned different worlds. Hillary Rodham graduated from college and law school and worked outside the home for her entire adult life. Mrs. Bush dropped out of college after one year and never held a full-time job outside her home. Her choices were her husband's and her children's. Mrs. Clinton's career began first, and family came later (Caroli, 1995).

Hillary Clinton is in a sense a typical First Lady in terms of what she brings to her role and how she enacts it. As with all of her predecessors over the past two centuries, she is a woman of her times.

Branson (1998) suggests that Americans still want a "First Lady who captures hearts, not heads" and that "they need a Princess Diana, A Queen of Hearts. A Tipper Gore" (p. 12). However, Means (1995) counters that this will not last: "Most women do good things for their family but only one woman is First Lady with the opportunity to do good things for the nation. Nancy Reagan and Barbara Bush were typical of their time, but that time has gone. Pretending that Hillary Clinton is an aberration rather than the beginning of a permanent generational trend will be politically impossible to sustain."

The daughters—and, for that matter, the sons—of the past half-dozen or so First Ladies are now in line to become First Partners to American presidents. This century will not likely see a chief executive born before 1940 or listen to a First Lady describe her life as "beginning when I met my husband," as Nancy Reagan did, or say they "married the first man I kissed," as Barbara Bush did (Caroli, 1995, p. 308).

The future First Ladies will, like all First Women before them, be persons in their own right, fulfilling their roles as their hearts, minds, and generation dictate, just like Martha, Jackie, and Hillary before them. Who is to say what kind of First Partnership might have existed between Abigail and John Adams, or Sarah and James Polk, or Grover and Frankie Cleveland, or even Ike and Mamie had these women become First Ladies in 1996 or 2000 or 2004 instead of 1797, 1845, 1885, or 1953? Brant and Thomas (1996) speculate that if Hillary Clinton had lived in the nineteenth century, she would have "saved souls in Africa" (p. 2).

Lady Bird Johnson once argued that the First Couple will "do what life has shaped them to do" and that they will find among the "many choices available to them those to which they may align themselves with the most enthusiasm and understanding" (quoted in Anthony, 1990–1991, p. 42). That, in short, is what all American First Couples have done since Martha and George, and is what Hillary and Bill are doing today.

Chapter Two

Politics and Mediated Realities

Through the unpredictable operations of fate—the accidents of marriage and the electoral process—presidents' spouses have found themselves in the public eye, whether or not they wished to be there. Without set duties, they nevertheless are expected to improvise suitable roles, knowing they will be scrutinized closely as symbols of administration style or tone. Journalists stand foremost among the scrutinizers. Both influencing and reflecting public opinion, they watch the performances of the presidential spouses, measuring their success or failure by the media's own standards. (Beasley, 1987, pp. 3–4)

NARRATIVE AS SYMBOLIC ACTION: MEDIATED STORIES

According to Nimmo and Combs (1990), "To study politics without making communication a key feature of the political is, indeed, to take the 'breath' out of political science" (p. xi). Because few people learn about politics through direct experience, language activity is a mediator of it. Political experiences are generally mediated through mass and group communication, a process that results as much in the "creation, transmission, and adoption of political fantasies as it results in independently validated views of what happens." While individuals reach different personal judgments about what political reality means, the tendency is to accept the mediated, "secondhand" (p. 18) world as real without question (p. xiii). Journalist Walter Lippmann (1922) believed that humans act according to pictures in their heads of the way they perceive things. These pictures evolve from and may be changed by direct experience or, since much happens in life that is not firsthand knowledge, mediation. Therefore, the "pictures we have of politics are rarely the products of direct involvement"; rather, they "are perceptions focused, filtered, and fantasized by a host of mediators" (Nimmo and Combs, 1990, p. 2). Essentially what the public generally considers its taken-for-granted reality is "delusion"; reality is "constructed" through communication, not expressed by it; and for any situation, there is no single reality or one objective truth but "multiple, subjectively derived realities" (p. 4), many of them fashioned by the mass media.

Narratives or storytelling, as a particular form of symbolic action, have been staples of political communication. These are stories that people can relate to about the nature of a political leader. They usually involve common sense or courage, qualities with which the leader wants to associate. With symbols and values, the narrative encourages the viewer, listener, or reader to interpret an issue or leader according to the reality presented in the story. There is usually a setting or context in which an activity takes place, with main figures engaged in the activity or involved in events, at times with conflict. These carry a major meaning: the moral of the story along with an emotional edge. Jamieson (1992) believes a successful narrative controls the interpretation of reality by "offering a plausible, internally coherent story that resonates with the audience while accounting for otherwise discordant or fragmentary information" (p. 41).

In addition, the story must be believable and "internally coherent" to have impact. The "character" of the main figure is often the main point of the stories, and usually a pattern of tendencies for action is core to what the main character is about (Alger, 1996). Fisher (1989) argues that a contradiction or major change in the main figure's tendencies may breech trust in that figure. Alger (1996) illustrates this point by noting that when Ross Perot debated Vice President Gore on television in the fall of 1993 over the North American Free Trade Agreement, Gore pointed out the Perot family benefited from such free trade and Perot displayed an "antagonistic style of interaction" at odds with the public persona he had constructed. Perot's "characterological coherence" in his story or narrative suffered, and "he lost favor with the public in the aftermath of that event" (Alger, 1996, p. 54).

The nature or temper of the times—events, trends, and patterns of developments—influences how Americans accept persuasive political communications in general and the use of symbols in particular. During the 1980s and 1990s, such events included civil rights activities and conflicts, the Vietnam War, Watergate, and the Iran-contra affair, as well as the Wall Street and corporate scandals. Many Americans longed for a past that was remembered as more peaceful and honest. They also developed a growing skepticism about political and corporate issues, which became full-blown cynicism in the 1990s. Accompanying this was a tendency to condemn traditional parties, leaders, and institutions and to look for leaders and solutions untainted by "politics as usual" (Alger, 1996).

Ronald Reagan used word and visual symbols to feed into the public's longing for a country about which they could again feel pride, and Jimmy Carter played to the public's longing for a reduction of the imperial presidencies of Nixon and Johnson and untouched by the corruption of Washington. Carter tapped those feelings with the visual and action symbols of walking the parade route at his inauguration for the first time in history. The ultimate expression of what Alger (1996) calls the "symbolic of doubt about 'politics as usual'" was Ross Perot in 1992, with his plain talk, his frequent use of word symbols such as "restoring the American Dream," and the visual symbols of his "volunteers" and their various headquarters.

FRAMING: AGENDA SETTING, PRIMING, AND SUBTEXTS

In 1922, Walter Lippmann argued that the news media are a major source of the "pictures in our heads," giving people impressions of the world of public affairs that is "out of reach, out of sight, out of mind" (p. 29). According to McCombs and Estrada (1997), Lippmann's "intellectual offspring" includes agenda setting, a salience-focused mass communication theory grounded in the notion "that elements prominent in the media picture become prominent in the audience's picture" (p. 237). Agenda setting, defined by Jamieson and Capella (1997) as "a memory-based process in which accessibility of topics increases with their availability in the news environment," results in a consistent correlation between topics that the news media treat and problems the public identifies as important (p. 81) and enables the media "not only to tell us what to think about" but also "how and what to think about it, and even what to do about it" (McCombs and Estrada, 1997, p. 247). The media, particularly television, have the power to influence the public's political attitudes. Political life for most Americans is a mediated experience; the news media educate Americans about national institutions and government officials (Rozell, 1996, p. 4).

By covering some issues and ignoring others, the media set the public agenda and influence what Americans consider important issues. "Even modest amounts of television news" increase public perception of the importance of newsworthy issues. Most significant, the issues highlighted in the news are adopted by the audience as the standards by which they judge politicians. For example, when the United States "liberated" Kuwait from Iraq, military and security concerns were at the front of the public's mind; on the basis of these issues, President George Bush's performance "appeared exemplary." However, as the media later focused on the U.S. economy, citizens began to worry about the economy. "Seen in this light, President Bush appeared as a mediocre and ineffective leader" (Iyengar, 1997c, p. 213).

According to Jamieson and Capella (1997) how the news is covered is as important as what it covers. They employ the term *frame* to describe the schema or script created by the media in order to structure receivers' views of the world. Framing becomes a means of inducing a "particular kind of understanding about events in the news" (p. 85). News frames influence the public's attributions of responsibility for issues and events (Iyengar, 1997c) and are created through journalists' inclusion or exclusion of images, opinions, examples, or actors to package information for their audiences (Winett, 1997). Visually, episodic stories provide good pictures. Thematic framing depicts political issues more generally and abstractly by placing them in some appropriate context, such as historical or geographical. Reports on reductions in government welfare, changes in federal affirmative action policy, and the backlog in the criminal justice process are examples of thematic coverage. In production, a story framed thematically becomes a background report delivered by "talking heads" (Iyengar and Simon, 1997, p. 251).

Televised political news in particular, "a twenty-one minute 'headline service' operating under powerful commercial dictates" relies extensively on episodic framing as a visually appealing and on-the-scene way to make news. Conversely, thematic coverage is less frequent because of its interpretive analysis component, which "would simply crowd out other news items" (p. 251). Miller and Krosnick (1997) report that a large increase in news media coverage of an issue results in that issue's having more impact on presidential evaluations in terms of job performance and assessments of competence and integrity. News media coverage also increases its salience and the impact of related issues and sometimes decreases the impact of unrelated issues (p. 268). Edwards (1983) suggests that journalists "frame the news in themes" as a way to simplify complex events and reinforce these themes through repetition so people perceive reality stereotypically (pp. 159, 166).

News publications and broadcasts have become the dominant sources through which the electorate learns about its public officials. While such sources do not change most people's basic political orientation, they can "dramatically affect *what* people think and *how* they approach a given subject" (Sabato, 1991, p. 207). Framing is therefore a quintessential rhetorical tactic. It is a way to manipulate symbolic reality by controlling its content through discursively setting boundaries, after which the rhetor manipulates the symbols within that finite discursive territory.

There is a consistent relationship between "salience influence" (McCombs and Estrada, 1997, p. 247) and media priming (the "prominence that the news media give to a topic—and the importance of that topic in the public mind") as evidenced by the correlation between the frequency of a topic covered by the news media and its ranking in public opinion polls (Jamieson and Capella, 1997, p. 51). In addition, political issues receiving more news attention are given greater weight in people's judgments of politicians who had some direct responsibility for issues. In short, what is covered in the news affects what the public thinks and how it judges its leaders. For example, judgments of the president's performance may depend on the handling of economic, domestic, international, and political issues. A single strategically framed news story can activate cynical attributions to the subject of that story by the public. As an example, the negative reactions to President Clinton's plans for health reform could be explained in part as stemming from the electorate's cynicism about government trustworthiness (p. 231) as well as Bill Clinton's trustworthiness.

Media priming correlates the attention the news media give to an issue and the importance the issue has in evaluations of political actors (Jamieson and Capella, 1997, p. 81). The mass media shape not only what the public perceives as political reality but also how political elites understand what voters and opinion leaders are thinking about. The public therefore relies on the press's near monopoly as sources of information about political actors and events (Kuypers, 1997). The media-priming effect shows that if a particular domestic issue, such as balancing the budget, is receiving a good deal of press attention, the electorate's judgments of overall performance will depend more on how they feel the president is doing on balancing the budget than on an issue getting little attention. Therefore, the media are responsible for the ranking of issue importance as well as for the use that voters make of the issue in judging their leaders (Jamieson and Capella, 1997). The priming effect also refers to the ability of news programs to affect the criteria by which political leaders are judged. It addresses the impact of news coverage on the weight assigned to specific issues in making political judgments. Generally, the more prominent an issue is in the news media, the greater is its influence on citizens' political judgments (Ivengar and Simon, 1997).

Miller and Krosnick (1997) assert that the rapid topic-to-topic movement in news media produces dramatic changes in the public's evaluations of the president's performance. This change occurs through priming. When people make daily decisions, they rarely consider all the relevant evidence that could be used to reach a conclusion. Instead, they usually opt for decisions based on subsets of available information. To save time and effort, most people, when faced with complex problems, choose to "satisfice" or make "adequate" decisions based on only a few considerations. And just as people might make decisions about what investment to pursue or what college to attend, they also satisfice when making political judgments. For example, to decide how well President Bush was doing his job, a citizen could have evaluated how well he handled all of the issues relevant to him and his office. But given all of the issues involved, this would be a hard, if not impossible, task for the average person to accomplish, so most would satisfy their curiosity by judging how he handled only a few issues.

The media influence the process by determining in varying degrees which issues citizens use in making their overall evaluations. In 1992, the news paid much attention to the U.S. economy, which probably encouraged many Americans to think often about American economic factors, to talk with family and others about them, and to believe that the economy was a significant political issue. When deciding how good a job President Bush was doing, Americans may have been especially inclined to think of the economy as one criterion. However, had the media focused on President Bush's Gulf War success during that time, citizens may have leaned toward evaluating him on that basis and overlooked the economic situation, considering the "victory" over Iraq to be the more significant issue and therefore the more important standard against which to judge George Bush's presidency. Miller and Krosnick (1997) conclude that most of the issues that the media cover end up being primed and so become the "predominant bases for the public's evaluations of its president" (p. 260).

Episodic frames focus on specific instances and individuals rather than general or thematic information, while thematic frames depict collective or general concepts. Episodic frames attribute responsibility for the cause and treatment of problems to individuals rather than society or situations and depict issues in terms of specific instances, such as a terrorist bombing or a homeless person. An episodic frame for an issue such as poverty would encourage constituents to attribute responsibility for that state to individual factors such as laziness instead of societal factors such as underemployment. Capella and Jamieson (1997) explain this effect by what has been called "the fundamental attribution error and actor-observer differences." When viewing others' behavior, there is a consistent tendency to explain actions in terms of a person's characteristics rather than the surrounding situation (p. 84). The news frame most Americans focus on pertaining to government officials is generally episodic—an organized set of assumptions that state leaders are often self-interested to the exclusion of the public good, that their votes can be swayed by monied or special interests that do not serve the public's ends, and that political actors are dishonest about what they are trying to accomplish and driven privately by a desire to stay in power (p. 39).

Subtextual Framing

Sabato (1991) contends that the diminished threat of successful libel suits has empowered reporters to publish their "frank" evaluations of a public persona's basic character. These episodically framed portrayals often produce an "accurate or not" general consensus about a politician's personality, complete with stereotypes, which becomes that individual's subtext, or the "between-the-lines character sketch that guides and sets the tone for press coverage." Reporters then look for circumstances that fit the stereotype, particularly in terms of shortcomings. Therefore a major incident that "validates the subtext" as mediated by the press has a good chance of being magnified into a journalistic "feeding frenzy" because it seems to validate the press's own judgment.

For example, most of the journalists who covered the "plagiarism scandal" surrounding Joseph Biden's presidential bid shared the same conventional wisdom vision. ABC's Brit Hume described Biden as a "blowhard" who did not have much to say and "wasn't very deep," and E. J. Dionne, formerly with the *New York Times* (which played a major role in the senator's political demise), described Biden as "mostly talk." Columnist Jack Germond stated that Biden was known only as a "guy who gave a good speech," which, as it turned out, was a speech that "other people had already given." *Time* described him as a "gabby lightweight" who "might talk himself out of the nomination" (Barrett, 1987); *Business Week* headlined, "Is Joe Biden More Than 'Just a Speech'?" (Harbrecht, 1987), and the *Economist* challenged him to prove he was "not just a pretty face and articulate voice" ("More Urge," 1987). According to Sabato (1991), although this common vision of Joseph Biden may have had elements of truth in it, a fairer evaluation of his qualifications for the presidency might have been achieved if the judgment criterion had been his long and substantive legislative career rather than typecasting based on stereotypes. A more balanced assessment of Joe Biden was prevented because the media "nearly universally embraced" the "substance of his subtext" (p. 74).

Other political actors who were negatively influenced by their subtexts include Geraldine Ferraro and Dan Quayle. President Gerald Ford's subtext began to gel after Lyndon Johnson's remark that Ford "couldn't walk and chew gum at the same time." He had been ridiculed in the popular media because of what appeared to be his innate clumsiness, ranging from bumping into things to tripping and falling getting off airplanes and on ski slopes. In fact, Gerald Ford, a Yale Law School graduate, possesses a keen intellect, and Sabato (1991) calls him one of the most fit and athletic presidents of the twentieth century.

Nor was Jimmy Carter, Ford's opponent in the 1976 presidential election, free from the negative results of being caught in a subtextually created mesh. He was negatively stereotyped because of prejudices against his southern roots and his religion, Southern Baptist. Even before the "lust in the heart" *Playboy* interview, which was given to reframe Carter's religious beliefs, he had received much criticism because of the phrase "ethnic purity," which he had used to describe his support for the preservation of ethnic neighborhoods. The phrase was contextualized by the press to confirm their vision of Jimmy Carter as yet another racist southerner. *Time*'s Walter Shapiro, an aide during the Carter administration, criticized the press at the time for their bizarre journalistic notion that "these two words negated" Jimmy Carter's impressive civil rights record and his strong support among black leaders (quoted in Sabato, 1991, p. 74).

During his term of office, President Jimmy Carter also became evidence that an insignificant incident could "become a debilitating frenzy, given the right press subtext and spin." In the summer of 1979, after an AP story about a swamp rabbit's "attack" on his Plains rowboat, the "killer rabbit" became a "press parable" of Jimmy Carter's political impotence—"a perfect metaphor for a president at the mercy of political plagues, big and small" (quoted in Sabato, 1991, p. 75).

Occasionally, one scandal may create a subtext for the next. The *Washington Post*'s Bob Woodward considered "Debategate" as the precursor to the Iran-contra scandal since it demonstated that some of Ronald Reagan's staff were willing to use "subterfuge" to get what they wanted. In addition, Iran-contra may have reversed the dominant subtext of the Reagan presidency up to that point: Ronald Reagan as an astute delegator and superb manager (Boot, 1987).

In addition, Sabato (1991) believes that media frenzies feed on one another. As they weave topics from previous scandals into stories about emerging scandals, reporters are able to develop precedents from one scandal or frenzy to justify creating another. As an example, the Gary Hart–Donna Rice scandal story set the tone for publication of the "George Bush mistress" rumor.

By the time Gary Hart emerged as a possible front-runner for the 1984 Democratic presidential candidate nomination, his subtext was already well established. A veteran political journalist for the *Los Angeles Times,* Bob Shogan, considered the Democrat to be "one strange and quirky person." The *New Republic*'s Fred Barnes called Gary Hart "a weird man" and described him as the "strangest guy I ever talked to." The *Washington Post*'s George Lardner, who first tracked Hart's misrepresentation of his age, described him as "strange," and the *Post*'s Richard Cohen thought of him as a person who "doesn't make sense," a major negative, since "you're talking about the guy who's sitting next to the [nuclear] button" (quoted in Sabato, 1991, pp. 76–77). A major subtextual theme surrounding Gary Hart was his image as a womanizer. Despite the existence of such rumors for years, this subtext did not become a frenzy until the 1988 presidential campaign; by that time, the press was primed since Hart was the clear Democratic front-runner. Having gone "on record" in 1984 with his "I love danger" statement, perceived by some reporters as a challenge, the womanizing subtext became the full-blown scandal that took out his candidacy when the story of Gary Hart's relationship with Donna Rice was headlined by the *Miami Herald* (Sabato, 1991, p. 78).

MEDIA AS A GOVERNMENT INSTITUTION

Sparrow (1999) considers the news media to be a fourth component of the American political system. Rather than being a fourth branch in the sense of being part of the government itself or a fourth estate that checks the excesses of the other three government branches, it is a "fourth corner" in the "iron triangle" model of the policy process. The metaphor of an iron box better represents the role of the media, which become a part of the threesome of congressional committees, special interests, and public administrators in policy making and outcomes. The media conglomerates, with huge commercial stakes, engage in political action to protect or further their own positions, as do other large corporate or societal entities. The effect of the bottom-line orientation on news production points to the "institutional existence" of the news media (p. 94). In this view, the news media are private actors representing a narrow slice of the American public who have power over matters that affect the entire country. Although there are important differences among the political news media, the various newspapers, newsmagazines, broadcast and cable television, and radio broadcasters constitute a political institution that produces "remarkably consistent news coverage across separate organizations—no matter the medium." Editors and producers are thus employees of organizations and television; newsmagazine newspaper offices and newsrooms are places of bosses and subordinates "with shared conformity" (Sparrow, 1999, pp. 130–131). The news media influence elections, Congress, the federal bureaucracy, the Supreme Court, foreign, economic and public policy as well as the president so much that they "cannot maneuver without factoring in the presence and potential actions of the news media" (p. 133).

Kurtz (1998) argues that the Clinton White House acknowledged four power centers in Washington: the White House, Congressional Hill, lobbyists, and the press. An administration official had to deal with all of them. By the summer of 1997, Clinton had acknowledged and played to the "press party," the White House journalists who considered themselves essentially members of Congress. Such "proper presidential attention could yield dividends" (Kurtz, 1998, p. 242). Because of this awareness, Clinton asked Paul Begala, a consultant from his first presidential campaign, to return to sell the administration to the media (Kurtz, 1998). Begala "spoke press, understanding the rhythms and needs of reporters, the art of the leak" and the "slashing humor" required for regular appearances on television.

Part of Begala's role was to explain the nature of journalism to the president. He believed the "elite press" was like a "Gang of 200" who talked mostly to each other but whose opinions mattered. The president needed to learn that his power derived not only from the ballot box but from journalists as well (Kurtz, 1998). To that end, Clinton lit the candles in the Cabinet Room for Helen Thomas's seventy-seventh birthday and sent CBS producer Mark Knoller a signed copy of a newspaper picture featuring Knoller at a bill signing, saying, "You're always there when history is made." Clinton had dinner with ABC's Cokie Roberts and her husband, Steve Roberts, of the *New York Daily News*. He called to congratulate Carl Rowan on his final day as a panelist on television's *Inside Washington*. Clinton sent Wolf Blitzer a note when his mother died and had an off-the-record talk with the *Washington Post*'s chief political reporter, Dan Balz. The president also provided the *Post*'s Ceci Bonnolly with an "unusually frank" interview about Republican House leaders during which he referenced Newt Gingrich as "the only guy who can give us a run for our money on the vision thing" but who sometimes "just checks out" and talks outrageously (quoted in Kurtz, 1998, pp. 242–243).

The history of American news media development reveals how the media are treated as an institution by government, with subsidies and privileges. The pressures of uncertainty and the rise of professionalism also force most news organizations to look alike so that "we can then speak not of the news media as organizations or as institutions in the plural, but as a single—and quite singular—institution" (Cook, 1998, p. 15). The strong similarities of news processes and news content across the modalities (television, radio, newspapers and newsmagazines), size of organization, national or local audiences, and the like "point to the news media as a single institution" (p. 84), or a true "fourth estate." In Press and Verburg's (1988) view, how governments organize themselves determines the access the media have to political information. Separation of powers mandates a splintering rather than a concentration of American political power. The president, legislators, judges, and administrators reach office in different ways and are accountable to different constituencies. The terms of office are different lengths; the legislature is divided into two bodies, partly to check each other. Legal powers are distributed so that officials in one branch check and balance the powers of officials in other branches.

Major coordinating powers were given to only the presidency by the Founders. The chief executive is the only official who can give some direction to the government. However, even the president leads as much through persuasion as by command, which in turn rests on the president's legal powers, political skills, and, in particular, popular support.

The result is a government with an antiorganization bias composed of competing politicians with diverse career ambitions, different power bases, and unique constituencies. As power in the American system is splintered, so is information about policymaking. As a result, the president is a major source of stories, and the reporter is both recorder of government and participant in that government.

The media operate in a system in which power is divided. A reporter becomes an "indispensable broker and middleman" among the subgovernments of Washington, a person who can "illumine policy and notably assist in giving it sharpness and clarity; just as easily, he can prematurely expose policy and, as with an undeveloped film, cause its destruction. At his worst, operating with arbitrary and faulty standards, he can be an agent of disorder and confusion. At his best, he can exert a creative influence on Washington politics" (Cater, 1959, p. 7).

According to Cook (1998) the "fourth branch" metaphor is ironic because it was created by nineteenth-century British journalists to provide them with a legitimate political role. Although the ideas of independently checking governmental power are similar, American journalists have been wary of accepting a "fourth branch" designation because it would place them within government. They work hard to discourage perceptions of them as political actors. They attempt to argue their product is neutral news, but the twin concerns that news should be both important and interesting cannot be divorced from politics. Important news is often certified as such by persons in a position to know based on their official position within government. Therefore, powerful officials are best positioned to create news events, certify issues as newsworthy, and make news on their own terms.

Although these political actors are best able to verify the importance of issues, journalists are the final arbiter of what is interesting. Officials stage media events with particular coverage in mind, but the ultimate news story depends on what the journalists desire. Production values—drama, novelty, timeliness, vividness, color, easily described stories with two distinct sides, terseness, good visuals, pithy sound bites—often set the angle of the story or the play or spin given it. In this view, contemporary American news media are not only part of politics; they are part of government (Cook, 1998).

Some of the presidential staff may now be more loyal to the media branch rather than the executive branch of government. Nixon had "Deep Throat," who leaked inside information to investigative reporters. Essentially all modern presidents have experienced damaging leaks from within, often from those whose goals and careers conflict with the president's. Few members of Congress feel obliged to keep a president's confidences on all issues. In addition, the president may not be able to locate those who reveal administration secrets to the media and may not even be able to silence them if found. Nor are political secrets of the administration's opponents protected from leaks. However, journalists often find separation of power beneficial as it guarantees them a great deal of news and multiple perspectives from which to access information (Press and Verburg, 1988).

The mass media's concern is how to be independent as White House correspondents when there is a dependence on the president and his offices for information. Scholars who study political communication wonder about two major presidential mass media conflicts: the executive's manipulation of the American mass media and the overriding power of the national press—an unelected "other government" (Winfield, 1994, p. xii).

The American electorate tends to regard the office of the president as a national symbol while simultaneously distrusting the political actor who is the president and the practice of politics. They are inclined to see the president as more than chief political and executive officer; he is the national symbol, someone "we all must rally around," someone whose message much be heard and whose leadership is primary in the nation and must not be fettered. On the other hand, Americans have a long tradition of being suspicious of politics; they think that political matters are inherently less-than-honorable, even dirty activities—sentiments that have especially focused on Congress, although the pattern seems to have been extended to the president. The word *politician* itself has a negative ring to it in American political culture. Further (at least in form), there is a long tradition of suspicion of governmental power, especially in the hands of a chief executive, which is the principal reason for the nonparliamentary, separation-of-powers form of government established in the U.S. Constitution. Such perceptions have created a tough rhetorical environment for American presidents.

The changing nature of journalism increasingly has altered the coverage of the president and the relations between press and president. At various points in history, presidents have had a rough time with press coverage. Politicians have long claimed that journalists distort information to get the public's attention. George Washington's early drafts of his Farewell Address included attacks on journalists. And Thomas Jefferson said he would "not hesitate a moment" to choose a nation with newspapers and no government over one with a government but no newspapers" (quoted in Press and Verburg, 1988, p. 10).

However, a new stage in press-president relations began in the late 1960s and, despite a hiatus during most of the Reagan and Bush years, solidified and deepened in the Clinton years. Through the Kennedy administration, the news media's coverage of the president in the twentieth century was fairly positive, and presidents were able to control the use of their communications, particularly in press conferences. Through at least the early part of the Eisenhower era, they exercised strong control over the use that newspeople could make of presidents' comments in press conferences. And through the early years of Lyndon Johnson's presidency, the basic orientation of the press toward presidents was relatively positive and constructive. But Vietnam and newspeoples' perceptions that President Johnson was not telling the truth about that war raised profound doubts about the relationship. President Nixon's problems with the truth, in regard to both Vietnam and Watergate, shattered the positive orientation of newspeople toward presidents, turning them into skeptics about what presidents say. That investigative reporters, especially the *Washington Post*'s Woodward and Bernstein, were at the center of exposing the wrongdoing in Watergate resulted in much emphasis on efforts to expose official conduct that might be illegal or unethical (Alger, 1996).

In the aftermath of the Nixon years, the new orientation manifested itself in a negative coverage of the Carter presidency. But with the help of a sophisticated public relations operation and Ronald Reagan's own personality, there was an easing off during the coverage of the Reagan administration and a much less critical press response, at least for the first two and a half years, of George Bush's presidency (Alger, 1996).

This all changed with the Clinton administration. Some origins of the bad relations between President Clinton and the press originated in the 1992 election campaign, but in general, "in coverage of the Clinton White House, the news media returned to the orientation of abiding skepticism and intensified it to the point of unbridled attack journalism founded on a bedrock of cynicism" (Alger, 1996, p. 202). Even the traditional honeymoon period of at least a few months, at the beginning of the president's term, which even

Carter enjoyed, was eliminated in Clinton's case. Patterson (1994) believes that Bill Clinton's presidency from its inception was the victim of "hypercritical news coverage" (p. 21).

Politicians and journalists define "political news" in different ways. Garrison Keillor, of PBS's *Prairie Home Companion*, summed up his reasons for being wary of the press during an address at a journalism convention: "We see things differently. If I were to suffer a violent death, you would regard it as a professional opportunity" (quoted in Press and Verburg, 1988, p. 11).

Politicians complain about the kind of events the media deem newsworthy. Journalists, they say, are generally interested only in political events that attract readers and viewers. There is a focus on the superficial—political items that shock or amuse—rather than substantial issues. "Human interest" stories are sought out. Press and Verburg (1988) recall that once following a broadcast of a presidential nominating convention, the television anchor booth switched from covering the political notables on the platform to an interview with a bearded "candidate for president" who said he campaigned in favor of free silver while riding on Greyhound buses between Utah and Oregon. They also noted stories concentrating on a mayor's peculiar habit of breaking crackers into his coffee, while generally ignoring the policies he was proposing.

Political actors also complain that much news coverage gives citizens oversimplified and overly moralistic pictures of a complex political process. Issues and ideas are turned into a "good guys versus bad guys horse opera . . . building in extraneous drama." Some have suggested that television journalists in particular have difficulty deciding whether they are in the information or entertainment business (Press and Verburg, 1988, p. 14). Bill Moyers, President Lyndon Johnson's press secretary and PBS news commentator, argues, "The rules of politics are negotiation, weaving, subtlety, nuance, trading, advancing, retreating, and so on. These are the things with which you sustain the political process. But television doesn't like nuance. And television doesn't like subtlety. . . . Television deals in a world of simplicity and insists politicians play by the rules of television and not the rules of politics" (quoted in Shales, 1980, p. B11).

Nevertheless, American government increasingly relies on the news media to communicate among and within its parts. Among national institutions, according to Cook (1998), all three branches—executive, legislative, and judicial—now devote more time and energy to media relations and to "going public" than they did in the late 1950s. The entry of journalists into governing and their emergence as a fourth estate is costly to the working of the "other" three branches, given reporters' ultimate control over the news product and their potentially divergent sense of what is news.

The news media are "political"—that is, they enter "into the authoritative allocation of values" (Cook, 1998, p. 86)—by reinforcing political power or otherwise providing resources to official actors to pursue their agendas. The political role of the news media generally lies in augmenting the reach of those who are already politically powerful. However, the media are at least partially independent from their sources in producing the content of the news and so may influence who is authoritative, what the values of politics are, and which allocations are made. According to this perspective, like the other three constitutional branches of government, the fourth estate news media are partially independent from and partially dependent on other institutions in accomplishing their own task. So the media are not only political in the United States; they are also part of government.

The news media are generally successful in mirroring the outside world and are thus "governmental" when they emphasize "official action." Yet the news is also political because it sometimes presents and interprets such actions in a way not always beneficial to the actors. As a result, the news is often the result of "recurring negotiations between sources and newspersons, the daily results of which favor only certain authoritative allocations of values" (Cook, 1998, p. 87). In other words, the news media are political because the choices they end up making do not equally favor all political actors, processes, and messages. In this sense, not only do they reflect external political actions; they are directly involved in instigating them. Individual journalists' biases and omissions become less important if journalism is conceptualized as a collective enterprise across individuals and organizations that implicitly contains a set of assumptions about how the world works and how the world should work and so bring with it a finite number of political interpretations. The American press becomes a political institution because individual news outlets reinforce each other's coverage, and the processes of news making become similar from one medium organization to the next. Most significant, the news media are a political institution because of their central role in the American political and social process as the producer and arbiter of communication.

The modern White House is information driven. According to Richard Reeves (1997b), reporters have made driving that information their business. Decision making has become high speed and interactive, while analysis and adjustment is reactive and continuous. The checks and balances and "cumbersome" process devised in the eighteenth century to slow governance are now "like flags snapping under an out-of-control skier" so that "too much is happening too quickly to be seen much less understood." For example, the "old newspaper staple, the story behind the story" has been overtaken by the "story before the story." When *Los Angeles Times* reporters Bill Rempel and Doug Frantz were in Little Rock, Arkansas, in 1993 checking on rumors about Bill Clinton's sex life when he was governor, a Republican congressman from California, Robert Dornan, went on Rush Limbaugh's radio program announcing that the paper was about to publish a story on the new allegations. Reeves continues:

It is, simply a great time to be a reporter—if you are at the top. In the middle ranges, however, journalists are losing freedom—the freedom to roam. There was a time . . . when reporters sitting around in the middle of the day would be asked why they were not out scaring up some news. Now, if they are not at their desks scanning the screen, they are asked where they have been and why. Why do you have to go out and talk to people, including senators and presidential advisers, when it is all on C-Span and the Internet? (pp. xii-xiii)

THE ELECTORATE'S RELIANCE ON PRESS-MEDIATED REALITIES

The press is most influential in mediating perceptions about the world in areas where people have little direct experience, such as politics. Accordingly, public perceptions of national politics depend on the mediation of journalists and news organizations. The practices and procedures of news organizations "take on a life of their own, influencing the conduct and character of national politics" (Sparrow, 1999, p. xii).

The first true medium of mass communication was established and took hold in America during the middle third of the nineteenth century: the mass circulation newspaper, originally called the "penny press." The twentieth century brought further developments in the communications capacities of radio and television—dramatic developments considering the scope of the audience reached by these broadcast media and their pervasiveness in modern life.

When Truman was born in 1884, metropolitan newspapers, following the example of Joseph Pulitzer and the *New York World*, were just beginning to blend sensationalism and solid news reporting characteristic of the era's new journalism. The wireless of Marconi and his rivals loomed just over the horizon, but commercial radio's news coverage did not begin until 1920, when KDKA in Pittsburgh broadcast the results of the presidential election. Television, successfully demonstrated by several of its various fathers during the 1920s, required more than two decades of development before it became a national medium of news communication at midcentury. Televison's predecessor, newsreels shown in motion picture theaters, brought first the sights and then the sounds of the news until their demise a few years before Truman's life drew to its close in 1972. The dramatic changes in technologies and networks of mass media that developed in the 1990s, including cable TV and information technologies, gave promise of further changes in communication across boundaries of time, space, and status and in learning about public affairs and society more generally.

A basic question is what role the mass media play in a democracy. The centerpiece of a representative democratic system is the process of selection of representatives by the public through elections, intended to be the principal form of political participation by the public. There are other vital dimensions of the democratic political process. A primary purpose of elections is to hold government officials accountable for their performance in office. But both elected and appointed government officials must be held accountable between elections as well. The ways people come to respond to political communications and to perceive political leaders, institutions, and issues are key elements in how the system works.

Most people have neither the time nor will to search for detailed, authoritative sources of information on candidates, issues, and governmental performance. In the past, much of this information has come from political parties and their organizations. But as the parties have declined greatly over the past twenty-five years as influences on American's political behavior, people increasingly have relied on the mass media for such information. Even when decisions are partly based on conversations with others, the media still are an indirect information source. In Capella and Jamieson's (1997) opinion, few Americans have close contact with election campaigns or the performance of their leaders; knowledge about them comes primarily through news reports.

Full access to information is a major principle of a democracy. The mass media's role in providing adequate information for people to make the democratic process work is imperative in the United States. In addition to the decline in political parties as information networks and guides to political options, society has become more mobile, and the economy is dominated by national and international corporations. These factors, combined with job changes, travel and other factors, have resulted in an extremely high percentage of Americans who do not have the benefit of long-term, stable social networks that might help share information about and interpret political matters (Alger, 1996).

The general public has minimal levels of political attention and information, minimal mastery of abstract political concepts such as liberalism and conservatism, and minimal political preference stability. In addition, people develop political opinions based on the ideas that are the most prominent or important to them—which has major implications for how the media cover public affairs (Alger, 1996). People's low levels of attention to and knowledge of politics and issues, combined with the decline of the role of political parties as a means of helping them sort out political choices, suggest a reason for the reliance of most Americans on mass media for their political ideas.

Many Americans lack long-term ties to community and social networks that help their members interpret occurrences in the world in a constant and stable manner. In the contemporary political climate, with national organizations and media dominant, Americans tend to look to remote leaders and institutions and to invest their hopes and feelings in them. Presidents are a prime example. People know about matters with which they have little or no experience only "with considerable difficulty," and so symbols carry great weight in helping them "learn" about such things (Alger, 1996).

Murray Edelman (1967) wrote of symbolics and politics:

For most [people] most of the time politics is a series of pictures in the mind, placed there by television news, newspapers, magazines, and discussions. The pictures create a moving panorama taking place in a world the mass public never quite touches, yet one its members come to fear or cheer.... There is ... the immediate world in which people make and do things [and] can check their facts.... Politics is for most of us a passing parade of abstract symbols.... It is central to its potency as a symbol that it is remote, set apart [distant, in the psychological as well as geographical senses from the mass public]. (pp. 5–6)

The impact and outcomes of political actions are difficult for most people to figure out because of political actors' remoteness. The impossibility of checking "real conditions" makes the use and effect of symbols and narratives or stories on the American public a major element in political communication (Alger, 1996). The news is what economists call a *credence good*: a product that has to be consumed on faith, since it is difficult for the customer to evaluate the quality of the commodity, even after it has been consumed. Medical treatment, automobile and appliance repairs, and a liberal arts education are other examples of credence goods. Consumers of such goods are generally unable to distinguish high quality from low quality at the point of consumption and for a short while after. Individuals cannot inspect the news (unless they are "there" in person), and most of the news is beyond their experience, so they rarely have a real-world comparison for evaluation.

That the news is a credence good means that news organizations have much latitude in deciding what news to present. They therefore define "news" largely by "breadth of appeal" or whatever story sells best. News that is easiest to cover for commercial reasons (for example, the O. J.

Simpson trial, crime in general, natural disasters, and other sensational stories) can be presented and often accepted as "genuinely serious current events," even though the consumers may actually be taken advantage of or misled (Sparrow, 1999).

THE POWER OF THE MEDIA: INFORMATION CONTROL

The majority of the public's knowledge, political and otherwise, comes from the mass media. According to Winfield (1994), free expression is a necessary concomitant to self-government, dependent on public information so that the bulk of the electorate's knowledge comes from the mass media. In addition, the media's control of information is a source of power. The public learns most of what it knows about politicians from news reports. What reporters write or say in interpretive or investigative stories can directly influence political careers (Press and Verburg, 1988).

The media trumps those its reporters interview, particularly on television, because of production techniques and framing. Journalists hide their influence from outside actors and themselves by "following standard routines of newsmaking." By adhering to what Cook (1998) identifies as the "strategic ritual of objectivity," journalists can persuade their readers and themselves that their report is as neutral as it can be. In fact, the opposite is true. The final news product therefore gives little sense of the individual choices that reporters work hard to protect in their work. Furthermore, the separation of editorials and "news analysis," on one hand, from straight news, on the other, suggests that only the former is subjective. The camera framing of television journalists is a visual translation of this strategic ritual of objectivity, shot in "close social distance," which allows for discussion without intimacy. The language of news as well as television framing enable journalists to present themselves as "coolly dispassionate in contrast to the intensity, color, and subjectivity of their subjects." As a result, journalists work hard to "maximize their autonomy" and even harder to present a news account that seems largely beyond their individual control (p. 7).

In pursuing objectivity, reporters end up implicitly adding a structural bias to the news—one that favors certain actors, events, programs, and issues. The most prevalent bias of the news is its concentration on the events, ideas, preoccupations, strategies, and politics of powerful officials. According to Cook (1998) this is what enables the news media to be not "merely" political but governmental as well. The availability of the media provokes officials to think of them as a potential help to accomplish their goals and therefore assists the conversion of the news media into an "institution of governance" (p. 111).

However, the mostly private ownership of the news media and its profit orientation provide a counterweight to official governmental power as journalists apply standards of newsworthiness beyond importance to interest their audiences. It follows, in this view, that the authority or power of government officials rests on their ability and willingness as political actors to fit their activities to the production values of the news. If they do not, the politicians risk losing control of their agenda and/or being portrayed in negative terms. Cook (1998) notes that American news in particular tends to vacillate widely between news that "deeply reinforces the officials' aims and news that undercuts them" (p. 111).

The basis for a free press in a democracy may be the right to criticize government, yet citizens must have enough information on which to base an opinion before criticizing. For example, the lack of information during World War II did not stop either the public or the press from holding the president accountable, but the criticisms might have been more credible had there been more reliable information. Thus, control of information is a source of tremendous political power. In the United States' populist conception of a democratic government, a supreme value has been placed on critical information to permit the people to decide issues and vote so that the government, in giving out information, cannot be superior in the information process, nor can the press (Winfield, 1994).

The major media carry much that their owners personally disagree with. However, this does not prevent emphasis of certain issues and deemphasis of others. Owners hire and fire those who make the everyday decisions on content, and "it is a rare corporation that hires an influential executive known to be inimical to the owner's heartfelt social values" (Bagdikian, 1997, p. 71). This narrowing of political and social content in the media stems not from reporters' being told to write something that is false, but from their being told what stories to focus on and what stories to ignore.

Dominant media corporations "operate at the highest levels of national and international power and have political and social goals crucial to that power." Their agendas, which include favoring lower corporate taxes, lower levels of social services for the general public, and governmental and market advantages for large corporation owners, have affected media content and public opinion on major issues. For example, the media were "notoriously slow" to report seriously on post–World War II phenomena like structural poverty, McCarthyism, and resistance to racial segregation. Most of the major media resisted overwhelming evidence of U.S. policy failures in Vietnam or the early evidence of the Watergate scandal in the Nixon administration (Bagdikian, 1997).

Hearst, Pulitzer, Scripps, and Dana in the nineteenth century and Frank Gannett, Colonel McCormick, and Henry Luce in the twentieth all pursued their own political aims while collecting large audiences and high profits. For example, Henry Luce influenced his generation's attitudes toward China. By stressing the American fear of communism and support for Christianity, he deemphasized the Chinese communists' popular support and rejection of Stalinist doctrine and the emphasis on opposition of the nationalists' corruption. Luce did so while making *Time* magazine so profitable it became the flagship for his media empire of Time, Inc. (Bagdikian, 1997).

The press is biased toward a "good story" because that makes its product more marketable. In that way, reporters can counter the power of politicians who can feed stories to the press. The press is then able to choose both what stories to cover and how to frame or present them. In effect, the "logic of the market" (Cook, 1998, p. 112) biases, maintained by the commercial pressure to attract and keep audiences, counterbalance the effect of political actors' power on the media. The making of news not only transforms happenings into events and then into stories but also takes the original occurrence out of its initial context and places it into another context of the journalists' choosing. One of the consequences is that issues and occurrences that do not easily become narratives or "good" stories are likely to be neglected in favor of those that do. Cook (1998) cites as an example how a reform-minded interest group initially captured reporters' attention by evidence of how nursing homes defrauded Medicare. Soon, however, this angle was transformed into an NBC report focusing on how nursing homes abused patients—partly because of the media's "need for clear villains and victims" and partly because of their inability to present fraud visually as well as they could present abuse. The executive producer of NBC News said when the producer unveiled a fraud piece, "It's just too complicated. Where are the victims?" (quoted in Cook, 1998, p. 112).

In addition, frames are used to structure and organize the contents of "policy-relevant" political news stories to support one position over others. For example, an article about pesticides headlined "New Double-Duty Insecticide" would be perceived much differently from one headlined "Nerve Gas in the Orchards." It therefore becomes imperative to determine which frame or frames dominate media coverage. Paletz (1998) argues that "policy makers know this" and points to an example from Bill Clinton, who framed the issue of gays in the military as a question of status when he called for a lift of the ban. Clinton argued, "Should people who have served their country with distinction—many of them with battlefield ribbons—and who have never had any kind of question about their conduct, be booted out of the military?"(cited in Cannon, 1993, p. 46). His opponents counter-framed the issue in terms of disrupting military discipline and morale, undermining combat readiness, and negative images of homosexual behavior. Finally, the media framed it as intergroup conflict, with the military on one side and gays on the other (Paletz, 1998, pp. 224–225).

PRINT AND ELECTRONIC CHANNELS OF MEDIATION

There are significant differences and impacts in the nature of each of the mass media. The printed word comes in several specific forms as mass media; those of principal political interest are newspapers and magazines. The news reaches essentially all adult Americans. According to Iyengar (1997c), newspapers and magazines reach 100 million Americans every day, while access to television is "near universal and, at times, so is the audience." The funeral of John Kennedy, the moon landing, the marriage of the prince of Wales, the U.S. Senate hearings on charges of sexual harassment against Supreme Court nominee Clarence Thomas, and the announcement of the verdict in the O. J. Simpson trial were watched by nearly all Americans. And since the networks and print sources report on the same issues, events, and people, regardless of medium, the messages conveyed in the news are homogeneous. The news carried through these outlets is also increasingly about national events. Radio and television depend on networks with their nationally advertised products. They feature national news to hold their audience. Local stories are often given national twists, and even the smaller dailies, with the help of the Associated Press, feature national and international news. Nationalizing the news means that more of the stories reported are politically themed (Press and Verburg, 1988).

Sparrow (1999) observes that editors pay attention to their competitors at the most elite and influential publications, particularly the *New York Times*. The *Times* is considered to be the standard by which other media decide how to handle or if to handle a story. Many of the *Time*'s front-page stories become lead stories for television news shows and magazines. The *Washington Post*, the *Los Angeles Times*, and other papers also consult the front page of the *New York Times* when they assemble their own front pages. There are a limited number of leading journalists and news organizations that report authoritatively to Americans, either directly through the television networks, subscriptions, and newsstand sales or indirectly through newspaper news services and local news programs. Along with the *New York Times*, the *Washington Post*, the *Wall Street Journal*, the *Los Angeles*

Times, AP, Reuters, the newsmagazines, ABC News, NBC News, CBS News, and CNN are considered political authorities (Sparrow, 1999). Pertschuk (1997), while arguing that commercial television "may be the medium that matters most," notes that newspapers shape the agenda of television journalists, who "still read newspapers even if their viewers do not" (p. 391). Although the United States is only beginning to have national newspapers, the *Washington Post* and the *New York Times*, through their prestige and use by elites, have a much greater scope of influence than the base of their circulation would suggest. Television networks usually follow the lead of these two major elite newspapers, which get most of their news from the wire services. Stories that the editors of these papers opt to put on their front pages usually become the lead stories on the evening television network news (Robinson and Sheehan, 1983). When the *New York Times* "commits itself" to a scandal involving the president of the United States, the rest of the media invariably follow, guaranteeing partisan political operatives and opportunistic opponents a free ride (Lyons, 1996, p. 25).

Sabato and Lichter (1994) argue that how the mainstream press handles a story about a scandal determines the life of that story and influences its impact. For example, the February 11, 1994, news conference of Paula Corbin Jones was not carried on CNN, while "Troopergate" was. This may have assisted media organizations in ignoring Jones's allegations until the filing of the lawsuit and the hiring of an attorney by President Clinton. Conversely, CNN played a vital role in generating media focus on "Troopergate," which the *New Republic*'s Fred Barnes believes would have been "successfully submerged" had it not been by CNN's running of the story in December 1992, which led other stations to go with it and soon after also received the attention of the White House (Sabato and Lichter, 1994).

In Lyons's (1996) view, the "Clinton scandals" were the result of "one of the nastiest and most successful political 'dirty tricks' campaigns in recent American history." Aided and abetted by a group of Arkansas Republicans "whose hatred knew no bounds," the scandals originated in a planned campaign underwritten by right-wing organizations such as Floyd Brown's Citizens United, Reed Irvine's Accuracy in Media, and evangelists Jerry Falwell and Pat Robertson. In addition, an irony of the Clinton presidency is that as a centrist and a compromiser, President Clinton had "almost no natural allies in the press," liberal or otherwise:

With *The Washington Post* and *The American Spectator* flogging the Whitewater story on one side, even *The Village Voice* and *The Nation* joined in the attack. Why? Because while the majority of voters say they're in the middle, most of the passion and all of the good rhetoric is on either end of the ideological spectrum. Once the

Times and the *Post* committed their prestige to the Whitewater scandal, there was almost nobody left to question its provenance. (p. 5)

Mark Penn was a pollster who joined the Clinton staff during the 1996 campaign to track front-page stories in the *New York Times, Washington Post,* and *USA Today.* He focused on the last because its 2 million copies were sold daily at newsstands and airports, and as a "more populist" medium, it was more likely to reflect what Americans were focused on and what was covered in local papers. Penn believed the typical *USA Today* reader "didn't read page A-12" and was too busy to read long, complicated articles about Webb Hubbell. If Bill Clinton made the front page of *USA Today*, he was likely to do well in the *Miami Herald, Kansas City Star,* and *Seattle Post-Intelligencer.*

During Clinton's first term, Susan Page of *USA Today* had been given three interviews. With its billboard-style format of short front-page stories, the daily would present "little scooplets" about a forthcoming speech or announcement pertaining to the administration. Page would often call up on Thursday, trying to snag an exclusive for Friday's paper, reminding the White House that *USA Today* didn't publish on weekends. The White House, realizing there would be little room for details, was "usually happy to comply" (Kurtz, 1998, p. 205). Penn also monitored ABC, CBS, and NBC to assess where administration stories ranked during each of their nightly newscasts. A typical page from one such report would note how on April 15, NBC profiled Clinton's appearance at Shea Stadium for the fiftieth anniversary of Jackie Robinson's breaking baseball's color barrier, and CBS showed him addressing an antismoking rally but also showed White House chief of staff Erskine Bowles preparing to testify in the Hubbell case. On April 16, CBS focused on the president's initiative on seat belt enforcement, and ABC reported on the First Lady's early childhood development conference. On April 17, all three networks covered Mrs. Clinton's meeting.

Early in the third week of May 1997, White House aide Rahm Emanuel called the *New York Times*'s Alison Mitchell to offer her an advance scoop on President Clinton's upcoming speech calling for the United States to develop an AIDS vaccine within ten years. Emanuel had counted on the *Times*'s interest in breaking the story first, and Mitchell initially seemed to want to do the story. A big story in the Sunday *Times* would guarantee major network television coverage. Later in the week, Emanuel, banking on the reporters' competitiveness for a good story, called the reporter to warn that other papers were interested in the AIDS story. However, the *Times* had cooled on the story after Mitchell learned that Clinton was offering no new spending for AIDS or new researchers;

his address was nothing "except another speech" and not front-page *New York Times* material (Kurtz, 1998).

That evening, Emanuel was contacted by the *Washington Post*'s John Harris, who pressed him for more information about the story, saying the *Post* had many gay readers. Although Emanuel initially refused the details, hoping to hold out for Mitchell and the *Times,* Harris's pressure for the story combined with the reluctance of the *New York Times* to report the speech on the front page resulted in its coverage by the *Post.*

According to Kurtz (1998), Mitchell was not pleased when she saw the *Washington Post*'s front-page Sunday story, a relatively straightforward account of Clinton's forthcoming speech, with the caveat that he was not planning any new AIDS funding. Mitchell had treated the speech in three paragraphs on page 19, citing it as one more example of how President Clinton was unfocused and forced to piece together an agenda for his second administration.

Mitchell had reduced Clinton's AIDS vaccine from a "big idea" to a Kennedy-like posturing and combined it into a story about the president's second-term drift. Emanuel was concerned that often reporters failed to search for more story background and details such as whether a vaccine was feasible and how much it might cost to develop one. If he had told reporters before the second-term inauguration that the president would get a balanced budget deal, a chemical weapons treaty, and an agreement on NATO expansion in the first 125 days of the new term, they all would have agreed that was dramatic progress. Now they were "demanding an encore in time for the next deadline" (Kurtz, 1998, p. 208). Still, in this case, the *Washington Post* story strategy worked. Both CNN and MSNBC carried the AIDS speech live, and it was "all over the network news" Sunday evening and the front-page banner headline in Monday's *USA Today.*

The difference in attention that print and electronic media require leads to their handling news events differently. The print media carry many political stories and other features that are completely ignored by the electronic media, including editorials, recipes, financial news, and sports data. They also carry political stories that appeal to many minority tastes and can feature political news for specialized groups—Spanish speakers, women, business executives, or labor, for example. The print media also cover political stories in depth and generally have space for extended political analysis, with the only restrictions on such reporting being the cost of news gathering and limited space (Press and Verburg, 1988).

A major concern regarding over-the-air electronic media is boring the mass audience and losing viewers or listeners. Television in particular requires lures—visual presentations that attract viewers. This requirement mandates industry standards such as brevity. Televised reports are generally brief. One minute and fifteen seconds per item—about 100 to 120 words—is the usual outside limit on the evening news. Press and Verburg (1988) point out that one such broadcast would fill slightly more than two columns on the front page of a standard newspaper. Network television and radio stories must have general rather than special interest—national is favored over state news. Stories must also have emotional content and be presented dramatically, with structure and conflict, problem and denouement, rising action and falling action, a beginning, a middle, and an end. Electronically mediated stories also tend to be more heavily edited than print media, with news often "manufactured in the television newsroom" (Press and Verburg, 1988, p. 80).

There are other differences between the two media. Printed matter is more lasting than material that is broadcast on radio or televison. The former may be preserved for years for quick reference, while rarely does anyone record a news broadcast, and only the most memorable footage is ever rebroadcast. Print journalists pride themselves on being the medium of permanent record and generally say they feel pressure to be accurate. Print media depend on reports of hours or days previous, while electronic media often allow consumers to experience a political event even as it occurs. The actors in the story can be seen and heard while the "cameras may [also] distort reality with false rosiness " (Press and Verburg, 1988, p. 81).

Print journalists may base their reports on what politicians confide to them in private rather than on only what the camera is able to film or the microphone record. Print reporters can inform readers about the "subtler forms of politicking"—those not easily shown visually (Press and Verburg, 1988, p. 81). The media also differ in news-gathering ability. Print media need details, so the typical newspaper is labor intensive; television needs pictures and depends on sophisticated equipment for its abbreviated coverage of politicians and political events. Finally, getting stories into print, even with modern technology, is a generally slow process, while the major struggle among electronic media is over which network or television reporter will be the first to break the story.

Nacos (1990) contends that most political actors as well as the public believe the news media—electronic and print—have the power to make or break politicians, including presidents, while Neustadt (1976) believes that a president's influence and power, as well as effectiveness to govern, stem from public perceptions of prestige and reputation. If these assertions are valid, the president's political well-being is directly linked to press mediation. Capella and Jamieson (1997) argue that political events, like all other social events, are the objects of interpretation by the press and the public through journalistic frameworks of presentation. Understanding the social and political impact of events depends on comprehending how those events are interpreted for the public in the stories the press tells. This interpretation or framing becomes "a kind of sense-making that creates one interpretation of political events while ignoring others" (p. 228), a sort of "interpretation of an interpretation" (Edleman, 1988, p. 95). Entman (1993) argues that framing involves taking some aspects of a "perceived reality" and making them "more salient in a communicating text, in such a way as to promote a particular problem definition, causal interpretation, moral evaluation, and/or treatment recommendation for the item described. They define problems, diagnose causes, facilitate moral judgments, suggest remedies and function by making some information more salient than other information" (pp. 52–53) and are " located in the communicator, the text, the receiver, and the culture at large" (Kuypers, 1997, p. 44). The problem in what Capella and Jamieson (1997) consider "cynical rather than skeptical" press framing is that when a singular perspective becomes the dominant one, there is a risk of "crowding out the substantive engagement and discussion that helps the public understand the relative merits and practical consequences of political decisions" (p. 237).

Print and electronic mediation of political news has resulted in the loss of one of the presidency's critical powers: control over the flow of information to the American people. As an example, Reeves (1997a) describes President Clinton's first "shot in anger" of ordering a missile strike on Baghdad in retaliation for a planned assassination of former President George Bush during a visit to Kuwait. Clinton wanted to tell of the strike live on the nightly news but could not get information on whether the missiles were on target. White House counsel David Gergen suggested "calling CNN rather than the CIA," and by that evening, the "president of CNN, was able to tell the president of the United States" that the missiles had done their job. Shortly afterward, President Clinton went live on CNN and the three other networks to "announce the news to the people who had told him" (Reeves, 1997a, p. 5).

TELEVISION AS MEDIATOR

Former *Washington Post* editor Ben Bradlee asserts that the news media, and major television networks in particular, could "cause big trouble" for the White House virtually anytime they wanted simply by focusing sustained attention on any of the scandals, inequities, dangerous or bankrupt policies, or shortcomings common to every Washington administration (Sparrow, 1999). With 50 percent of Americans relying on television for their news, 24 percent on newspapers, and 14 percent on radio and with television being the "more trusted medium," the values of video, which are emotional and personal appeal, dominate the values of print, which are reflection and dispassion. Newspapers and newsmagazines also choose dramatic news stories and respond to the video media, "since it is television that interprets politics for most Americans" (p. 109).

Media scholar John McManus (1994) suggests that the job of producers and editors is evolving into constructing news as entertainment so that the defining trait of news becomes drama. This is grounded in the assumption that consumers' interest is probably best maintained through easily identified images and most likely to become distracted by unfamiliar or confusing images. An additional assumption is that conflict appeals more than quieter images. Stories depicting confrontations between two easily recognizable sides in conflict—blacks versus whites, uniformed police versus demonstrators—are preferable to ones in which the issues are less easily identified. And when the conflict involves more than two sides, it can usually be reframed into a polarized format. In this way, news stories may reduce complex issues or occurrences to political contests with two distinct sides (to focus coverage on the competitive process itself rather than on the substance of the contest), such as elections, legislative battles, controversial cabinet or Supreme Court nominees, and major court trials. A final assumption is that viewers' attention span is limited but may be prolonged by action (Sparrow, 1999).

The distortion caused by compressing complex issues into simplified stories means that both reporters and consumers become the "victims of sound bite editing" because of newsroom pressure to present a coherent report in inadequate time. As a result, the news media decontextualize the news and then recontextualize it on their own terms (Sparrow, 1999, p. 111).

In the past two decades, presidents have lost the power to control the flow of information to the nation so that "pretty much everybody finds out everything at the same time and in the same way." Modern presidents must then function first as an explainer of events and then as a political actor who must compete with another American who gets in front of a camera. In Reeves's view, television becomes a great equalizer because everyone is the same size on television—the president, the correspondent, or any citizen who seems "at that moment" to be making more sense than the "man in the White House" (1997b, pp. x- xi). As a result, there is an electronic revolution "seizing control of flow of information" to the country so that "the president and Rush Limbaugh, the *New York Times*, the *National Enquirer*, the CIA, the Pharmaceutical Manufacturers Association, Larry King, and you and I find out at the same time these days: All information is created equal" (p. xvi).

Television, "the handmaiden and perhaps the mother to the age of personality politics," has been a major contributor to Americans' desire for more information about their public officials' private lives. The medium has conditioned audiences to thinking about the private lives of the rich and famous, whether they reside in Hollywood or Washington, D.C. (Sabato, 1991). Presidents Johnson, Nixon, Ford, and Carter all failed in trying to apply the technique of cooperation and conflict in a television-dominated media environment. Robinson and Sheehan (1983) believe that televised network news began in 1963 to modify how Americans looked at politics and politicians in that it made citizens more "political, more volatile, and more cynical" than during the traditional print or radio eras (p. 262). Hallin (1997) argues that modern television news is much more mediated than the television news of the 1960s and 1970s, when the journalist's role as a communicator was relatively passive. The earlier period of television journalism was dominated by the words of political actors rather than journalists. For example, Walter Cronkite would introduce long, uninterrupted sound bites from speeches and press conferences and spend much time quoting politicians. Today words are not simply reproduced and transmitted to an audience but become "raw material to be taken apart, combined with other sounds and images, and reintegrated into a new narrative." In addition, film and graphics accompany visuals, while journalists use outside material they bring to a story rather than only that provided by a public official to "put the statements and actions of the latter into perspective" (p. 61). This packaging produces a news story much more "journalist centered" than its predecessor, whereby the reporter rather than the political actor is the primary communicator (p. 62).

The mediated style of modern campaign reporting is disturbing, according to Hallin (1997), because the public never has a chance to hear a candidate or anyone else speak for "more than about twenty seconds." Not only are analysis and background information curtailed, but the rise of mediated television news facilitates a preoccupation with technique and an "inside dopester" perspective that moves image making to the center of politics and "pushes real political debate to the margins." This results in a cynicism that both "debunks the image and the image-maker, yet in the end seems to accept them as the only reality we have left" (p. 65).

As the advance of cable television and other developments in electronic media reached a crescendo in the 1990s, the elite newspapers, newsmagazines, and network news shows found themselves just one of many venues in which presidential candidates were presented to the public.

The candidates made appearances on morning news entertainment shows, TV talk shows, radio talk shows, MTV, and so on, and various of these new media gave the public the opportunity to ask questions directly of the candidates instead of the traditional situation where only elite reporters had such contact and hence mediated the communication (Alger, 1996).

Print and televised media have different natures. Print is linear and sequential and has a content; it encourages rationality and analysis. A moving-picture-based medium poses no proposition to think about, but "just the assertion of a vague, pleasant image projected through television pictures" (Alger, 1996, p. 73). The main politically relevant print media consist of ink words on a page and still photos, with more photos and more in color in news magazines. The written word is the main element in these media. The print medium comes printed on a page of paper. One significant consequence is that the reader can go back at any time and reread a statement by a candidate and so reflect on what the person said. Under normal circumstances, people do not do this with communication through the electronic media, which are transmitted over airwaves or cables. Sometimes a political figure makes a statement, preserved on video or audiotape, that directly contradicts a previous statement or her or his own or the accepted facts on some significant matter—or the person makes a foolish statement. If replayed by a new show, this does allow people to reconsider the statement. The view and hearing of it may give the contradiction even greater impact because of the nature of the electronic medium. The majority of political communications over electronic media do not receive such attention. Generally such communications pass by on the airwaves without any chance for reconsideration.

Television is also fundamentally visual. The moving pictures accompanying sound are central. They are the primary material sought for TV news. Alger (1996) notes that the nature of the dominant medium of televison has influenced the "splashy, colorful layout" of *USA Today* in that the dominant national newspaper of the late twentieth century "felt the need to emulate television to make a go of it" (p. 71). Boorstin (1962) believes that television encourages the "pseudo-event," which is planned and executed only to be shown in the media (p. 11). And Press and Verburg (1988) suggest that television has brought to the surface tendencies that have been part of the American system of governing from the beginning. American politicians have always brought an element of theatrics and symbolism to the political stage, and "television merely increases their opportunities" (p. 203).

Meyrowitz (1985) distinguishes between "discursive symbols"—words and languages—which are abstract, arbitrary, and developed by convention to stand for certain meanings people learn through education and practice, and "presentation symbols"—pictures—which are more directly connected with the meaning of the symbol and are experienced holistically, with "no logical links" such as "if-thens" or "either-ors" (pp. 38–39). Television is a primarily visual medium, which is fundamentally presentational and expressive in nature. Print media require different kinds of attention and involvement. With a newspaper or magazine, the choice of what story to read is up to the news consumer. Main headlines and front pages may grab attention, but readers can skip to another story from the one they first see. Reading a given story requires an active effort to link letters on a page while watching stories on television news requires no such "affirmative effort" (Alger, 1996).

There is also evidence that people process visual images in a different manner than they do verbal. The reason many watch a given television news program is simply that the television was already tuned to that station. The television viewer cannot choose which news story to watch, since the stories are not all laid out for selection, as in a newspaper. The viewer sits and is exposed to each story as it comes. Selective exposure and, to some extent, selective attention are more difficult in the case of televison, even though this has been modified to some extent by the wide use of remote controls. An additional characteristic of television is that it enables a communicator to reach an enormous mass of people, but does so by entering their homes in a "seemingly close and personal fashion" (Alger, 1996, p. 76).

When print was the sole or dominant mass medium, certain types of political leaders with certain natures and skills found advantage and certain types of activities and modes and techniques of communication were favored—perhaps even certain types of issues as well. Different people, modes of communication, and types of activities find natural advantage with the medium of radio as well as for the medium of television (Alger, 1996). For example, it was no accident that Franklin Roosevelt's reign came during the height of the radio era, and Ronald Reagan found strong advantage in the medium of television. Alger (1996) asks, "Could Lincoln have been elected in the TV age? Would three-hour debates, with hour-statements and half-hour to one-and-a-half-hour replies, 'play' on TV today? In fact, would they be accepted and attended in any fashion?" (p. 77).

Well over half of Americans rely on television—more than any other medium—as their main source of news in general and political news particularly. In addition, between 70 and 80 percent of Americans indicate the press is "generally believable" (Davis, 1996, p. xvii). Television affects viewers' political choices by "priming the pump"—emphasizing certain aspects of national politics and ignoring others. The audience is more inclined to give weight to concerns in direct proportion to the attention paid these issues in the media and to use such measures to assess the performance of national government, particularly the president. Therefore, agenda setting can influence public approval in that the way an issue is mediated by the press determines the public's frame as well. Television news has both local (local stations) and national (network news) dimensions. On average on a weekday, about 50 million people watch the ABC, CBS, and NBC (the three "traditional network") news shows. Radio has been primarily local but does have a national dimension, with the network affiliations and an increasing level of syndicated programs. Television news shows, with reports of institutions and their officeholders and of classic symbols of the nation, serve as socializing and mediating instruments. They can also change attitudes by their coverage and portrayal. Alger (1996) cites as major examples President Nixon and Watergate, President Reagan and the Iran-contra affair, and much of the coverage of President Clinton.

By the 1990s partisan magazines, radio talk shows and "televison shoutfests," and Internet chat groups with "raw opinion and sheer attitude" made it difficult for President Clinton to connect with the public. He had "all the accoutrements" of high office but did not command the public stage as had his predecessors. Press secretary Mike McCurry and his staff worked to hone Clinton's message and hype each proposal into news cycles. The competition was intense: Dennis Rodman, Courtney Love, and David Letterman, among others. "In a hundred-channel world the president had become just another piece of programming to be marketed, and high ratings were hardly guaranteed" (Kurtz, 1998, p. xxiii). The Clinton-Lewinsky story illustrates the "new media" at work on the brink of the new millennium: the hourly, instantaneous news cycle made possible by cable television, CNN, and the Internet. With the news organizations posting their stories on the Internet as they are being composed, news is released at a rapid-fire pace, meaning that there is less time for critical assessment. News organizations are pressured, to get the story out as soon as it breaks (Sparrow, 1999).

Television news, with nightly viewership in the tens of millions, is the principal vehicle by which political and social values are transmitted to a national audience (Sparrow, 1999). Market journalism drives the networks and their affiliates. Ratings are what management use to measure news media success. Research by media scholar John McManus (1994) confirms the focus on ratings in news organizations. A study of four West Coast television stations revealed four general rules of broadcasting: (1) seek images over ideas; (2) seek emotion over analysis (with corollaries being to avoid complexity and to dramatize where possible), (3) exaggerate, if needed, to add appeal, and (4) avoid extensive news gathering. McManus says that journalism has been displaced by economics, with the main goal of news production becoming the making of money. Sparrow (1999) agrees there is increasing movement toward "scandal, celebrity [and] gossip" among television newscasts (p. 234).

POLITICAL NEWS: REPORTERS AS MEDIATORS

Journalists rhetorically compete in the public area as political actors who frame a "good story." Journalists seldom, if ever, witness an entire event they cover. It must be reconstructed from conflicting assertions, evidence fragments, and possibly eyewitness accounts (Sparrow, 1999). Press and Verburg (1988) suggest four aspects of political journalists' jobs: getting the facts, interpreting for readers and viewers, investigating or uncovering buried information, and, on occasion, becoming active participants in the political process. Many journalists believe that reporting only facts is an illusion because space or time does not allow them to report all details. In deciding what to include or leave out of their stories, they screen information and prioritize data. In addition, some journalists see themselves as representatives of the public who look out for the "ordinary citizen's interests." Some create news, while others believe that reporting facts, interpreting events, or discovering information influences political outcomes as much as the behaviors of politicians themselves. Patterson (1998) believes journalists are increasingly influential political actors, chiefly because of the emergence of television as a major medium and the weakening in the grass-roots strength of political parties. However, finding a story to tell is the "first fact of journalistic life." Although journalists may claim that their stories mirror society, news is a "highly selective account of events" and a "construct": "It is a version of reality shaped in significant part by journalistic norms and conventions. Through the frames they employ and the gatekeeping role they play, journalists help to shape public opinion and debate" (p. 17).

Reporters are employees of complex organizations who see their copy go through layers of editors. As an illustration, newsmagazines get far more copy than they can use in any one issue, and their reporters usually have their work rewritten by their section editors and possibly senior editors. As a result, news writers learn what kind of stories, particularly regarding important political and economic themes, will survive the screening and become published (Sparrow, 1999). Only a handful of reporters, editors, and producers are employed by the leading news conglomerates in the United States and are therefore in positions to "explain and interpret political reality" (p. 115). For example, the *Miami Herald* reporters who tracked Gary

Hart and Donna Rice radically changed the 1988 presidential race (Press and Verburg, 1988). Ultimately which issue is covered becomes the reporters' choice, often determined by criteria that have little or nothing to do with the political significance of a story (Graber, McQuail, and Norris, 1998). Sabato (1991) indicates that Watergate, as well as the social movements of feminism and fundamentalist Christianity, have affected the public opinion that "feeds" pack journalism scandal-based frenzies. In this view, the post-Watergate generation of Americans is more cynical about politicians and less tolerant of perceived corruption. These perceptions contribute to the subtextual vision within which a contemporary First Couple functions. ABC's Peter Jennings believes that contemporary media play "against a backdrop of a fairly righteous" if not "self-righteous" public, which holds individuals to higher standards than in the past (quoted in Sabato, 1991, p. 122).

Politicians face a dilemma in their relationships with journalists: they often think the media cannot be trusted to report fairly. When reporters talk about the public's right to know, some politicians think they actually mean the media's right to boost circulation and audience by printing or broadcasting sensational stories. Mike McCurry, late in 1997, came up with an opportunity for Bill Clinton to vent his spleen about the *New York Times*, the newspaper that "most consistently ticked him off." However, the president backed away and granted *Times* reporters a lengthy interview. Still, a culture of distrust remained between the Clinton administration and the press (Kurtz, 1998).

Political reporters can illuminate or prematurely expose policy and, if operating with arbitrary and faulty standards, may be agents of disorder and confusion (Cater, 1959). Some reporters try to make politicians look sinister or stupid, or they reveal strategies and secrets that interfere with the governing process in order to attract attention (Press and Verburg, 1988). During a 1997 television interview, Ted Koppel was "clearly mystified" as he questioned Clinton media consultant Paul Begala about why the president was still so popular with the American people when the press was "obsessed" by the DNC fundraising scandal and strongly suggesting a cover-up. Kurtz (1998) reports the administration considered remarks such as Koppel's evidence of a media agenda. For example, many journalists wanted a special prosecutor, "if only to validate their scandal-mongering" and "needed to make an impact because that was how you won Pulitzer Prizes " (p. 273).

While there were apparently few statements by journalists at the time about President Washington's treatment of the press, poet and editor Phil Freneau described Washington as "the man who is the source of all misfortune of our country," and the editor of the Philadelphia *Aurora* wrote in 1796, "If ever a nation was debauched by a man, the American nation was debauched by Washington" (quoted in Press and Verburg, 1988, p. 18). Investigative reporter Jack Anderson has said of politicians:

One of the seemingly irreversible currents I have observed during 32 years of covering Washington politics is the hankering of our leaders to transform themselves from servants to sovereigns, to replace Abraham Lincoln's "government of the people" with a government of privilege, majesty and omnipotence.... The common practice has been to pursue aggrandizement and usurpation, often with mock humility. (1980, p. 12)

In Press and Verburg's (1988) view, journalists operate on the maxim that only their constant "criticism, nagging, probing, digging and exposing, or the threat of it" keeps politicians from retreating to their default mode of dishonesty (p. 19). Common complaints from journalists include that politicians want the media to report only what they believe should be reported. In this view, politicians suppress all news that may cast them in an unfavorable light. A related complaint is that politicians try to control not only the news but the media as well, so that there is an atmosphere of "barely concealed warfare" between some leaders, such as Presidents Nixon and Johnson, and the American press (Press and Verburg, 1988, pp. 18–20).

Before television, few Americans followed politics closely. Many voted traditionally, supporting the parties of their parents and grandparents. However, a number did follow news events closely. These opinion leaders—including labor union shop stewards, religious leaders, and local business leaders—acted as political guides for others. With the advent of mass television consumption, political cues began coming from the media more than from private individuals. Reporters, particularly television journalists, became opinion leaders. This encouraged contemporary reporters to become increasingly "politically independent" due to increased competition for mass audiences, which created a new style for reporting the news. Press and Verburg (1988) argue that political news now penetrates all levels of society, with journalists "beaming" more information to ordinary citizens so that citizens become superficially familiar with political events as no one could conceive possible in the past.

Journalists often become more than objective observers of political events and, in the case of superstars such as Peter Jennings and Mike Wallace, frequently dominate the stories they report. Press and Verburg (1988) contend that viewers begin watching more for the interpersonal dynamics in an interview than for substance of the news, which reinforces the tendency to view issues and events in terms of personalities. In such an atmosphere, journalists wishing to advance their careers may be tempted to opt for the dramatic and personal publicity rather than the substantial and news-gathering approach to issue coverage. There is also the possibility that media stars may influence the news itself. For example, that Tom Brokaw or another well-known national reporter handles a story may give a political candidate more credibility and legitimacy than she or he may deserve (Press and Verburg, 1988). Opinions expressed by such journalists may affect the outcome of political events and situations. Lyndon Johnson was said to have believed the United States lost the Vietnam War after Walter Cronkite announced on the nightly news that America could not win it (Press and Verburg, 1988). Cook (1998) believes governmental processes provide the stages, the actors, and the lines for the accounts that journalists create. But the journalists cut and paste these elements together according to their own standards of quality and interest, which may well diverge from the optimal spin of the politicians. Although they may be dependent on government sources for their basic ideas, political reporters in particular put their own spin on stories, which may be entirely different from the original version.

As newspapers evolved into businesses, the value of nonpartisan stories increased. In the early 1900s, Associated Press required nonpartisan reports because newspapers representing such diverse political opinions subscribed to the service. Reporters were to address only the facts, and opinions belonged only on editorial pages. According to Press and Verburg (1988) the strength of an objective approach was to back stories with facts. Because reporters were discouraged from writing their perspectives into reports, official political news—the voices of incumbent officials eager and willing to be heard—was most emphasized.

Some, however, argued that not only was such writing often dull but also far from objective because deciding what facts to emphasize automatically builds in a bias. Reporters also believed that objective reporting sometimes left them apologists for a system that left them "captive to the public officials who provided the facts." Nor were facts interpreted according to their significance. For example, much of Senator Joseph McCarthy's charges of communist subversion in the United States were reported without comment in the 1950s, despite lack of any substantial proof on his part (Press and Verburg, 1988).

To address such criticisms, newspapers, and ultimately television newscasts, added feature stories by analysts and commentators with bylines and easily recognizable faces. Generally built around a theme, such pieces provide details and include the reporter's opinion. For political reporting, this often means asking incumbents and candidates embarrassing and even hostile questions. The value of such analysis depends on the qualifications of the media source.

Adversarial reporting allows journalists to include more personal attitudes, including hostility and cynicism, in their stories than the interpretive style. The public image of most politicians is often suspect by such reporters, who may also view politicians' rhetoric as "disingenuous, their moral pronouncements hypocritical, their motives self-serving, and their promises ephemeral" (Press and Verburg, 1988, p. 87). The "facts" provided by public officials are often considered more self-serving than not. Therefore, adversarial reporters generally believe in doing more than "just" recording a politician's statements for the public: they must also watch out for the public.

Since adversarial journalists must get the truth, no matter what, Press and Verburg (1988) contend that the influence of legal and self-restraints grounded in friendship, loyalty, and civility affecting other reporters is often missing. Fred W. Friendly, an associate of investigative reporter Edward R. Murrow, said, "A good journalist has a lot of shoe leather, a conscience and the ability to see the world from the wolf's point of view" (quoted in Henry et al., 1983). Robert Pious, in his book about the presidency, argues that "the legacy of Watergate is wolfpack journalism" (1979, p. 417). Timothy Crouse, who tracked coverage of the 1972 presidential campaign, criticized journalists for following the wire service lead and filing the same reports. If filed pieces differed from the wire story, they would sometimes get calls from their home offices inquiring why they were interpreting events differently. In his view, reporters "tend, after a while, to believe the same rumors, subscribe to the same theories and write the same stories" (p. 7).

Although apparently not dependent on the bias of official sources, adversarial reporters often become entrapped by their dependence on leaks for their stories. Such (often unnamed) sources may also provide suspect information because anonymity facilitates sloppy fact gathering and, on occasion, reporting of charges. Press and Verburg (1988) recall a reporter who said, when asked if a story about a politician was really true: "That's the kind of story that's too good to check out." Adversarial reporting may also result in news that is less reliable than under objective reporting because reporters with "chips on their shoulder" often cut themselves off from official sources of information (pp. 88–89).

For the elected politician, the media world is not as friendly as it was a generation ago. The pressures to get the news first and best the competition increasingly has moved journalists from objective to interpretive and even adversarial reporting (Press and Verburg, 1988). How a reporter "reports" may depend on the medium as well as the competitiveness of the job situation. Most print editors prefer generally objective reporting with interpretive pieces in distinct, byline columns or with opposing views in alternating paragraphs. However, major exceptions include the *Washington Post* and the *New York Times*. Their competition for readership depends on investigative as well as adversarial journalism (Press and Verburg, 1988).

During the 1992 campaign, Clinton cultivated a group of young, "New Democrat–style" reporters and columnists such as *New York Magazine*'s Joe Klein; the *Washington Post*'s E. J. Dionne, and Ron Brownstein of the *Los Angeles Times*, all of whom helped shape "elite opinion" (Kurtz, 1998, p. 72). Such reporters also helped shape the dialogue of national politics because their books and columns influenced other reporters and, in particular, television producers.

The media set the agendas of political actors by portraying an event as a crisis and imposing deadlines. The satellite transmission of news as it happens guarantees that the public and policymakers know about it at the same time, which may force onto the agenda subjects that political actors might prefer to ignore. It also forces them to make a quick response rather than one based on waiting and seeing what develops (Sigal, 1973, p. 185). The media can also move issues off a political actor's agenda by not covering them any longer or by giving the impression that the issues are no longer serious or deserving of a reporter's attention. Paletz (1998) argues that the interplay between politicians and the press produces the policy agenda or issues that public officials perceive as warranting government action or attention. During the first three years of the Clinton administration, the executive branch led on the foreign policy subjects of Bosnia and the North American Free Trade Agreement (NAFTA) and Congress led on the domestic issues of Medicare and Whitewater. However, *New York Times* coverage "led political activities" more than it followed them, with particularly strong agenda-setting influence for Whitewater and NAFTA (Bartels, 1996)

Bill Clinton, after his 1992 success in at least momentarily deflecting media inflammation of the Gennifer Flowers scandal by appearing with Hillary Clinton on *60 Minutes*, may have thought he could one day govern by appearing on news or talk shows. However, as Richard Reeves points out (1997b), "those folks" do not cover government and the White House as correspondents do, but "with their own agenda."

Miller and Krosnick (1997) argue that competence and character, particularly in terms of integrity, influence the public's judgment of the president. If the prime issues are scandals, this judgment is particularly influenced by press-mediated issues. On March 24, 1994, President Clinton held a press conference, only the sixth of his first fourteen months in office. He began by saying that since Congress was beginning its Easter recess the next day, "this is a good time to assess" the "real work we are getting done." Reeves notes, "It had been the kind of day that defines what it is like to be president." On that day, an Air Force transport had crashed in Texas, killing ten; the leading candidate for Mexico's presidency had been assassinated; and statistics revealed that 2 million new jobs had been created in the United States in 1993. The president also reviewed the progress of health care and welfare reform bills, a crime bill, and campaign reform legislation being debated in Congress. He concluded, prior to taking reporters' questions, by mentioning a political accord between the Muslims and Croats, stopping North Korea's nuclear program, American troops' return from Somalia, and human rights in China. Reporters responded to the president's statements with twenty-one questions: one on health care, one on American efforts to block the development of nuclear weapons in North Korea, one on the assassination of the Mexican presidential candidate, and eighteen on Whitewater (Reeves, 1997b).

Chapter Three

Mitigating Factors in Press Mediation

This is a very exciting time to be involved in American politics. It is not an easy time for those of us who are involved, as we all are, because it is a challenging time. . . . I think in large measure it is because there are great issues at stake. They sometimes become obscured in the daily back-and-forth of what makes the news headlines, but what's really going on under the surface are tectonic shifts that are very much going to determine what kind of politics and nation we have in the next century. (Hillary Clinton, 1997b)

REPORTING FOR PROFIT

In Sparrow's (1999) view, news organizations are constrained and shaped by the political and economic environment in which they operate. The myth of the wall of separation between news organizations' editorial content and financial matters, the monitoring of media markets with the goal of matching editorial and programming content (and therefore audiences) with advertiser, and the turn toward soft and "feature-y" news (away from serious news) are media practices found throughout the United States. With three-fourths of newspaper revenues, half of magazine revenues, all of television income, and much of cable revenues coming from advertising, the media market is not where the audience's political news demands are met by the supply of editorial content. Instead, it is a market where news organizations match audiences with advertisers. The reader or viewer as a potential customer of goods and services (rather than as a voter and citizen) determines the economic life of news organizations (Sparrow, 1999).

Factors that influence a political journalist's reporting include that media organizations are generally capitalistic, for-profit enterprises, that media have sought technological advances in printing and electronic communication, and that media coverage has expanded to new audiences and that government regulation has varied. In short, the elite press—the major networks and newspapers—are large corporations governed by economic rather than political concerns (Davis, 1996).

Sparrow (1999) addresses the 1997 economic performances of the leading news organizations as evidence of their commercial stakes. Among the Fortune 500 U.S. companies, the New York Times Company, which owns five network television stations, two radio stations, five forest product companies, twenty-two magazines, twenty-seven newspapers, and information services, ranked 487th in revenues ($2.8 billion), 281st in net profits ($262 million), and 267th in market value ($6.4 billion). The Washington Post Company, which own *Newsweek*, four network and fifty-three cable television stations, two other newspapers, Kaplan Learning Centers, information services, other media affiliates, and book publishing companies, ranked 628th in revenues ($2.0 billion) but was 282nd in net profits and 354th in market value. The Dow Jones Company, owner of the *Wall Street Journal* and twenty-three other newspapers, was 520th in revenues ($2.6 billion), lost money in 1997, and was 369th in market value ($5.2 billion). The Times-Mirror Company, owner of the *Los Angeles Times* and seven other daily newspapers, ranked 434th in revenues ($3.3 billion), 289th in net profits ($250.0 million), and 282nd in market value ($5.7 billion). Time-Warner, the conglomerate composed of *Time*, Turner Broadcasting and CNN, motion pictures, and news media services, among others, was 110th in gross sales ($13.3 billion) and 49th in market value ($42.5 billion) in the United States; it was 295th in net profits ($246.0 million). *U.S. News* is owned by publisher and real estate investor Mortimer Zuckerman, who also owns the *Atlantic Monthly* and the *New York Daily News*.

Among network television owners, General Electric (GE) owns NBC as well as six television stations, cable channels, electrical equipment, communication satellites, and networking software. GE was 5th in revenues ($91.0 billion), 1st in net profits ($8.2 billion), and 1st in market value ($260.0 billion) among American companies in 1997. CBS Corporation has fourteen television stations (mostly all in major markets), thirty-nine radio stations, cable interests, and financial services firms. It was 159th in revenues ($9.6 billion), 156th in net profit ($549.0 million), and 91st in market value ($22.0 billion). The Walt Disney Company, which bought Capital Cities/ABC for $18.0 billion in 1995, owns ten newspapers, cable channels, nine television stations (almost all in major markets), and a 14 percent interest in Young Broadcasting, which has eight television stations of its own. Disney ranked 51st in revenues ($22.5 billion), 43rd in net profits ($2.0 billion), and 23rd in market value ($73.0 billion). In 1995, television and radio profit margins reached 33.2 percent on average, cable TV had a 39.4 percent profit margin, and magazine publishing margins were 14.4 percent—their highest in five years. More than fifty media companies (print, broadcast, and cable) took in more than $1 billion each in annual revenues in 1995. In one year, 1994–1995, corporate mergers included Time-Warner with Turner Broadcasting, Westinghouse's purchase of CBS for $5.4 billion, Disney's purchase of Capital Cities/ABC, Gannett's buyout of Multimedia, Inc. (newspapers, television and radio stations) for $1.7 billion, and the New York Times Company's purchase of the *Boston Globe* for $1.1 billion.

The result of the monopolization of American media is that more individuals have a stake in a company's commercial performance, so that the economic pressures become even greater. Institutional investors such as pension funds and insurance companies, own 72 percent of Gannett and Knight-Ridder, 57 percent of the New York Times Company, 51 percent of the Washington Post Company, 47 percent of the Times-Mirror Company, and 43 percent of the Dow Jones Company. These economic pressures affect family owners as well—as the Sulzbergers of the *New York Times*, the Grahams of the *Washington Post*, the Chandlers of Times-Mirror, and the Bancrofts of the *Wall Street Journal*. Family firms are as concerned with their companies' bottom lines, so they too experience constantly increasing commercial pressures. Ultimately, the drive for profit predisposes most American news organizations to give favorable coverage to their own interests and those of corporate America and less favorable coverage to redistributive policies, pro-labor issues, and most political and economic reforms (Sparrow, 1999). Such a pro-business bias might account for some of the negative press spin on Clinton initiatives such as health care reform.

Contemporary politicians face journalists who function in a competitive market and whose careers depend on their ability to ferret out attention-grabbing pieces about political actors. Profit-oriented news organizations (as well as their nonprofit counterparts to a lesser degree) search for advertisers to whom they will sell access to their audiences. Cook (1998) identifies this "economic imperative" as the instigator of "production values" shared by essentially all news outlets. The corresponding consensus on how news is to be "made" in order to "crank out a predictable regular product" results in an institutional bias toward certain political policies and away from others (p. 167). Therefore, contemporary news organizations are most geared toward their audiences as consumers rather than citizens because advertisers rather than readers or viewers pay the salaries of media owners and employees.

In this view, far from being free from governmental involvement and intervention, the evolution of the American news media has always been and continues to be intimately tied to political sponsorship, subsidization, and protection and shaped by government action. In colonial times, establishing and operating a newspaper was risky. Those who tried often turned to politicians for underwriting. The price was partisan loyalty. News in such papers was sparse and biased toward sponsors, and stories often berated the opposition. Such party newspapers reached their peak during President Andrew Jackson's 1828–1836 administration. Two actions by the Lincoln administration in the 1860s signaled the beginning of the end for the American partisan press. Lincoln declared he would have no administration newspaper and later opened the U.S. Government Printing Office, ending national government printing contracts for loyal editors. The relationship has evolved from one of sponsorship to subsidies. Direct sponsorship prevailed through the mid-nineteenth century, when newspapers were funded generally by a party and received patronage, such as printing contracts and postmasterships. Access to politicians at this time, particularly those in Congress, was selective and politicized.

Political help was replaced by the more indirect subsidies such as those provided by the colonial era post office to deliver newspapers. As the media became commercialized and politically independent and as government's goals became enmeshed with publicity, indirect institutional subsidies completely replaced sponsorships. The wire services organized from 1900 on, loosening party ties by emphasizing nonpartisan objectivity in reporting, because reports went out to all papers, regardless of party. The Jacksonians expanded suffrage by the 1830s, inspiring newspapers written to attract "the common man." Simultaneously, new technology made longer and less expensive press runs on inexpensive paper possible. In 1833, the *New York Sun* began charging a penny a copy at newsstands, when established papers were sold only by subscription for six cents a copy. This "penny press" changed the content of newspapers in that editors chose particularly lively issues and exploited sensational stories to attract readers. Lithography and woodcut surfaces facilitated the production of drawings and cartoons for long press runs. Editors paid reporters to dig up news rather than wait for "handouts" from politicians or their surrogates. Political news was packaged as entertainment for the public and stressed crimes, corruption, and scandals. Editors openly expressed political prejudices and labeled themselves political independents.

The penny press began to change in the late 1800s when publishing became a business rather than a hobby. In the 1880s and 1890s, the "Great Editor" papers of Joseph Pulitzer and William Randolph Hearst appeared in cities where new immigrant groups upset old social patterns. Some had difficulty learning English, and papers in native tongues developed to meet the demand. Pulitzer and Hearst designed their papers to appeal to other immigrants with the style called "yellow journalism." They challenged the more traditional papers by exploiting technological advances, making their papers easy to read and understand, with pictures and comics. (The name *yellow journalism* derives from one of their color innovations—printing a comic strip, "The Yellow Kid," in color.) They introduced photo engravings and used eye-catching devices geared toward sensationalism. After World War I, tabloid-size papers designed to be read on streetcars and buses entered the urban media scene. What had begun with the postal subsidies for newspapers in the late eighteenth century developed from the middle of the nineteenth century and dominated the twentieth century, which saw the development of press offices and officers who provided the raw material for reporters working in limited news beats. The news media, instead of depending on daily favor or disfavor of political patronage, entered a more stable period of subsidies and entitlements from government. Current public policy toward the news media now works "very much to the profitability of the industry" so that "one must question" the idea of "freedom of the press" as meaning "untrammeled and independent development" (Cook, 1998, p. 14). Some editors until World War II maintained partisan affiliations in one-party enclaves such as the Democratic solid South or the Republican Midwest. Others recognized that too strong a tie could antagonize some readers or advertisers. Editors began using "Independent" or "Independent Republican" on their mastheads.

Radio and news magazines aimed at a more general audience who wanted to be better informed as well as entertained. From the crystal sets of the 1920s, radio evolved to the networks of the 1930s with newscasters from Lowell Thomas to Edward R. Murrow. Presidents from Coolidge on used radio to address the nation, and radio newscasters reported political events. National newsmagazines, beginning with *Time*, targeted professionals and emphasized lively, personal writing styles and editorial opinions.

After World War II, rapidly increasing numbers of Americans owned television sets, and televised news broadcasts focused on capturing viewers and their money. Early television news broadcasts were low-budget, fifteen-minute unopinionated reports—"talking heads" reading wire service bulletins. Coverage of the assassination of President Kennedy in 1963 revolutionized television news broadcasting. News directors began to realize new potential in techniques of presentation and the enormous potential audience for action-based news. This occurred at the time that television producers were looking for programs to fill the gaps left by game shows, which had become disgraced after the revelation that many, such as *The $64,000 Question,* were rigged.

Soon the networks developed half-hour news shows. They substituted visual clips from news files and added announcers as news anchors who tied wire-service reports together. Televised news reporting grew from unprofitable public service broadcasts to competitive profit-making endeavors with an increasingly dramatic and aggressive style in reporting political events. Specialized audiences were targeted by public radio and television, and new market identification techniques made profitable numerous publications targeting specific groups. Weekly papers reminiscent of the yellow press appeared, and radio changed its format, in order to survive, by specializing in music and, on occasion, twenty-four-hour news broadcasts.

In 1982 the Gannett chain began *USA Today*, a national newspaper with a "frozen television" format of brief stories. The same newspapers are printed at the same time in several locations throughout a state or nation, through microwave and satellite signal transfer. National newspapers like the *Wall Street Journal* can be produced as quickly as a local paper, and national magazines such as *Newsweek* can produce special issues with advertising targeting specific regions.

The peak number of dailies was 2,600 in 1909. The number of American cities with competing dailies dropped from 61 percent in 1880 to 21 percent in 1930 (Press and Verburg, 1988). In addition, many publishers purchased or developed their own stations when radio became popular. By 1923 new technologies made syndicates possible, and chains published 31 percent of the daily circulation. By 1984 chains controlled 79 percent of the daily and 88 percent of the Sunday circulation. However, the government limited the number of local radio or television stations that the networks could own, and so independent stations became network affiliates rather than be owned outright (Press and Verburg, 1988).

Publishers and media executives began establishing holding companies for multiple media: newspapers, magazines, television channels, radio stations, and movie production companies. Changes in the Federal Communications Commission rules, which expanded from five to twelve the number of television stations a corporation could own, resulted in numerous acquisitions. In 1985, Gannett Company, the largest newspaper chain at the time, owned eighty-seven daily newspapers, including *USA Today* and the *Des Moines Register,* as well as sixteen radio stations, six television channels, and the Louis Harris opinion polling organization. Federal law allows the development of conglomerates combining nonmedia and media enterprises. In 1988, the electronics company RCA owned NBC and formerly owned the publisher Random House. Xerox acquired the *Weekly Reader*. The *Los Angeles Times* organization includes the New American Library, a forest products corporation (a source of newsprint), Denoyer-Geppert maps, *Newsday,* and several other newspapers. CBS owns the New York Yankees. The *Chicago Tribune*, which already owned WGN radio and television stations, purchased the Chicago Cubs. Real estate developers Boston Properties owned *Atlantic Monthly Press* and *U.S. News and World Report*. Also, because many media companies are stock companies whose shares are traded on stock exchanges, some media firms also have come under the partial but influential ownership of general holding companies (Press and Verburg, 1988).

Monopoly and concentrated media ownership reduces breadth of information. Bagdikian (1997) identifies a "steady succession" of known incidents of owners' suppressing or distorting "journalistically legitimate" stories, or books killed at the corporate level out of corporate prejudices, or of producers, editors, and reporters fired or demoted for offending owners with accurate stories, articles, and programs. Major media owners differ among themselves, as do their corporations, in personality, style, and outlook, but these differences are "minor on any realistic scale of the total values of society." Theirs is a narrow and common outlook fueled by economically and politically driven common goals and outlooks. "They have self-interest, as does every individual and institution, but they have more power to pursue that self-interest, and they control access to the public mind." Such control produces not only self-censorship but also "professional practices ... that last after the originating incident has faded" (p. 69). Press and Verburg (1988) believe the major implication of contemporary media ownership is that media bureaucrats are pressed more than ever before to concentrate on profit and loss. Stockholders and managers may grow intolerant of firms that do not improve profit margins. Therefore, newspaper and television journalists will often be pressured to become more aggressive in their reporting and to substitute entertainment stories rather than substantive stories in order to sell papers and expand audience.

Newspaper executives now regularly survey their readers about their tastes and interests and then "retail" their news content, newspaper format, and newsroom beat systems to meet those perceived interests. There is a reciprocal effect that the individual decisions of a few editors, producers, publishers, and news executives have on national politics. Sparrow (1999) believes the attention shown by the leading American news organizations to the "scandalous rather than the sober, to the sordid rather than the serious" suggests the importance of the bottom line to contemporary journalism (p. xiv). This move toward market-oriented journalism is a continuation of a trend that has seen American journalism grow more commercialized, more focused on audience interests, and more fixated on profit making (Underwood, 1998). In addition, profit pressure may produce pressure on journalists from advertisers who object to certain news reports. Despite the tendency toward larger conglomerates, the media are still competitive, and individual outlets generally have adequate resources for gathering and reporting political news. One threat may be that the less successful media organizations will use the same techniques employed by the high-profit media organizations, such as Ted Turner's CNN, which are inclined to revive the "great-editor yellow journalism" approach to information presentation (Press and Verburg, 1988, p. 45).

The efforts of journalists to appease the conflicting pressures of business and profession increase the standardization of press coverage through story formulas. Reporters follow politicians around in packs, picking up information and consuming staged media events designed to put spins on the news. In Bennett's (1997) opinion, what passes for a critical press is actually "attack journalism" in which the "press pack turns surly, snarling at press conferences and attacking politicians hapless enough to have poor media handlers or foolish enough not to heed the advice of good ones" (p. 109). According to this view, the major media bias is neither liberal nor conservative but corporate and in favor of profit. The opinions of reporters are trumped by the interests of the organizations for which they work. Media conglomerate owners and executives are responsible for and in control of both the news and advertising content of their organizations. One CNN executive stated that it was in reaction to the "not only perceived but actual appeal to audiences" that CNN ran "so much of the O.J. trial" (quoted in Sparrow, 1999, p. 78). CNN's viewership increased by more than fourfold during the coverage of that trial. NBC News and CBS News also ran the Simpson trial as their biggest 1995 news story.

When President Clinton followed a "corporate-friendly line" on health care and trade, he was rewarded with enthusiastic media support. However, although a majority of the public and many in Congress favored a Canadian-style single-payer health care plan and opposed NAFTA, these positions were often barely visible in media coverage. Press discussions reflected the corporate consensus rather than the public or governmental debate. When the president attempted to pursue policies that were of less interest to the business community—for example, putting job creation ahead of deficit reduction—the media response was critical and instrumental in persuading him to change his course. And the "obsessive coverage" of allegations about Clinton's private life kept the president "weak and malleable." The "scandal mongering" avoided serious questions about how Clinton's public decision making might be influenced by private interests, while creating the impression that "a hard-hitting press was fearlessly investigating the powers that be" (Naureckas and Jackson, 1996, pp. xvi-xvii).

THE TABLOID PRESS

Sabato and Lichter (1994) describe reporters for "prestigious national publications" as being "perched in elite positions at the top of journalism's hierarchy" while "at the bottom . . . are those who work for tabloids' overly ideological publications." This hierarchy, however, breaks down whenever the mainstream press is "forced" to follow the lead of tabloids—members of the "new media"—as with the *Star*-generated Gennifer Flowers story in early 1992, which first emerged in tabloid newspapers, then on local television news, and finally in the mainstream or elite news media. The mainstream media backed into the story by publishing a piece on media coverage of the breaking scandal—a story about a story—rather than on the scandal itself and by reacting to the coverage of local affiliates. In providing background for these stories, the mainstream media rationalized their reporting of the scandal. In what would become a pattern in addressing Bill Clinton's alleged infidelities, the media covered the Gennifer Flowers story indirectly: media critics and political reporters wrote about the controversy in their own newsrooms, mulling over whether allegations of infidelity were relevant to judging a candidate's fitness for public office. This allowed them to publicize the tabloid allegations through the "tasteful prism of a journalism seminar." For example, Ted Koppel's *Nightline* did a segment on whether the story should be covered and in the process aired the charges to millions of viewers (Brock, 1996, p. 254).

The national mainstream news media's reporting of the *Star*'s payments to Gennifer Flowers for her story, as well as of the Clintons' response on *60 Minutes*, and of Flowers's counterresponse on *A Current Affair* were the first public signs that the elite media were losing control of the political agenda (Lemert et al., 1996, pp. 43–44). Former *New York Times* political correspondent Christopher Lydon commented on how the "old news," or elite media, and the "new news," including the tabloids, fed off each other in covering the Clinton-Flowers scandal: "The upscale media baited the trap with hints about womanizing" while "their downmarket cousins bagged the trophy" (1992, p. 58). Shortly after the Flowers story broke, the *Boston Globe*'s Thomas Oliphant said that in the past, it was "unthinkable" that a rumor published in a tabloid "could be lifted whole, undissected" into "what we like to think is the mainstream quality press" but has now "metastasized like a cancer" so that the political news media are "simply acting as a transmission belt for gossip and scandal" ("Politics and the Media," 1992).

The "old media" are not obsolete. Although they have "diminished in importance," they are not irrelevant. While the "new media" usually are supplemental, theirs can become a "momentarily dominant" role, depending on the situation (Rosentiel, 1994, p. 2). This was evidenced by the *Drudge Report*'s " breaking of the Lewinsky story on its Internet site. The tabloid/"new media" pressures the mainstream/elite/"old media" to lower standards so much that, according to Rosentiel (1994), it becomes "more likely that rumor and innuendo will be printed or aired" (p. 25). As an illustration, in March 1994 "conservative interests" succeeded in "peddling" the idea that White House deputy counsel Vince Foster's suicide was linked to the Whitewater deal. It began when a "right-wing group" sent a fax newsletter to news organizations around the nation passing a rumor that Foster had actually died at a White House "safe house" and was later moved to the park in Virginia where his body was found. The rumor was attributed to unnamed sources in Democratic Senator Daniel Patrick Moynihan's office, which later denied the allegation. But radio talk show host Rush Limbaugh picked up the rumor and repeated it over the air that day. So did others, including a talk show host in Florida who "freely suggested" that the report, which was now relayed as more than a rumor, raised the specter that Foster's death was not a suicide but murder. The rumor, "now conveyed over radio," provided an opportunity for stock market speculators to make a "little profit by trading on gossip." The next day the "old media" *Washington Post* ran a story about the rumor on the grounds that it had moved the stock market (Rosenstiel, 1994, p. 35). Reporter Tom Oliphant commented on the state of the news media and its focus on covering scandals:

I don't see Gennifer Flowers as one incident but as a continuum. As you go down that continuum ... the standards of the media have gone down rather than stayed the same.... [These episodes] teach us that the ethical distinctions at the editorial level, as opposed to the journalistic level, between, say the *Los Angeles Times* and the *National Star* are not as clear as they once were. (Cohen et al., 1997, pp. 55–56)

The *New York Times*, *Wall Street Journal*, and *Los Angeles Times* have all undergone major redesigns in the past two decades to become more reader friendly. For example, they cut down the number of columns, increased the type size, offered more colorful writing, added new graphics, and put in new sections as well as expanded coverage of areas such as food, sports, and fashion. Newsmagazines also modified their focus. A former *Time* editor remarked that the basic question at the magazine has become determining a cover story that would "sell on the streets." *Newsweek* has revised its look by cutting the length of its text by 20 percent, enlarging pictures, headlines, charts, graphs, and excerpts from its articles, and simplifying the news. For example, CBS offered to tailor its Gulf War specials to provide better lead-in commercials and to insert the ads after story segments that were produced with upbeat images or messages about the war (Sparrow, 1999).

Such media format innovation has influenced the content of the public debate issues. Iyengar (1997b) notes that in the 1896 election, the public was galvanized by policy issues such as free trade versus protectionism and the power of corporate monopolies. By contrast, during the presidential campaigns of 1988 and 1992, the public was bombarded with data relating to candidates' personal character. Their private lives and "bedroom behavior" are subjected to "ever-increasing scrutiny," and "even minor indiscretions can dash electoral prospects." Modern political contests are "waged over the candidates' 'good behavior' quotient rather than the substance of their policy proposals or visions for the future" (p. 145). Modern political communication is frequently aimed at the lowest common public denominator, thereby diminishing public dialogue.

This is significant for many reasons, not the least of which is that the media, as framers of the public's "political realities," can be manipulated. In Manheim's (1998) perspective, the political communication being distributed through news organizations has been systematically reduced to its lowest common denominator of audience appeal. Much of that information has also been "stripped of its substantive content and packaged in verbal and visual symbols." In addition, "negatives trump positives" in presenting the news because of their inherent appeal to journalists or their "prurient appeal" to the public. This produces a "diminution of the quality of political dialogue" and, ultimately, an impairment of the political life of the society in which that dialogue is voiced. In contemporary democratic politics, the media have been accepted generally as the principal gatekeepers and meaning givers for political information. However, the reality of journalism is that its dependence on the "most superficial forms of information gathering" renders most reporters vulnerable to would-be image managers. In addition, the increasing sophistication of the image managers and their growing record of success bring together the means and the incentive for them to exercise their influence, thus guaranteeing that "these news shapers" have emerged as a third force in the news-politics relationship.

The result is that "political 'news' is surely not what the public believes it to be" (pp. 106–107).

A case in point is the media evolution of a major Clinton administration scandal. A former White House aide, Kathleen Willey, told *Newsweek* reporter Michael Isikoff that Bill Clinton had propositioned her and that they had had sex in the White House Oval Office. Isikoff had been the first national reporter to break Paula Jones's charges when he worked for the *Washington Post* in 1994. He had gotten his tip from Jones's lawyer, Joseph Cammarata. Isikoff tracked down Willey, a former campaign volunteer, who told him off the record that she had succumbed to Clinton's advances in 1993. The alleged encounter took place the same day that Willey's husband, an attorney accused of embezzling $275,000 from a client, committed suicide. The president sent Willey to summits in Copenhagen and Jakarta, despite her lack of expertise. The story stalled because Willey would not go on the record, and Isikoff could not level such a serious charge with an anonymous source.

Isikoff's confirmation came through Matt Drudge, who ran his own World Wide Web site, the *Drudge Report*. While Drudge often used material from the tabloid *National Enquirer* and "Clinton haters," Kurtz (1998) notes he had "become fashionable among the media elite" (p. 236). One of Isikoff's colleagues leaked word of the Kathleen Willey story to Drudge, who reported that Isikoff was "hot on the trail of a woman who claims to have been sexually propositioned by the president on federal property" (Kurtz, 1998, p. 236). Shortly afterward, the story "spun out of control," and Kathleen Willey was subpoenaed as a witness in Paula Jones's sexual harassment suit. Isikoff (1999) argues that Drudge would "steal" stories from the mainstream or elite press and reprint or interpret them. The *Report* contained "'exclusives' you'd never find anywhere else," such as the "imminent indictment of Hillary Rodham Clinton." And "while his exclusives were often demonstrably false," he was "right just often enough so that most politicos . . . would wonder if there wasn't some kernel of truth to what he was reporting" (p. 146). Both the official ruling of Vince Foster's death as suicide and the Clinton-Lewinsky affair were "broken" first in the *Drudge Report*.

Bill Plante reported the subpoena, without naming Willey, on the *CBS Evening News*, and "within minutes," Wolf Blitzer was on the story. Bennett confirmed the subpoena soon after, and Blitzer's story made the CNN evening newscast. The *Washington Times* named Kathleen Willey in a front-page story the next morning, and "the New York tabloids" soon "joined the fray." Bennett believed the media were using the subpoena, and the *Drudge Report* to justify publishing unsubstantiated charges they would otherwise "never touch" (Kurtz, 1998, p. 237). The subpoena angle made the unconfirmed allegations fit to print and pursued by the *New York Times*, the *Washington Post, Newsday,* and *USA Today. Newsweek,* which had initiated the original story search, moved to publish the Willey story. McCurry argued that it was going to publish a story involving a charge of inappropriate sexual behavior by the president of the United States, which "your own story says you don't have any idea whether it's true" and that the magazine had an "institutional investment" in and was "pumping up" the Paula Jones story. In addition, Isikoff had clouded the issue by quoting another former White House aide who said that Kathleen Willey had emerged from the Oval Office the day of the alleged tryst "disheveled and happy," suggesting that Clinton's best defense was that he was a successful seducer and not a harasser. And Willey's attorney said she had a good relationship with the president, while Bill Clinton had no recollection of ever having seen Ms. Willey in the Oval Office. The story deadened, and reporters "quietly let it drop" (Kurtz, 1998, p. 140).

In what turned out to be a fallacious, if not ludicrous, twist on the 1997 Democratic National Committee fundraising scandal story, allegations were made that the White House had been selling burial plots at Arlington National Cemetery to big Democratic donors and friends of the Clintons. Initially, press secretary Mike McCurry thought the rumors were so absurd that no one would take them seriously. This was not the case. The false story originated in the conservative magazine *Insight*, a part of the *Washington Times* organization, and then "ricocheted" to Rush Limbaugh, Oliver North, and G. Gordon Liddy, on to Republican lawmakers in Washington, and finally to the *New York Times, Washington Post, Los Angeles Times,* and CNN. Few acknowledged the administration's denials that it was auctioning off the grave sites and the military had allowed the rumors to fester by not releasing the list of those who had received special waivers for Arlington burial. When the army finally released the list of sixty-nine people, it included only one Democratic donor, former ambassador Larry Lawrence, who was allegedly wounded during World War II.

The White House contacted *Nightline, USA Today,* and the *Washington Post* to get the facts out and set the story right. However, according to Kurtz (1998), essentially no one in the press expressed remorse because, given the president's record, the charges could have been true and "it did not seem such a stretch to think that this White House would even peddle eternity" (Maureen Dowd quoted in Kurtz, 1998, p. 281). Kurtz argues that by this time, "plausibility, it seemed, was the new journalistic standard" for media treatment of the Clinton White House for a press corps that "would run the story without running it down" (p. 281). Still, the cemetery plot mini-scandal would not go away. Substantiated rumors surfaced that Lawrence had invented his war injury and never served in the merchant marine, as he had claimed. Although there was no evidence that the administration knew of Lawrence's deception or even that the White House had supported his Arlington burial, it "smelled once again like a coverup" and critics, including the *New York Times*'s Maureen Dowd, "had a field day" (Kurtz, 1998, p. 282).

Lyons (1996) notes that Bill Clinton "pretty much admitted having sinned" in the *60 Minutes* interview following Gennifer Flowers's allegations but believes "how much more the public needs or wants to know is arguable." Where a figure like the president of the United States is concerned, the national media's standards of proof are lower, not higher, than standards of regional or local media. This is because, unlike a state or regional political actor, the president and the First Lady are national celebrities. Therefore, their real or imagined personal strengths and weaknesses draw the interest of a public that embraces celebrity. This in turn brings in the tabloid media, which "brings considerable sums of cash into the equation." Although Gennifer Flowers threatened a libel suit against a Little Rock radio station that broadcast her name in connection with an election-year smear against Bill Clinton in 1990, for $140,000 she told a different story to the *Star* tabloid. Similar incentives were offered to the Arkansas state troopers who in December 1993 told their stories about the president to the *Los Angeles Times* and *American Spectator*. Another reason that the Clinton administration was more scandal plagued than previous presidencies may be the national media's declining standard of proof in the contemporary "cable-TV-and talk-radio-driven twenty-four-hour-a-day news cycle." Rumors are broadcast or printed so frequently in contemporary political coverage that, according to Fred Barnes, the public finds it difficult to distinguish them from fact (quoted in Lyons, 1996, p. 7). Norris (1997) argues that the past decade has been marked by the tabloidization of news due to commercial pressures. For instance, television news has been absorbed into the entertainment television culture because of increased competition-based economic pressures as well as the proliferation of "reality-based programming." Economics has "eroded the barrier between journalism and the profit-making business of selling audiences to advertisers," so that the news media have become part of media conglomerates "for which news is only one more form of 'software'" (Hallin, 1994, p. 177). The result is that television news is now a subgenre of television rather than a branch of journalism. Tabloid television, seen in most markets in the evening at the beginning of prime time—such as *A Current Affair*, *Hard Copy*, and *Inside Edition*—are inexpensive to produce and successful in the ratings. And while they "borrow the form and aura of journalism," they are "produced purely as commercial products" (p. 178) so that television news "is both journalism and show business, a key political institution as well as a seller of detergent and breakfast cereal" (p. 88).

Rupert Murdoch's Twentieth Century Fox was among the first media conglomerates to transfer to television the sex and violence that sold copies of Murdoch's *National Star* and *New York Press*. Fox became a television ratings winner with its "tabloid TV" shows *A Current Affair*, a sensationalized account of "true" crime and scandal, and *America's Most Wanted*, where "real" fugitives were hunted down and sometimes apprehended. NBC News "crossed the line" when it presented a prime-time special, "Scared Sexless," in December 1987. Hosted by news correspondent Connie Chung, the show was watched by nearly a third of the viewing public, something no network news show had done in a long while. On her "quick tour" of the subject, Chung reported on singles bar, gay sex, and AIDS; sat in on sex education classes; and spoke with sex "experts," including actors Alan Alda and Goldie Hawn, as well as Los Angeles Raiders running back Marcus Allen. Within a week, NBC News announced specials including "Women Behind Bars" and "American Men in the 80s." Although there were some sober documentaries on the homeless and Islam hosted by Tom Brokaw during the same period, the "traditional barriers between news and entertainment would continue to collapse" (Auletta, 1997b, p. 78)

Networks were responding to what they conceptualized as audiences who were bored, had short attention spans, and craved excitement, surprise, or shock to keep their attention. Networks increasingly pressured local stations to promote network entertainment shows and stars on its newscasts, creating what one *Newsday* reporter called the "big shrill factor" (quoted in Auletta, 1997b, p. 78). News re-creations and docu-dramatics began to appear. Media owners "speeded the trend" to hold news to the same ratings standards as entertainment shows. If a news program did not achieve the desired numbers, it usually disappeared. Ultimately the "center of gravity—the value system" shifted within much of network news. In Auletta's (1997b) view, this is why NBC in April 1991 aired an extensive exposé on Senator Charles S. Robb's alleged extracurricular "escapade" and closed an earlier newscast with an "exclusive interview" with a man who asserted he had been Merv Griffin's lover or why ABC News re-created news events.

As a result, a tabloid journalism has evolved that focuses on an "endless diet of crime, scandals, and sex" as well as "infotainment." As small news organizations are consumed by larger national and international media conglomerates, the news becomes more commercial and created with drama and entertainment values geared toward drawing large audiences. Bennett (1997) suggests that the economic pressures on journalists encourage political coverage that is easier and cheaper to report as well as easier and less challenging for consumers to digest. As a result, the news has been transformed into a hybrid of information and entertainment. Publicity is focused particularly on the personal lives of political leaders, "so that personal peccadilloes of presidents or congressional representatives that would have remained discreetly hidden a few decades ago are now emblazoned on the front page" (Norris, 1997, pp. 6–8). According to Rosenstiel (1994), tabloidization is "entertainment and gossip rather than news" and has to do with news organizations' devoting time, resources, and prestige to "covering subjects in proportion to public fascination rather than significance" (p. 36). The media are "losing their authority" as gatekeepers; the reason is that they feel pressured to account in their outlets for what the public is learning about from other sources. So if the *American Spectator* publishes a story "full of innuendo, second-hand speculation, and reporter fancy about the love lives of the President and the First Lady," which gets picked up on talk shows and eventually the local news, the networks and other news organizations feel more pressure to air it. Conversely, news organizations that decline to run a story that is "gaining wide currency" are criticized for "sticking their heads in the sand." For example, even its own reporters criticized the *New York Times* for not covering the Gennifer Flowers story in 1992 more aggressively (Rosenstiel, 1994).

SENSATIONALIZED AND SCANDAL-DRIVEN MEDIATION

Begala (1995) reveals that a Nexis search indicated that Whitewater appeared in more than 31,000 news stories, while the 1994 health bill was mentioned in only 2,400. Just as they do to candidates in presidential elections, journalists now challenge, criticize, and condemn American presidents, in contrast to the deferential treatment they generally showed to presidents in the past. In Sparrow's (1999) opinion, the Lewinsky scandal story is a "study of the media sinking to a new (low) standard of sensationalist news coverage." Stories of President Clinton's relationship with Monica Lewinsky dominated the front pages and front sections of newspapers, newsmagazines, and television news programs. Many of the stories were reported secondhand, and articles had to be retracted from the *Wall Street Journal* and the *Dallas Morning News*. The *New York Times*, ABC News, *Newsweek*, *Time*, and other news outlets ran the story that Lewinsky had a dress given to her by the president that was stained with semen. None of these news organizations independently verified the report before the publication or broadcast. Lucianne Goldberg admitted to having leaked the story "to shake things up" (cited in Sparrow, 1999, p. xiii). Scandal-based news sells. *Time* devoted 43 of 80 pages to the Lewinsky scandal in its February 2, 1998, issue and 37 of 112 total pages in its February 9 issue; the *New Yorker* devoted all of its "Talk of the Town" section on its 8-page lead article to the story. The *New York Times* defended its front-page coverage by insisting that President Clinton's involvement and unconvincing response to the situation merited it. Sparrow (1999) believes this defense ignores the "extraordinary" resources the *Times* devoted to the story and the anecdotal accounts that were reported in the paper's coverage of the Lewinsky scandal. "The tabloid niche is becoming less and less a niche" (p. xiii).

During a March 1995 television interview with Rita Braver of CBS News, Tim Russert of NBC News, syndicated columnist Charles Krauthammer, and former vice president Dan Quayle argued that the news media were biased to rely on four things for political stories: attacks, flip-flops, gaffes, and polls. Charles Krauthammer added "one more":

Sex. You talk about cynicism in the press, I think a lot of it is prurience. The way that the politicians and any public figure is covered now is simply astonishing compared to, say, the way that JFK or FDR or Lyndon Johnson were covered. Had we excluded in the past leaders who had these unsavory things in their past, we would have lost some of the great leaders of American history. (quoted in Braver, 1997, p. 38)

Scandal coverage in particular drives much of the press's attention, reinforcing the public view of political actors in general as corrupt (Rozell, 1996). For example, news media coverage of Congress focuses on scandal, partisan rivalry, and conflict rather than the more complex subjects such as process and policy. Lichter and Amundson (1994) see the tendency to dwell on scandal reporting rather than process and policy in television as well as print media coverage of politics and government. One reason for the intense interest in sensationalized stories is the emergence of a more aggressive, scandal-conscious news media, which endorses a post-Watergate code of ethics. Such an ethic encourages honing in on scandal, delving into the personal lives of political actors, and investigating areas once considered off limits to reporters (Rozell, 1996). Rosen and Taylor (1992) argue that the tabloids "feast on political stories that come packaged as morality plays, soap operas, or 'gotcha' cat-and-mouse games." They suggest that the "more trivial" and "simple-minded" and "trashy," the better because the mission is to pander to "populist outrage." As such, the "new news" fails to maintain standards of "balance, nuance, perspective" (p. 40). One journalist described this environment in 1992 as "the idiot culture" of "sleazoid info-tainment" and "journalistic titillation" "in which the lines between Oprah and Phil and Geraldo and Diane and even Ted, between the New York *Post* and *Newsday*, are too often indistinguishable.... We teach our readers and viewers that the trivial is significant, that the lurid and the loopy are more important than the real news" (Bernstein, 1992, pp. 24–25).

Another reason for scandal-centered reporting might be to counter the tedious nature of covering the day-to-day routines and rituals of the legislative process. Reporters may avoid covering process and policy stories unless they are connected to "conflicts, rivalries among colorful personalities on Capitol Hill, or scandal" (Rozell, 1996, p. 129). David Broder (1987) believes that a reporter will have an easier time selling a scandal story to an editor than those of "larger consequence ... because they fit stereotypes of graft and sin on Capitol Hill" (pp. 216–217). The press has become the primary power broker in determining politicians' fates. This power is evidenced by reporters' ability to frame—and thereby set the agenda for—scandals in which political actors have center stage. Sabato (1991) believes the news media "go after a wounded politician like sharks in a feeding frenzy." Journalists create the news as much as report it and in the process change the contours of elections and government. They have replaced political parties as the "screening committee for candidates and office-holders," propelling some officials toward power and eliminating others (Sabato, 1991, p. 1). Late-twentieth-century journalists have emerged as full-fledged gatekeepers, which has empowered them to act in lieu of party leaders in deciding "which characters are virtuous enough to merit consideration for high office" (p. 4).

Times have changed. When the *New York Times*'s editors created the slogan, "All the News That's Fit to Print," many reporters believed they should not publish information that was in poor taste or "incivil," including personal scandal. Most Americans did not learn about the extramarital affairs of Presidents Franklin Roosevelt or John Kennedy until long after both were out of office. CBS's John Pierpoint and AP reporter Douglas Cornell opted not to report on a Kennedy affair they discovered because at the time such stories were not generally considered appropriate material for news (1981). Press and Verburg (1988) observe that Franklin Roosevelt was protected by the press to an unprecedented extent. He was wheelchair bound due to polio, but of thirty-five thousand press photographs of him, FDR appeared only twice in his wheelchair. Aides carrying the president, out of view of the public, once lost their hold and dropped him, but no one photographed the event.

Still, media interest in scandal has been a staple of the American news industry since the eighteenth century. Some of the contemporary press abuses have a "long and distinguished history." Like every other American institution, the "power, promise, and performance" of the press has varied greatly from era to era. For example, Thomas Jefferson was treated especially harshly by the early American press. His attempt as a young man to seduce a neighbor's wife became a "character issue" for a partisan press (Sabato, 1991, p. 27). Yet he was instrumental in establishing the *National Gazette*, the newspaper of his political viewpoint, created to compete with a similar paper founded earlier by Alexander Hamilton and his anti-Jefferson Federalists. This era of party newspapers lasted through Andrew Jackson's presidency.

The partisan press gave way to the penny press, typified by the 1833 founding of the *New York Sun*, which cost a penny at the newsstand. Such publications, with few direct ties to specific parties, were the precursors of the modern press, built through mass circulation and commercial advertising for profit. This nonpartisanship, however, did not guarantee more respectable news organizations. Since mass circulation dailies needed wide readership and readers were "clearly attracted" by the "sensational and the scandalous," the "sordid side of politics became the entertainment of the times" (p. 28). Yellow journalism and then muckraking become the journalistic fashions of this period. Pioneered by publishers such as William Randolph Hearst and Joseph Pulitzer, yellow journalism highlighted pictures, comics, and color in order to appeal to immigrants in particular. The front-page editorial crusade became popular. Muckraking, named by President Theodore Roosevelt after a special rake designed to collect manure, became reporters' style of choice in the early 1900s. Journalists such as Upton Sinclair ferreted out and exposed "real and apparent" misconduct by government and businesspersons, presumably to "stimulate reform." One side effect of this crusade of moral investigation was a growing tendency to violate public actors' "legitimate privacy rights" (Sabato, 1991, p. 28).

As the news business evolved, its focus changed from "passionate opinion to corporate profit." In order to make money, newspapers did not want to alienate their advertisers and readers who produced the organization's revenues. The result was less harsh, more "objective" reporting, and the media barons became members of the establishment. World War I also changed the rules of engagement for many journalists, whose patriotism made victory the "common cause for newsmen and politicians alike" (p. 29), although the press excitement surrounding the Teapot Dome and "mistress" stories connected with President Warren G. Harding represented a brief but intense example of pack-mentality journalism at the time.

In the modern age, since World War II, the breadth, depth, and influence of the news media have expanded and evolved. From about 1941 to 1966, journalists engaged in "lapdog" journalism—reporting that reinforced the political status quo and establishment. During this time, mainstream journalists rarely challenged the orthodoxy of the day and accepted at face value a great deal of what authority figures communicated to them. Politicians were more protected from scandal because little was revealed in the media about their nonofficial lives, even when personal behavior affected public performance.

By the 1940s, this mentality, which became a necessity because of war, had already been established in Franklin Roosevelt's earlier administrations during which "the rules of engagement for the relationship between the press and the politicians they covered" were rewritten (Sabato, 1991, p. 29). That relationship became more diplomatic and the tone of coverage more sedate during FDR's presidency. This may have been due in part to the crisis atmosphere and sobering effect of the Great Depression. In addition, many reporters were strong personal supporters of the president, and those who were not still knew he was immensely popular with the American people. After the beginning of World War II, reporters self-censored themselves, refusing to publish any information about the presidency that might aid the Axis powers. The Rooseveltian rule of thumb for press coverage of politicians endured for forty years: the private life of a public figure should stay private and undisclosed unless it seriously impinged on his or her public performance (Sabato, 1991). This produced a post-Roosevelt press that was "rather sleepy" and would, if it hinted at all, suggest "private impropriety" by code words or euphemisms. The *Baltimore Sun*'s political columnist Jack Germond recalls that during this time, "A politician who was a notorious drunk would be described as somebody with a reputation for excessive conviviality. A politician who chased women was known as someone who appreciated a well-turned ankle. And this was the way we went at this. Everybody knew except the reader" (quoted in Sabato, 1991, p. 31).

Sometimes the rule did not apply, as when Louisiana governor Earl Long became involved with stripper Blaze Starr in an affair "so flagrant that publicity became almost unavoidable." Nor were financial scandals, such as that surrounding Lyndon Johnson's aide Bobby Baker and Richard Nixon's secret fund, which became a major media-fueled scandal in 1952. The most taboo topic in the 1950s and 1960s was sex, and John F. Kennedy's presidency "provided the most severe test ever of the rule" (Sabato, 1991, p. 33), which essentially remained unchallenged during his administration.

Watchdog journalism, typified by scandals surrounding the Vietnam War and Watergate, was the "reporting of choice" style from 1966 to 1974.

News organizations tracked major political actors' behavior through independent investigations. It was during the later years of this period that discussions of politicians' private lives appeared, albeit mostly in the context of public performance. John Kennedy's successors, Lyndon B. Johnson and Richard M. Nixon, are considered by some to have been mistreated by a hostile and aggressive press, particularly when compared to journalists' hands-off approach to JFK. However, this treatment usually reflected coverage of political matters, most noticeably Vietnam for Johnson and Watergate for Nixon. The private lives of presidents by and large still remained off-limits for political reporters, the results of a "liberal expansion of the Rooseveltian rule under Kennedy" (Sabato, 1991, p. 42). Richard Nixon was one of the last presidential politicians not to be challenged on a major private matter. By the 1970s, the standards were changing, due in part to the relaxation of libel laws, but mostly because of Ted Kennedy's accident at Chappaquiddick, which produced not only a major feeding frenzy but also was the catalyst for public press scrutiny of political actors' character.

For years Senator Edward Kennedy, like his brother Jack, had enjoyed an adoring press, who ignored rumors ranging from cheating on Harvard exams to excessive drinking to "compulsive womanizing and erratic behavior" that was "so obvious to the newspeople who covered him." The press became "even more protective" after his brothers' assassinations. However, after the accident at Chappaquiddick, in which a young woman lost her life, the press "never looked the other way again" because Ted Kennedy had been "too flagrant, his actions too costly, and his excuses too flimsy and insulting" to a press corps that was criticized for concealing the character "weaknesses" that had preceded the senator's own cover-up of the facts surrounding the fatal accident (p. 46).

Since Chappaquiddick, "junkyard-dog" journalism—harsh, aggressive, and intrusive political reporting where gossip is printed and broadcast—has generally replaced the better-mannered and more praiseworthy watchdog media type. Since about 1974, feeding frenzies have flourished, and "every aspect of private life potentially becomes fair game for scrutiny as a new, almost 'anything goes' philosophy" prevails (Sabato, 1991, p. 26). With Chappaquiddick, many in the political media began to consider private life and individual personality traits to be so influential on public behavior that they could no longer be ignored. This perception was reinforced by the dumping of Senator Thomas Eagleton from the 1972 Democratic ticket because of his previously hidden psychiatric history, and the Watergate revelations, about the corruption within Richard Nixon's administration as well as the distasteful aspects of his personality. Sabato (1991) argues that a "new godhead" emerged "from this 'unholy trinity' of Chappaquiddick,

Eagleton, and Watergate" to replace the "Rooseveltian one," which was "as open as its predecessor had been closed" (p. 46). "Everything is fair game" in contemporary political reporting, since any aspect of private life is potentially relevant to an official's personal relationships and private behavior—anything reflecting character or judgment—including unproved rumors and innuendo. These private stories flesh out one's personal life, which, the thinking goes, flesh out their public life. Therefore, the new "anything goes" rule became established and has pushed the frontiers of what is considered appropriate for press scrutiny. For example, Richard Nixon's possible psychotherapy was not an issue in 1968, yet after the 1972 Eagleton scandal, the "mere hint," which turned out to be false, that Gerald Ford had also been in therapy became one of the major issues investigated in his 1973 Senate confirmation as vice president (Lyons, 1973). And after Chappaquiddick, alcohol abuse and sexual misconduct became a "permanent part of the reportable political landscape" (Sabato, 1991, p. 47). Sparrow (1999) asserts that because "politics is uglier now," news coverage is uglier than before. Politicians have the worst motives ascribed to their actions, and bad news about them "drives out the good." Speeches with substance and successful visits to diverse audiences around the country have no integral worth, and all become media events. The result is the "attack dog" method of reporting applied to much of a president's time in office.

There have been far greater concentrations of media character scandal-based "frenzies" in recent years. The classic American scandal, which once focused on financial impropriety (as in the Teapot Dome scandal)—has been superseded by "gaffes, 'character' issues, and personal life-style questions." As a consequence of Watergate and other recent historical events, political actors' character has come under increasing press scrutiny. Contemporary journalists often view the presidencies of the "three tragic but exceptionally capable figures" of John Kennedy, Lyndon Johnson, and Richard Nixon as "failures . . . not of intellect but of ethos" (Sabato, 1991, p. 64). The party affiliations and ideologies of these presidents varied, but "in common they possessed defects of personality, constitution, and disposition." While the issue of character has always been present in American politics, it rarely made such a mark for so many consecutive elections as it has since 1976, during which Jimmy Carter's campaign was characterized by "much moral posturing." Edward Kennedy's 1980 candidacy was in part destroyed by "lingering" character questions; Walter Mondale overcame Gary Hart's 1984 challenge in the Democratic preliminaries by "using character as a battering ram"; and 1988 "witnessed an explosion of character concerns so forceful that several candidates were eliminated and others badly scarred by it" (Sabato, 1991, p. 64).

News departments of the national American television networks have been cutting back their news operations since the mid-1980s, when new corporate ownership began downsizing the news staffs at CBS, NBC, and ABC. This left network news dominated by marketeers focused on keeping the dwindling network audiences through the mass appeal of "infotainment." The resulting demands of television "as an entertainment medium first and foremost," and so as a medium for visuals, ratings-grabbing news formulas, and emotion-laden themes has resulted in a preclusion of reporting on complex governmental and political issues. Underwood (1998) reports that this trend toward sensationalism over substance has grown as local television operations—under pressure from declining ratings, cable, and alternative news networks—have adopted tabloid formulas to hold their audience. Local television has "become the leading force in moving mainstream American journalism away from coverage of public affairs and into ratings-driven content." As a result, serious coverage of government or politics has virtually disappeared from local television coverage, replaced with stories that "emphasize hot-button controversy, promote other shows and devote a lot of time to teasers for upcoming stories and tend to tout the lurid, sensational, and the touchy-feely" (p. 173). Dahl and Bennett (1995) believe the media highlight certain events, particularly "scandals and outrages," that stand for governmental policy inadequacies or failures. These "news icons" dramatize and play to cultural fears, tensions, and politically "marginal ideas" so that "the news can become a cultural broker, defining the problem" and "redefining the policy situation" (p. 1).

Americans often construct their vision of government from television news, which, with its ratings-oriented "crime and celebrity coverage," portrays government in a negative light, and ignores the complexity of public issues (p. 174). Kimball (1994) argues:

What is going on in network television is a redefinition of news, driven by financial considerations and ratings. News is what networks feel they can afford to cover and what will get on the air as determined by ratings. The wall of separation between the business side and the news side, which had always been under siege, has now been significantly breached. (p. 165)

Because of competition, contemporary media entrepreneurs reward journalists who attract large audiences. For their own career advancement, reporters try to satisfy these demands. Political news as entertainment that shocks, reveals secrets, has human interest, and is dramatic has high value. Contemporary political reporting concentrates on personalities and media celebrities, and a major target of such personalized news coverage is the president, who is never offstage. James (1999) argues that politics and show business have bled together so completely that the question *Tonight Show* host Jay Leno asked of President Clinton throughout his impeachment hearings ("What the hell were you thinking?") "seemed more commonsensical and to the point than anything Congress cooked up" (p. C3).

The demand for more news results in the creation of media news events as political events, designed for visual appeal. Journalists are supposed to inform readers and viewers about events of which they know nothing. Timeliness counts, especially when media outlets compete; a delay in getting out the news increases the likelihood that people will learn about it from other sources. Therefore, political news often occurs in the form of a breaking story that creates a demand for new facts. The Watergate and Iran-contra scandals of the Nixon and Reagan administrations were "kept alive for months" because of the persistent digging by journalists, which turned up fresh details (Press and Verburg, 1988, p. 73).

This demand for filling hourly and around-the-clock newscasts expands politicians' outlets for such news. Whether a mayor's ribbon cutting or an act of terrorism, such media events are staged for the benefit of reporters as well as the politician. However, some contemporary journalists contend that any news gathered should be published and that essentially any way of gathering news is justified; they should not be subject to outside restraint or expected to show any self-restraint (Press and Verburg, 1988). Still, only a few television stations broadcast footage of the Pennsylvania state treasurer, R. Budd Dwyer, who committed suicide during a press conference. Some journalists have a sense of social responsibility and face hard choices. On the other hand, former *Time* correspondent Charles Eisendrath "vehemently disagreed" with those who withheld footage of Dwyer: "To deny the public an image of what happens in such a disaster is to deny them the basis for accurate judgement of their officeholders and the strain and tragedy they may encounter" (quoted in Fleming and Gunther, 1987). The *Washington Post*'s Charles Seib also believes that controversial stories should be covered unless they threaten national security, the personal security of those whose lives are influenced by the story, and an individual's right to privacy (Press and Verburg, 1988).

Some politicians seem to be perennial sources of scandal reports. Any story that can be turned against them gets that treatment. Their negative public image seems unshakable. Journalists embellish minor incidents and may tag their targeted politician with a label he or she cannot shake. One such victim was presidential adviser and later attorney general Edwin Meese III. President Reagan claimed the media were creating a "lynch atmosphere." Although a special prosecutor cleared Meese of all criminal charges, the "journalistic sniping" continued.

Reporter Richard Reeves (1983) notes that the traditions of journalism require that the media report the words and actions of public figures without comment, even when reporters think they are "a danger to the Republic and small children in school yards." Reporters "must wait for an opening—a mistake made by a public figure—to say, indirectly, what they really think" (p. 126). Reeves says the "crime" Meese committed was that he violated the media's social bias by being one of those "hardhearted millionaires and would-be millionaires who could not care less about the poor, the weak or the hungry." Meese, as the 1983 Christmas season approached, told reporters he had never seen "any authoritative figures" showing there are hungry children in the United States. Comments such as these earned reporters' contempt. The *New York Times* and other papers began running stories comparing Meese's words with those of welfare experts and with headlines such as "True Hunger and Malnutrition Cases Are Growing Problems, Experts Say." Other "violators of social norms" included James Watt, President Reagan's first secretary of the interior. Although environmentalists disliked his policies and reporters may have been unsympathetic to his fundamentalist Christianity, the statement that earned the wrath of the press, which ultimately drove him from office, was his reference to members of a special coal commission as including "a black, two Jews, a woman, and a cripple."

Earl Butz, secretary of agriculture under Nixon and Ford, was targeted because he told ethnic jokes, and Governor Richard Lamm of Colorado for seeming to suggest that older people with terminal illnesses had a "duty to die." Jesse Jackson publicly apologized for his reference to New York City as "Hymietown" in a statement he assumed was off the record to a *Washington Post* reporter, and Louis Farrakhan, because of anti-Semitic remarks, was dealt with harshly in the media (Press and Verburg, 1988, p. 127).

The unique circumstances of the presidency account in great part for the vulnerability of the First Couple to pack journalism mediated "frenzies," which feed on scandals (Sabato, 1991, p. 81). The president's power, the First Family as a national role model perennially under investigation, and histories of past presidents, particularly their flaws, produce the subtextual lens through which the political press interprets the presidency. When a political actor is "wounded" during a pack press, scandal-generated "frenzy," essentially any potentially damaging piece of news, related or not to the first offense, can be published. ABC News's Jeff Greenfield says that once a politician is "bloody," it becomes "awfully easy to assume that seven other assertions are true" (quoted in Sabato, 1991, p. 118).

The "Quayle frenzy" represents what Sabato (1991) calls the "paradigm of pyramiding," the "resurrection of dead-and-buried" charges. Immediately after the Republican convention in 1981, the vice-presidential candidate faced accusations that had previously disappeared or been disproven, including allegations of a role in a "sex-for-influence" scandal; challenges to how he achieved his National Guard status during the Vietnam War; criticism of his academic record; possible favoritism in his admission to law school; and continuous rumors about drug use and encounters with women other than his wife. The tone of the Quayle frenzy had been set by the media-generated subtexts that produced the previous vice-presidential frenzies surrounding Geraldine Ferraro and Thomas Eagleton. In addition, other parts of the Quayle feeding frenzy subtext included Gary Hart's womanizing, Joe Biden's grades, Pat Robertson's war record, and Supreme Court nominee Allen Ginsburg's drug use (p. 119).

The prominence of scandal-based political reporting by the media during the Clintons' tenure in the White House is evidenced by tracking the evolution, development, and framing of sex stories. Bill Clinton's press secretary, Mike McCurry, and other Clinton staffers and surrogates became familiar with rumor management. A rumor would develop in a column or tabloid or British newspaper and "make its way up the media food chain." McCurry's job was to stamp it out before it reached critical mass. Allegations about both of the Clintons' infidelities had a life of their own, with the president cast as the "First Playboy" and media coverage of his relationships with women such as Gennifer Flowers and Paula Jones. After Vince Foster's suicide, there were whispers that Hillary Clinton had been having an affair with the late White House aide and her former law partner. Shortly before, the rumor had appeared in the *American Spectator*, a conservative monthly. The source was David Watkins, a former White House aide who had been fired after being photographed using a marine helicopter to check out golf courses near Camp David for presidential use. Watkins had also written a piece blaming Hillary Clinton for the firings at the White House travel office.

He had planned to write a book about the White House, and after a publication deal failed to develop, Rebecca Borders, hired as his coauthor, began using the interview material for the *Spectator* article. She quoted Watkins as saying that Hillary Clinton and Vince Foster had been intimate. The story also reported Watkins saying that his wife had been told by Marsha Scott, an Arkansan named to a $95,000-a-year White House job, that she was having an affair with Bill Clinton. A *Washington Times* reporter had given McCurry an advance copy of the *Spectator* story, which would probably be put though the British "laundromat": American reporters would shy away from some sex story involving Clinton, which the London tabloids would run with. Then the "most aggressively" conservative American news outlets—the *Washington Times, New York Post,* or *Wall Street Journal*—would attribute the latest sleaze to the British papers, and "from there it would hit the talk shows and the rest of the mainstream press." McCurry realized that if he acknowledged the Watkins piece at all—even if only to deny it—his "official" presence would give the media license to write about an article that would "otherwise be untouchable" (Kurtz, 1998, pp. 96–97).

When reporters called to discuss the story off the record, McCurry told them there wasn't much new and that the "sex stuff" was all attributed to "a very bitter source," Watkins's wife. Within a day, the "transatlantic conveyor belt" went into action. Ambrose Evans-Prichard, Washington correspondent for London's *Sunday Telegraph*, wrote a story about the *Spectator* article. He called President Clinton a "phony" and the official account of Vince Foster's death "a tissue of lies." The charges were becoming "news" of sorts. The *Washington Times* reprinted the Evans-Prichard article on its front page. The gossip page of the *New York Post* followed suit. While the Watkins story faded, the process by which such stories were laundered did not. Clinton's staff recognized a pattern to the dissemination of gossip about the president and Mrs. Clinton. Some of it never moved beyond fringe publications and Internet chat groups. Some stories were filtered through British papers, as with Gennifer Flowers in 1992, as a story that "had nearly sunk Clinton's candidacy." Flowers sold her story to the *Star*, a tabloid, and within days the report spread to the *New York Post* and *New York Daily News*, other big papers, and on to CNN, which provided live coverage of the news conference staged for Flowers by the *Star*. Sally Perdue, who claimed that unnamed Clinton staffers tried to intimidate her into silence over their affair, could not convince the *National Enquirer* to print her story. But Ambrose Evans-Prichard included it on the front page of the *Sunday Telegraph*, which encouraged coverage by the *Washington Times*.

Evans-Prichard also reported that an Arkansas state trooper said that Chelsea Clinton's nanny, Helen Dickey, had called the trooper about Vince Foster's death hours before his suicide was supposed to have been known—and said he had shot himself in the White House parking lot, not in the Virginia park where his body was found. The Western Journalism Center, funded by conservative financier Richard Mellon Scaife, reprinted the *Sunday Telegraph* story in a full-page ad in the *Washington Times*. Next, a *New York Post* writer picked up the story and then urged Al D'Amato, head of the Senate Whitewater Committee, to call Dickey as a witness. The initial press interest eased when the White House released a deposition from

Dickey, who said that she had called the trooper about ninety minutes after White House aides said they had learned of Foster's death.

It was hardly news in 1995 when White House staffer Chris Lehane compiled three hundred pages of such articles and wrote a lengthy memo, "The Communication Stream of Conspiracy Commerce." He described the cycle as the mode of communication employed by the right wing to convey their fringe stories into legitimate subjects of coverage by the mainstream media. After Congress "looked into the story, the story now has the legitimacy to be covered by the remainder of the American mainstream press as a 'real' story" (quoted in Kurtz, 1998, pp. 98–100). In January 1997, the memo was mentioned in a *Wall Street Journal* editorial that accused the White House of trying to intimidate the press. Shortly afterward, the *Washington Times* headlined its front page with the story. Conservative publications "loved the report" because it demonstrated that "they mattered, that they had gotten under the administration's collective skin" (Kurtz, 1998, p. 100). Chris Lehane, the originator of the "conspiracy" story, had left the Clinton staff, and Clinton White House press officer Lanny Davis was left to practice damage control of the growing "conspiracy" report scandal. He got seventy-five media calls regarding the memo in one day, including from the *Washington Post*'s Warren Strobel, who asked, "You folks have always denied that there's a bunker mentality here, paranoia regarding Whitewater and these other issues. Isn't that exactly what this looks like? 'Here are our enemies, they're out to get us'" (quoted in Kurtz, 1998, p. 101).

Lanny Davis spoke mainly with investigative specialists who dissected official explanations about crisis-related issues: the *New York Times*'s Jeff Gerth, the *Washington Post*'s Susan Schmidt, the *Wall Street Journal*'s Glenn Simpson, the *Los Angeles Times*'s Alan Miller, ABC's Chris Vlasta, and AP's John Solomon. In Kurtz's (1998) view, their job was to "dig up dirt" because each time they "nicked a White House official, they helped their own careers" (p. 177). *Inside Politics* had been launched by CNN to cover campaigns, but in odd-numbered years, it reduced "everything, even serious policy matters, to crass politics" in order to justify its existence (Kurtz, 1998, p. 184). Mike McCurry believed the scandal press tried to beat the prosecutors to the punch. Reporters had been on the Whitewater/Travelgate/fundraising trail so long they started to "think like Ken Starr (Kurtz, 1998, p. 186). Ultimately scandal-centered journalists were so invested in the crisis stories of the Clinton administration that they had to believe in their importance.

While competitive pressures, media-generated subtexts and tendencies to search for patterns, and the persistence of the character issue guarantee frenzies will generally feed on one another, there are occasions when the momentum of a scandal may be channeled so that it causes less damage. For example, if the public fallout from a pack reporter–generated scandal is heavy enough, that scandal may not harm a political actor as severely as it would if the public embraced its subtext. In addition, Sabato (1991) argues that there may be a "build-down" in addition to a "buildup" of press scandal–based feeding frenzies. As an example, many in the press were unhappy with the severe criticism the news media received after the Donna Rice–Gary Hart stories, and some were reluctant to pursue similar stories in the immediate aftermath. This attitude may have accounted for the reluctance of some reporters to run with the stories of Senator Chuck Robb's "womanizing" and President George Bush's "mistress."

Public opinion does contribute to the press's mediation of scandals. The *Washington Post*'s Paul Taylor believes the American public ultimately decides if reporters have "gone too far or whether we've hit the nail on the head," which "determines whether the target [of the "press frenzy"] survives or doesn't survive" (quoted in Sabato, 1991, pp. 123–124). The lack of balance in the coverage of most frenzies produces a "trial by media, with an inherent presumption of guilt" (Sabato, 1991, p. 138). Yet if the press determines that the electorate is intolerant to charges made against a political actor, which will, at the very least, cause the public to ignore a story, the charges and the story will be deemphasized or dropped entirely. Referring to the fact that Pat Robertson's first child was born three months into his marriage, ABC's Jeff Greenfield recalls the public "decided, 'who cares?'" and the story disappeared within hours. Even when most Americans consider the accusations to be serious, as they did in the 1972 election about Watergate, they may choose to overlook the implications.

According to Sabato (1991), voters prioritize issues about which they are concerned regarding elected officials, with the taking of money for political favors as the "most serious questions about the ethics" of a political actor. While "lying" is not taken lightly, "extramarital sex" is the issue that generates least concern (p. 125) and is the only offense most Americans argue isn't "any of the press' business" (p. 265). The public may be genuinely interested in reading or hearing about private-life scandals but condemns the media for spinning the scandals into a frenzy, particularly if the coverage is perceived by the electorate to be an invasion of a political actor's privacy" (p. 126). And certainly the American presidency has afforded both the media and the public ample opportunity to test this assumption.

Chapter Four

Crisis Management Rhetoric

> One of my favorite quotes of [Eleanor Roosevelt's] is as follows, "To undo mistakes is always harder than not to create them originally, but we seldom have foresight. Therefore, we have no choice but to try to correct our past mistakes." She lived by that. In many, many ways she kept reminding the people of her time, those in power, that they could reverse their mistakes. (Hillary Clinton, 1995)

From the early twentieth century, when Theodore Roosevelt called the White House a "bully pulpit" from which to "preach" his principles and policies, presidents have acted as interpreters-in-chief. The latter part of the century has factored in tailoring presidential rhetoric, visually as well as verbally, for television (Alger, 1996). Press and Verburg (1988) identify four media styles—cooperation, warfare, the loss of control of and respect from the media—that presidents may employ in their interaction with the media during scandal or crisis.

MEDIATION OF AMERICAN PRESIDENCIES

Theodore Roosevelt pioneered the cooperation-control approach that many successful presidents in the twentieth century used. He provided them with stories and dealt with the press in a generally friendly, personal manner, but he also recognized limits in the relationship. His "reporter's cabinet" illustrates how Roosevelt succeeded in getting reporters, off the record, to advise him on how to handle breaking stories, as if they were part of his administration. Teddy and Franklin Roosevelt and John Kennedy also established rapport with the press and usually functioned as their own best representatives with the media. Press and Verburg (1988) note that all three approached reporters with friendliness and confidence rather than suspicion.

Presidents Truman and Ford were less successful in part because of Truman's natural scrappiness and Ford's lack of media skill. Woodrow Wilson began his term of office saying he was for "pitiless publicity" but ultimately used America's entry into World War I as justification for backing away from the press. And when he suffered a massive stroke in 1919, reporters were deceptively informed that the president had been stricken by a nervous breakdown and would be back at work soon (Kurtz, 1998). Lyndon Johnson's media relationship disintegrated as reporters criticized the Vietnam War (Press and Verburg, 1988).

While most presidents experience crises and scandals during their terms of office, not all made bad news worse by their reactions. Franklin Roosevelt survived the attack on Pearl Harbor and criticism of his packing of the Supreme Court as well as his 1938 attempt to "purge" some members of Congress. John Kennedy weathered the Bay of Pigs invasion of Cuba; Dwight Eisenhower endured the USSR's capture of a U-2 spy plane and pilot and being caught in lies about the event. And after a serious 1955 heart attack, the press was initially informed he had a "digestive upset" (Kurtz, 1998). Ronald Reagan survived the loss of hundreds of marines in Lebanon. According to Press and Verburg (1988), any one of these incidents would have "unraveled the media influence of a Taft, Harding, Carter or Hoover" (p. 181). Of the late-nineteenth and earlier-twentieth-century presidents, Grover Cleveland and Warren Harding perhaps provoked the most scandal-honed media coverage.

During the 1884 presidential campaign, the *Buffalo Evening Telegraph* headlined "A Terrible Tale" about Democratic nominee Grover Cleveland. In 1871, while sheriff of Buffalo, the Cleveland bachelor had allegedly fathered an illegitimate child. Although the woman in question had been seeing other men as well during the time, Cleveland accepted responsibility since the other men involved were married, and he paid child support for years. "Fortunately" for a competitor newspaper, the *Democratic Sentinel* broke a story that counterbalanced his own scandal: Republican presidential nominee James G. Blaine and his wife had had their first child only three months into their marriage. Cleveland won the election (Sabato, 1991).

Warren Harding liked to interact with the press. However, his ineptitude was revealed as a *St. Louis Post-Dispatch* reporter ferreted out facts about the Teapot Dome oil reserves scandal. When faced with a scandal over disputed Alaskan land claims, William Taft "threw up his hands in helplessness," while Herbert Hoover became "petulant and largely ineffective" as the depression continued during his administration (Press and Verburg, 1988, p. 180). After World War I, the Teapot Dome scandal occupied American journalists in the muckraking tradition. Although the press was apparently unaware of the scandal during his term of office, the 1927 revelations about Warren Harding's White House mistress, Nan Britton, and their illegitimate child provoked another frenzy among the political press corps (Sabato, 1991, p. 29). Essentially all modern presidents have had their brushes with mediated-news coverage as well, some more serious and historically precedent setting than others.

Franklin Delano Roosevelt

Winfield (1994) believes that Franklin Roosevelt's communication artistry and successful persuasion provided the baseline in the contemporary evolution of the relationship between the presidency and the press. Roosevelt's presidency marks the historical yardstick for measuring how well contemporary presidents communicate and mold public opinion. Foremost a great communicator, FDR knew when to speak and when not to, how to use his charm and how to withdraw it. Succeeding presidents, regardless of political party, have compared their communication tactics and their leadership abilities to Franklin D. Roosevelt's (Winfield, 1994).

Roosevelt had the same kind of presidential struggle between the American mass media and the chief executive and his administration as have more recent presidents. The dilemma is how to get a message out to the people unhampered. A strong president such as Roosevelt can influence journalists' news gathering, the reporters' reactions, and the final news stories. If FDR was as tactically adroit in handling the press as so many journalists and scholars have said he was to have been, did this president actually reduce the press to a mere publicity arm of the government? The argument here is that the type of crisis made a difference—that Roosevelt's openness, his news management, and his adroit handling of the mass media of his day changed as his administrative focus switched from economic to military crisis (Winfield, 1994).

Interpretive journalism had been created by New Deal reporters as a method of explaining the era's political, social, and economic revolution. Winfield (1994) suggests that the rise of interpretive reporting was the most important press development of the 1930s and 1940s; the new reporting style challenged the old-style objective of sticking to a factual account of what had been said or done. "Why" and "how" became important because readers wanted background information and context about the new government agencies and the flurry of New Deal activity. Despite the president's own statement—"I have not tried to create a publicity bureau for the administration or to 'plant' stories on its behalf"—Franklin D. Roosevelt did just that. His administration aided journalists personally so they maximized positive results for FDR's agenda. Despite the efforts of some correspondents to look beyond the official versions to other news sources, the president's attempts to coordinate information and set the news agenda worked well (Winfield, 1994). Some of the crises to which Roosevelt's media acted and reacted were his 1936 reelection campaign, the Court-packing plan, Justice Hugo Black's appointment, the 1937–1938 recession, the 1938 congressional election, the growing international war, and his 1940 reelection campaign (Winfield, 1994).

The idea of lying politicians is not new, but printing that politicians lie is. The modern press, like modern candidates, is candid. Many of the same things were said of Franklin D. Roosevelt that were said of Bill Clinton—but in private. Roosevelt told reporters at his first news conference in 1933 that he did not want to be quoted directly but would provide "background" and "off-the-record" information. Kurtz (1998) believes this was "remarkable—the president, as chief source, setting strict ground rules that enabled him to shape the news agenda. For the twelve and a half years of his presidency Roosevelt was treated with deference and affection by the press. In 1944, as a "desperately ill" Franklin Roosevelt campaigned for a fourth term, publishers such as Republican Henry Luce refused to print photos hinting at the president's poor health. And although many in the press either "knew of or strongly suspected" his estrangement from Eleanor Roosevelt, as well as the president's relationship with Lucy Mercer, no mention was made in virtually any report—this despite the fact that Mercer at times resided in the White House and was with Franklin Roosevelt at his death (Sabato, 1991).

Turner Cateledge, the White House correspondent of the *New York Times* in the 1930s, once said that FDR's first instinct was to lie, but that halfway through an answer, he would realize he could get away with the truth and would shift gears (quoted in Reeves, 1996, pp. 68–69). As a benchmark, Roosevelt showed the importance of a dynamic personality, which became an integral part of his news management abilities, skills that might have created unreasonable expectations for less personable presidents (Winfield, 1994).

Harry Truman

With Roosevelt's death and Truman's assumption of the presidency eighty-two days into FDR's fourth term, the preoccupation of the press with the Trumans became constant and unrelenting. Bess and Harry Truman received a rude reception by the media upon their arrival in Washington as the First Couple, labeled as "social butterflies" and treated as Missouri "rubes" out of place. Bess Truman made little, if any, personal effort to reconfigure the media's images of herself and her husband, short of calling one reporter a "skunk" for his insulting article (quoted in Mitchell, 1998, p. 27).

The media began looking almost immediately for any scandal within Harry Truman's administration. During the next seven-plus years, journalists, motivated by noble as well as malicious interests, investigated essentially all aspects of the president's personal life. The search involved matters as diverse as his ancestry, education, reading interests, finances, tastes in music and art, religious practices, and marital fidelity (Mitchell, 1998). Many of Truman's contemporaries held him in low esteem, and the public accorded him one of the lowest ratings among the modern presidents. The American news media played a primary role in this denigrating portrayal of the president. While a portion of the press supported his policies, understood and lauded his leadership, and valued his personal character, more did not. For them, Truman's rise to power in political alliance as a result of his connections with the corrupt political machinery of Kansas City in the 1930s tainted his record of public service. The conservative press in opposition to Truman's administration, principally the publishing empire of William Randolph Hearst, the McCormick-Patterson newspapers, the Scripps-Howard chain, and the newsmagazines of Henry R. Luce, contested the president's efforts to preserve and expand the New Deal. Its opposition presented Truman with his greatest challenge in gaining election to a full term in 1948 (Mitchell, 1998). His election triumph, the greatest upset in American politics, produced the greatest miscalled election in journalistic history.

Between 1945 and 1953, the news media's coverage of the president and national life registered significant innovation and development. The Washington news corps nearly doubled in size from a decade earlier in response to the growing importance of the federal government in the lives of the American people and the emergence of the United States as the ascendant global power. White males working for newspapers still dominated, but radio and television broadcasters and women and minority journalists gained power and influence during the immediate postwar period. These developments foreshadowed an expanding role for broadcast journalism in the news media at the expense of newspapers, photojournalism, and newsreels, as well as a greater democratization of the journalism profession (Mitchell, 1998).

Truman's full term occasioned the onset of a nuclear arms race in the developing cold war, war in Korea and the recall of General Douglas MacArthur, failed efforts to secure legislative enactment of the administration's domestic Fair Deal, and the revelation of corruption in the federal government. News media reportage and editorials on these events and developments produced celebrated instances of acrimony and brought censure of the president and several members of his official family by elements of the fourth estate. By extension, press coverage of the First Family and the kin was designed—in significant part, Truman believed—to diminish his power and the family's good name. The press—the "one-party press," according to Truman—had unfairly consigned him to the company of "charlatans, demagogues, and traitors" (quoted in Mitchell, 1998, p. x). During the final years of his presidency, he pledged himself, with some seriousness, to spend the rest of his life "in an endeavor to cause a return to truthful writing and reporting" (quoted in Mitchell, 1998, p. x).

John Kennedy

Reeves (1997b) argues that John Kennedy "played the press, with engaged and determined enthusiasm, as if it were a great theater organ, a mighty Wurlitzer" (p. x). Berry (1987) believes that because of television's focus on a political actor's communication qualities, including ability and presentation, the Kennedy administration is remembered more for style than substance:

Do they remember that Kennedy backed the first signing of a limited Nuclear Test Ban Treaty with the Soviet Union, or do they remember his bad back and famous rocking chair? Do they remember that he, for the first time on television, participated in The Great Debates with Richard Nixon, or do they remember the great beauty and culture of his wife . . . ? Do people remember that he had an eye for establishing the Peace Corps, raising the minimum wage, increasing aid to education, or do they remember that he had an eye for the ladies? (p. 75)

Kennedy was the first president to hold live televised press conferences, an innovation that permanently altered the nature of White House communications by staging a regular drama, with the reporters as extras, that reached into every American living room. He also befriended reporters (including *Newsweek*'s Ben Bradlee), marketed his wife, Jacqueline, as a cultural phenomenon, and drew "stunningly positive" coverage by today's standards (Kurtz, 1998, p. xx). Nor was Kennedy averse to keeping his own staff in the dark in order to hide a truth. Pierre Salinger, JFK's press secretary, complained he had not been told about the 1961 invasion of Cuba and so unwittingly misled the press about the Bay of Pigs crisis. According to Press and Verburg (1988) John Kennedy instructed his press secretary, Pierre Salinger, to be on the lookout for "hidden bomb" questions from the press about matters that were bothering them and might surface in later reports. Media manipulation was also a key factor in Kennedy's political career. He used television to overcome what Berry (1987) identified as the three major obstacles to his being elected president: to become a nationally recognizable political figure, to prove a Catholic could be elected by discussing his Catholicism openly, and to show he was not too inexperienced to become president.

Sabato (1991) suggests that John F. Kennedy was "not King Arthur but Sir Lancelot in the Camelot of his presidency" and that it is the "recklessless" in pursuing his sexual dalliances rather than their large number that "stuns" (p. 33). However, during his lifetime, John Kennedy's enactment, along with Jacqueline, as the First Couple of Camelot went essentially unchallenged, despite the facts that "every major journalist" at the time "heard and suspected plenty" (p. 36). For example, one of his principal mistresses was Judith Campbell (later Exner), who was introduced to Kennedy when he was a senator by Frank Sinatra in early 1960. Shortly after becoming Kennedy's mistress, Campbell also become the mistress of Sam Giancana, the Chicago mob boss and successor to Al Capone as head of a billion-dollar crime syndicate. There is evidence that both men were aware of the other and that Campbell acted as a courier between the two as there "was no lack of business to be conducted between" the two. Giancana assisted JFK's presidential campaign with financial contributions before the crucial West Virginia primary and later in Cook County, Illinois, where Kennedy won a "squeaker election." In addition, Sam Giancana had been recruited by the CIA for a mafia–U.S. government collaborative effort to assassinate Fidel Castro. These revelations did not come out during the Kennedy administration or as the result of a "scandal-hungry" press. Instead, more than a decade after John Kennedy's assassination, the U.S. Senate Select Intelligence Committee was investigating the CIA's plans to kill foreign leaders when Campbell's role was uncovered.

There was at least one incident during that period when political reporters went into investigative high gear. Ironically, this was to clear President Kennedy of rumors widely circulated in private that he had been secretly wed to a twice-divorced socialite in 1947 before his marriage to Jacqueline Bouvier in 1953. Although the rumor had been published only in fringe outlets, the White House feared it would eventually reach the mainstream, since the story was based on a privately published book, *The Blauvelt Fam-*

ily Genealogy. Kennedy friend Benjamin Bradlee, at the time a *Newsweek* reporter (later executive editor of the *Washington Post*), believed the story untrue and arranged through press secretary Salinger for temporary use of "some solid FBI documentation" about the character of those spreading the rumor. In return, Bradlee promised John Kennedy the "extraordinary right of approval and clearance of the story before publication." The president had no problem with the September 1962 article, which concluded that Kennedy had been all but legally slandered by hate groups and gossip columnists (Sabato, 1991). Pierpont (1981) argues that one reason the press chose to ignore this, as well as the many other personal and potentially politically explosive actions, was that the "basic feeling" of the press at the time "was that we shouldn't touch it because it wasn't our business or the public's business" (p. 194).

Lyndon Johnson

Lyndon Johnson made major efforts to cajole the press, dispatching military aircraft to pick up anchor David Brinkley and *Washington Post* publisher Katharine Graham and fly them to his ranch for private meetings and dinners. However, his "mounting deceptions" over Vietnam produced disillusionment among the press corps and the public, "saddling the White House with the dreaded phrase 'credibility gap'" (Kurtz, 1998, p. xxi). Being caught regularly in or suspected of lying is a major crime to reporters. Press and Verburg (1988) recall how journalists referenced Lyndon Johnson's credibility gap and jokingly asked: "How can you tell when the president is lying? Is it when he tugs his ear like this, or when he rubs his hair in the back or when he touches his nose? No. Then when is it? It's when Johnson moves his lips" (p. 128).

While the political press was more than willing to skewer Lyndon B. Johnson on issues linked to the Vietnam War, his less than admirable personal attributes were generally ignored, including a "lack of couth [that] was legendary and for the most part went unreported" (Sabato, 1991, p. 43). For example, the *Boston Globe*'s John Mashek recalls that when presented with a prize bull by Tennessee's governor, LBJ "punched" a male reporter in the ribs and in earshot of the entire press corps, female and male alike, is said to have asked, "Hey, how'd you like to be hung like that?" Even in formal settings, Lyndon Johnson might "exhibit foul-mouthed coarseness that made Nixon sound like a piker when he cursed in the taped privacy of the Oval Office." Once, when pursued by a persistent reporter at a press conference, an irritated LBJ responded with, "What are you trying to do, fuck me?" (quoted in Sabato, 1991, p. 43).

The political press corps was aware of Johnson's acting out of his attraction to women other than his wife. Former *Atlanta Constitution* reporter Douglas Kiker remembers a White House secretary's account of how President Johnson "used to chase her around and around his desk," while his attempts to "corral" NBC News's Nancy Dickerson as well as many other women was "no secret in the White House Corps" (quoted in Sabato, 1991, p. 43). Nor were Lyndon Johnson's occasional binge drinking sessions—both while Senate majority leader and president—revealed by the press. This includes one time recalled by CBS News's George Herman when a visibly drunk LBJ, "the man whose finger *was* on the button," came "reeling out of the plane and climbed up on a truck bed and made a speech anyway":

But none of us reported it. . . . Got back to Washington and called my bosses in New York, and I said, "I want some guidance: what do I do under our First Amendment responsibilities when the President of the United States is drunk in public?" . . . They said, "Oh Christ, let's think about it and we'll call you back," and that was twenty-five years ago and they haven't called me back yet. (quoted in Sabato, 1991, p. 44)

Richard Nixon

Richard Nixon conducted what Kurtz (1998) considers a "virtual war against the press" by ordering wiretaps and tax audits of selected journalists, had CBS's Daniel Schorr investigated by the FBI, demanded an immigration probe of household help employed by *Los Angeles Times* publisher Otis Chandler, and moved to revoke television licenses held by the Washington Post Company. For Nixon, Watergate reporting was "outrageous, vicious" and "distorted." His press secretary, Ron Ziegler, dismissed the Watergate break-in as a "third-rate burglary," fed the press lies about scandal, and attacked reporters for unfairly maligning "all the president's men" (quoted in Kurtz, 1998, p. xxi).

Although possibly best known as the president brought down by the media, Richard Nixon also benefited from the political press corps' reluctance to mediate a political actor's private life. In both the 1960 and 1968 campaigns, information was never made public about the Republican presidential candidate's consultation with a New York psychotherapist in the 1950s and possibly later as well. This line not to be crossed remained intact even during the Watergate scandal. Several respected White House correspondents received an anonymous but apparently credible telephone call claiming Richard Nixon was having a homosexual affair with his close friend Charles ("Bebe") Rebozo. While Sabato (1991) notes that at the time the charge "appeared ridiculous on its face"—and no evidence has ever surfaced to validate it—many other "ludicrous allegations" were nonetheless investigated and printed during the time (p. 45).

Gerald Ford

Some presidents who are clumsy or inept during interactions with reporters are framed by the media as people who are or will also be inept in office, as was the case with Gerald Ford whose every stumble seemed to be headline and photo-op fodder. Mediation of a more serious nature occurred when Jerald terHorst, spokesman for Gerald Ford, resigned in protest after Ford's staff lied to him by denying that Ford was considering pardoning Richard Nixon (Kurtz, 1998). In addition, during the 1976 presidential debate with Jimmy Carter, President Ford insisted that Poland was not then under Russian domination, a major gaffe. Pollsters interviewing a random sample of citizens immediately afterward discovered that most believed President Ford had "won" the debate. The next day, reporters mediated Ford's statement as a major blunder. Public opinion shifted, and Jimmy Carter was perceived as the debate winner. The outcome led some to suggest, "somewhat in jest, that the public should elect newscasters also" (Press and Verburg, 1988, p. 8).

Jimmy Carter

Jimmy Carter's press secretary, Jody Powell, told the *Los Angeles Times* in 1980 that a rescue mission to free American hostages in Iran would make no sense only two days before that very mission ended in disaster (Kurtz, 1998). Germond and Witcover (1980) wrote that President Carter had been using "newspeak," the term George Orwell invented in his novel about totalitarianism, *1984*. For evidence, they noted Carter's description of the fatal 1982 helicopter mission to rescue American hostages in Iran as merely "an incomplete success" when it was the exact opposite. They also addressed Carter's statement to North Carolina tobacco growers angry at his antismoking campaign: Carter said his goal was to make cigarette smoking "even safer than it is today" (p. 18).

During his term of office, Carter commented that he had "two unpleasant surprises . . . the inertia of Congress . . . and the irresponsibility of the press" (quoted in Press and Verburg, 1988, p. 10). Although the president, as the most powerful of American politicians, has the advantage over journalists, the tables may turn. Sometimes presidents mistake a reporter's friendship or political preference as a professional trait, as did President Jimmy Carter when he confided to *Playboy* magazine that he sometimes looked at women with "lust in his heart" (Press and Verburg, 1988, p. 180).

Press and Verburg (1988) believe that journalists search out any hint of scandal so that the "president is always on the run." During the first term, it is for reelection and during the second for what history will record about the presidency. The attention drawn by television increases the pressure for quick action. During the Iran hostage crisis, the network nightly news announcements giving the "days in captivity" count put constant pressure on Jimmy Carter, resulting in a "hastily conceived and inadequately planned rescue attempt" (p. 202).

Ronald Reagan

Ronald Reagan was considered by some to be a "great president" even though he did not possess many of the characteristics Americans think "great" presidents should have. This was due in part to his rhetorical ability to make Americans feel good by telling stories. Despite Reagan's landslide victory in the 1984 presidential election, major public opinion surveys showed majorities of the public holding opinions on policy issues that were contrary to positions or actions he had taken. In areas such as increased spending for Medicare and the nuclear freeze, as well as many others, Reagan's positions and actions were at odds with public opinion. The electorate has a general concept of what candidates for high office, especially the presidency, "ought to be like," including the appearance of competency—having sufficient knowledge and skills for the job (Alger, 1996).

Honesty and intelligence have been identified as ideal traits of presidents, yet Ronald Reagan, one of the most popular recent presidents, "frequently gave incorrect statements of facts, made up stories and/or took them from movies and told them as real, and generally demonstrated a weak grasp of the substance of issues, policies and processes." Larry Speakes, spokesman for Ronald Reagan, said in 1983 that an American invasion of Grenada would be "preposterous." Marines landed the next day (Kurtz, 1998, p. xxi). Yet the public in 1984 perceived President Reagan as a strong and competent leader. While good economic times were a factor in the 1984 election results, Reagan's use of symbols may better explain the paradox of the disagreement between Reagan and the public on policy issues. Ronald Reagan's success was due, at least in part, to his tapping into Americans' desire to replace painful memories with more pleasant ones. He accomplished this by "using symbols effectively" (Alger, 1996, p. 43) and reaching voters through the media by influencing their perceptions of candidates and office holders and their actions through the use of narrative.

Kurtz (1998) believes that the modern practice of spin has come to occupy a gray zone between candor and falsehood. The Reagan administration revolutionized the staging of news, by selecting a "story of the day" and providing television with the pictures to illustrate it. One prime example is when Reagan stood in front of a senior citizens" housing project built under a program he had tried to abolish; although reporters "duly noted" the contradiction, the White House was happy with the pictures on the evening news. Larry Speakes sometimes declared members of the press who were critical of the Reagan administration "out of business" and refused to deal with them. And after Reagan's 1985 summit with Mikhail Gorbachev, he quoted President Reagan's private remarks to the Soviet leader—which he later admitted he had "simply" made up (p. xxii).

Ronald Reagan developed a particularly unique television age public relations style, which enhanced his advantages and minimized any aspects of reporting that put him at a disadvantage. Reagan's staff based their strategy for media handling on the conclusion that President Carter spent too much time addressing daily crises and not enough time on long-term planning. Early in the Reagan administration, press secretary James Brady and deputy secretary Speakes planned future and daily strategies to maximize good news and minimize the bad. When polls showed the public disapproval of Reagan's education policy because of cutbacks in federal aid, the Reagan staff countered with a report on merit pay for teachers and speeches on school discipline (Press and Verburg, 1988, p. 182).

A daily theme was presented as a newsworthy event, and reporters were kept at a distance and managed with carefully staged media events. Some were allowed to cover one event while kept away from others. The pool reporters sometimes found the Secret Service kept them out of hearing range of President Reagan, while others claimed that helicopter motors were revved up intentionally to drown out their questions so the president could legitimately ignore their queries (Press and Verburg, 1988).

Because senior media staff believed the "prestige press" set the national news agenda, which the nightly news transformed into visuals to become the average American's source of information, part of their strategy was to feed stories to the prestige print media. As an illustration, prior to a summit conference, Hedrick Smith, *New York Times* chief Washington correspondent, had lunch with Ronald Reagan's communication adviser Michael Deaver. Shortly after, the front page story in the *Times* explained how hard President Reagan was preparing for the summit. Visuals were strategically set in "comfortable" environments, as when the president was photographed sitting in the dugout of the world champion Baltimore Orioles on opening day, taking a bite out of a hot dog. Although there might be accusations that such visuals were blatant attempts at manipulation, Press and Verburg (1988) believe the White House spin doctors correctly assumed the important fact that what viewers would remember were the pictures rather than the spoken words of criticism. The visuals were of high technical quality, and Ronald Reagan's experience as an actor guaranteed he was a media professional, aware of how minute details can affect photographic images.

Reagan also adopted a major feature of the cooperative-control style. In public he maintained a friendly, nonconfrontational personal persona with the press, sometimes calling reporters by their first names. To the television viewers, he seemed comfortable and connected with reporters. A secondary purpose of creating a friendly public television image was that daily activities in which the president "congratulated some Olympic wrestler on behalf of the nation" kept Reagan in the public eye and deflected media criticism that he was controlling and evasive. On occasion, such public relations strategies are not fail-safe, particularly when a presidential policy or action is questionable, as evidenced by his administration's handling of the Iran-contra scandal (Press and Verburg, 1988). Regardless of such strategic missteps Ronald Reagan is still popularly perceived as a great president, primarily because he was considered the "Great Communicator."

MEDIATED REALITIES OF THE CLINTON PRESIDENCY

George Reedy, press secretary for Lyndon Johnson, said that the presidency was no longer only the "bully pulpit" of Teddy Roosevelt but was now "a great stage": "A pulpit is a platform for persuasion and exhortation. A stage is a setting for a presentation which may or may not carry a message. It can be an instrument for education and leadership or an attention-getting device for entertainment" (1970, p. 105). Press and Verburg (1988) call advertising and entertainment experts who provide technical advice to the president *media technocrats*. These are individuals who realize that "as a stage, the White House has no equal in the electronic age" (Reedy, 1970, p. 105).

The enactment of the presidency on a stage has other implications as well. Television encourages a public relations style of politics grounded in exploiting a president's personality and relying on "gimmicks and stunts." In Press and Verburg's (1988) opinion, "one may almost say that the duties and responsibilities of being president today require being the nation's chief political entertainer" (p. 200). Howard Kurtz, media reporter for the *Washington Post*, considers President Clinton's administration to be a "tabloid presidency" (1998, p. 295). In addition, Alger (1996) argues that two elements may account for the "frenzied, extremely critical" coverage of President Clinton. First, in the heat of such news practice, there is a tendency to "shoot first and ask the more detailed questions later"—and when the media have gotten it wrong in regard to a specific fact or some sensible perspective, they "all too rarely" make prominent note of their error. For example, there was much media focus on a haircut Clinton got in *Air Force One* on the tarmac at the Los Angeles Airport in summer 1993, with the claim that he had held up traffic at the airport. As *Newsweek*'s Jonathan Alter (1993) has noted, the *Washington Post* mentioned the haircut episode fifty times in the paper, including nine times on the front page. But "when *Newsday* reported that a review of FAA records showed that the haircut had not in fact held up traffic at [the] airport, the *Post* ran one measly paragraph on it. Same with other big papers."

Journalists became more skeptical after each spin and less willing to allow the president the benefit of doubt. "At some point, even a reelected president dogged by endless scandal can no longer defy the laws of political gravity" (Kurtz, 1998, p. 302). The group of journalists who questioned press secretary Mike McCurry each day in the White House briefing room had an agenda focused on scandal—"the malfeasance and misfeasance and plain old embarrassments" that had followed the Clinton administration from the start (p. xix). When reporters had the upper hand, headlines were dominated by scandal news—Watergate-style charges that drowned out almost all else. Kurtz continues:

Even the best spin cannot work if it is totally untethered from substance, and, in the absence of hard information about the president and the intern, the loyalists' spin had become surreal. The press wasn't buying it, and neither was much of the public. The journalists were caught up in a frenzy of unprecedented intensity, with all sorts of uncorroborated allegations echoing through the headlines and the newscasts. (p. 302)

PRESS MEDIATION OF THE CLINTONS' AGENDA

The most wealthy and best-known reporters in the Clinton press room at the end of Bill Clinton's first administration were the network correspondents, including Rita Braver, Brit Hume, and Jim Miklaszewski. Correspondents who had worked the beat—Dan Rather, Tom Brokaw, Lesley Stahl, Sam Donaldson, Chris Wallace, Judy Woodruff, Brian Williams—had gone on to big anchor jobs and bigger paychecks. The most dramatic stories—war, recession, diplomacy, scandal—were there for the picking. Reporters' ninety-second segments for the evening broadcasts "skated along the surface of the news" with clear story lines and visuals that could be "capped with a couple of pithy remarks on whether the president was sinking or swimming" (Kurtz, 1998, p. 36).

Reporters for the elite newspapers—Alison Mitchell and James Bennet at the *New York Times* and John Harris and Peter Baker at the *Washington Post*—did the most to set the overall tone of the media coverage. A front-page exclusive would dominate briefings and most likely wind up on network news. Newsmagazine reporters were not as influential as in the past, but could still alter dialogue with a cover story or behind-the-scenes report.

Other White House regulars, although not in attendance at briefings, included columnists such as Jonathan Alter at *Newsweek*, Joe Klein at the *New Yorker*, William Safire and Maureen Dowd at the *New York Times* and E. J. Dionne and Richard Cohen at the *Washington Post*. Kurtz (1998) believes that with only a few "mocking phrases," these journalists could change the tone or direction of a story and declare Clinton a failure or deeply flawed because they were "unconstrained by conventions of objectivity" (p. 37). Other influential journalists included investigative reporters such as Jeff Gerth at the *New York Times*, Bob Woodward at the *Post*, Glenn Simpson at the *Wall Street Journal,* and Alan Miller at the *Los Angeles Times*, who "immersed themselves in the minutiae of scandal and on any given morning could drop a bombshell on the White House" (Kurtz, 1998, p. 37).

Much of what Americans saw of Bill Clinton in the headlines and in the evening news was orchestrated by a staff who "worked relentlessly at presenting the president in a favorable light and deflecting the scandal questions that seemed constantly to nip at his heels." The modern presidency was ultimately a "media presidency" (Kurtz, 1998, p. xxiv) with staff playing to cameras and placating journalists. In previous eras, American presidents were graded on such traditional measures as their relations with Congress or dealings with foreign leaders. For Clinton, the mass media became the arbiter of political success, and "his every move filtered through someone else's ideological lens" (Kurtz, 1998, p. xxiv).

Much of the information about the presidency comes from the official media representative, the White House press secretary who heads and organizes the press office, subject to presidential approval. Deputy or assistant press secretaries may be specialists, as in foreign affairs. Another may serve as communications director, planning and coordinating the public affairs activities of the president with executive agencies. The Office of Media Liaison, headed by an assistant secretary, prepares news releases on specialized topics. Press office aides prepare the White House news summary for the president, a daily briefing of news and comment.

The secretary may also pass along the president's criticisms of the press of individual reporters and might serve as the reporter's advocate by arguing that some information should be released or that the president should hold a news conference. In several administrations, the press secretary has prepared the president for questions asked at press conferences or following speeches. For much of Bill Clinton's first term, efforts to control the media were clumsy (Kurtz, 1998). The core of Clinton's original team—chief of staff Thomas "Mack" McLarty, confidant Bruce Lindsey, senior adviser George Stephanopoulos, counselor David Gergen, and press secretary Dee Dee Myers—had trouble developing a consistent media message, and the president "seemed unfocused and error-prone." For example, his "casual" response, at his first postelection news conference in 1992, about his plans to change the Pentagon's policy toward gays in the military sent his administration into a "long and bruising battle" that pushed other issues off the radar screen.

Myers was popular with reporters but widely viewed as ineffective and "out of the policy loop." By the time Mike McCurry became press secretary, Clinton's growing press operation needed to deal with an expanding media universe, including all-news cable networks, on-line magazines, and weekend chat shows to more than 1,200 talk radio stations. The White House press staff also needed to address television's emphasis on dramatizing stories and tendency to focus the camera on a "single leader doing battle against the forces of politics and nature." The Clinton press staff faced a White House press corps of 2,000 accredited correspondents, "all of whom had to be serviced" (Kurtz, 1998, p. xxiii).

In the second half of the term, the president's new chief of staff, Leon Panetta, imposed order; Mike McCurry smoothed relations with the press; communications director Don Baer focused on long-range planning; deputy chief of staff Harold Ickes oversaw the political operation; special counsel Mark Fabiana deflected scandal stories; consultant Dick Morris steered Clinton toward the political center; and the president became more disciplined and less willing to answer any question when talking with reporters. For example, Clinton carefully measured his words about the Oklahoma City bombing and the two government shutdowns. He would stick to the script; repeat campaign priorities about protecting Medicare, Medicaid, education, and the environment; brush off scandal questions; and keep his "famous temper" in check (Kurtz, 1998, p. xviii).

Second-term media staff included senior adviser Rahm Emanuel, who assumed George Stephanopoulos's role of "behind-the-scenes press handler." Special counsel Lanny Davis, under the supervision of deputy chief of staff John Podesta, became the "chief spinmeister" on the growing fundraising scandal, Ann Lewis became communications director, and chief of staff Erskine Bowles presided over the entire operation. Counselor Doug Sosnik provided political advice, joined by strategist Paul Begala and former journalist Sidney Blumenthal. McCurry stayed on to "broker a cease-fire" between the president and a hostile press corps. The staff were daily engaged working to control the agenda, seize the public's attention, and "package the presidency in a way that people would buy the product" (Kurtz, 1998, p. xix).

The packaging was a crucial element of the Clinton presidency, particularly because of the less-than-hospitable press environment—a "Beirut without guns" was the Washington that Hillary and Bill Clinton first encountered in 1992. They were exposed to what the *Washington Post*'s E. J. Dionne, Jr., described as "the politics of moral annihilation":

It's no longer enough to simply defeat, outargue or outpoll your political opponent. In this new approach to politics, the only test of victory is whether an adversary's moral standing is thoroughly shredded and destroyed. A foe cannot simply be mistaken, foolish, impractical, or wrongheaded; he or she has to be made into the moral equivalent of Hitler, Stalin, the Marquis de Sade or Al Capone. (quoted in Reeves, 1996, p. 74)

This produced a sort of seige mentality in the Clinton administration, particularly after the discovery that during President Clinton's first two years, the nightly news was mediating "bad" things about this president about twice as often as they reported "good" things. In his third year, a quieter Clinton was on the nightly news programs about half as much as he had been before—the media focus was on Newt Gingrich, Robert Dole, and the murder trial of former football hero O. J. Simpson—and his good-bad survey ratings improved. Reeves (1996) observes that the president's new stillness was not popular with the White House press corps, who wanted regular televised press conferences from the president, which would get them on television as "momentary equal of the president" (Reeves, 1996, p. 62). Clinton continued to resist, telling his own press office staff that all the reporters would do was try to trip him up with questions on women and Whitewater. He was right. One of the few conferences Bill Clinton agreed to do during the latter part of his first administration was on March 24, 1994.

In his opening statements, the president touched on the day's events: the assassination of the leading candidate for president in Mexico, an Air Force transport crash, statistics showing two million new jobs in the United

States, fighting in Bosnia, nuclear weapons in North Korea, human rights in China, and the return of American troops from Somalia. He reviewed the progress of health care and welfare reform bills, a crime bill, and campaign reform legislation being debated in Congress. Then the press began a series of twenty-one questions: one on health care, one on American efforts to block the development of nuclear weapons in north Korea, one on the assassination of Luis Donaldo Colosio—and eighteen on Whitewater and Clinton family finances (Reeves, 1996).

Many journalists at the time believed the president and his staff played "fast and loose with the truth"; many of the press corps covering Clinton had been in the White House during Watergate and Iran-contra. Some believed both Bill and Hillary Clinton "had a particular tendency to fudge facts" and watched as various administration explanations were voided by embarrassing disclosures and damaging stories. With their former Arkansas business partners heading for jail, their close friend Vincent Foster a suicide, and congressional investigators and a special prosecutor "breathing down their necks," the Clintons "lived a precarious existence in what they once promised would be the most ethical administration in history" (Kurtz, 1998, p. 38).

A new breed of White House reporters for the major papers were younger, less driven, and less awed by the job than journalists of previous eras. They were journalists like James Bennet, who got the assignment only five years after joining the *New York Times*. He was struck by the tight controls on information in the Clinton White House and the "daily feeding" so a "pool report" could be filed by the correspondent; reporters were dependent on a small circle of aides and colleagues' pool reports, and had little access to the president and First Lady (Kurtz, 1998). Even more senior reporters were dismayed by the "culture of suspicion" that permeated the White House. Rita Braver of CBS was struck by how hard White House officials worked to keep unfavorable stories off television. They would go to "unbelievable lengths" to prevent her from breaking a story, which was hard enough in a tightly controlled environment where no reporter could wander around unescorted. The White House seemed to think bad stories came across as more sensational on television or that TV reporters were "just plain stupid." At the very least they understood that the three network newscasts reached 30 million households, more than any print media source (Kurtz, 1998).

From the onset of her tenure as First Lady, Kurtz (1998) says, Hillary Rodham Clinton viewed the media with animosity. Early on she moved the White House press corps out of its West Wing offices into the "bureaucratic Siberia" of the Old Executive Office Building across the street. Media suspicion of the First Lady seemed apparent in early pieces about topics such as her non-orthodox decision to include her maiden name and be known as "Hillary Rodham Clinton" as well as her decision to keep her office in the West Wing, while First Ladies traditionally remained in the East Wing. Kurtz (1998) recalls one cartoon that had Hillary Clinton erecting a ten-story annex to the White House, a clear message that "this was one power-grabbing broad" (p. 82).

Lisa Caputo, Mrs. Clinton's press secretary, lobbied for reporters to accompany the First Lady on domestic trips but was overruled by chief of staff Maggie Williams. The official policy toward the media was one of estrangement, which resulted in a defensive posture from many reporters. Staff manipulated coverage by controlling access to Hillary Clinton. While most political figures had done this in the past, none had done it as blatantly as Mrs. Clinton, who granted her first newspaper interview to the *New York Times* on condition that she be asked only about her hostess duties. The resulting front-page story featured the First Lady's plan to ban smoking at White House social events. She also gave interviews to *Time* and *U.S. News* but refused to talk to *Newsweek*, angry at the magazine for printing unsubstantiated gossip about her having supposedly thrown a lamp at her husband.

Initially media coverage was positive about Hillary Clinton. *Time* described her as "the icon of American womanhood," *Vanity Fair* said she was "arguably the most important woman in the world" and the *Washington Post* suggested she was "replacing Madonna as our leading cult figure." *Parade* devoted an issue to Mrs. Clinton as "one of the most influential women of our time" and joined other periodicals such as *Mirabella, TV Guide, Good Housekeeping, Redbook,* and *Vogue* in anointing her "Saint Hillary, media superstar" (Kurtz, 1998, p. 83).

However, the *New York Times Magazine*'s Michael Kelly "turned the image on its head" when his "Saint Hillary" cover story cast the First Lady as a supermoralist, lecturing on ethical and religious values. Describing her as fiercely ambitious, he criticized what became known as the policy of meaning, saying, "The meaning of the politics of meaning is hard to discern under the gauzy and gushy wrappings of New Age jargon that blanket it" (quoted in Kurtz, 1998, p. 83). Kurtz (1998) acknowledges that Mrs. Clinton may have "asked for" such coverage, "prattling on" about "spiritual vacuums" and the like. However, she had also recently suffered the death of her father and so "was in mourning, trying to talk about human values, and Kelly had treated her as if she was a navel-gazing college sophomore" (p. 83).

As the second administration evolved and despite budget, education, and Medicare advances, Clinton and his staff felt columnists in particular refused to give the president credit. Maureen Dowd dismissed the president's second term as "shrunken," "defeated," "aimless." Joe Klein wrote of a "mystifying torpor," a "weariness" an "odd lack of ambition," and a "sense of physical and intellectual exhaustion" that began "in the Oval Office" (quoted in Kurtz, 1998, p. 200). First, President Clinton had been chided for tackling impossibly large tasks such as health care reform and encouraged to take on more realistic projects. However, the progress in more modest areas resulted in a ridicule of Clinton as a "political pygmy" (Kurtz, 1998, p. 200). Kurtz (1997) suggests that many in the Clinton White House considered the true motives of the press in their attack journalism to be "in the end, purely personal" (p. 200). Any upbeat headlines about the administration disappeared. Stories about the balanced budget agreement disappeared in forty-eight hours, while scandal coverage dragged on for months. Since the 1994 "electoral debacle," when they had lost both houses of Congress, Democrats had saved Medicare from slashing reductions, extended health insurance to children, and won enough education aid to make college more affordable (Kurtz, 1998). None of these stories had the staying power of scandal.

News accounts, including scandal stories, are symbolic constructions of political realities that most people never experience firsthand. Walter Lippmann (1922) argued that opinion is shaped not by direct experiences of politics but through images planted in minds by news accounts. According to Bennett (1997), the symbolic makeup of the political universe allows strangers to identify with each other and decide which side they are on in dramatic struggles over abortion, civil rights, health care, and dozens of other national issues mediated by the news, which ultimately becomes "a divisive battleground in which the symbols of society and government are hotly contested and redefined" (p. 104).

The "news" therefore is a negotiation among various actors occupying different niches in the "information ecosystem": political actors seeking to control news content, journalists who operate simultaneously within a profession geared toward informing citizens and a business that sells a product to consumers, and those citizens and audiences who are also members of a culture for whom the news must "ring true with what they believe about themselves as a people" (p. 108). The mediated realities of the scandals surrounding the presidency of William Jefferson Clinton became turf over which Hillary Rodham Clinton rhetorically battled with the American press.

THE DISCURSIVE MANAGEMENT OF POLITICAL CRISIS: THE FIRST COUPLE AS SYMBOLS

Press secretary Mike McCurry was astute at deflecting questions about Whitewater, Travelgate, and other scandals, deferring often to Mark

Fabiana and, later, attorney Lanny Davis, who joined the White House staff. Fabiana had handled Travelgate and Filegate and "all the other gates" so effectively that press secretary McCurry had dubbed Fabiana "my garbage man" (quoted in Kurtz, 1998, p. 56). Both Davis and Fabiana were hired to defend the president against whatever accusations were made against him. When Davis asked McCurry, "Where does your job end and mine begin?" the press secretary responded, "You know the expression 'Shit Happens?' ... well, when shit happens, it's your job" (quoted in Kurtz, 1998, p. 56).

McCurry did not want the questions themselves dominating the daily briefings from the Clinton White House. The sessions became a sort of "running mini-series" on C-SPAN, and the press secretary wanted to keep the damaging material off camera. He insisted on this control as a condition of taking the position because he believed that once the White House press corps obsessed with the day's scandal story, they would wipe out any other news the White House was trying to make. By directing all scandal questions to attorneys, McCurry could "stay on the high road while Lanny Davis shoveled the shit" (Kurtz, 1998, p. 45).

Gould (1996b) contends that Hillary Rodham Clinton's 1992 campaign experience was unusual among prospective First Ladies because inquiries into the life of a potential president's spouse usually develop after the election or in the beginning of the new administration. Mrs. Clinton's professional career, her role as adviser to her husband, and her espousal of feminism made her seem a "harbinger of the new American woman" who forced Americans to face their perceptions about strong, forceful women, an experience that "provoked intense passions that carried over into the White House" (p. 641).

During the 1992 presidential campaign, the media also focused not only on Clinton's alleged affair with Gennifer Flowers, but on his shifting stories about whether he had dodged the draft during the Vietnam War and his belated admission that he had, in truth, once tried smoking marijuana. These, along with the first reports on Whitewater, which both Hillary and Bill Clinton "had trouble" explaining, "drove some columnists into outright opposition" and into making statements such as that made by the *New York Post*'s Mike McAlary that "everyone seems to agree this guy is a fraud" (quoted in Kurtz, 1998, p. 71). Bill Clinton's election galvanized American right-wing politicians, who challenged his presidency partly because he had gained only a plurality of the popular vote in 1992. They labeled him a draft dodger, a philanderer, and an "opportunistic politician," with an animosity that extended to Hillary Rodham Clinton. For example, in a fundraising "Hillary Alert," the American Conservative Union said that her "radical agenda include special privileges for homosexuals, feminists, abortionists, and other left-wing kooks" (Gould, 1996b, p. 642).

According to Richard Reeves (1996), the farther south white males lived, the worse the numbers and perceptions became for Bill Clinton. The passion of the people who hated what was happening heated up when some of these individuals came to power in Congress and in the press and began reacting to the president and First Lady as symbols of "civil rights and feminism, sexual tolerance and abortion. For a lot of people that's when America went wrong. And the Clintons were right there" (Reeves, 1996, pp. 76–78).

Bill Clinton became president when many Americans had tuned out the political world out of disgust with what seemed irrelevant to their lives. The 1996 political conventions and presidential debates had drawn the smallest audiences of the televison era. Most Americans were "resigned" to Clinton's victory over Bob Dole but still did not trust him. McCurry also knew that many viewed Bill Clinton as a "lying, scheming, pot-smoking crook." Kurtz (1998) observes there was no shortage of conservative media outlets "all too happy" to stoke fires of resentment, publishing a seemingly never-ending list of allegations about Bill Clinton's personal life, a "litany of overlapping scandals and the work of four special prosecutors."

Kurtz (1998) suggests that Clinton initially modeled his second term on Theodore Roosevelt's "big stick" approach. By leaking selective bits from the president's supposedly confidential conversations, McCurry shaped the speculation about Clinton's legacy in that direction. The *Washington Post*'s John Harris wrote in January 1997 of three categories of presidents: those such as Lincoln and FDR who shone in times of crisis; those such as Coolidge who managed only caretaker status; and those, like Teddy Roosevelt—and Bill Clinton—who steered the country through periods of transition.

Clinton's staff linked him to Teddy Roosevelt whenever possible. No longer a "flabby, blabby baby boomer," his legacy would be played out in history. The president told reporters that the Rough Rider had helped guide America at a time when "we changed the way we worked" and "we changed the way we lived" (quoted in Kurtz, 1998, p. 102). Soon, the *New York Times* was "morphing" Bill Clinton into Theodore Roosevelt, and press secretary Mike McCurry was being quoted referencing Clinton's use of the "bully pulpit." The White House press team set the president on the high road. For example, he responded with empathy to Speaker New Gingrich's reprimand by the House Ethics Committee, saying he just wanted the scandal to be over and that "way too much time and energy and effort is spent on all these things, leaving too little time and emotional energy for the work of the people" (quoted in Kurtz, 1998, p. 103).

Don Baer, Clinton's communications director at the beginning of the president's second term, followed the "old Michael Deaver rule." Deaver, the mediator of much of Ronald Reagan's presidency, held that television pictures mattered much more than anything said in the media. Much of Reagan's administration was "made-for-TV"—what Kurtz (1998) describes as a daily staging of visuals for the networks. Still, Baer tended to believe that what Clinton said erased what was said about him. Initially a speechwriter in the president's first administration, Baer, with seven years of experience as a *U.S. News* writer and editor, was one of the few journalists in the White House. By 1997, he had become disturbed over what seemed shoddy, if not brutal, journalistic coverage of the Clinton White House.

Ann Lewis, who took over from Don Baer in May 1996, believed the media were impatient and hostile with the president and Mrs. Clinton. Lewis saw her job as generating news when things were going smoothly and the president wasn't fighting with anyone. According to Kurtz (1998), reporters had "loved the endless warfare of 1995," when the battle lines were clearly drawn and Clinton was taking on the Republican revolution. In 1996, however, they suffered from a "sort of postpartum depression" after the campaign. Lewis felt the real problem with the media was that things had never been better. The country was in the sixth year of a robust economic expansion. Yet if the economy were in a tailspin, it would be on the nightly news with President Clinton as the cause. If the reporters needed a "strategy" story, Lewis and her colleagues would stage events—"bundling," they called it—to break into the headlines. They would bring out charts and graphs filled with "upbeat statistics" and hold news conferences and devote radio addresses to the "surging economy." Reporters were not moved. Some even walked out of a news briefing.

The president also "retailed" the news. The *Wall Street Journal*'s Gerald Seib called Rahm Emanuel and said he had put together a "tong"—a group of like-minded columnists interested in having background conversations with administration officials—which included E. J. Dionne, Ron Brownstein, and David Shribman of the *Boston Globe* and Susan Dentzer of *U.S. News*. Clinton's staff advised him to meet with these "centrist" journalists, who ended up writing of Clinton's "nuanced blend of government activism" and "new purpose" (quoted in Kurtz, 1998. p. 202).

Rham Emanuel increasingly became the behind-the-scenes broker with the press for the Clinton administration. According to Kurtz (1998) Emanuel considered the notion of objective reporting "hogwash" and believed Washington journalists biased and almost unanimously of the opinion that Bill Clinton was a "petulant little child with an uncontrollable appetite" (p. 108). As a result, when dealing with the press, Emanuel would "spin so hard" he often insulted them. Nor was he shy about name calling or leaking a story to a competitor if a journalist used something that had been off the record. In short, he viewed politics as a "contact sport," considered press room atmosphere poison, and believed the media were "really pissed" that Clinton was at 60 percent in the polls. If President Clinton was still popular, their "daily scandal stories" had not been on target (p. 109).

Cook (1998) observes that for all political actors, "working with the news is part of the job of governing" (p. 162). In addition, news making becomes a "way to govern," a means to accomplish political and policy goals for officials and their surrogates. As a result, the needs of the news become priorities and influence options and decisions. There actually were two conversations going on in the country: the daily dialogue—grounded in maneuvering over minute details—between reporters and political operatives, and the president's attempt to talk—via the media—to Americans about the "real" issues in their lives. Like Don Baer and Dick Morris, Rahm Emanuel believed that mastering the second conversation would rhetorically empower Bill Clinton to neutralize the first (Kurtz, 1998). And since Hillary Clinton was, as in her first term as First Lady, an equally as frequent target of scandal reporting as her husband, she also adapted a rhetoric of personal and political empowerment through the news media.

Chapter Five

Crisis Management Styles of First Couples

Ike runs the country, I turn the porkchops. (Mamie Eisenhower quoted in Anthony, 1990, p. 563)

I had always had the satisfaction of knowing almost as much as he about the politics and intricacies of any situation in which he found himself. (Helen Taft quoted in Anthony, 1990, pp. 318–319)

Presidents, along with other major political actors, daily face news events—some potentially damaging—to which they are expected to respond. Breaking stories, particularly scandals, can be the most difficult to manage: Ronald Reagan and the U.S. Marine barracks bombings in Lebanon; Walter Mondale and the financial statements of his running mate Geraldine Ferraro; Jimmy Carter and brother Billy's ties to Libyan leaders; Richard Nixon and Watergate; Ronald Reagan and Iran-contra; Bill Clinton and Monica Lewinsky. As each addition to the story is revealed, the president wants the public to think the problem is under control. Politicians also want to put opponents on the defensive and state the case so that others may support their view. The goal is to influence reporting so that, at best, their stories will help control the scandal or crisis—or at least not make the situation worse.

To counter the mediated view that his administration was not prepared, Reagan emphasized that no one could protect a marine base in Lebanon and be totally effective against suicide attacks. Geraldine Ferraro argued that any mistakes she and her husband may have made paying their taxes were honest ones, the Nixon staff initially spun that the Watergate break-in had no connection to the reelection campaign, and Carter argued that being president did not mean he could control his adult brother's actions (Press and Verburg, 1998).

First Ladies have always exercised private influence over their husband's administrations if they wished. Some have been publicly influential. Abigail Adams was the first of a series of copresidents in the guise of a presidential spouse and was much criticized by the press of the time for her role. First Ladies in the late nineteenth century also exerted influence, albeit private, over their husband's political policies, and in the twentieth century, they became more overtly political. The Office of First Lady was institutionalized when Edith Roosevelt, First Partner to Teddy, hired a "social secretary," the first salaried government employee required to answer to the First Lady alone (Burrell, 1997).

The idea of the First Lady in American politics joins in a unique way the public and private domains of life. The position has the potential to alter the notion of what is private and what is public in the political arena. The First Lady is there because of her relationship to a man, not having attained a public position through her own achievements. Traditionally she represents the "expressive, supportive traditional role of women as wives, mothers and homemakers." The word *First* suggests she is a role model for others, while *Lady* suggests a "certain kind of appearance and demeanor" connected to "middle-and-upper-class respectability" (Burrell, 1997, p. 14). Together, these expectations set up conflict for First Ladies: as presidents' wives, they inhabit the political stage with a public persona, but as ladies—and women—they are expected to stay out of politics. As a result, "unelected and unappointed, the political influence of First Ladies is questioned" and "their participation becomes suspect and controversial" (Burrell, 1997, p. 14). But participate they do.

MARY (TODD) AND ABRAHAM LINCOLN

Mary Lincoln's greatest contributions came in the years after her husband's first defeat for the U.S. Senate during which she encouraged his public career. A newspaper reporter who shared a ride with Lincoln during the 1850s quoted him as saying that his wife insisted that he would be senator and even president, at which "Lincoln shook with laughter" (Baker, 1996, p. 179).

In 1858 Mary Lincoln's predictions became more realistic when her husband ran for the Senate, and she traveled to hear the last of the campaign debates, in which Lincoln took the "ethical high ground," arguing that his opponent, Stephen Douglas, did not care about the immoral institution of slavery. Throughout the 1850s, there is additional evidence of what Baker

(1996) identifies as Mrs. Lincoln's "unusual interest and support" of her husband's political career. She wrote to friends to clarify his position on slavery and explained his ideas about the Know-Nothing party, which opposed the immigration of Irish and Catholics. With numerous opinions on several specific issues, Mary Lincoln was ahead of her time as a First Lady because of her interest in the platform of the Republican party. She also took an active role in discussing with her husband the political prospects of his competitors, "perceptively noting in the mid-1850s that the Democrats were losing ground in the state of Illinois" (p. 179).

Mary Lincoln intruded into areas previously reserved for men with persistent efforts to influence patronage matters, an important subject since her courtship with Lincoln. She might intervene in behalf of a friend or acquaintance and encourage her husband to appoint her two Democratic brothers-in-law to official posts, which resulted in complaints that the president placed his family in government jobs. She believed women's intuition gave them a keener understanding of character than men and continued to try to influence Lincoln's appointments until the public men of Washington acknowledged a role that kept Mary Lincoln at her desk writing several letters a day. A *New York Times* reporter at the time wrote that Mrs. Lincoln "is making and unmaking the political fortunes of men and is similar to Queen Elizabeth in her statesmanlike tastes" (Baker 1996, p. 186).

Baker (1996) notes that patronage seekers recognized "this First Lady had influence" and that claims with her for positions in the army as well as for civilian jobs multiplied during the Civil War. However, Mary Todd Lincoln's role was not popular, and she was frequently humiliated by the press about her assertiveness. She became an election issue because of her bills and spending on the White House. Nevertheless, Abraham Lincoln won reelection with 55 percent of the vote. Mary Todd Lincoln's First Ladyship summarized themes of domestic women in public roles during the Civil War era. Her interpretation of the First Lady role involved an expansion of the First Lady's authority as she "straddled the male sphere of public affairs and the female's secluded habitat of homemaker" (Baker, 1996, p. 189). President Lincoln's prominence made her "public property" at a uniquely trying time in U.S. history. Although Mary Lincoln referred to herself as a domestic woman, as First Lady she also had ambitions for the White House, which she greatly improved, and for herself.

ELIZA (McCARDLE) AND ANDREW JOHNSON

Andrew Johnson's relations with Congress deteriorated as the executive and legislative branches of government argued over the development of post–Civil War reconstruction policy. Moderate and Radical Republicans lost patience with the president when he vetoed bills extending the life of the Freedmen's Bureau and a civil rights bill abolishing black codes. After Congress took responsibility for Reconstruction and placed the South under the jurisdiction of five military districts, Johnson dismissed government officials favorable to the new policy. This provoked congressional Republicans to impeach Johnson in 1868.

Eliza Johnson had little contact with the public or government officials during her tenure as First Lady. Her daughter Martha Johnson Patterson established a friendly tone for White House affairs and saw her father's administration through a significant restoration period after the Civil War. While never taking an active role in her husband's political life and perhaps like several other nineteenth-century First Ladies who consciously used their physical condition to avoid public official responsibilities (Young, 1996), Eliza Johnson was nonetheless a devoted defender of her husband.

Mrs. Johnson, with much concern, followed the congressional impeachment proceedings closely and daily provided moral support to her husband. She read newspapers and clipped material for his examination, displaying favorable articles at the end of each day and negative ones the following morning. Young (1996) observes that the president sought advice from his wife and daughters instead of his political colleagues and reports one witness's description of the First Lady's reactions to her husband's acquittal:

The frail little lady ... rose from her chair and in both her emaciated hands took my right hand. Tears were in her eyes, but her voice was firm and she did not tremble once as she said: "I knew he'd be acquitted; I knew it. Thank you for coming to tell me." That was all she said, and I left a moment later; but I shall never forget the picture of that feeble, wasted little woman standing so proudly and assuring me so positively that she had never doubted for one instance that her beloved husband would be proved innocent. (quoted in Young, 1996, pp. 199–200)

LUCY (WARE) WEBB AND RUTHERFORD B. HAYES

For Lucy Webb Hayes, the hardest part of being First Lady was reading unfair comments about her husband. She said, "I keep myself outwardly very quiet and calm, but inwardly there is a burning venom and wrath," and that she forced herself to hide anger "under a smiling and pleasant exterior" (quoted in Hoogenboon, 1996, p. 228). Possessing a sense of history, she identified with First Ladies before her and influenced those who followed. Mrs. Hayes visited Sarah Polk; slept in Martha Washington's Mount Vernon home; admired the landscape of Dolley Madison's Montpelier;

asked Julia Tyler to cohost a White House reception; was on friendly terms with Julia Grant, Lucretia Garfield, and Ida McKinley; and introduced the future wife of President William Taft, Helen "Nellie" Herron, to White House living at the age of seventeen (p. 228).

FRANCES (FOLSOM) AND GROVER CLEVELAND

Grover Cleveland's First Lady, Frances Folsom Cleveland, was initially apolitical, with her life centered on home, family, and friends, but acted as her husband's surrogate during their tenure as First Couple. Early in Cleveland's 1884 presidential campaign, a Buffalo newspaper published, under the headline "Terrible Scandal," an account of a minister's charge that Grover Cleveland had fathered and abandoned an illegitimate child. Eleven years earlier, a widow named Maria Halprin had wanted Cleveland to marry her when she became pregnant. He admitted the child might be his, but several other married men were also possible fathers. Cleveland assumed financial responsibility, supported Halprin until the child could be adopted, and paid her expenses to return to her family in New York. Despite the "exaggerated stories" that appeared in many newspapers, Grover Cleveland told his campaign managers to "tell the truth" about Maria Halprin, which was defended, most notably, by Henry Ward Beecher. The scandal did not prevent Cleveland's election in November (Severn, 1996).

However, the election of 1888 did not end as well for Cleveland. Not only was his campaign in trouble because of an unpopular stand against the protective tariff, but also because of a recurring rumor that the president abused his First Lady. Frances Cleveland wrote a letter in defense of her husband and critical of his chief accuser, which was carried in much of the popular media of the day:

Every statement made by the Reverend C. H. Pendleton in the interview which you send me is basely false, and I pity the man of his calling who has been made the tool to give circulation to such wicked and heartless lies. I can only wish the women of our country no greater blessing than that their homes and lives may be as happy, and their husbands may be as kind, attentive and considerate, and affectionate as mine. (quoted in Severn, 1996, p. 253)

Shortly afterward, Cleveland wrote to a friend:

My wife sits by me and bids me send to you her affectionate regards. I tell you . . . I am sure of one thing. I have in her something better than the presidency for life—though the Republican party and the papers do say I beat and abuse her. I absolutely long to be able to live with her as other men do with their wives. (quoted in Severn, 1996, p. 253)

Despite winning a majority of the popular vote, Cleveland fell short in electoral votes and lost his second presidential campaign to Benjamin Harrison. In 1892, Cleveland was again nominated for the presidency and ultimately defeated both Harrison and the Populist candidate.

New problems emerged during the summer of 1893 when President Cleveland was diagnosed with cancer of the mouth. At the time, he was in a tough battle with Congress, and his vice president was publicly at odds with Cleveland's position upholding the gold standard. It was decided that announcing the president's illness would complicate his delicate politicking, and Cleveland said he would not go into a hospital, even in secret. Instead, a wealthy friend put a yacht at Cleveland's disposal, and a team of physicians and a dentist arranged an operation on board. The media were informed that the president was going on a fishing trip and the family traveled together to New York, where the president was photographed boarding the yacht to "go fishing" and the First Lady and children went on for their summer vacation.

For five days, "during which she dealt with reporters and had to appear unconcerned that there was no definite date" for the president's return, Frances Cleveland "stoically" fielded reporters' questions about the "strangeness" of a fishing trip when there was so much to be done in Washington, because "everyone agreed that there must be no communication between the yacht and land." Ultimately, the "fishing trip" was successful, the yacht docked, and the "president walked off under his own power, unable to speak because of the cotton stuffing in his mouth, but alive and well" (Severn, 1996, pp. 255–256).

CAROLINE (LAVINIA) SCOTT AND BENJAMIN HARRISON

One press-covered incident during Caroline Harrison's tenure as First Lady evoked much criticism. In the summer of 1889, she and President Harrison spent a weekend with Postmaster General John Wanamaker at Cape May Point, New Jersey. The First Lady was so impressed by the seaside resort that the following spring, Wanamaker put together a group of friends who planned to construct a large cottage for the First Lady, which they gave to her the following year. Mrs. Harrison accepted the gift, with little thought about any political complications that might arise for Benjamin Harrison because of doing so. Reporters, when they learned of the cottage, implied that the "gift" exposed the president to charges of being a bribe taker and demanded to know the names of the "gift givers," most of whom were business associates of Wanamaker who expected no favors from the president. To defuse criticism, a "media event" was staged: three hundred reporters were given a free tour of the resort during which Caroline Harrison personally entertained the entourage. Afterward, favorable stories of the resort and the Harrisons appeared in many of the reporters' home papers.

Still, critics persisted in charging that the president and First Lady had played into the hands of developers who had begun to advertise Cape May as the official summer home of the president. Caroline Harrison practiced damage control through a news conference that Calhoun (1996) believes "probably made matters worse." In the interview, Mrs. Harrison alluded to former president Grover Cleveland—but did not mention him by name—and said he had bought a summer house in the Washington suburbs, which he had sold for a substantial profit upon leaving office. Her husband had "decided scruples" against following a similar course. Accepting the cottage, she said, "does not involve the President in any money-making for her personal benefit. How others may be benefitted does not concern us. If our presence at Cape May Point may be a benefit to any persons they are welcome to it" (quoted in Calhoun, 1996, p. 270). Although, in a final attempt to quell criticism, President Harrison paid Wanamaker $10,000 for the cottage, the public relations damage was already done.

Media attention to her family generally offended Caroline Harrison, who thought reporters' inquiries an invasion of privacy. Journalists particularly focused on President Harrison's times spent playing with his grandchild on the White House grounds. The First Lady was most unhappy with suggestions that her family encouraged such attention to court public favor and once said, "I have about come to the conclusion that political life is not the happiest—you are [so] battered around in it that life seems hardly worth living" (Calhoun, 1996, p. 270).

IDA (SAXON) AND WILLIAM McKINLEY

During the particularly mean-spirited 1896 presidential race between William Jennings Bryant and William McKinley, Ida McKinley was targeted with rumors that she planned to undermine her husband's candidacy. While McKinley was rumored to be anything from a drunk to a swindler, his wife was accused of being everything from an English spy, to a mulatto, to a Catholic, to a battered wife, and a lunatic. Although some of his staff feared a public response to the gossip would do more harm than help, the Republican party produced a campaign biography of Ida McKinley as the principal strategy to counter the rumors.

The sixty-one page pamphlet, *Sketch of the Life of Mrs. William McKinley,* became the first campaign biography ever published of an American presidential candidate's spouse. It was primarily an ethos-building attempt grounded in framing her as a member of a hardy American pioneer family and a woman who had survived and been strengthened by personal tragedy. The pamphlet concluded with a description of America's joy when William McKinley won the Republican nomination, recalling the telegraphs—"a torrent of yellow slip"—of congratulation, which came "not from men along to the [then] Governor, but from men and women to Mrs. McKinley; from friends she had known, and from another multitude of those whose hearts had been melted by the pathos in her story, and in whose aspirations her husband's name stood transfigured as the symbol of deliverance and hope" (Leffler, 1996, p. 287).

The publication of the pamphlet coincided with the Republican candidates' "front porch" campaign during which thousands traveled to the McKinleys' Ohio home to shake his hand and, on occasion, even meet and be photographed with Ida McKinley, who, but for the exigence of the rumors, would have remained out of sight. Although William McKinley was known to leave the premises when "tactless questions" about his wife were asked by visitors, his staff's handling of the "whispering campaign" against the McKinleys was successful, and they traveled to Washington in 1897 as the First Couple.

HELEN (HERRON) [NELLIE] AND WILLIAM HOWARD TAFT

Helen "Nellie" Taft was a substantial influence on her husband, William Howard Taft, primarily through her aspirations for his ascension to the presidency. After winning the presidential election in 1904, Theodore Roosevelt announced he would not run again. It was not until March 1907 that Roosevelt supported Taft as his successor. Nellie Taft believed the president had unconscionably delayed his backing, which caused her to mistrust Roosevelt. She realized that her husband could become president only with Theodore Roosevelt's aid and had purposely blocked Roosevelt's attempt to place Taft on the Supreme Court. When Taft hesitated, the president met with Mrs. Taft, hoping she would influence her husband to accept the appointment. Roosevelt soon after wrote to William Taft that after spending thirty minutes with Helen Taft, he understood why Taft would wait and try for the presidency (Cordery, 1996, p. 331).

Even after Roosevelt backed him for the presidency, Taft was reluctant because he still wanted his friend Roosevelt to run again. Helen Taft began a campaign to assist Republicans who advocated her husband's nomination. She met formally and socially with President Roosevelt to urge his public support for Taft. In 1906, the president chastised Mrs. Taft for being overly ambitious. Mrs. Taft was suspicious that Roosevelt's decision to surrender the presidency voluntarily was an attempt to use her husband as a foil for his personal ambitions. During Taft's campaign, his wife read and corrected his speeches, monitored his popularity in the newspapers, and watched Washington politics closely in case Theodore Roosevelt withdrew his support for Taft. She provided moral support when Taft's public speeches were poorly received and urged him to state his candidacy firmly and allow Republican party machinery to support him. Her attention to detail was illustrated by a "frantic" concern over the potential scandal that would ensue if newspapers discovered she and Taft had "inadvertently played bridge on a Sunday" (Cordery, 1996, p. 331).

While William Taft campaigned, Nellie Taft tracked the newspapers to determine the media's assessment of her husband. Journalists satirized Taft as a reluctant campaigner and Mrs. Taft, who "wanted more than anything to be First Lady," could not let him be nonchalant about the nomination. She constantly advised him on his performance, while his other chief adviser, President Roosevelt, looked more and more to Helen Taft for advice. Despite his own doubts, William Howard Taft was elected president on November 3, 1908, and Nellie Taft "confessed that she had never been so happy" (Cordery, 1996, p. 332).

As First Lady, her husband's career always took precedent over traditional chores of entertaining and overseeing civic improvements. She often sat in on and contributed to Taft's conferences with politicians and diplomats and attended essentially all important public and private White House meetings. Helen Taft also continued to listen to congressional debates, as she had done in the past. She directly influenced her husband, and at the swearing in of new Supreme Court justices, she requested and received a seat within the bar of the Court, the first woman ever to do so (Cordery, 1996).

ELLEN [LOUISE] (AXSON) AND WOODROW WILSON

When Governor Woodrow Wilson became a potential Democratic presidential nominee, Ellen Wilson joined him during the Democratic primary campaign, a first for a political spouse on the national level. When Wilson's increased popularity resulted in criticism from party members who found him too progressive, Mrs. Wilson blocked attempts to undermine the nomination.

Ellen Wilson became the target of rumors when reports appeared that she condoned women's smoking at a time when such behavior was controversial. Sallee (1996) notes that she took her own press release to the newspapers to counter the rumor because her realization of the link between perceptions of her and Woodrow Wilson's political image. Until her death, Mrs. Wilson demonstrated skill at manipulating the press to create political realities that favored her husband's administration. When she died of kidney failure on August 6, 1914, the *Washington Post* reported she had told President Wilson she would "go away" more cheerfully if a bill to improve alleys was passed. The Senate adopted the bill in silence the day Mrs. Wilson died, followed soon by the House (Sallee 1996, p. 352).

EDITH BOLLING (GALT) AND WOODROW WILSON

Gould (1996a) contends there is no doubt that Edith Wilson acted as a surrogate chief executive during husband Woodrow Wilson's serious illness from 1919 to 1921. Mrs. Wilson's impact on policy decisions during this time provoked some of the earliest serious criticism of American First Ladies' exercising "real power" (p. 366). For Wilson's friends and advisers, the prospect of a presidential marriage less than a year after the death of his first wife was politically risky. There was concern that Wilson's chances in the 1916 presidential contest might suffer if a new romance were seen as a betrayal of his late wife's memory.

Part of the problem went back to Wilson's first marriage to Ellen Axson. Between 1907 and 1910, Wilson had been seeing Mary Allen Hulbert Peck. The extent of his friendship with Mrs. Peck is in dispute, and both denied a physical relationship. However, the letters they exchanged suggested a "more passionate tie than a married man ought to have displayed" and became "political dynamite." In 1912, rumors about the relationship had been circulating among Republicans but had not been picked up by national newspapers. The existence of these letters provided Wilson's advisers with the leverage they hoped would deter his marriage with Edith Galt. Under pressure, in September 1915, Wilson told her about Mrs. Peck and offered to release Edith Bolling from their engagement, after which she pledged to stand by the president and said, "I am not afraid of any gossip or threat, with your love as my shield" (quoted in Gould, 1996a, p. 361). Wilson announced his engagement to Edith Bolling Galt, and the marriage took place in December 1915 with little adverse reaction. The 1916 election was close partly due to rumors, circulated by those Republicans who perceived Wilson as weak on foreign affairs, that Wilson and Edith Bolling Galt had known each other before Ellen Wilson died. Still, Woodrow Wilson was elected to a second term in November.

In 1919, President Wilson's health was breaking under the stress of lobbying for Senate approval of the pact that contained the League of Nations with the United States as a full member. At one point, he complained of a severe headache. When he later awoke with paralysis in his face, he was ordered to cease his campaigning and begin immediate rest. Edith Wilson decided not to disclose to either her husband or the United States the extent of his illness.

The president suffered a major stroke on October 2, 1919, after which he was able to function only minimally as president, "his political skills ... diminished" and his capacity to govern lost (Gould, 1996a, p. 363). Some allege that Edith Wilson functioned as the first woman president during her husband's illness, a charge that she later denied: "I myself never made a single decision regarding the disposition of public affairs.... The only decision that was mine was what was important and what was not, and the very important decision of when to present matters to my husband" (quoted in Gould, 1996a, p. 363).

One of the initial major decisions made by Edith Wilson, possibly in consultation with her husband's physicians, was that Woodrow Wilson should not resign his office. At the time, there was no provision in the Constitution concerning the physical disability of a president. In addition, Wilson's vice president, Thomas Riley Marshal, was not considered politically strong.

Although Edith Wilson indicated that she asked doctors directly for their advice Gould (1996a) believes that it is more likely she acted alone, as "from the first," Edith Wilson "was determined that her husband should not leave the presidency" (p. 363). A second major decision was to construct a disinformation campaign so that neither Wilson's cabinet nor the American public would learn the extent of the president's illness.

In an attempt to relieve her husband of stress, Edith Wilson took on as many presidential responsibilities as possible. Although some significant state documents were presented to Wilson "when he felt strong enough to look at them," all materials—as well as visitors—were personally screened. Despite her efforts, the government began to work less effectively during President Wilson's slow recovery; governmental and diplomatic appointments remained vacant, while many domestic and foreign policy questions were postponed.

Ultimately the public was informed of the seriousness of Woodrow Wilson's health problems, and rumors began circulating that he was being held captive and his wife was running the country. Some worried that "our government had gone out of business." Gould (1996a) believes the institutional legacy that Edith Wilson left for future First Ladies was the historical conviction that she had overreached the limits for a presidential spouse's responsibilities. "Petticoat government" and "first woman president" became clichés to describe her efforts, which were applied to later First Ladies when they "intruded on what was believed to be the masculine realm of national politics" (p. 365).

FLORENCE [MABEL] (KLING) AND WARREN G. HARDING

Except for Frances Cleveland, who had been a bride, and "legendary hostess and war heroine Dolley Madison," Florence Harding was the most popular woman to have lived in the White House and married to a man often considered to be America's most scandalous president. "Doomed to be known as wife of the greatest failure in the presidency" and historically overshadowed by Eleanor Roosevelt's persona as the "ideal modern woman," Mrs. Harding as First Lady initiated informal press conferences for women reporters, flew in an airplane, identified herself as a feminist, publicly argued for women's political, social, and economic equality, and, in 1920, became the first woman to vote for her husband for president (Anthony, 1996a, 1998). She wore no wedding ring, "shockingly" encouraged women to be as physically fit and as competitive as men, and envisioned an America where wife and husband would be equal partners in private and public life. According to Carl Sferrazza Anthony in his biography of Florence Harding, "Few First Ladies had such an acute sensitivity to the nations' pulse." She introduced to the White House "everything from jazz music to mah-jongg to the radio" and had a "brilliant sense of public relations," inviting "Hollywood stars to the White House for the first time, using them to political advantage" (1998, p. xii).

Although she pushed her husband to remain in the 1920 primaries despite losses, when he received the nomination, Florence Harding told reporters, "I see nothing but tragedy," and indicated regret over his candidacy. She emphasized her cooking and housekeeping skills to some reporters, while highlighting her business sense and refusal to wear the "bond" of a wedding ring to others. And while "eagerly" serving as a media source, she refused to allow reporters to quote her directly in their stories. Mrs. Harding was a "visible presence" during the campaign, attending most of her husband's speeches, greeting women's groups, and continually declaring her support for suffrage and women's involvement in politics.

When a whispering campaign emerged in the newspapers that Warren Harding had African American ancestors, Florence Harding led the campaign staff's response by stating she was "telling all you people that Warren Harding is not going to make any statement." During her First Ladyship,

Florence Harding "openly and regularly" spoke with both women social reporters and male political reporters. She escorted groups of women reporters through the state dining room and, while accompanying her husband on official trips, befriended the male press corps who covered the president's activities, to the point that she knew them all by their first names. She was parodied in one newspaper cartoon with her husband as "The Chief Executive and Mr. Harding," and publicly criticized for sending a donation to keep "Clover"—rumored to be the oldest horse in America—alive, while ignoring a plea for a contribution to an old age home in the same town (Anthony, 1996a).

According to Anthony (1998) there had always been another woman during the Hardings' marriage. Three years after their wedding, Warren Harding had impregnated his wife's best childhood friend. Next was his relationship with Florence Harding's closest adult friend, Carrie Phillips, the only "known mistress in U.S. history who successfully blackmailed a presidential candidate" (p. xiii). Anthony (1996a) suggests that Florence Harding experienced emotional problems from her husband's affair with Phillips. Although the relationship did not become fully public until the 1960s with the appearance of several "love letters" between President Harding and Mrs. Phillips, the letters indicate Florence Harding's knowledge of the relationship. The Harding marriage survived not only because a divorce would have threatened the president's political future, but also because Florence and Warren Harding "had become, if not romantic, at least political and business partners" (Anthony, 1996a, p. 373).

While other presidents have been accused of affairs, there was tangible documentation of his fifteen-year relationship with Phillips: love letters that included his "acquiescence to blackmail." Phillips received a lump sum of twenty thousand dollars from Warren Harding's supporters, as arranged by the National Republican Committee. Accused of being a German spy during World War I, she was the president's "favorite mistress"; they sometimes made love "with Florence just a wall away." Mrs. Harding "kept the devastation of this to herself, confiding only to her private diary," which was discovered in 1997, rather than in her private papers (p. xiii).

Another paramour, Senate staffer Grace Cross, had been unsuccessful in her blackmail effort. There were many others, including Augusta Cole, whose pregnancy by Harding was terminated in an abortion; Rosa Cecilia Hoyle, who claimed to have a son by him; a New York woman so distraught when Warren Harding would not leave his wife for her that she committed suicide; a prostitute who was accidentally killed in President Harding's presence when she was hit with a glass bottle during a "raucous party"; and Nan Britton, the most famous of his mistresses, who claimed that both of her children were by President Harding. Although Britton, the daughter of one of Florence's friends, was "one of the few Harding girlfriends Florence did not know about," Mrs. Harding did respond to her husband's adultery. For example, she hired a Justice Department agent who "moonlighted" as a private detective to spy on the president's extramarital activities (Anthony, 1998, p. xiv). In 1911, the discovery that her best friend and husband were having an affair so "devastated" and "enraged" her that she sought an immediate divorce, although "both Hardings kept up appearances, continuing to live under the same roof." In her private journal, Florence Harding wrote: "Most of the pain in this world is located in the hearts of women. Many women are forced into mute acceptance of disloyalty, faithlessness and humiliation because this is, after all, a 'man's world,' and up to the very recent years woman has had no redress since she must depend upon the man for support" (quoted in Anthony, 1998, pp. 97–98).

The Hardings mutually decided to remain married. Warren Harding realized his wife's "demands were to protect, improve, and promote *his* business, political aspirations and personal well-being" and that without her "he would not even *have* the life he had." Conversely, Florence Harding had "invested everything she had into the very idea of 'Harding' as her career" and perhaps, acknowledging she could not sexually satisfy her husband, would ask no more about what he did on trips without her. Years later, Florence Harding alluded to the importance of forgiveness in continuing a marriage, with only the "vaguest of references" to her husband's infidelity: "The broad point of view is to understand each other's weaknesses, to be tolerant and to understand that there are other *demands* upon your husband. There are things outside of yourself. You know I am speaking of a woman" (quoted in Anthony, 1998, p. 98). Anthony (1998) observes that, after that point, "in every way except through sexual fidelity and his honesty about that," Warren Harding displayed increased respect for his wife and "would honor, cherish, and obey if she asked no questions." And while Florence Harding's "jealousy never actually abated," her "attempts to keep him from other women became more a matter of protecting his career and *their* work on the career's behalf" (p. 98).

One of the most dramatic examples of Florence Harding's contribution to her husband's career was her vote getting in 1920, the first presidential campaign in which millions of women were eligible to vote. With no formal agendas or professional staff and only nominal support from the Republican National Committee, she became the most visible candidate's wife in history to that time. Mrs. Harding relied on instinct, drawing on a "devoted middle-aged middle-American wife yet progressive feminist working businesswoman" ethos in appealing directly to the press and public. In so doing, she both reflected and appealed to a wide spectrum of potential women voters. She exerted a political influence unprecedented at the time, saying that while her husband was "the statesman," she was "the politician" (quoted in Anthony, 1998, pp. 211–212).

The media even hinted at a Harding copresidency. One reporter speculated that "if Warren G. Harding is elected there will be two p———, well, *personalities* in the White House," while another wrote that Florence Harding was "an active element" in the campaign and that what Warren Harding might accomplish as president "will be the result of both their efforts, of an active partnership" (quoted in Anthony, 1998, p. 213). The media also dogged Florence Harding and tracked her history, looking for any scandalous item. That item and her "deepest held secret" was initially discovered by muckraker William Chancellor, who learned that she had entered into a common law marriage years earlier after learning she was pregnant. She and the child's alleged father "were separated by the Court, though no marriage was proven" and "her neglected son died" (p. 223). The revelation and attempt to control it fueled the issue of divorce in a presidential campaign, particularly since Harding's campaign had targeted the press by spinning "sugar halos around the Harding marriage" (p. 224). Anthony notes that Florence Harding's initial reaction was to "shut it away in my mind's secret cupboard and lock the door upon it" (p. 224). That Florence Harding did have children from a previous marriage—and grandchildren as well—was never mentioned to the press. As pictures of the grandchildren appeared in newspapers, "gossip became rife," and Harding staffers "begged and importuned" her to issue a "bare factual statement" to be issued before it harmed the campaign. Mrs. Harding "reacted with anger and conclusiveness, saying more than she ever had or would again on the issue of her first marriage":

That is my own private affair. It never had anything to do with Warren Harding. He knew nothing about it. He had nothing whatever to do with it and it has nothing to do whatever with this campaign. It has no bearing upon his ability to be President. That short, unhappy period in my life is dead and buried. It was a great mistake. It was my own mistake. I did all that was possible to correct it and obliterate it. No man, father, brother, lover or husband can ruin my life. I claim the right to live the life the Lord gave me, myself. I never lived ... until after I was thirty.... That other chapter was over and dead and buried long before that time. (quoted in Anthony, 1998, p. 225)

Still, the more the Hardings refused to discuss the issue of divorce, the more the press spun the story as one in need of further investigation. The story that the wife of the Republican presidential candidate had not only been divorced but had been a "pregnant bride" as well soon became known to the national Democratic campaign, which held it as insurance in case the Republicans chose to make an issue of the fact that Democratic presidential candidate James Cox had been divorced. The story of the first marriage that Florence Harding finally agreed to publish implied she had "simply" married a man who later died, leaving her with a son.

Other mediated scandals about Florence Harding, aside from her "nonmarriage" and pregnancy, included attacks on her Jewish ancestry, her reliance on astrologists and psychics, and her acceptance of her husband's adultery.

Florence Harding strove, above all, to protect her husband's public image, even though "his appetites could not always be controlled." Still, the scandals surrounding President Harding's public and private life were overwhelming. He had been drunk in the Oval Office during a meeting with union leaders; was whispered to have "black blood" but also rumored to have been a member of the Ku Klux Klan; had lost heavily in the stock market; and had been "permanently tarnished" for allegedly profiteering from "dirty deals" connected with "secret" leases of naval oil reserves (p. xix). Anthony (1998) indicates that the vigilance Florence Harding displayed about protecting her husband's image during his campaign only increased when he became president. She feared assassination and blackmail as well as "devastation" of their "public fortunes" from public knowledge of his drinking, promiscuity, and other illicit activities. As a result, Mrs. Harding strove to track and manage her husband's "every move" (p. 284).

Perhaps the major scandal directly connected with Florence Harding was the rumor that the First Lady had poisoned the president, at whose "sudden and mysterious death" in 1923 she was present (Anthony, 1998, p. xiv). At the time the scandals of the Harding administration were at a "breaking point," and impeachment might have occurred had he lived (p. 462). However, Anthony concludes that although Warren Harding's death was "innocent and accidental" and "she did not poison or in any other way murder him," the death was negligent homicide, the result of medical incompetence on the part of his chief physician and covered up by Mrs. Harding and the president's staff for fear of public humiliation.

LOU (HENRY) AND HERBERT HOOVER

Although Lou Henry Hoover often spoke of her deference to husband Herbert and her sons, Cottrell (1996) considers her an independent woman who broke new ground in communications, protocol, and special projects during her tenure as First Lady—someone Alice Roosevelt Longworth believed was the first president's wife to find her own public voice. Lou Hoover's use of the media—primarily the radio—and open support of her husband's programs established significant precedents on which succeeding First Ladies would build. She actively campaigned with Herbert after he received the Republican party's presidential nomination in 1928. Unlike any of her predecessors, as First Lady she delivered formal speeches on subjects ranging from Hoover's depression policies to her work with the Girl Scouts. Cottrell (1996) believes Mrs. Hoover "made history" with these speeches because she broadcast them over the radio and reached a national audience.

At the same time, Lou Hoover was chastised for her poor relationship with reporters because she refused to grant interviews. By the time she became First Lady, Mrs. Hoover was suspicious of what she considered an intrusive press corps that devalued accuracy. She would sometimes meet reporters about her Girl Scout work and allow them to cover state functions in advance, but would not permit them to witness events firsthand. According to Cottrell (1996), this resulted in one reporter's sneaking into the White House in 1930 dressed as a Girl Scout Christmas caroler to observe how the president and his family celebrated Christmas. By 1932, although Eleanor Roosevelt, the wife of the Democratic contender, granted daily interviews, Mrs. Hoover's policies were unchanged.

Ultimately the contrasting styles of Lou and Herbert Hoover complemented their effectiveness as a First Couple. Her outgoing personality humanized Hoover's "engineering mentality and distant, shy air." Mrs. Hoover fought to protect the president's interests by moving discussions away from topics she knew her husband wished to avoid and accepting engagements only after clearing with him. She supported his policies in public and private. For example, after 1929, she made several speeches and radio addresses on behalf of voluntarism, which she believed would help in Hoover's approach to dealing with the country's deepening depression.

(ANNA) ELEANOR AND FRANKLIN ROOSEVELT

Long before they became a First Couple and she began acting as a political stand-in for her husband, Franklin and Eleanor Roosevelt's relationship had moved away from one defined by marital responsibilities to one of a professional collaboration between peers after Mrs. Roosevelts' discovery, in 1918, of her husband's affair with Lucy Mercer, her social secretary. "Competing pursuits and divergent communities" facilitated the Roosevelt's development of separate personal lives. In 1930, when asked by *Good Housekeeping* to define "a wife's job today," Mrs. Roosevelt responded, "to develop her own interests, to carry on a stimulating life of her own" (quoted in Black, 1996, pp. 430–431).

FDR's administration had many spokespersons. The most preeminent and closest to the president were two members of his secretariat and his wife (Winfield, 1994, p. 79), who played a far more active publicity role than had other First Ladies. As the president's roving emissary, she functioned as FDR's physical contact with the outside world and as information gatherer. More than any other administration spokesperson, she became a public figure in her own right with her activities. One of her most innovative steps was to hold her own weekly press meetings. When her traveling companion and White House guest, Lorena Hickok of the Associated Press, originated the idea of regular press conferences that would be limited to women reporters, FDR's secretary, Louis Howe, was delighted and gave Mrs. Roosevelt pointers on handling "loaded questions" (Winfield, 1994, p. 81).

The First Lady was so newsworthy that journalists wanted access to her. Since she limited the meetings to women, all-male Washington press bureaus like the Associated Press were forced to hire women to cover her. Initially journalists labeled those early meetings as "girlish"; the White House menus, the social events, and the children were discussed. Eleanor Roosevelt soon changed the focus to political news by holding joint press conferences with female governmental officials, such as Secretary of Labor Frances Perkins. She also gave political insights into the president's new programs and her own current projects. Newspaperwomen traveled with her on her inspection tours, such as to the capital's depressed areas. Her exposure of problems set a news agenda, and Washington correspondents were then forced to ask the president about the situation at his press conference. Although FDR did not attend her meetings, Eleanor would sit knitting and then comment at some of his press conferences, during which she would give greetings, answer the president's questions directed at her, make remarks to correct a potentially erroneous impression, and even ask FDR questions herself (Winfield, 1994).

During her husband's first term of office, Eleanor Roosevelt provoked the media through her nontraditional First Ladyship, which included such unorthodox activities as driving her own car and meeting with trade unionists as well as miners. Franklin Roosevelt's "overwhelming victory" in the 1936 election represented an endorsement of his wife's First Lady enactment. Some of Roosevelt's staff—but not the president himself—wanted to "keep Mrs. Roosevelt" in the background during the campaign. Such reasons included her advocacy of better treatment for African Americans as well as her extensive traveling. One critic "pleaded with the Almighty that

Mrs. Roosevelt 'light somewhere and keep quiet.'" The Republican party, trying to make an issue of Mrs. Roosevelt's performance as First Lady, pledged that Mrs. Alfred M. Landon would not travel but would "spend her time in the White House" if she and her husband became First Couple. After the media publicized the claim that Mrs. Landon would be a stay-at-home First Lady, the controversy over Eleanor Roosevelt's interpretation of the role expanded into a "public debate over the political influence of the First Lady" (Beasley, 1987, p. 103).

Eleanor Roosevelt did tone down some aspects of her First Ladyship in 1937. For example, the number of her press conferences fell from a high of thirty-eight in 1934 to twenty-one in 1938. And she repeatedly denied that she had any political influence, although the role she played in numerous political appointments by suggesting names of possible candidates was common knowledge. Still, by 1940, she had transformed public expectations for a First Lady from a woman primarily concerned with social form to one concerned for "social ills" (p. 135). In addition, lectures and a willingness to meet local reporters while on tours enhanced Mrs. Roosevelt's First Lady ethos.

When the Roosevelts were running for an unprecedented third term as First Couple, the Republicans attempted to transform Eleanor Roosevelt and her children into a campaign issue by labeling them as mercenaries who had profited from FDR's position. One popular slogan at the time was, "We don't want Eleanor either!" By 1940, after Franklin Roosevelt had been identified as "one of the five 'best husbands' in the country" and Eleanor Roosevelt had been identified as "one of the five 'most fortunate wives,'" it was clear that her celebrity did not stand apart from her status as a wife, albeit to the President of the United States. She was "known for what she did, but she was also known for who she was, which in turn influenced what she did" (Beasley, 1987, p. 138). During the 1944 campaign, Republicans again tried to make Eleanor Roosevelt a negative in her husband's campaign by introducing Frances Hutt Dewey, the wife of their candidate Thomas E. Dewey, as a traditional woman who believed a First Lady should "stay put in the White House" (quoted in Beasley, 1987, p. 161). After Roosevelt's victory, the First Lady lobbied the press for more productive use of wartime news and coverage of postwar issues.

Eleanor Roosevelt made concerted efforts to avoid news that would embarrass herself or her family. She thus exerted firm control over the image that she presented to the public. Her daily syndicated column, "My Day," was a channel through which she could offer "charming glimpses of her family," which, in Beasley's (1987) opinion, made it "a low-keyed but effective political weapon." It was a device through which Mrs. Roosevelt could disarm critics of her family by both preempting potentially negative stories (as when she confirmed the impending divorce of her daughter in 1934) while casting herself as the "prototype" of a wife and mother" (pp. 88–89). She also used the column to defend herself. For example, she was accused of sullying the "dignity of our country" by serving hot dogs to a royal couple at a picnic. In her column, she told her "dear readers" that "the more important guests will be served with due formality"—even if they dined on hot dogs (quoted in Beasley, 1987, p. 129).

Relationships between Eleanor Roosevelt and society writers were often strained during her tenure as First Lady. The gulf widened in part because of different attitudes toward personal appearance: the reporters valued makeup and dress; Mrs. Roosevelt did not. One *Chicago Tribune* writer railed about Mrs. Roosevelt's attire during the 1932 Democratic convention, commenting that "she was so long and so tall" and was wearing a "very simple, unchic" dress with a "pedestrian handbag" (quoted in Beasley, 1987, p. 55). While in the White House, she attempted to update her wardrobe by arranging with a New York store to obtain fashionable clothing at reduced rates in exchange for being photographed in outfits identified with the store's name. However, even for the photo shoot, she never bothered to look at herself before the pictures were taken. Questions about her wardrobe were raised repeatedly at press conferences, and when she was selected as one of the "best-dressed" American women of 1934, she told reporters that she "didn't know it." Generally Eleanor Roosevelt was more inclined to work with "hard news" women reporters, for whom "matters of style and grooming held little personal appeal" (Beasley, 1987, p. 56).

In 1937, while she refrained from discussing the truth about her marriage and her husband's affair with Lucy Mercer, Eleanor Roosevelt did publish an autobiography that addressed aspects of an unhappy childhood, including her father's alcoholism and her mother's disappointment in her daughter's "lack of looks." However, the book was generally an inoffensive, if not rose-colored treatment based on political realities. For example, there was no reference to infidelity in connection with her brother's divorce or of her husband's "delirium at the onset of polio" (p. 111).

While the political press of a later era may have made much out of Eleanor Roosevelt's agreement to serve as a director of her son James's insurance company, which did business with corporations that held federal contracts, the press duly reported the story without comment. The First Lady made it clear that she believed a president's family should not be compelled to give up normal business ventures (Beasley, 1987). By 1944, Mrs. Roosevelt was adamant that she did not want press conferences to "bog down into fishing expeditions" for intimate information about her family that might fuel scandals. When reporters asked about a *Washington Post* story alleging her daughter had ordered priority travel on a military plane for a dog, Eleanor Roosevelt quipped, "I wouldn't know, and I wouldn't comment if I did know" (quoted in Beasley, 1987, p. 162).

Years after her tenure as First Lady, Mrs. Roosevelt wrote to a biographer of Franklin Roosevelt that

there are certain things you did not entirely understand and of course, certain things that neither you nor anyone else knows about outside of the few people concerned. Whether it is essential they should ever know is something on which I have not made up my mind since they are personal and do not touch on public service. (quoted in Lash, 1973, p. 150)

BESS [ELIZABETH VIRGINIA] (WALLACE) AND HARRY TRUMAN

While scandals in the Truman administration were comparably mild in relation to those in other presidencies, there were controversies nevertheless. Walter Trohan, chief of the Washington Bureau of the *Chicago Tribune*, sought information to discredit Truman for the *Tribune*. Trohan had gathered both incriminating stories and revealing photographs of national politicians for political purposes and had hoped to accumulate private derogatory information on Truman for use at a future critical time. The reporter had heard rumors of sexual high jinks that occurred on a junket to Central America and Mexico in 1939 when Truman and other senators and congressional representatives visited the region. In an account obtained from a member of the junket, Trohan learned that "ladies of the evening" had entertained the Americans during their visit. Truman had apparently "discreetly absented" himself from the group during this time and supposedly retired to his room to write to his wife, Bess, about the "cavorting" of the others and of his own fidelity to her. The real story was of Truman's fidelity, but Trohan could not use it for partisan advantage (Mitchell, 1998, p. 186).

Truman's liberal use of *hell* and *damn* and its reportage in the press earned him a reputation as a "profane" man, and his angry letter threatening physical harm to one venomous critic's coverage of daughter Margaret's singing inspired media attacks on Truman's "deplorable state of mind" (quoted in Mitchell, 1998, p. 200). Other would-be scandals that Trohan and other reporters toyed with included Truman's playing poker and moderate drinking of bourbon and scotch. Mitchell (1998) describes a widely reported statement in which Senator Joseph R. McCarthy insinuated that

President Truman was intoxicated when he fired General MacArthur, resulting, according to McCarthy, in "a Communist victory won with the aid of bourbon and Benedictine" (p. 187).

In July 1941, Harry Truman added Bess to his office staff at an annual salary of $2,400, which exceeded the pay of other aides. The practice of putting family members on congressional payrolls was not uncommon but usually received adverse press coverage. Mrs. Truman opposed her husband's nomination for the 1944 vice presidency in part out of fear that her father's suicide would be targeted by the press during the campaign. Although the "payroll scandal" did arise as a campaign issue for Truman, the press did not explore the circumstances surrounding the suicide of Bess Truman's father, David Wallace, while she and Harry were First Couple. Despite some written inquiries submitted to Mrs. Truman through her secretary in 1947, which included questions about her father's business, Mitchell (1998) reports that "by politeness or an assumption similar to Margaret Truman that Bess's father had died a natural death, no additional inquiries were made by the distaff side of the White House press corps" (p. 207). Beasley (1996) notes that Bess Truman decided on the response to accusations of nepotism and told Harry Truman to "say that like most Americans, the Trumans weren't rich and that she had to work to make ends meet" (p. 455).

Unlike her predecessor, Eleanor Roosevelt, Bess Truman consciously avoided reporters. When Mrs. Roosevelt offered to hold a last press conference to introduce Mrs. Truman to the female White House corps, she was appalled and requested exemption from having to hold her own press conferences. This upset reporters, who were under pressure to produce copy about the First Lady. To make amends, Bess Truman held a tea for women in the Washington press corps but said little to them. When asked how they could get to know her, she told the reporters they had no need to, because she was "only the President's wife and the mother of his daughter" (quoted in Beasley, 1996, p. 456).

Because she was in Missouri at the time, Bess Truman was not in Washington when her husband made the decision to drop the atomic bomb in 1945 and was allegedly angry because he had not first consulted her and usually did not take action on important issues without a mutual discussion. For example, she was instrumental in persuading the president to increase research funding at the National Institutes of Health (Beasley, 1996).

Bess Truman initially failed to recognize the connection between her activities and those of her husband, which resulted in a 1945 scandal. She had attended a tea given for her by the Daughters of the American Revolution (DAR) despite protests from Representative Adam Clayton Powell, who revealed that his wife, pianist Hazel Scott, had been told she could not perform in the DAR's Constitution Hall because she was African American. Mrs. Truman issued a statement, carried in the *New York Times*, saying, "I deplore any action which denies artistic talent an opportunity to express itself because of prejudice against race origin," but would not cancel her appearance. Powell responded by labeling Bess Truman "the last lady." However, the president, who would have liked his wife to have declined the invitation, still backed her decision. The episode resulted in unflattering comparisons between Mrs. Truman and Eleanor Roosevelt, who had resigned from the DAR in 1939 to protest discrimination in Constitution Hall.

Harry Truman's protectiveness of his First Lady, Bess, earned for two of her critics—Clare Boothe Luce and Adam Clayton Powell, Jr.—a permanent ban from the White House during his administration. In 1944, Luce had incurred Truman's wrath by writing that Washingtonians had nicknamed Mrs. Truman "Overtime Bess," a reference to her well-compensated service on the senator's office staff. And in 1948, Luce ridiculed the president and Mrs. Truman during a speech at the Republican National Convention in which she called the president "a gone goose" and Bess Truman "an ersatz First Lady" (quoted in Mitchell, 1998, p. 192).

In Beasley's (1996) opinion, Bess Truman's tenure revealed it was possible for an American First Lady to remain herself yet also win public esteem. In an era before spin doctors and image makers, she was an effective political communicator for her husband's administration through her embodiment of 1950s middle-class values as a "housewife who loved her family, protected her own privacy, and declined to speak out as an individual" persona and "refusal to let herself be made into something that she was not" (p. 461).

MAMIE [GENEVA] (DOUD) AND DWIGHT D. EISENHOWER

In 1942, when husband Dwight was appointed commanding general of U.S. forces in Europe, Mamie Eisenhower was introduced to Americans in a *Washington Post* article saying, "She is a career woman: Her career is Ike" (quoted in Teasley, 1996, p. 469). She saw Dwight Eisenhower only once between 1942 and 1945, and received over three hundred letters from him during this time, which her son, John Eisenhower, later published in large part to counter the story of Eisenhower's alleged liaison with Kay Summersby, his wartime British driver. Although no evidence exists that such an affair occurred, the rumors plagued Mamie Eisenhower through her two terms as First Lady and continued until her death. When questioned about the alleged relationship, her response was, "If I had believed that for one minute, I would have gone after General Montgomery and believe me, I would have gotten him," (quoted in Skiba, 1998). Caroli (1998) reports that when questioned about her husband's relationship with Summersby, Mamie Eisenhower "calmly insisted" that nothing inappropriate could have happened between them because "I know Ike." The reporter printed Mrs. Eisenhower's answer without comment.

JACQUELINE [LEE] (BOUVIER) KENNEDY [ONASSIS] AND JOHN F. KENNEDY

During her husband's presidency, Jackie Kennedy became the "nation's paragon of virtue, one of the most splendid First Ladies ever" (Sabato, 1991, p. 40). However, former CBS News correspondent George Herman recalls that the reality of the First Lady was very different from the mediated version:

Jackie would skip out on a White House dinner and the word would be that she was ill or that she had other responsibilities. And the next day the New York newspapers would show pictures of her dancing at a ball in New York or water-skiing while the president was entertaining some head of state she wasn't anxious to meet. And yet everybody was talking about what a wonderful First Lady she was.... She was one of the worst First Ladies. (quoted in Sabato, 1991, p. 40)

Caroli (1996) says that although Americans occasionally commented that John and Jacqueline Kennedy appeared not to have a close marriage, the media failed to report on what they believed were his liaisons with other women. These rumors may have convinced Mrs. Onassis to avoid writing memoirs of her White House years, something each of her predecessors did (except Pat Nixon, whose daughter Julie wrote them for her). Jacqueline Kennedy Onassis apparently kept no diary and for the three decades that followed her White House years generally refused to discuss that period of her life with reporters. Despite her public silence, there is evidence she was aware of rumors regarding the president's adultery. Robert Pierpoint, CBS's White House correspondent during the Kennedy administration, recalls a conversation with a French magazine correspondent who had been invited to have lunch with the Kennedys in the White House. At the time, John Kennedy said, "Jackie, why don't you show our friend around?" after which she brought the reporter to the West Wing. She then took the reporter to a small room where secretaries were working and said in French, "And there is the woman that my husband is supposed to be sleeping with" (Pierpoint, 1981, p. 192).

There were occasions when Mrs. Kennedy acted as a surrogate for her husband. Over one hundred reporters followed her during her 1962 trip to India as she attempted to represent the Kennedy administration by smoothing relations between the United States and India after the latter's seizure of the island of Goa. *Newsweek* wrote a story asserting that Jackie Kennedy had spent too much time touring with the prime minister and seeing the sites rather than visiting the poverty-stricken areas of India. President Kennedy was "bitterly" disappointed in the coverage and complained to Benjamin Bradlee:

That wasn't one of your best efforts, was it? She's really broken her ass on this trip, and you can always find some . . . NBC stringer to knock anything. I don't get all this crap about how she should've been rubbing her nose in the grinding poverty of India. When the French invite you to Paris, they don't show you the sewers; they take you to Versailles. (quoted in Berry, 1987, p. 65)

LADY BIRD [CLAUDIA ALTA] (TAYLOR) AND LYNDON B. JOHNSON

Although Lyndon Johnson was, according to Gould (1996c), unfaithful to his wife, Lady Bird Johnson gave no public indication she was aware of his infidelities. She knew a divorce would ruin Johnson's political career and believed the extramarital relationships were transitory and would eventually stop. Caroli (1998) reports that Lady Bird Johnson publicly argued that an extramarital affair by a husband was as "only a little fly on the wedding cake." The long process of waiting facilitated the development of Lady Bird Johnson's "unusual self-control and patience" (Gould, 1996c).

One incident in Mrs. Johnson's term as First Lady sparked a national controversy. In January 1968, she held one of a series of "Women Doer Luncheons" at the White House, which convened women who had achieved distinction in their fields or were interested in social issues. This luncheon's topic was crime in the streets, a controversial one as urban rioting was commonplace at the time. Eartha Kitt, the African American entertainer, one of the guests, made an extended comment about the impact of the Vietnam War on young people, accusing the Johnson administration of taking children and sending them off to war. Lady Bird Johnson, remaining "calm and dignified," informed Kitt that the existence of war in Southeast Asia should not mean that all efforts to improve society should be abandoned. Although the First Lady's response was applauded on the scene, the exchange was mediated by the press into a major issue as it played to the polarized opinion in the country regarding the war (Gould, 1996c).

PATRICIA [THELMA CATHERINE] (RYAN) AND RICHARD M. NIXON

After Richard Nixon's 1952 nomination as the Republican vice-presidential candidate, reporters claimed he had a secret fund to provide for political expenses. Pat Nixon, responding to calls for her husband to leave the ticket, advised him, "We both know what you have to do, Dick. You have to fight it all the way to the end, no matter what happens" (quoted in Anthony, 1996b, p. 525). He took her advice and planned to explain the fund to the nation during a televised speech, at which time the Nixons' personal finances would have also been made public. Mrs. Nixon spoke against the plan, arguing, "Why do we have to tell people how little we have and how much we owe? Aren't we entitled to at least some privacy?" Despite her protests, the speech was delivered as planned, with President and Mrs. Nixon appearing on televison, he apologetically candid and she "strong but silent." Nixon referred three times to his wife, noting she was Irish and someone who didn't quit easily, that she was not on the Senate payroll as many other Senate wives were, and that she had a cloth coat rather than a mink coat. This "Checker's speech"—named after a family pet given Nixon as a "gift"—enabled him to remain on the Republican ticket and made Pat Nixon a national figure (Anthony, 1996b, p. 525).

In Anthony's view (1996b), media portrayals of Mrs. Nixon failed to depict her personality because the First Lady did not want a high press profile and so responded with often bland, general answers to reporters' questions. She was uncomfortable appearing on television and also prevented her print interviews from being taped. This, combined with the dominance of issues such as Vietnam, women's rights, and ultimately Watergate, resulted in media perceptions of Pat Nixon as not being a very worthwhile subject for stories.

The Watergate scandal overshadowed the second Nixon administration. Pat Nixon insisted she "only [knew] what [she] read in the newspapers" after the events surrounding the Watergate investigation. When she learned the details, she became a staunch defender of Richard Nixon to the press, saying he was innocent of the charges against him. Pat Nixon did, however, suggest that the secret tapes from her husband's office should have been destroyed when they were still private property. While privately deeply disturbed about the scandal, she publicly presented an upbeat image about her Watergate reaction, saying, "By blocking out the negatives, the positives focus more prominently in my mind. A long time ago, I learned that if I worry about what might happen, my energies are sapped" (quoted in Anthony, 1996b, p. 533).

[ELEANOR] ROSALYNN (SMITH) AND JIMMY CARTER

Rosalynn Carter's interpretation of the First Lady role as the president's closest adviser was an advance in what Smith (1996) calls the evolutionary history of First Ladies. While other First Ladies had been active advisers to their husbands, no president prior to Jimmy Carter was as open in acknowledging use of a First Lady's advice. Although Mrs. Carter was determined to eliminate the stigma of mental illness and eventually made good on her promise to have Congress enact a President's Commission on Mental Health, she drew most attention for being "strong-willed" and "goal-oriented," a First Lady "ahead of her time . . . perceived as 'Mom' to Jimmy's 'Pop' and trying to run the store they lived above" (p. 249). Her advice to Hillary Clinton about being First Lady was that "you're going to be criticized no matter what you do, so be criticized for what you think is best and right for the country" (quoted in Radcliffe, 1993, p. 249).

Precedents included being sent to Boston to greet Pope John Paul II on the first visit of a pope to the United States as well as her 1977 journey to Latin America. The latter was a ground-breaking example of a First Lady representing the president in a policymaking situation with a schedule that covered seven Latin American countries and twelve thousand miles in less than two weeks. While Eleanor Roosevelt acted as her husband's surrogate and traveled abroad during World War II, her mission was not to explain American foreign policy to heads of state. Such was not the case with Rosalynn Carter. The president openly discussed how he turned to his wife for her feedback regarding issues and strategy. As a result, except for some high security matters, Rosalynn Carter was kept fully informed of virtually everything in her husband's administration, (Smith, 1996). For example, she suggested the termination of U.S. oil purchases from Iran after the 1979 hostage crisis; after cabinet members agreed, the sales stopped. Mrs. Carter was also consulted on major administrative appointments, including the vice president, and acted as Carter's surrogate, as had her predecessors, on numerous occasions.

President Carter also broke precedent when he invited his wife to attend cabinet meetings, which she often attended, silently taking notes. Critics pointed to her attendance at these meetings, as well as her inclusion in certain national security briefings, as evidence of Rosalynn Carter's "copresidency" role (Smith, 1996). She responded to questions of her qualifications to serve as the chief adviser to her husband by asking, "And who is closer to the president, who better has his ear than his wife?" and stated, "I was determined to be taken seriously" (quoted in Smith, 1996, p. 571).

NANCY [ANNE FRANCES ROBINS] (DAVIS) AND RONALD REAGAN

Media spin during the Reagan administration is credited with transforming First Lady Nancy Reagan's image from one who buys expensive china and donates old gowns to charity for tax breaks, to a woman who cares about disabled children and fights drugs (Press and Verburg, 1988, p. 184). The initial "crisis" surrounding Nancy Reagan stemmed from what Benze (1996) believes was a confusion of elegance with elitism. Reporters, who initially seemed enthusiastic about her plans for the White House decor, began accusing the First Lady of being ostentatious. For example, although the redecorating was paid for by private monies, the bill ultimately exceeded $800,000. With much of the donated money being tax deductible from tax returns at the 50 percent tax bracket, money was indirectly being spent from the public treasury. The same could be argued for the $200,000 Nancy Reagan spent on china.

Ultimately the harshest criticism was aimed at her pricey taste in clothing, such as the $5,000 gown she wore at an inaugural ball. Rumors spread that the First Lady accepted a number of dresses on loan from favorite designers that she did not return, a departure from the practices of her predecessors. The Internal Revenue Service investigated whether such actions violated the Ethics in Government Act. Mrs. Reagan defended herself by saying that such practices were common in Europe and would also be good publicity for the American fashion industry. She then offered to donate the dresses to museums but after "very publicly donating a couple of gowns ... promptly returned to her previous habit" (Benze, 1996, p. 596).

While she had critics and fans, Ronald Reagan's Campaign '84 reelection team was concerned about the "Nancy problem" and set about "rehabilitating" Mrs. Reagan's image. Their initial suggestions including minimizing contact with "her fun-loving California crowd" and easing up on parties, designer dresses, and traveling hairdressers. A second strategy included turning the press in Nancy Reagan's favor, a prime example of which occurred in March 1982. The First Lady appeared on stage at the annual Gridiron Dinner wearing old, poorly fitting clothes and sang a self-mocking song (to the tune of "Second Hand Rose"). The media event was a success and press reviews outstanding (Benze, 1996).

Finally, the Reagans' reelection staff believed his wife needed a cause—something "common to First Ladies that would show the serious and caring side of her personality." Nancy Reagan's previous involvement in the California antidrug movement transformed into her national "Just Say No" to drugs campaign. By 1985, she had appeared on twenty-three talk shows, cohosted an episode of television's *Good Morning America,* and hosted a two-hour documentary on drug abuse for the Public Broadcasting Service. She also hosted a drug summit attended by seventeen First Ladies of other nations and established, through a tax-exempt foundation, the Nancy Reagan Drug Abuse Fund. The reframing of Nancy Reagan's First Lady persona was a huge success: press coverage became much more positive, as did public opinion polls, so that when respondents asked what they most admired about Nancy Reagan, the most frequent response was that she supported the president and acted as a First Lady should (Benze, 1996).

The media crises nevertheless continued. The revelation by Donald Regan in a 1988 book that she relied heavily on an astrologer for advice provided the press with a major ongoing story. National newspapers suggested the White House might have fallen under the control of Nancy Reagan's astrologer, and the theme became the major political story of the summer of 1988 (Benze, 1996).

BARBARA (PIERCE) AND GEORGE BUSH

Like most other contemporary spouses of national politicians, Barbara Bush campaigned throughout the 1988 presidential primaries with and without her husband. When the media complained of an "affection gap"—that George and Barbara Bush were not publicly affectionate and that Democratic nominee, Michael Dukakis, and his wife, Kitty, were—the Bushes countered by holding hands, smiling more at one another, and touching frequently. At the Republican National Convention, Barbara Bush was introduced through a video presentation and then presented a speech to educate delegates about the human side of their candidate—his family and values.

Less than three weeks before the election, a rumor circulated that the *Washington Post* was about to report on George Bush's alleged extramarital affair with a former staff member. Mrs. Bush's response to staffers was initially one of surprise that they "were even disturbed" by the stories and that the allegations were ridiculous and to ignore them. She humorously told the press that her husband couldn't even stay up past ten o'clock at night. When the rumors would not disappear, Barbara Bush labeled them as "malicious and vicious." Bush's staff finally referred the press to an interview in which George W. Bush said he had asked his father if he had ever been in a relationship with another woman after his marriage to Barbara Bush and that his father said "no" (quoted in Gutin, 1996, p. 618). Still, the rumors followed Bush into office and re-surfaced again, along with other allegations, in Campaign '92.

In 1988, Barbara Bush was "furious" when Ann Richards, later the governor of Texas, sarcastically described George Bush during the keynote address to the Democratic National Convention and was "equally incensed" at those who labeled her husband "a wimp." At the 1992 Republican National Convention, Mrs. Bush told reporters to give her son Neil a chance to clear his name in the Silverado Savings and Loan Scandal.

One media crisis during Barbara Bush's term as First Lady stemmed from a commencement address she delivered to Wellesley College in June 1990. Two months prior to the address, 150 Wellesley students petitioned to protest Mrs. Bush as commencement speaker, charging the First Lady's recognition stemmed from her marriage to the president rather than her professional achievements. Because Mrs. Bush did not represent the type of woman Wellesley hoped to educate, they said, her invitation to speak should be revoked. Mrs. Bush's response was that the protestors were "looking at life" from the perspective of twenty-one year olds, and while she didn't "disagree with what they're looking at," she still might have some worthwhile ideas to share with them. George Bush told reporters that the young Wellesley women could learn from his wife's model of unselfishness, her outstanding conduct as a mother, her advocacy of literacy, and, most of all, that Barbara Bush was "not trying to be something she's not" (quoted in Gutin, 1996, p. 620).

As First Lady, Mrs. Bush was aware that essentially anything she did or said would reflect on the president and was wary of his having to "expend any of his political capital to clean up after her" (Gutin, 1996, p. 624). Therefore, except on rare occasion, Barbara Bush deflected comments or refrained from commenting to the press entirely. The latter was a reaction to the 1985 "Ferraro debacle" in which she became annoyed with Democratic vice presidential nominee Geraldine Ferraro, who had told the press that the Bushes' wealth insulated them from the problems of most Americans. Mrs. Bush replied to reporters that Ferraro's family was probably more affluent and that while she couldn't say the word that best described the Democratic vice-presidential nominee, it rhymed with *rich.* The story went national, and Barbara Bush personally apologized to Ferraro (Gutin, 1996). By 1992, Mrs. Bush was assuring the press that "the poet laureate has retired" (quoted in Gutin, 1996, p. 624).

A SIGNIFICANT RELATIONSHIP

Because the media has essentially replaced political parties and other organizations and institutions in presenting government actors to the public, it can ultimately make or break an elected official. It therefore becomes exceedingly important that those who represent and recreate mediated images about the president are talented communicators. The evolution of the First Couple's relationship, traditionally that of the president and his wife, reveals a progression in both the First Lady's mitigation of her husband's crises as well as in the press's mediation of the First Lady as a political actor in her own right, complete with her own crises. That the press controls a president's future through framing techniques such as agenda setting and priming is perhaps most evident in the mediation of a First Couple's political scandals. How these crises are rhetorically re-presented determines whether they bring down the political actor or even a presidency.

Chapter Six

Mini-Scandals to Whitewater: The Early Crisis Management Discourse of Hillary Rodham Clinton

> The harder they hit, the more encouraged I get. (Hillary Clinton quoted in Osborne, 1997, p. 74)

A crisis is by and large a rhetorical creation. Windt (1973) notes that aside from a military attack on the United States, a crisis exigence is a "political event rhetorically created by the President" with discursive responses limited by "precedent, tradition, and expediency" (p. 127). Crisis rhetoric is distinguished by an "obligatory statement of facts," the establishment of a "melodrama" between "good" and "evil," and the framing of the announced policy and "asked-for support" as moral acts. Since crisis rhetoric is not necessarily situationally constrained, it may be applicable to "circumstance other than international discord" and may be motivated by a president's "desire to maintain political popularity" more than by "international events themselves" (Blair and Houck, 1994, p. 95). In addition, such discourse by presidents may be viewed as constructing an image of crisis "often regardless of the situational characteristics spawning such discourse" (Cherwitz, 1980). While Kuypers (1997) observes that much crisis rhetorical theory is conceptualized as situation based—as in Windt's lines of argument, which evolved from an analysis of John Kennedy's and Richard Nixon's discursive responses to Soviet military buildup—they might also serve as a strategy for the management of other exigences in a presidency, such as major scandals, by a presidential ally, such as the First Lady.

HILLARY CLINTON'S EXIGENCE: BILL CLINTON

The American presidency is rhetorical in particular because the chief executive must reach the public. This occurs through persuading the press to frame the president's message in a positive manner. Media coverage can influence or create a public mood that may or may not be favorable to a political actor by mobilizing public opinion about whatever the press deems important for a story (Cook, 1998). The framing of these stories also tends to be long-lasting and influences later choices for both the media and its consumers. A public actor who influences the media's framing to favor her or his preferences can "boost their likely success" and "enhance their reputation for future battles" (Cook, 1998, p. 130). The presidency, according to this view, is an office empowered by speaking. And since interpersonal, face-to-face interaction is so rare in the public sphere, particularly for political actors, discursive management of the media is crucial for presidents and their surrogates, including First Ladies. Political actors must therefore devote more effort to discovering ways to reach Americans indirectly through the news media. This communication-driven imperative, mass-mediated strategy of governing may now be central to the American presidency.

Columnist Richard Reeves believed, in 1996, that a fundamental mistrust existed between politicians and reporters about Bill Clinton's manipulation of the truth and the "annoying arrogance" of Clinton's young White House staff. Liberals accused him of selling out to conservatives; moderates accused him and his wife, Hillary Rodham Clinton, of being closet radicals. Some "northerners" did not trust southerners and the way they talk, and some southerners thought Bill Clinton a "phony" southerner and a phony Baptist (Reeves, 1996, pp. 72–73). Reeves argued there seemed to be something like a computer virus hidden in the generation that produced Bill Clinton. The "1960s people" possessed a "generational suspicion and jealousy of each other, some of it related to who served, who dodged, and who protested during the Vietnam years." For example, *Newsweek*, columnist Joe Kein, a peer of the Clintons, wondered in 1996 whether anyone of his generation deserved to govern because their common life experience was so thin compared with the generations that survived the Great Depression and World War II (Reeves, 1996).

Clinton once said of himself: "I acted forty when I was sixteen, and I acted sixteen when I was forty." Reeves calculated in 1996 that "that would make him twenty-four now." John Brummet, a columnist for the *Arkansas Democrat-Gazette*, described Clinton, a politician he had followed for fifteen years, as "an insecure over-grown boy, who seems to lack grounding or certainty about who or what he is" (quoted in Reeves, 1996, pp. 86–87).

Margaret G. Hermann, a professor of political science at Ohio State and author of two books on the psychology of political leaders, has tried to catalog the elements of what she calls "the Clinton Factor," coming up with a short list: "His perpetual lateness . . . his quick temper . . . his talking to the very last person at an event . . . his complaining about lack of free time when all those he invited actually drop by . . . his limitless energy . . . his love of politics, cajoling, log-rolling, and trench fighting that make up consensus building . . . his desire to be in the center of everything . . . his perseverance and dedication . . . his thriving on chaos and uncertainty" (quoted in Reeve, 1996, p. 87). In Brock's (1996) view, Bill Clinton was "extremely talented, intellectually facile" as well as "an unparalleled campaigner, organizer, and silver-tongued orator" who was also "a wayward child, requiring continual emotional support and moral supervision." Since the beginning of their personal and political relationship, he has "looked to Hillary" as his "moral compass" and "listened to her carefully," a bond "tested in Fayetteville, solidified in the depths of Bill's defeat in 1980, and institutionalized after 1989 in the full-fledged co-candidacy" (p. 416). Denton and Holloway (1996) believe one of the major reasons Bill Clinton earned his nickname "The Comeback Kid" (p. xiv) was his resiliency in rebounding from the critiques of his character as well as the incessant scandals that occurred during his presidency. A major factor in that "coming back" was the rhetorical intervention of Hillary Rodham Clinton.

A biographical video of Bill Clinton shown at the 1992 Democratic National Convention reintroduced him to the American people after the news media ran numerous scandal stories on him in early 1992 and his image had suffered serious damage. By mid-June, only 16 percent of registered voters viewed him favorably and 40 percent unfavorably, a standing "normally devastating." This dramatically changed after the Democratic convention, with general support and specific perception of Clinton's honesty and trustworthiness to become president rising to 70 percent by August (Alger, 1996).

Perhaps the initial successes of Bill Clinton's image-making team, as evidenced by the 1992 video, explains why political opponents and the press soon focused on one of the president's primary "handlers": the First Lady. At one point, Hillary Clinton was angry with the *Washington Post*'s coverage of her husband's presidency and argued that its editors had a vendetta against the First Couple. When the president of CBS News, Andrew Heyward, met with Mrs. Clinton, she complained that in the current climate, it was hard to get attention for the president's programs and policies. While she frequently turned down print interviews out of concern that her words could be edited and paraphrased, the First Lady did occasionally make live appearances on radio, CNN, or network morning shows, where she believed her message would be unfiltered. For example, in a National Public Radio interview with Diane Rehm, Hillary Clinton criticized Whitewater as a "never-ending fictional conspiracy that honest-to-goodness reminds me of some people's obsession with UFO's and the Hale-Bopp comet some days" (quoted in Kurtz, 1998, p. 187). She realized that "you can be very involved and on the front lines like Mrs. Roosevelt and be criticized. Or you can be totally concerned with your family and not venture forth and be criticized. It is a no-win situation" (Hillary Clinton quoted in Osborne, 1997, p. 74).

The Clintons had "set themselves up for a fall" when Bill Clinton announced his would be the most ethical administration in the history of the United States (Brock, 1996, p. 304). Although post-Watergate political actors and attorneys had learned that political scandals could best be diffused by openness and full disclosure and although she was said to have kept a copy of *How to Impeach a President* on her bookshelf, Hillary Clinton was "understandably reluctant to apply these lessons to her own situation." Instead, drawing on her Watergate experience, scandal damage control involved manipulating legal procedures, stonewalling, "artful dodging" and an occasionally sympathetic press (p. 305). Despite complaints about the press's distorting "her" messages, Hillary Clinton ultimately proved herself a masterful mediator. The intense and frequently oppositional media scrutiny mandated Hillary Rodham Clinton's rhetorical responses and produced several exigent situations.

Sabato (1991) believes that the political news media participate in "feeding frenzy," a type of group thinking triggered by any political event or circumstance where a "critical mass of journalists leap to cover the same embarrassing or scandalous subject and pursue it intensely, often excessively, and sometimes uncontrollably" (p. 6). Most of these are drawn from presidential politics. Others come from state and regional levels and, more often, government scandals or personal acts of nationally recognized political figures. Examples of such feeding frenzies from presidential politics include Ted Kennedy's Chappaquiddick; Edmund Muskie's "New Hampshire cry"; Thomas Eagleton's mental health; Jimmy Carter's "lust in the heart" *Playboy* interview; Jimmy Carter's "killer rabbit" and brother Billy ("Billygate"); "Debategate" (Reagan's use of Carter's debate briefing books); Jesse Jackson's "Hymietown" remark; Geraldine Ferraro's family finances; Jack Kemp's sexual orientation; Gary Hart and Donna Rice; Joseph Biden's plagiarism and Michael Dukakis's "attack video"; Pat Robertson's "exaggerated resumé"; Dukakis's mental health; Dan Quayle's National Guard service and academic record; and George Bush's alleged mistress. During the Clinton presidency, frenzies included Gennifer Flowers's allegations; Whitewater; "Travelgate" and the role it played in

Vince Foster's death; the First Lady's decision to remove papers from Foster's office and the resulting appointment of a special prosecutor; Paula Jones's allegations that spawned "Troopergate"; the cattle futures investment; William Kennedy and Nannygate; Zoe Baird; Web Hubbel; Monica Lewinsky; and, finally, the impeachment of William Jefferson Clinton. Many of these exigencies required discursive intervention at various times, in varying degrees and with varied tactics by the First Lady.

THE MINI-CRISES

The Cookie Gaffe

Gould (1996b) references one incident in March 1992 that highlights the significance of Hillary Clinton's role in her husband's presidential campaign. "I suppose I could have stayed home, baked cookies and had teas," Hillary Clinton replied to a reporter in Chicago on March 16, 1992. "But what I decided was to fulfill my profession, which I entered before my husband was in public life" (quoted in Flaherty and Flaherty, 1996, p. 157). The comment was a reaction to the reporter's reference on the eve of the 1992 Illinois and Michigan primaries by former California governor Jerry Brown that Bill Clinton had steered state business to the Rose Law Firm. The accusation came only days after former Massachusetts senator Paul Tsongas charged that the Clintons had improperly benefited from a land deal, which later became known as Whitewater (Flaherty and Flaherty, 1996). The statement was "instantly seized" by the media (King, 1996, p. 157) and spun into "angry denunciations of Hillary Clinton as having demeaned traditional women and their homemaking priorities" (Gould, 1996b, p. 639). The *New York Times*'s William Safire wrote that Hillary Clinton, although a "successful lawyer," was coming across as a "political bumbler" in great part because she was showing such contempt for "women who work at home" (quoted in King, 1996, p. 158).

After this statement became public, Republican strategists targeted Hillary Clinton as her husband's weak spot and began investigating her writings and life more closely. By the time of the Democratic National Convention, Mrs. Clinton had become a key force in her husband's campaign and the object of mounting criticism from his opponents (Gould, 1996b, p. 640).

"I Didn't Inhale"

The week before the April 1992 New York primary, Bill Clinton, who had answered previous questions about his use of marijuana with denials that he had ever broken any drug laws, was asked if he had ever tried the drug in England. He replied with the now infamous "I didn't inhale it" statement (Popkin, 1997).

George Bush's Mistress

Further controversy surrounding Hillary Clinton's role in the 1992 campaign evolved from a *Vanity Fair* interview with Gail Sheehy in which Mrs. Clinton explained how annoyed she was that the media dogged her husband because of infidelity rumors while ignoring those about George Bush. She was referring to the fact that during the 1988 presidential campaign, the media had investigated rumors of a longtime Bush liaison with an aide. The rumor was never substantiated, and when the article was published, Hillary Clinton immediately apologized for discussing rumors about President Bush:

It was a mistake. Nobody knows better than I the pain that can be caused by even discussing rumors in private conversation. . . . I shouldn't have been drawn into a discussion under any circumstances. It was in a private conversation. After what my husband and I have been through, I don't think the media should go after anybody. (quoted in King, 1996, p. 159)

The Throwing of the Lamp

The press tracked the Clintons for any signs of marital discord, in Arkansas and during their terms as First Couple. One of the most infamous examples of such scrutiny was when both the *Chicago Sun-Times* and *Newsweek* reported that Hillary Clinton had thrown a lamp in the White House residence during an argument with her husband. According to Brock (1996), the items were "sourced" to the Secret Service, who "confirmed to this author" that after the tossing of the lamp, Hillary Clinton was "mortified" that she had been seen by a security officer. Soon after, the Secret Service agents were permanently moved out of parts of the White House residence. Although the incident was never officially acknowledged, one source told congressional investigators that Hillary Clinton felt "compromised" by the breach of security and threatened to find a new agency to guard the First Couple if the "tongue-wagging" did not cease (p. 321).

Nannygate

Problems arose early in 1993 during the process of selecting a woman as attorney general when two female candidates were forced to withdraw over their hiring of illegal aliens as domestic employees. While Janet Reno was ultimately appointed, questions were asked regarding Hillary Clinton's political instincts and influence in appointments (Gould, 1996b).

Brock (1996) believes that Hillary Clinton's insistence on the appointment of a woman as U.S. attorney general led to an early impression of "gross incompetence" when a series of "trial balloons were cast aloft only to embarrassingly burst" (p. 310). Circuit Judge Patricia Wald, a research colleague of Hillary Clinton at Yale, had declined the nomination after refusing to approve the First Lady's choices for second-tier Justice Department appointments. Prior to her nomination, the White House had known that Zoe Baird, a friend of Clinton adviser, attorney and confidant Susan Thomases, had not paid social security on a nanny who was an illegal alien. After the fact was disclosed, talk show hosts had a field day talking about the $500,000–a-year corporate attorney who wouldn't pay her nanny's social security. Baird soon withdrew.

Next, a classmate of Susan Thomases, Kimba Wood, was considered. She was never nominated because of similar "nanny tax" concerns. When word leaked that she would receive the position, the media picked up the name and soon revealed that she too had hired an illegal alien in 1986 (King, 1996). Ultimately Janet Reno, who had been introduced to Hillary Clinton during the campaign, and was supported by Hillary Clinton's mentor Marian Wright Edelman, was named attorney general.

Reno's tenure became controversial two weeks into her appointment with her dismissal of all U.S. attorneys nationwide. While a standard practice, the timing suggested to some that the White House was manipulating the attorney general for political ends. The replacement of all ninety-three U.S. attorneys by personnel "handpicked" by Hillary Clinton's appointees was a "brash act," which suggested an "unprecedented level of partisanship and distrust" of anyone who had ever served in a Republican administration. Some also suspected the firings were a way to cover the replacement of the Little Rock U.S. attorney with Paula Casey, a former law student of Bill Clinton. Casey was named as a decision was pending regarding action on the criminal referral targeting associates of Madison Guaranty, including Clinton friends the McDougals, for prosecution (Brock, 1996).

The West Wing

During the "extended confusion" over the selection of an attorney general, Hillary Clinton "broke with precedent" and established her primary office in the West Wing rather than the traditional "First Lady" location, the East Wing of the White House. King (1996) notes that the move "sent out messages of status to those in the know" because of its proximity to the Oval Office, which "allowed her to see any member of the domestic policy staff headed downstairs to see the President" (p. 192).

The Haircut

Alger (1996) observes that while media attacks on presidents are not a new phenomenon, the coverage of the Clinton White House represents an "unbridled attack journalism founded on a bedrock of cynicism" characterized by "hypercritical news coverage" focused on innuendo and scandal. There was much media ado about a $200 haircut Clinton received on *Air Force One* on the tarmac at Los Angeles International Airport in the summer of 1993, over the claim that he had held up traffic at the airport. "Condemnation of his imperial arrogance rang all around." The *Washington Post* mentioned the episode fifty times, with nine accounts headlined on its front page. However, when *Newsday* reported that a review of FAA records revealed that no airport traffic had been held up because of the incident, the *Post*, as well as other big papers, allotted the story one "measly paragraph" (p. 238). Still, the Clinton staff ended up having to "prove that it was not incompetent" after the "haircut incident" merged with "Travelgate" into a story mediated as a crisis (Rosenstiel, 1994, p. 112).

Lani Guinier's Nomination

The nomination of University of Pennsylvania professor and Yale classmate of the Clintons, Lani Guinier, as head of the civil rights division of the Justice Department was defeated by moderate Democrats. They considered the appointment of Guinier, who believed racism was endemic in the United States, to be "yet another betrayal" of Bill Clinton's original campaign stance as a moderate and demanded its withdrawal. A major criticism of Guinier was her supposed support for electoral districts shaped to ensure a black majority (Richie and Naureckas, 1996).

Brock (1996) reports on Guinier's recollection of how Hillary Clinton withdrew her support for the appointment after it came under such fire. She had seen Hillary Clinton during the height of the controversy, at which point, according to Guinier, the First Lady "breezed by me with a casual 'Hi, kiddo.'" She continues that "when it was pointed out that we were in the White House to strategize on my nomination," Hillary Clinton turned and said, "Oh . . . I'm thirty minutes late to a lunch" (p. 315).

Richie and Naureckas (1996) consider the aborted nomination an example of media framing, suggesting that Guinier was "abandoned in the face of widespread media distortions of her record" (p. 132). Rather than revealing the First Lady as "unprincipled" in her rejection of Lani Guinier's appointment, Brock (1996) believes this incident shows that the First Lady "values the political cause over personal loyalty" and notes that Guinier's less controversial successor, Deval Patrick, a partner in the Boston law firm Hill and Ballow, still followed many of the same policies she might have been expected to impose. In this case, Hillary Clinton circumnavigated Lani Guinier in favor of a person who was not a potential source for media-spun scandal either.

Conversations with Eleanor Roosevelt

Throughout the Clinton presidency, the First Lady received occasional media flak regarding "mythical conversations" with Eleanor Roosevelt, "one of my favorite predecessors" and "someone whom I have been accused of talking with from time to time" ("United Nation International," 1999). The issue of Hillary Clinton's "conversations" with Mrs. Roosevelt initially developed after a January 1995 address when the First Lady declared she was a "die hard Eleanor Roosevelt fan":

Over the past few years I have felt an even greater affection for her. And have taken on occasion to having imaginary conversations with her. Now I am sure that there will be a talk show host somewhere who will point out with great glee that I have gone over the edge and am talking to myself and talking to Mrs. Roosevelt on a regular basis, but I believe the world, and particularly our country, would be better off if we all spent a little time talking with Mrs. Roosevelt and less time yelling at each other and listening to people yell at each other. (Clinton, 1995)

In late 1998 Hillary Clinton acknowledged media spinning of her revelation through a humorous explanation of its origin:

When I first told people a few years ago that I sometimes held imaginary conversations with Mrs. Roosevelt, there were some—particularly, I must say, in the journalistic community—who thought they finally had irrefutable evidence of my having gone off the deep end. Well, I can only commend to you this imaginary conversation technique, whether it is with a parent, or a grandparent or a beloved former teacher or a famous person. It does help to get your ideas straight because you think, Now what would my grandmother say about this? or What would Mrs. Jones (who desperately tried to prevent me from dangling participles) have to say about this? So talking to Mrs. Roosevelt, even in my imagination, has proven to be a very great source of strength and inspiration. (Clinton, 1998).

THE DRAFT SCANDAL

During the presidential campaign in 1991, the *Washington Post*'s Dan Balz had pulled Bill Clinton's Selective Service records and thought it "odd" that the candidate had managed to remain 1–A for a full year—from the summer he graduated to the fall of 1969. When Balz questioned Clinton directly, he "casually brushed the question aside," suggesting that it was "just a matter of luck" that his number never came up in the lottery. In the same interview, Clinton talked about his later decision to "patriotically" give up his ROTC deferment in the fall of 1969 and how he had requested to be put back in the draft. Within weeks of the story, which had headlined in the *Post*, the "real story" emerged: Clinton had "maneuvered mightily" to avoid the Vietnam War. He had "pulled influence" with his local draft board, recruiting help from Arkansas senator William Fulbright and others, to avoid being called. He had enrolled in an ROTC program only after being classified 1–A. Although Clinton was "correct" in telling Balz that he had surrendered his deferment, he had done so, according to Isikoff, only after major American troop withdrawals and "his chances of being called had substantially diminished" (1999, p. 27).

On February 5, 1992, the *Wall Street Journal* reported that in the summer of 1969, Bill Clinton had gained a crucial deferment from his draft board by enrolling in ROTC at the University of Arkansas for the fall, suggesting that Clinton had been less than forthcoming on the circumstances surrounding his avoidance of military service. It had been an issue as early as the 1978 gubernatorial race, during which Clinton falsely claimed he was never drafted.

Despite a two-hour interview with the commander of the program in 1969, Colonel Eugene Holmes, Clinton did not tell him that he had already received an induction notice. Holmes said in 1992 that he believed Bill Clinton "purposely deceived" him, using the possibility of joining ROTC as a ploy to work with the draft board to delay his induction and get a new draft classification. Bill Clinton's draft status was changed from 1–A to the protected category of 1–D, for students taking military training, but he did not report for ROTC, returning to Oxford for a second year. He reverted back to 1–A status on October 30, 1969, after a September announcement by President Nixon that there would be no more call-ups.

Fuel was added to the draft controversy when ABC disclosed a December 3, 1969, letter of "apology" and "explanation" to Holmes from Clinton explaining why he didn't report. The letter was written two days after the lottery, when Clinton's chance of being drafted was gone. Where campaign staffers saw "only disaster," Hillary Clinton argued that her husband's letter supported his previous statements that he had made himself available to the draft but was never drafted, the position Bill Clinton himself took on ABC's *Nightline*. Although the episode did not help Clinton, the fact that it was faced head-on stabilized the situation and allowed the campaign to continue (Flaherty and Flaherty, 1996).

The First Lady also turned to friends producer Harry Thomason and Hollywood scriptwriter Linda Bloodworth Thomason to help in managing the fallout from the *Nightline* story. The Thomasons had practiced "damage control" once before. In 1988, after Bill Clinton had delivered a "disastrously ineffective" nominating speech for Michael Dukakis at the Democratic National Convention, he was considered "politically dead." Shortly after, Linda Bloodworth Thomason had arranged for him to appear on Johnny Carson's *Tonight Show*, where he was an "instant hit." And during the 1992 campaign, she had developed the idea of Bill Clinton's showing off his saxophone playing in television venues like the *Arsenio Hall Show* (Brock, 1996).

By the time Mrs. Clinton had consulted again with the Thomasons in early February, the positive reaction to her *60 Minutes* interview had elevated Hillary Clinton's public role in her husband's campaign, and the nature of the "cocandidacy" was being openly recognized. The "power-couple idea" had become part of their campaign strategy as the Clintons promised a "new Camelot" (Brock, 1996, p. 260). The Thomasons created a thirty-minute paid spot for the New Hampshire primary in which Hillary and Bill Clinton appeared together before a panel of ten undecided voters and answered questions on a broad range of subjects. Shortly after winning the Illinois primary a few weeks later and essentially tying up the Democratic nomination, Hillary Clinton spoke "plainly in the plural voice of the co-candidacy" when she said, "We believe passionately in this country and we cannot stand by for one more year and watch what is happening to it" and introduced her husband as "the messenger" (quoted in Brock, 1996, p. 260).

THE GENNIFER FLOWERS SCANDAL

During the time in which Bill Clinton lost his race to be reelected to a second term as Arkansas governor, reports of his alleged extramarital affairs also began to surface. However, after his 1982 comeback, some Democrats had speculated about the presidential race for the Clintons in 1988. While he said their decision not to run in 1988 was grounded in commitment to family, others noted that since marital infidelity had destroyed the political career of Senator Gary Hart during his bid for the presidency, Bill Clinton might have held back for similar reasons (Gould, 1996b).

By 1991, Bill and Hillary Clinton had reconsidered and announced his entry into the presidential contest in October after a September meeting with reporters during which the Clintons confided that their marriage had its share of problems but that they were committed to each other. Although Californian Jerry Brown upset Bill Clinton in the Connecticut primary on March 24, Clinton won the April 7 New York primary and locked up the nomination. Flaherty and Flaherty (1996) argue "that Clinton was still alive at all politically was nothing short of a political miracle" (p. 159). Either one of the "twin crises" that erupted before the February New Hampshire primary—over the draft and Bill Clinton's infidelities—"might have been fatal to any other campaign" (p. 159). By January 1992, the question of Bill Clinton's extramarital relationships reappeared as tabloid newspapers and television programs continually queried Hillary Clinton about the stories in Arkansas that he had been unfaithful.

The "bombshell" media event occurred with the publication of the January 23, 1992, edition of the *Star* about a woman named Gennifer Flowers. Although aspects of Flowers's story later proved false or erroneous, she repeated her story that she and Bill Clinton had engaged in a twelve-year sexual relationship. The revelation threatened to destroy Bill Clinton's candidacy just as he was emerging as the Democratic front-runner for the presidential nomination. Hillary Clinton agreed to a one-on-one interview with *Newsweek* in which she framed Bill Clinton as a good family man and said any previous marital problems were private; she said that "we don't talk about this kind of stuff in our marriage with family and friends" and thought that was the "way most people live." When asked about how she felt about defending her husband against sexual allegations, she replied: "I'm bewildered by the kind of press attention that they've generated. But I recognize that we don't set the rules, and that is the way the whole situation has developed in the last couple of years. I feel very comfortable about my husband and about our marriage" (quoted in Nelson, 1993, p. 32).

She also refused to answer specific questions about her marriage and how she and her husband had addressed their problems: "I really don't want to open that up. I don't think that is anybody's concern. What is important to us is that we have always dealt with each other. We haven't run away or walked away. We've been willing to work through. And I think it is inappropriate to talk about that" (quoted in Nelson, 1993, p. 33).

The *60 Minutes* Interview

Hillary Clinton pulled off what Flaherty and Flaherty (1996) considered the "public relations coup" (p. 159) and Nelson (1993) called the "defining moment"(p. xviii) of the campaign on January 26, 1992. Polls at the time showed the Gennifer Flowers allegations had raised serious questions in voters' minds about Bill Clinton's character. At the end of January, the ABC/*Washington Post* poll revealed that 26 percent of respondents would not vote for a candidate who committed adultery and 54 percent said Bill Clinton should withdraw from the race if it was shown he had lied about Flowers. At this point, the Clinton candidacy was in free fall because "the proliferation of populist news outlets ... from tabloid television to talk radio" guaranteed a full airing of the scandal, whether or not the "elite" press ran with the story (Brock, 1996, p. 254). The crisis mode strategy was to have Hillary Rodham Clinton declare her unconditional support for her husband.

Voters were much more likely to accept infidelity in a candidate's past if "the wife had been made aware of her husband's infidelity," one *USA Today* poll revealed (cited in Brock, 1996, p. 254). The Clinton campaign's James Carville believed Hillary Clinton to be "our ace in the hole" and the holder of "the ultimate trump card"; *Newsweek*'s Bruce Lindsey argued that the Clinton campaign would fold under the weight of the "womanizing allegations" only "when Hillary says it's too much" (quoted in Brock, 1996, p. 255). To counter Flowers's accusations, both Hillary and Bill Clinton appeared on the CBS television news program *60 Minutes* three days after the *Star* article appeared. According to Reeves (1996), reporters "flocked to new Hampshire" to watch Clinton "do a Gary Hart—that is, quit with a usable mea culpa"—but "he stood up there and told them to shove it," and "with Hillary by his side," he went on " to explain and blur the stories, much preferring public humiliation to private life" (pp. 58–59). The interview was shown after the Super Bowl, virtually guaranteeing a massive nationwide viewership.

The broadcast version opened with a teaser from the interview—Kroft asking Bill Clinton, "Are you prepared tonight to say that you've never had an extramarital affair?" to which Clinton replied he was "not prepared tonight to say that any married couple should ever discuss that with anyone but themselves." Both Clintons were introduced and the audience informed that they would talk about their marriage and allegations that had been made against him that were stalling his presidential campaign as Democratic front-runner. Mention was made of the *Star*'s publication of marital infidelity rumors of an affair with Gennifer Flowers from the late 1970s to the end of 1989 and their widespread circulation in the press. The Clintons' private life had become a major, if not *the* major, campaign issue.

Kroft asked both Clintons if they knew Flowers, and both said they did. Bill Clinton claimed the allegations were false, and Hillary Clinton talked of how she initially felt badly for Flowers, who "got caught up in these charges" through "no fault of" her own. He indicated that "she changed her story" only "when the tabloid went down there offering people money" (quoted in King, 1996, p. 143). Bill Clinton denied any sexual relationship with Flowers and seemed to confirm other infidelities when he said, "You know, I have acknowledged wrongdoing. I have acknowledged causing pain in my marriage" (quoted in Flaherty and Flaherty, 1996, p. 159).

Hillary Clinton added that no more details were necessary: "I don't think being any more specific about what's happened in the privacy of our life together is relevant to anybody besides us" (quoted in King, 1996, p. 143). King (1996) notes this was one of "many statements" by Hillary Clinton that the editors cut when they put together the final tape: "She saw more clearly than Bill where Kroft was going. He was slowly loosening up the candidate. Clinton had already said that he was not going to talk about any specific case, and yet because he was a talker, always up front, he was about to go public on Gennifer Flowers" (p. 144). Her reminder "got through," and Bill Clinton later said he was "not prepared" to say that any married couple should ever discuss such matters with anyone but themselves. Hillary Clinton later added: "There isn't a person watching this who would feel comfortable sitting on this couch detailing everything that ever went on in their life or their marriage. And I think it's real dangerous in this country if we don't have some zone of privacy for everybody" (quoted in King, 1996, p. 144).

Kroft asked if her answer was "not a denial" to which she said, "Of course it's not." Later he noted that "fourteen percent of the registered voters in America say they wouldn't vote for a candidate who's had an affair." After Bill Clinton replied, "That means eighty-six percent . . . either don't think it's relevant to Presidential performance or look at whether a person looking at all the facts is the best person to serve," Hillary Clinton agreed, saying, "We've gone further than anybody we know of, and that's all we're going to say" (quoted in King, 1996, p. 144).

When Kroft suggested that the Clintons had "reached some sort of an understanding" after working out their difficulties, Mrs. Clinton replied that her relationship with Bill Clinton was "not an arrangement or an understanding" but "a marriage," which was "a very different thing":

You know, I'm not sitting here some little woman standing by her man like Tammy Wynette. I'm sitting here because I love him and I respect him and I honor what he's been through and what we've been through together. And, you know, if that's not enough for people, then, heck, don't vote for him. . . . I think if the American people get a chance and if they're trusted to exercise their vote right because people talk to them about real issues, this country will be okay. That's what we're betting on, and we're just going to roll the dice and see what happens. (quoted in King, 1996, p. 144)

Although the Clinton staff generally considered the *60 Minutes* appearance a good rebuttal to Flowers, the interview also made the story legitimate in the eyes of the establishment press. The lead story on ABC, CBS, and NBC the day after the *60 Minutes* piece was a live press conference of Gennifer Flowers's playing incriminating tapes of conversations between herself and Bill Clinton. Again, Hillary Clinton initiated damage control. "Putting on her lawyer's cap" she learned that shortly after the Little Rock station aired Flowers's name for the first time in 1990, her attorney had contacted the station and threatened to sue for falsely naming her as a Clinton intimate. Flowers's credibility was also hurt by falsely claiming a guest appearance on the television show *Hee Haw*. On the day of the press conference, Hillary Clinton commented to *Vanity Fair*'s Gail Sheehy: "If we'd been in front of a jury I'd say, Miss Flowers, isn't it true you were asked this by A.P. in June of 1990 and you said no? Weren't you asked by the Arkansas Democrat and you said no? I mean, I would crucify her" (quoted in Brock, 1996, p. 257).

According to King (1996), after the *60 Minutes* interview, both of the Clintons played down the Flowers scandal without "blatantly denying it," and Hillary Clinton continued as the "faithful wife" who believed in her marriage and her husband. Prior to Flowers's allegations, Hillary Clinton spent much of her time campaigning separately from her husband; after the allegations broke, she was "quite literally standing by him" and seldom campaigned alone (Nelson, 1993, p. 30). Although the public seemed far less interested in the intimate details of the Clintons' marriage than did the press—later that day, at a rally in Portsmouth, New Hampshire, more than three hundred people shouted down an audience member who raised the issue of infidelity—the interview produced a frenzy on the part of the press. Nelson (1993) suggests that if the press had held any doubts about the appropriateness of character questions, the Clintons' appearance on *60 Minutes* resolved them because "the candidate himself had put the issue into play" (p. 37).

The importance of the *60 Minutes* interview was seen in a Washington Post/ABC News poll taken four days later on January 29. Of those surveyed, 54 percent said that Clinton should withdraw from the race if it were found that he had lied in denying an affair with Flowers (Flaherty and Flaherty, 1996). Clinton strategist James Carville was pleased with Mrs. Clinton's performance on *60 Minutes* and suggested more single interviews without her husband (Nelson, 1993). While the reference to Wynette caused a major flap among country music fans and became fodder for critics, the *60 Minutes* appearance by the Clintons helped control the initial damage inflicted on Bill Clinton's presidential race by Flowers's charges.

Particularly helpful was Hillary Rodham Clinton's affirmation that their marriage was strong and that since she had forgiven her husband for any transgressions, the rest of America should do the same (Gould, 1996b, p. 639). Brock (1996), however, suggests that one reason she was perceived so negatively in the latter stages of Campaign '92 was the manner in which Hillary Clinton had been introduced to the American public on *60 Minutes,* "'spinning' her own marriage." While some were impressed by her firm, "even courageous" decision to "stand by her man," others may have suspected that he had been manipulated into sharing power with his wife in return for her agreement to support him through the Flowers scandal.

Regardless, the Clinton staff speculated that his wife's support might be the only thing keeping Bill Clinton's nomination "airborne" and scheduled several additional interviews. As an example, Hillary Clinton spoke with the upscale New York publication *Women's Wear Daily*, saying that while marital obligations included fidelity, the details of the Clintons' marriage were private: "We have really collapsed the space in which public people can live, to the detriment of our overall politics" (quoted in Nelson, 1993, p. 41). Nelson (1993) suggests Clinton's aim was to stake out private turf for herself, her husband's career, and "the health of the national conversation" (p. 41). She also indicated that whether one's marriage pulled down a political career depended on "the candidate and the marriage" and that "any stressful undertaking can either be made better or worse by the relationship between the spouses. But if it's a supportive one, if people believe in each other, if they love each other, if they have a commitment to what each is trying to do, it makes life a lot easier than it is alone" (quoted in Nelson, 1993, p. 42).

The *Prime Time Live* Interview

Some were arguing that Clinton did lie and that the media had chosen to ignore his deceit. Audio recordings of phone conversations between Clinton and Flowers released at a press conference the day after the *60 Minutes* interview presented the two "plotting to deny they had been intimate." On ABC's January 30, 1992 *Prime Time Live* with Sam Donaldson, in a segment entitled "The Other Woman" (meaning Gennifer Flowers), Hillary Clinton responded to the contents of the tapes and the probability that her husband had lied: "This was a woman who at least pretended that her life was ruined because somebody had alleged that she had a relationship at some point with Bill Clinton. Anybody who knows my husband knows that he bends over backwards to help people who are in trouble and is always willing to listen to their problems" (quoted in Flaherty and Flaherty, 1996, pp. 160–161).

According to King (1996), it was a "tough" interview and one that she was suited for. Donaldson wanted to "set up" Clinton as her husband's "helpmate, then the wronged woman, then ask questions that were actually directed at the candidate, though posed to her as his loyal supporter and defender." He pointed out how Governor Bill Clinton had become mired in an extramarital scandal that might compromise his chances of running for president. Still, she had stood by him and even fought against those who were trying to bring him down. Mrs. Clinton rhetorically "sidestepped" Donaldson's inquiry about whether she felt that infidelity was important enough for the American people to make an issue of it when electing their president by saying that she "would not presume to say what an individual ought not to take into account. That's what elections are for." She then added:

Bill Clinton has a record of accomplishment in a state that is a very small state. It's like living in a fishbowl, a very happy fishbowl, but nevertheless a small one, where people know him and they know him very, very well. And they've given him their trust and their confidence for eleven years in the highest position they could vote for him for. (quoted in King, 1996, p. 153)

Donaldson countered by pointing out that some might fear that cheating "on one thing" might lead to cheating on another—a "character problem." Hillary Clinton replied she thought "character" was a larger issue and

all that's really important is the relationship of honesty and openness and forgiveness between Bill Clinton and me. . . . If you're married for more than ten minutes, you're going to have to forgive somebody for something. And that's one of the things we've had to learn over sixteen years. There are a lot of big and little things that come up in a marriage that if you don't deal with right then and there, they can sink you. (quoted in King, 1996, p. 153)

Clinton once again deflected Donaldson's attempt to elicit a statement of forgiveness for her husband's "sexual transgression," but since such an admission would have been a tacit admission of her husband's infidelity, she "simply said that she had forgiven him for many things in the past, avoiding specifics" (King, 1996, p. 153). With the presidency on the line, Hillary Clinton was apparently "more than willing to stand by her man," a pattern followed by other Clintonites when confronted with damaging information during the campaign: deny everything and attack the messenger (Flaherty and Flaherty, 1996, p. 161).

THE HEALTH CARE SCANDAL

During the 1992 campaign, Bill Clinton pointed to an increasing number of uninsured Americans and skyrocketing health care costs as evidence of the need for a plan making affordable health insurance available to every American. The passage of health care reform legislation became the cornerstone of his first-term domestic policy agenda. In September 1993, a commission headed by the First Lady prepared a comprehensive health reform bill, the Health Security Act (Jamieson and Cappella, 1998). However, the intricacy of the "thousand-plus-page" plan "didn't make understanding easy," and neither did its scope, which included "everything from measles vaccines to MRIs." In addition, by early February 1994, there were competing plans "in the congressional hopper" (pp. 111–112).

Brock (1996) believes that Bill Clinton revealed his "naive expectation" that appointing his wife would at least end the need for downplaying the Clinton co-presidency when he said he was grateful that the First Lady had agreed to chair the task force and "not only because it means she'll be sharing some of the heat I expect to generate" (quoted in Brock, 1996, p. 326). As she had shown in the educational reform effort in Arkansas in the mid-1980s, Hillary Clinton had a "keen" intellect and was a "skillful and engaging public speaker" and advocate for causes. In addition, she was willing to make hard decisions and disappoint in order to achieve a political victory. Furthermore, she had an ability to present controversial ideas in the "language of traditional values" (p. 327).

Health care presented Hillary Clinton with the chance to trailblaze as the first First Lady to take a "line-authority" government job. In the first flush of the hundred-day effort, she framed the outline of the plan and talked to members of Congress, lobbyists, interest groups, and the public to gain momentum and rally support. She made dozens of courtesy calls on Capitol Hill, testified—to bipartisan applause—before committees in both houses of Congress, and went on a nationwide speaking tour. After meeting with individual legislators, she sent letters—and often autographed photos—thanking them for their input. At hearings, she would ask about family members by name and paid compliments on particular pieces of legislation. As the major spokesperson for selling the policy to the country, she appeared at events and in the media nationwide (Gould, 1996b) and during the process exhibited "political savvy and carefully planned attention to detail" (Brock, 1996, p. 331).

A week after the plan had been revealed, flanked by Senators George Mitchell and Ted Kennedy in the Senate's Lyndon B. Johnson Conference Room, Hillary Clinton stood as the only First Lady in history to confer with

Congress on a crucial domestic policy issue. Her Capitol Hill visit was high profile and a signal she would "not only be the shaper of the important health-care proposal but would shepherd the legislation through Congress as well." Initial congressional feedback was positive after the hour-long meeting for Mrs. Clinton, if not for the health care program. For example, Ohio senator Howard Metzenbaum called her "sharp" and "on the ball" (quoted in King, 1996, p. 195). But others worried about the electorate's reaction to change from her more traditional image in the latter part of the 1992 campaign. The *New Republic*'s Mickey Kaus complained about "creeping Rodhamism," calling Hillary Clinton a "false feminist" because "nepotism is not feminism" (quoted in King, 1992, pp. 195–196). A White House aide was quoted in *Newsweek* implying that "Hillary Rodham Clinton was not just in the loop, she *was* the loop" (King, 1996, p. 196).

Clinton campaign strategist James Carville commented on Hillary Rodham Clinton's influence in her husband's presidency: "If the person that has the last word at night is the same person who has the first word in the morning, they're going to be important. You throw in an I.Q. of a g'zillion and a backbone of steel, and it's a pretty safe assumption to say this is a person of considerable influence" (quoted in King, 1996, p. 196).

Initially by a margin of two to one, Americans approved of the First Lady's heading up the task force (Flaherty and Flaherty, 1996); her approval rating was higher than the president's, and most Americans considered her a positive role model (King, 1996). However, in February, the *Washington Times* argued that reporters had been denied access to the first task force meeting, a violation of the Federal Advisory Committee Act (FACA), a little-known law on the books since 1972. Shortly after, Hillary Clinton and the six cabinet members serving on the task force were sued in U.S. District Court for the District of Columbia by three groups: the Association of American Physicians and Surgeons, the American Council for Health Care Reform, and the National Legal and Policy Center (Flaherty and Flaherty, 1996). These groups filed suit during the winter of 1993 charging that the President's Task Force on National Health Care Reform, the panel headed by Mrs. Clinton, could not hold its meetings in secret because that violated FACA. The Justice Department responded that the First Lady was a de facto government employee and so not covered by the act. The federal court of appeals ruled that Hillary Clinton was essentially a government official, as the Justice Department had argued, a decision that set out for the first time the basis for the position of the First Lady in American government (Gould, 1996b).

On March 10, 1993, the court ruled that the task force had to open its meetings to the plaintiffs and the media. The ruling was appealed by the

White House and was overturned on June 22, after the task force had supposedly already disbanded on May 30. Justice Department lawyers argued that since Hillary Clinton "functions in both a legal and practical sense as part of the government," her participation in the task force should not trigger FACA (Flaherty and Flaherty, 1996, p. 191). The health plan was supposed to be unveiled on May 30, 1993, but was not officially presented to Congress until that autumn. On September 22, 1993, Hillary Rodham Clinton testified before a House committee on the health care program. She joined Eleanor Roosevelt and Rosalynn Carter as First Ladies who have appeared before Congress during their husbands' presidencies. Her adept handling of questions about the lengthy documentation of the plan, particularly from Republicans, showed that the program had "gotten off to a sparkling start" (Gould, 1996b, p. 644).

Yet the criticism of her role in formulating the health care initiative ranged from concern that she was stepping out of the traditional First Lady sphere or place to charges of political nepotism (Brock, 1996). After the Gennifer Flowers story broke, rumors had circulated of a "Treaty of Georgetown" between Bill and Hillary Clinton, whereby the First Lady was given a "sphere of influence" in exchange for remaining with the president despite the controversy. Such rumors, discounted by most who knew the Clintons personally, remained persistent and temporarily undermined the moral authority and position of Hillary Rodham Clinton.

While her staff felt that Mrs. Clinton was justified in her reluctance to discuss specifics about health care when, in most cases, there were not any complete enough to detail, many in the media interpreted her reluctance to be yet another example of an unelected woman, using secrecy in order to continue her "wielding power behind closed doors" (Kurtz, 1998, p. 84). Her responses included attributing criticism of the health care plan to sexists: "If somebody has a female boss for the first time, and they've never experienced that—well, maybe they can't take out their hostility against her so they turn it on me" (quoted in Kurtz, 1998, p. 84). Reeves (1996) contends that the idea that such grand-scale change in American life, arrived at in secret meetings of "experts," could be pushed whole through Congress or past the American people without debate, amendment, or consensus offended politicians. The budget battle of 1993 and Whitewater also negatively influenced media framing of the Clintons' health care program.

Jamieson and Cappella (1998) believe that news norms and conventions affected the shape and outcome of the health care reform debate of 1993–1994. These included that the use of labels for the alternative plans minimizes the likelihood that the public would understand the details of any of them; the conflict frame narrowed public focus to two plans, minimizing the viability of the others; and reporters emphasized the Whitewater scandal, a complex set of allegations surrounding business dealings during the Clintons' time as Arkansas First Couple, over the substance of health care reform. In late February through early April, Whitewater "became the lens through which broadcast news saw health reform." For example, after reporting a Chicago restaurant owner's concerns about required contributions from employers, a segment on ABC "might have explained such alternatives as a Republican plan requiring employers to offer coverage, but not pay for it." However, the reporters said instead, "The Clinton plan hasn't been helped by Whitewater either" (p. 116). At President Clinton's prime-time press conference on March 24, 1994, Whitewater was the subject of fourteen of the eighteen questions. Because of their framing, "Whitewater marauded around inside health stories," and in the process the media "insinuated the cynical assumption that the White House was pushing health reform because it wanted to duck Whitewater" (p. 117).

In addition, Gould (1996b) believes that the opponents of the president and First Lady often put the worst possible interpretation on their health plan without doing justice to the real reforms it hoped to achieve. Many of the criticisms of the plan were, in this view, exaggerated. For example, mandatory coverage for all Americans would have been required because such reform would have been impossible if much of the population were left out. In addition, many Americans under the plan would have been provided more choice in health care than they received from private insurance companies. The Clinton plan also tracked existing health care practices. And although critics said the system was functioning well and needed no improvement, health care costs did not rise as fast in 1993 as in previous years, partly because of expectations that Clinton would control them.

The much chastised complexity of the plan arose from the nature of the national health care dilemma. Complex problems require complex solutions. In Brock's view (1996), the "hard truth" about Hillary Clinton's role in the failure of the plan was that she could not get past the "language of a welfare advocate" and the public's distrust of the "idea that government could make the system better by getting more involved" (p. 331). By mid-1994, despite polls showing that Americans opposed the plan, "Hillary soldiered on," refusing to compromise with Congress and taking the universal health care issue into 1994, which proved to be "catastrophic" for the Democrats, who lost control of Congress for the first time in forty years (Brock, 1996, p. 366). The plan did not survive congressional scrutiny and by August 1994 was in trouble, partly because of the Clintons' initial "clumsy" handling of the press early on, which biased many reporters against providing a positive spin for the "plan." Hillary Clinton turned down interviews by health care writers for the *Wall Street Journal* and *USA Today*. The *Washington Post* reporter was asked to submit questions in advance.

Ultimately Hillary Clinton publicly accepted responsibility for the failure of the plan when she said, "I know that the perception of the health care plan, which I fully accept, was one of big government," and played to her critics in the press by explaining her actions:

One of the big mistakes was going along with the recommendation that we shouldn't brief reporters even off the record, in part because there was a legitimate concern, from both people in Congress and here in the administration, that trying to put together a health care plan to meet our original date . . . was a huge undertaking. Everybody felt that was going to be hard under even the best of circumstances and they worried that talking about it as we went along would create all kinds of false expectations or misunderstandings. But I think in retrospect that was the wrong call. (quoted in Osborne, 1997, pp. 166–167)

Still, Gould (1996b) suggests that Hillary Clinton deserves credit for taking the reform plan as far as she did and that "when health care reform is achieved in the future, she is likely to receive praise as a pioneer" (p. 645). Brock (1996) argues that the "health care debacle" revealed the Clintons' complementary relationship—that neither she nor he would be "able to succeed without the other": "Had Bill been more directly involved, his innate tendency to compromise—a weakness in isolated, but a strength in the context of the co-candidacy—would likely have tempered Hillary's zeal and made it possible to sell the plan politically" (p. 365). In this view, the defeat of the health care bill—"the single most important piece of legislation scheduled for the president's first term"—was also due to the fallout from another crisis jointly experienced by Hillary and Bill Clinton: Whitewater.

WHITEWATER

One of the dominant scandal stories of the Clinton administration stems from the president and Mrs. Clinton's financial and personal activities, primarily while he was governor of Arkansas. In 1978, Bill and Hillary Clinton used borrowed money and financial ties with Arkansas friend James McDougal to make a $200,000 investment in property in northwestern Arkansas. During Clinton's first term as governor, James and Susan McDougal and the Clintons formed the Whitewater Development Company. The company was not a financial success in the 1980s, and the Clintons continued making interest payments on their bank loan. James

McDougal had become involved with the affairs of Madison Guaranty Savings and Loan, an institution that went into federal receivership. In the 1990s, questions were raised about the links between the Clintons and Madison Guaranty Savings, which focused on whether Hillary Clinton acted ethically when her law firm engaged in negotiations over the future of the Madison. Concerns were raised about their losses from Whitewater as well as its connections to Madison Guaranty and the Clinton administration's overall handling of the Whitewater investigation itself (Sabato and Lichter, 1994). Evidence indicated that the First Lady's name was mentioned once in a letter from the firm to an Arkansas state regulator but that she did not become involved personally in the matter. Had she pressured state regulators for special treatment? Did she and Bill Clinton personally profit from the transactions?

Hillary Clinton knew there were going to be problems figuring out the tax status of the Whitewater investment when it came time to file financial disclosure forms on 1992 taxes in the spring of 1993. The Clintons' personal tax records from the 1970s documenting the $100,000 commodities profits had been shielded from public view for ten years. There were also rumors that the federal agency charged with cleaning up savings and loan failures from the 1980s had sent a criminal referral to the U.S. attorney in Little Rock in an investigation of an S&L with ties to the Clintons (Brock, 1996).

The Whitewater story first surfaced nationally during the 1992 campaign. The *New York Times*'s Jeff Gerth reported that the Clintons had been co-investors in Whitewater Development Corporation along with James McDougal. Jeff Gerth's Whitewater story was seen as a "dreaded 'third strike'" during Clinton's bid for the 1992 presidential nomination. While "strikes one and two"—the draft and Gennifer Flowers—were "Bill Clinton's doing," Whitewater "focused on Hillary Clinton" and mandated that she "rescue her husband" as "she had done in the past." Stewart (1996) speculates that because they feared a full revelation of all the Whitewater details might cost the nomination, the Clintons strove to contain the story. The primary allegation in the story was that while the Clintons were 50 percent owners of Whitewater, they had invested thousands less in the land deal than had James McDougal and his wife, Susan. The Clinton campaign denied any wrongdoing and assigned Denver attorney James Lyons the task of preparing a report on their investment. After Lyons concluded that the Clintons had lost approximately $69,000 on Whitewater, the story essentially disappeared for the remainder of the campaign. It reemerged in the fall of 1993 when the *Washington Post* reported that the Resolution Trust Corporation had asked the Justice Department to probe James McDougal for the possible misuse of depositor funds from his S&L, Madison Guaranty. Media speculation about

Whitewater became intense. Press reports said that the Resolution Trust Corporation had sent the Department of Justice a criminal referral about Madison Guaranty Trust Company and the Whitewater real estate venture in which the Clintons had been involved. The referral, leaked to the press, identified Hillary and Bill Clinton as possible witnesses in the investigation, although they were accused of no criminal acts.

Calls immediately were made by political opponents for the appointment of an independent counsel or special prosecutor to inquire further about the Clintons' involvement in Whitewater. Hillary Clinton argued that she and her husband should not condone a "partisan fishing expedition" into their Arkansas business activities. The investigation of a First Couple for actions that had taken place before they came to the White House was without precedent. In the end, political pressure resulted in both Clintons' accepting Robert Fiske's appointment as a special prosecutor. A few stories appeared in the mainstream press during November and December, documenting the Clintons' relationship with McDougal, including that McDougal had helped ease Bill Clinton's 1985 debt from the previous year's gubernatorial campaign, after which more serious allegations began appearing in the media. Former judge David Hale, under indictment for fraudulent use of loans backed by the Small Business Association, claimed that Bill Clinton had encouraged him to make a $300,000 SBA-sponsored loan to Susan McDougal so that some of the money could go into the financially strapped Whitewater Corporation. Of that money, $120,000 did go to Whitewater, although President Clinton said he did not remember meeting Hale.

The public's interpretation of the First Lady's interaction with the McDougals was a major catalyst for the criticism of her ethics, character, and reputation and resulted in a harsh portrait of Hillary that "stuck in the popular imagination" (Brock, 1996, p. 183). The *Wall Street Journal*'s Al Hunt described her as a "hard-edged, even mean-spirited money-grubber" (1996, p. 19), and the *Washington Post* (Powers, 1996) commented on a *Time* magazine excerpt of James Stewart's 1996 book, *Blood Sport,* which

> features a cover photo of Hillary Rodham Clinton looking like a Gothic fiend. At first glance, she's a vampire—ghastly white skin, scarlet lips, teeth slightly bared—coming at us cloaked all in black. In the eternal cliché of suggested guilt, her glance is averted. But study the image for a minute and you'll notice that the red "M" in TIME forms two perfect horns on the first lady's head. This is no mere bloodsucker: it's Satanella. (p. D7)

The *Washington Monthly*'s editor commented, "There was behavior that if not criminal was certainly embarrassing" and that "the principal sinner had been Hillary Clinton." The *New Republic* headlined a 1994 cover story, "The Name of the Rose: An Arkansas Thriller." *Time* told its readers that Whitewater had always been "more about Hillary than her husband," and the *Economist* tagged the scandal "Wifewater," while *Tax Notes* speculated that Bill Clinton might just be "an innocent spouse." Talk show host John McLaughlin said, "Whitewater translates in Hillary!" and a joke about Hillary Clinton's going to jail and "taking fat boy down with her" became a punch line on David Letterman's late night talk show. Columnist Jack Newfield wrote that Mrs. Clinton resembled "an Ozark Leona Helmsley," and the *Nation* editorialized a connection between the First Lady and Richard Nixon when it asked, "What did Hillary know and when did she know it?" (quoted in Brock, 1996, pp. 183–185).

In late March 1994, the president held a prime-time news conference to answer Whitewater questions, during which he revised his losses on the land deal to $47,000. The Clintons' tax returns, released at that time, supported that figure. In April 1994 Hale entered a plea agreement with special counsel Robert Fiske and pleaded guilty to a single felony count of fraud in exchange for his testimony regarding Whitewater (Sabato and Lichter, 1994, p. 8). In January 1996, the discovery of missing Rose firm billing records outside the First Lady's private office in the White House residence created a media-frenzied sensation. Under subpoena by Whitewater independent counsel Kenneth Starr and a Senate committee for two years, the records were covered with notations in Vince Foster's handwriting that detailed Hillary Clinton's involvement in Jim McDougal's Castle Grande development project (Flaherty and Flaherty, 1996) and revealed that her law firm might have had more to do with Whitewater and the firing of White House travel office employees than she or her friends and assistants had admitted (Reeve, 1996). While congressional Republicans accused her of obstructing justice in the disappearance and rediscovery of legal documents, journalist William Safire of the *New York Times* called her "a congenital liar" (quoted in Reeves, 1996, p. xiii).

With Whitewater, Mrs. Clinton's reluctance to meet with the press became a political liability. The *Wall Street Journal*'s Al Hunt wrote that "the bunker mentality at the White House is a reflection of Hillary Clinton," and Michael Barone of *U.S. News* complained of her "startlingly bad judgment" (quoted in Kurtz, 1998, p. 84). For her part, Hillary Clinton told aides that she felt she was in a "twilight zone," where reporters seemed only to want to talk about the scandal and became less reluctant to meet the press, asking, "Why should I talk to people who have no interest in getting the story straight and who only want to see the negative?" (quoted in Kurtz, 1998, p. 85).

She followed the Whitewater media stories closely and knew the bylines of all the Whitewater reporters. If Mark Fabiani, the special White House counsel handling the scandal, was quoted as saying something she did not like, she would contact him. In particular, Mrs. Clinton argued that Whitewater was more a vendetta than an investigation:

I personally do not believe that this level of paranoiac, conspiracy-driven investigation is appropriate—of anybody in public life, not just me. This is a matter that goes way beyond me. It is just absurd. If you take historical precedent, no president has ever had any of his activities before he became president investigated like this. And a lot of people came into office having made a lot of money, and with people knowing they made money through friends. We came in having lost money. We came in with very little in the way of resources. We are subjected to a whole new set of standards. We don't have a vacation house in Maine, we don't have a ranch in California, we don't have a cottage on the shore of Maryland—we don't have any of those things. So how many times do we have to say, over and over again, "Look—we spent our lives primarily in public service." Even my law practice was subordinated to our public service." (Hillary Clinton quoted in Osborne, 1997, p. 76)

Mrs. Clinton was particularly unhappy with the *Washington Post*'s Susan Schmidt, who in the fall of 1993 had reported that federal banking regulators had referred their inquiry into Madison Guaranty for criminal prosecution. Schmidt seemed to many at the White House the "most consistently unfair" of the Whitewater media who was personally invested in "pumping up" the scandal, at least in part because the *Post* ran more Whitewater stories on the front page than any other major paper (Kurtz, 1998, p. 87). At one point, Hillary Clinton decided to discredit Schmidt and the *Post* by preparing a document outlining the difference between its coverage of the scandal and that of other papers. Although an initial strategy was designed, the report was never published, under orders from Bill Clinton's staff. There was concern that by singling out Schmidt, the *Post* would only rally behind the reporter and publicize its take on an administration that was openly "going after" its critics (Kurtz, 1998, p. 89).

By January 1994, as a result of the impact of revelations about the removal of Whitewater-related papers from Vince Foster's office and media "picking through Whitewater with a fine tooth-comb," the Whitewater scandal was, according to treasury secretary Roger Altman, "exploding into a press frenzy." He wrote that administration "stonewalling" resulted in press speculation that there must be something to hide. Altman's concerns were about the independent prosecutor and speculation that Hillary Clinton was at the center of the mishandling in Arkansas (Brock, 1996). Hillary Clinton, according to Brock (1996), was reluctant to encourage her husband to take the lead in asking Attorney General Janet Reno to bring in a special prosecutor and investigate two decades of the Clinton's public life. Once the counsel began his investigation and a parallel inquiry on Whitewater began in Congress, the Clinton administration "ground to a halt," and Hillary Clinton became committed to containing the fallout from Whitewater, which "soon became an all-purpose term for Clinton political scandal" (p. 402).

In June 1994, Congress approved a new independent counsel law, which required that the counsel be appointed by members of the federal judiciary, not an attorney general beholden to the president. Janet Reno asked that a three-judge panel reappoint Robert Fiske. Also during that month, Fiske issued a report on the death of Vincent Foster, concluding there was no evidence to counter a verdict of suicide. But the report was attacked as incomplete and insufficiently skeptical, and there was a Republican call for Fiske's replacement. In August, Kenneth Starr, a conservative Republican, former solicitor general in the Bush administration, and a former appeals court judge appointed by Ronald Reagan, replaced Fiske as independent counsel. Stewart (1996) notes that although Starr appeared to be "one of the most partisan independent counsels of special prosecutors ever appointed," he vowed "to be fair and impartial, but thorough" (p. 424).

The White House would not publicly attack anyone who could bring charges against anyone in the administration, including Starr. But through whispered conversations and the use of surrogates, aides framed Starr as a persecutor rather than prosecutor. In early May 1997, the Clinton administration had some good news to announce after two and a half years of what Kurtz (1998) describes as "trench warfare." The president and the Republicans had struck a deal to balance the federal budget by 2002. The agreement was the first major victory of the president's second term. All of the networks led with the budget news. But the *Times*'s Rita Braver was talking about an appeals court ruling that the White House had to turn over some disputed Whitewater papers and observed that statements taken during discussions with Hillary Clinton included her assertion that the administration had made a "declaration of war against Kenneth Starr" (quoted in Kurtz, 1998, p. 192). Despite the fact that a historic budget agreement had just been struck and American unemployment had dropped to a twenty-four-year low, some reporters chose to "still wallow in Whitewater" (Kurtz, 1998, p. 192).

At this time, *Washington Post* reporter Bob Woodward interviewed some Arkansas state troopers who had been part of Bill Clinton's security detail and had once made sensational charges about his relationships with women other than Hillary Clinton. Two of the troopers told Woodward that

Ken Starr's investigators were pressing them for details of Clinton's sexual life, asking about a list of twelve to fifteen women, including Gennifer Flowers, whom Clinton was said to have slept with. The investigators had interviewed some of the women. White House counsel Charles Ruff declined to comment when questioned by Woodward, but the story was what the administration had looked to prove Starr "an overzealous fool" (quoted in Kurtz, 1998, p. 221). It would remind people of Clinton's sex life, but voters had been aware of his sex life for some time. Hillary Clinton had complained that the press held Kenneth Starr, attorney for the tobacco industry, to a lesser standard. The story led the next day's *Washington Post*. Mike McCurry deflected a question about Starr's tactics, saying the White House had no comment. When reporters tried to question him outside a conference in Nashville, Clinton "pulled the Reaganesque maneuver" of saying he couldn't hear over the roar of the helicopter engines. The administration also lined up Bob Bennett and James Carville to denounce Starr. Reporters, including Jeff Gerth and Sue Schmidt, who had spent five years following the Whitewater story, spun negatively. Chris Vlasto argued that ABC should not follow the Woodward piece because he believed Starr's approach to be a standard prosecutorial practice. The *New York Times*'s Steve Labaton also thought the story was blown out of proportion and that Starr was being treated unfairly (Kurtz, 1998).

One recurring theme in Hillary Clinton's mediation of this scandal was that the First Couple had always been proved right in other investigations—that they "told the truth":

The conventional wisdom about Whitewater always is take any straw you can to go on, so I don't have any doubt that there are those who will say this should go on. I just would like to tell them, go on where, we've been going on four years, and every time there's an official investigation of any sort . . . what my husband and I have been saying proves out to be the case. So I don't have any doubt that since so much of this is politically inspired it will go on almost regardless of what happens anywhere. It has a life of its own. (quoted in Osborne, 1998, pp. 137)

She also discursively attempted to create a reasonable doubt about her critics' version of Whitewater by first admitting she had made mistakes and that any perceptions of malice or criminal actions on the Clintons' part were the results of a conspiracy:

We ended up losing more than $40,000. So it was not a sweetheart deal. We were on the papers. The bank looked to us to make good if there was any default. We had to, over the years, put in money every time our partners asked, even though we were passive investors. We never should have made the investment. I suppose the other big mistake that I made was not appreciating how other people view their reluctance to publicly divulge information. . . . [The Whitewater controversy is] a well organized and well-financed attempt . . . to undermine my husband, and by extension, myself, by people who have a different political agenda or have another personal and financial reason for attacking us. (Hillary Clinton quoted in Osborne, 1998, p. 138)

She insisted that if "people" insisted on not believing the truth, that was "their" problem:

If they don't want to believe we lost money in Whitewater, that's their choice, but that doesn't change the truth. . . . If they don't want to believe that we paid back all our loans, and we never did business with an S&L, fine, they don't have to believe it—but that doesn't change the truth. . . . They can ask me from now to doomsday—they're going to get the same answer, because it's the truth. We went into Whitewater to make money, not to lose it. I mean, the embarrassing thing to me is that we ended up losing money and it keeps being beaten like the deadest horse there is over and over again. (Hillary Clinton quoted in Osborne, 1997, p. 140)

Her reply to an inquiry by Claire Shipman of CNN in January 1996 about how a savvy political spouse could have fallen for such a deal as Whitewater was that the media's asking the question actually framed the Clintons' involvement in Whitewater as wrong when the truth was that the business deal just didn't work:

In 1978 or 1979—maybe it was '77—when we got into that land deal there was nothing wrong with it. There's never been anything proven wrong with it. You see, the very question you ask assumes that there was something wrong about what we did. And we said, when the questions were first raised in 1992, we didn't do anything wrong. We were passive investors. We lost money. (Hillary Clinton quoted in Osborne, 1997, p. 138)

At "worst" the handling of the Whitewater investment was "reckless." After instigating the investment, Bill Clinton "largely abdicated responsibility" and left Hillary Clinton the burden of handling the details of the investment. However, nothing in their involvement with Whitewater explains the "pattern of evasions, half-truths, and misstatements that have characterized the Clintons' handling of the story, both during the campaign and in the White House" (Stewart, 1996, p. 432).

Three weeks after the special counsel was appointed in 1994, Jim McDougal, "heavily medicated and suffering from manic depression and acute memory loss," appeared on ABC's *Nightline* for an exclusive interview during which he claimed that Bill Clinton had never done anything unethical but refused to say the same about Hillary Clinton. Susan McDougal later appeared on a *Nightline* broadcast to contradict a sworn statement that the First Lady had made about the McDougals' Castle Grande project, in which she told Resolution Trust Corporation investigators that she did not recall doing work on Castle Grande. When confronted with billing records showing that she did work on the project, she said her involvement was known with the Rose firm as Industrial Development Company (IDC), the entity that had sold the Castle Grande property to a subsidiary of Madison Guaranty. Although Rose firm billing records showed the project was in fact billed as IDC, thus supporting her account, Susan McDougal argued that Castle Grande and IDC were the same, and viewers were left with the impression that Hillary Clinton had lied.

Sabato and Lichter (1994) believe the press created many "Whitewater tributaries" that branched out into auxiliary areas. Among these were the shredding of documents at Little Rock's Rose Law Firm, the former employer of Hillary Rodham Clinton and Vincent Foster; improper contacts between Treasury officials and the White House; and a phone call from White House aide George Stephanopoulos to the Treasury Department questioning the hiring of a former Republican-appointed U.S. attorney, Jay Stephens, to work on the RTC's investigation of Madison Guaranty.

Throughout the spring of 1994, the Clinton administration operated under a damage control mentality. Media coverage of Whitewater reached its crescendo in March 1994 and eclipsed issues such as health care and welfare reform. Sabato and Lichter (1994) note that "in classic scandal reporting style, Whitewater became an omnipresent context for stories on the president's every move or decison: 'still hounded by questions over Whitewater, the president departed for Europe today'" (p. 9).

The counsel's office, which had worked to shield the Clintons, was in disarray; Vince Foster was dead; White House counsel Bernard Nussbaum had resigned amid criticism of his handling of the Foster office search; William Kennedy had resigned, and returned to his position as the Rose Law Firm's managing partner following revelations he had failed to pay social security taxes on a nanny's wages; and Webster Hubbell, the "final Rose Firm recruit," went to jail for fraud (Brock, 1996, p. 405). And in May 1994, the *Washington Post* published the results of a three-month investigation based on the statements of an Arkansas state trooper who had identified a woman named "Paula" as someone he had taken to Bill Clinton's room at a Little Rock hotel in 1991. Jones denied she had consensual sex with Bill Clinton and claimed sexual harassment (Brock, 1996, p. 405).

Chapter Seven

Travelgate to Impeachment: The Later Crisis Management Discourse of Hillary Rodham Clinton

> You know, he's my President too. (Hillary Clinton quoted in Tumulty and Gibbs, 1999).

TRAVELGATE

By the end of Bill Clinton's third year as president, Hillary Rodham Clinton had become the focus of investigations of scandals involving the firing of several career White House employees, as well as Whitewater. One of her first 1993 appointments was friend and colleague Vincent Foster as deputy White House counsel. Foster was versed not only on the Clintons' tenure as Arkansas' First Couple but also served as their personal lawyer, handling their taxes, financial disclosure forms, and arrangements for putting their holdings in a blind trust. He also acted as White House liaison to the Justice Department. Another Clinton colleague, Bernard Nussbaum, the New York attorney who had supervised Hillary Clinton's work on the Watergate Committee, was appointed White House counsel. Nussbaum ran the litigation section at a New York firm that specialized in corporate mergers and acquisitions law, and the Clintons hoped his experience would help keep Washington press and congressional investigators within limits.

Foster and Nussbaum were joined at the White House by Rose Law Firm managing partner William Kennedy, who was offered a job by Foster. Brock (1996) suggests that Kennedy's "clumsy maneuverings" in the travel office firings played a central role in "Travelgate," which may have been the catalyst for Foster's suicide, which placed the First Lady at the center of several federal investigations, including that of Whitewater independent counsel Kenneth Starr. "Travelgate," as it was labeled by the press, fit what Brock (1996) called the "now familiar pattern" of the "Clinton scandals and co-candidacy." Like Whitewater, its roots were found in long-standing political and business ties between Bill Clinton and Arkansas acquaintances. When Hillary Clinton "stepped in" to defuse the "political fallout," she, rather than her husband, "got caught in the cross hairs."

In May 1993, seven long-time employees of the White House travel office, which makes arrangements for the press corps traveling with the president, were fired for "mismanagement" and replaced by individuals employed by World Wide Travel, a Little Rock, Arkansas, travel agency. The new office director was Catherine Cornelius, a cousin of the president. The firings touched off such a wave of bad publicity that replacing the travel office employees with the Arkansas group was abandoned, and the White House handed over the travel office operations to American Express. In addition, Cornelius never took control of the office; World Wide had moved into the White House the day of the firings but left two days later. Shortly after, the Clinton administration was "backpedaling furiously." For example, it was announced that five of the seven employees had not really been fired, but had been placed on leave. An internal review concluded that the charges against the five were baseless and they were placed in other government agencies, while the assistant director of the travel office filed for retirement (Brock, 1996).

Fitzwater (1995) considers Travelgate an example of a mistake that "could have been corrected or avoided" if the administration had "had a good read on press reaction":

When the Clinton staff professed total surprise at the press' hostile reaction to firing these people so loyal Arkansas followers could have the jobs and the airline contracts that go with them, it was clear the White House had a tin ear about how the Washington press view political patronage and an equal deafness to their feelings about the personnel in the travel office. (p. 240)

Billy Dale, the former travel office director, was accused of embezzling $68,000 but was acquitted by a jury in 1995, by which time a congressional investigating team had discovered evidence that the firings had been premeditated and the allegations fabricated to steer the travel office business to World Wide Travel and TRM, an air charter brokerage owned by Clinton friend Harry Thomason. According to Brock (1996), the First Lady "quickly brought the issue to a head" (p. 373), evidence of her "increasingly aggressive efforts to thwart politically damaging disclosures" (p. 380). A memo, which did not appear until after Dale's acquittal, indicated that she was the "driving force" behind the travel office firings (Flaherty and Flaherty, 1996, p. 213).

Thomason had initially met with both Clintons and was asked by the First Lady to "stay ahead" of the problem and told that rooting out corruption in the travel office and initiating a new money-saving system would make a "good story" (quoted in Brock, 1996, p. 374). The First Lady may have endorsed the firings because of the stories she was hearing about corruption in the Travel Office, which she may have accepted at face value. Under fire for her role on the Health Care Task Force and facing a "severe political test with the Lani Guinier nomination, the White House" did not want to face another scandal, and the First Lady may have felt that clearing out an allegedly corrupt travel office was the only course to avoid being trumped by the press. In addition, after the Secret Service leaked the lamp-throwing story, she may have been more inclined to replace staff from previous White House administrations with the "Clintons' own people as a protective impulse rather than as a ruthless and arbitrary attack by a latter-day Marie Antoinette" (p. 377).

Her previous denials of any involvement in the firings, coupled with the Dale trial, created doubts about the First Lady's credibility. By early 1996, for the first time in history, a First Lady's negative rating exceeded her positive (Flaherty and Flaherty, 1996). In the initial round of interviews for the internal White House review, investigators looked for and received little information about Hillary Clinton's role. The first version of events given to the White House investigators by Vince Foster left the First Lady completely out of the chain of events. Brock (1996) suggests the "air brushing" of her involvement was part of the "continuing struggle" to preserve Hillary Clinton's "public image and moral authority" as First Lady. How could a woman who "personified the self-image of an entire post-Watergate generation . . . that felt uniquely fit to bring the highest moral and ethical standards into government" be connected with a process that misused the FBI? She had worked on the Watergate investigation, which "ushered in a wave of reforms designed to ensure a more accountable government with higher ethical standards." One of the articles of impeachment drawn up against Richard Nixon, which had been crafted in part by Hillary Clinton, had charged misuse of the FBI and other executive personnel by ordering investigations unrelated to any "lawful function" of the presidency (p. 383).

The January 1996 surfacing of the Watkins memo implicating Hillary Clinton resulted in press caricatures of her as a manipulative, inhumane "Mommie Dearest" (Brock, 1996, p. 383) of a First Lady. This media framing was due in part to her continuing reluctance to give few interviews in which journalists—and therefore the public—could see the "real person." In addition, she rarely played the official hostess role of First Lady, saying, "I don't get out a lot in Washington and I didn't get out a lot in Little Rock, because when I have time that is not spent on my work and my public activities I want to be with my family" (quoted in Brock, 1996, p. 383).

A few days after the travel office firings, an article, "Saint Hillary," appeared in the *New York Times Magazine* describing the First Lady as heir to the social gospel tradition of Jane Addams and Dorothy Day. She was quoted as condemning the Reagan era "ethos of selfishness and greed" and called for a new "politics of meaning." In a speech shortly before the article appeared, delivered after her father's death, she spoke of calling up what one believes is "morally and ethically and spiritually correct" and relying on "God's guidance." She spoke of the commandment to "love thy neighbor as thyself" and of seeing as human and thanking others such as the "woman who cleans the restroom" (quoted in Kelly, 1993). Some criticized the First Lady's "new age mysticism" brand of Christianity from which she wielded political power, arguing that "returning to moral judgment as a basis for governmental policy must . . . mean curtailing what have come to be regarded as sacrosanct rights and admitting to a limit to tolerance. And that will bring the politics of meaning hard against the meaning of politics" (Kelly, 1993).

Brock (1996) argues that under such circumstances, which included the press's rejection of invoking a religious justification for progressive policies, it is easy to see why the White House downplayed Hillary Clinton's connection to Travelgate. Still, by mid-July 1995, Republicans were demanding congressional hearings and the appointment of a special counsel. All involved, including the First Lady who, unlike the president, could be compelled to give congressional testimony, could be drawn into the investigation. In addition, the press was spinning negatively.

On July 11, the *New York Times* ran an editorial focusing on the First Lady's involvement, asking, "When the White House was getting ready to fire all seven employees of its travel office, why was notice sent to Hillary Rodham Clinton and not her husband the President?" Brock (1996) notes the *Times* was wrong in singling out Hillary as the only Clinton notified about the firings and targets the editorial as a "prime example" of how the press was harder on Hillary Clinton, the "zealous Watergate reformer," than on her husband (p. 387).

In an effort to recast the story about the travel office firings, Hillary Clinton used the "Arkansas" connection to suggest that her "higher standard" of morality perspective stems from the not directly stated but subtly implied superiority of her "God fearing, apple-pie loving" roots:

There was petty cash left lying around. Cash ended up in the personal account of one of the workers. Now, that may not seem like something to people who spend lots of money, but coming from Arkansas, that sounded serious. And so, from my perspective, it was something worthy of being concerned about. Even if it was just the press's money, that money belongs to people and it should be handled appropriately if it is in any way connected with the White House. Although I had no decision-making role with regard to the removal of the Travel Office employees... I expressed my concern ... that if there were fiscal mismanagement in the Travel Office or in any part of the White House it should be addressed promptly. I am sure I felt such action could include, if necessary and justified, appropriate personnel actions so that this administration would not be blamed for condoning any existing fiscal mismanagement problems (Hillary Clinton, quoted in Osborne, 1997, p. 133).

She also defended the apparent "harshness" of her rhetoric in the situation as being a communication style honed in Arkansas, a style of frankness, and, again by implication, honesty:

Before I came to the White House, I dealt with people in a very direct way. If something was on my mind, I said it. That is an entirely different environment, and the mere expression of concern could be, I guess, taken to mean something more than it was meant. (Hillary Clinton quoted in Osborne, 1997, p. 133)

On July 14, Senate minority leader Bob Dole called for a special counsel to investigate, and on July 20, the day of Vince Foster's suicide, Democrats on the House Judiciary Committee deflected a Republican attempt to force the president to furnish documents concerning potential misuse of the FBI in the investigation. However, the House Republican Policy Committee adopted a statement calling for a special counsel on the issue to address concerns about who authorized FBI involvement and Hillary Clinton's role (Brock, 1996).

FOSTER SUICIDE AND FILEGATE

Although Brock (1996) believes the Republicans were misdirected in suspecting that Hillary Clinton took action on her own, without the knowledge of the president, her role would become a major issue in later investigations by the General Accounting Office and the Justice Department, if not by a special counsel. Vince Foster knew what that role had been and was "undoubtedly going to be compelled to describe it under oath," forcing him to "lie or give up Hillary" (p. 388).

Foster committed suicide on July 20, 1993, outside Washington. A seasoned corporate litigator, his clinical depression—from which he suffered prior to joining the Clinton White House—may have "shaded into desperation" when Foster realized that eventually Hillary Clinton would be compelled to testify before a federal grand jury (Devroy and Schmidt, 1995). Within days of his death, media reports linked White House aides to the removal of records and files regarding the Clintons and their Arkansas real estate investments from Foster's office. These stories fueled growing momentum for further investigation of the Clinton's Whitewater business dealings (Gould, 1996b).

When Hillary Clinton received the news of Foster's death, her press secretary, Lisa Caputo, recalled that the First Lady was so devastated that Caputo assumed the president had died. Hillary Clinton made a series of phone calls, the first to chief of staff Maggie Williams, who went immediately to Foster's White House office, arriving before law enforcement investigators. Patsy Thomasson, David Watkins's deputy, was already there, searching for notes that might have been personally embarrassing to the First Lady. Rumors had surfaced earlier of a romantic relationship between Foster and Hillary Clinton. True or not, the First Lady's staff, according to Brock (1996), "had to act as though they were true" (p. 390).

Lyons (1996) recalls Rush Limbaugh's March 10, 1994, broadcast to an audience of millions that White House counsel "Vince Foster was murdered in an apartment owned by Hillary Clinton, and the body was then taken to Fort Marcy Park." Although he said the story was based on a rumor, Limbaugh then claimed that a bogus crime scene was probably rigged to make Foster's death look like a suicide: "There's a Washington consulting firm that has scheduled the release of a report that will . . . be published, that claims that Vince Foster was murdered in an apartment owned by Hillary Clinton, and the body was then taken to Fort Marcy Park" (quoted in Koppel Covers, 1996, p. 139). The story, which Limbaugh and others repeated, resulted in a mass of conspiracy theories about Whitewater and Vince Foster's death, despite a series of official investigations that concluded Foster died by his own hand due to clinical depression that had nothing to do with the Whitewater situation (Lyons, 1996).

Distraught or not, Hillary Clinton exerted influence over the investigation of Foster's death. The removal of documents from his office to the White House residence prior to their being turned over to the Clinton's private attorney later precipitated the appointment of a special counsel to investigate Whitewater. She issued a precisely worded statement that she did not "direct" anyone to "interfere" with the investigation of Foster's death. Whether documents were actually removed from Vince Foster's office will probably never be known for certain. Although he claimed only to be exercising his duties as an attorney to review documents for privilege, Bernard

Nussbaum was most concerned with documents in Foster's possession that were related to Whitewater and the travel office firings, the latter already under investigation by the Justice Department.

By the time of Foster's death, the Clinton administration knew that the federal Resolution Trust Corporation, in charge of S&L clean-up, had sent a criminal referral mentioning the Clintons to the Justice Department for possible prosecution, raising the prospect of criminal or civil liability for Bill and Hillary Clinton in connection with the defunct Madison Guaranty S&L. The referral contained charges on which the McDougals and former Arkansas governor Jim Guy Tucker were convicted in May 1996. Although the Clintons were not implicated in the case, Tucker was called to testify as a witness for the McDougals, and the convictions became a political embarrassment. At about the same time as Ken Starr interviewed the First Lady at the White House regarding Travelgate, a 1982 check for $27,600 from Madison Guaranty, made out to Bill Clinton and alleged by the media to be a secret loan, was found in a car trunk in an Arkansas junkyard. Kurtz (1998) believes that by this time, scandal was such an integral part of the Clinton presidency that this discovery "hardly caused a stir" (p. 278).

When the search of Foster's office began on July 22, Nussbaum clashed over procedures with two Justice Department attorneys and, arguing from attorney-client privilege, insisted on examining the documents himself. Among the files was one labeled "Whitewater Development, Personal and Confidential VWF." Since December 1992, when the Clintons had sold their remaining interest in Whitewater to Jim McDougal for $1,000, Foster had been trying to figure out how to report the transaction on the Clintons' 1992 tax return. The main issue was that during the campaign, the Clintons had glossed over the extent to which they had been shielded from the Whitewater losses by the McDougals. Foster had been concerned that claiming a loss on Whitewater in their 1992 returns could trigger an IRS audit and open up their involvement to renewed scrutiny.

As efforts seemed to increase to "ferret out wrongdoing by the Clintons," the First Lady also increased her damage control efforts. Attorney Lloyd Cutler and Judge Abner Mikva were brought in as consecutive White House counsel, after Bernard Nussbaum's resignation, with a revitalized office of White House attorneys who stonewalled the Republican investigators and kept documents from public disclosure. The counsel scripted the Democrats on the congressional committees before televised Whitewater hearings were convened. An assistant White House counsel was assigned to monitor the question of Hillary's role in the travel office firings as it was being investigated by a House committee and the independent counsel. As the investigations proceeded, numerous Clinton staff members and associates spent much time preparing to give testimony in court and before congressional committees, distracting them from the business of government. In January 1996, the "lid was blown off" any doubt about Hillary Clinton's role in Travelgate with the release of a draft of a memo by David Watkins after the 1993 firings in which he said that Hillary Clinton had personally told him to fire the staff. Hillary Clinton stood by her unsworn statement that she had no role in the decision.

Republicans encouraged the dissemination of the memo to the press, which resulted in *New York Times* columnist William Safire's calling the First Lady a "congenital liar," which resulted in Bill Clinton's threatening to "punch the columnist in the nose" (quoted in Brock, 1996, p. 408). There were major "credibility problems" with Watkins, and although Hillary Clinton's denials of involvement in the travel office firings may not be correct "except in a very technical sense," Brock (1996) concludes that the characterization of the First Lady as an incessant liar was "a classic political smear" (p. 409).

Within a few days of the release of the Watkins memo, a copy of Hillary Clinton's Rose Law Firm billing records documenting her work for Madison Guaranty was discovered in the White House office of Carolyn Huber, an aide to the First Lady and former administrator of the Rose firm. Huber testified she had picked up the records in the White House book room in the Clintons' residency next to the First Lady's office in August 1995 and inadvertently carried them to her office to file. Not until a January 1996 office move did she find the records and realize what they were. The discovery of the records, last seen in the possession of Vince Foster, posed potential legal problems for Hillary Clinton. If she knew about them and failed to produce the records in order to obstruct the Senate committee investigation, she could be criminally liable.

In the Senate Whitewater report, the Republicans concluded that the First Lady, whose fingerprints were found on the records, probably hid them from investigators to conceal the extent of her role in representing Madison Guaranty. During the time the records were missing, RTC investigators were attempting to decide if she had any civil liability in connection with her work for the failed S&L. It was argued that she had a motive to hide the records because they contradicted her statements to investigators about the work. Hillary Clinton had labeled her work as "minimal" and said she did not believe she knew anything about the Castle Grande parcels and projects. The records revealed that she had billed Madison for sixty hours of work over fifteen months, including about thirty hours on Castle Grande. When asked to answer under oath "any knowledge" she had about the disappearance and discovery of the records, the First Lady said she had no idea the records had been found (Brock, 1996, p. 411).

In addition, a notebook recording Hillary Clinton's role in Whitewater was removed from Foster's briefcase and concealed by Nussbaum for over a year, despite travel office documents being under subpoena by special counsel since January 1994. The Justice Department, which was conducting an investigation of the FBI's role in the travel office firings, did not learn of the notebook until August 1996, two years after Foster's death, when the White House released thousands of pages of documents that had been withheld from congressional investigators under a claim of privilege. Whether Hillary Clinton played a role in deciding to keep the notebook a secret (until a leak of its existence forced it into the media) and whether she was facilitating criminal obstruction of the investigation into Foster's suicide, Brock (1996) suggests that her behavior during the Travelgate/Vince Foster/early Whitewater scandals represented a "serious infringement of the public trust" (p. 397).

CATTLE FUTURES TRADING

In March 1994, the *New York Times* reported that Hillary Clinton had made $100,000 in the cattle futures commodities market in the late 1970s. Several weeks later, after a report in *Newsweek* inaccurately reported she had put no money down on the deal, the White House released trading records showing that the First Lady had placed a $1,000 investment to create the profit (Sabato and Lichter, 1994, p. 9). Although no laws were broken and both Clintons had signed tax returns reflecting the trading profits and Bill Clinton was governor at the time, Hillary Clinton was singled out as the hypocritical partner in the presidency who, while criticizing the "decade of greed," was actually a "greedy yuppie" (Brock, 1996, p. 403).

The disclosure resulted in an approval rating drop for the First Lady to an unprecedented 44 percent. Not only had the Clintons made an extraordinary profit, but their advice had come from individuals with questionable backgrounds or connections. Portfolio management counsel had come from friend James Blair, a lawyer who later became associated with Tyson Foods, a major Arkansas employer, while Robert L. "Red" Bone, who handled Hillary Rodham Clinton's trading account, had a "checkered record" as a commodities speculator. Critics speculated that Mrs. Clinton had been "allocated" such large profits as a sort of "legal bribery" that directed money her way in return for influence with her husband, charges that she and the president denied (Gould, 1996b). In defense of her investments, she explained that she had followed the advice of Blair since she "only knew a little bit about" cattle futures and that when he "asked me what I thought we could afford to invest, I told him $1,000." Furthermore, "not all my trades made money" and "some of them lost money." She stopped trading during the summer of 1979 because "I could not keep up with it. It takes a lot of nerve to be in the commodities trading, and I just found out I was pregnant." And despite Blair's suggestion that she continue trading because it was "really still doing well," she stopped and was glad, "because he and other friends of mine who were trading ended up losing money":

It was a good investment offered by somebody who knew a lot, who could provide a lot of good advice, and I was lucky and made the decision to stop when I did. The fundamental facts have not changed: I opened an account with my money. I made the trades. It was nondiscretionary. I took the risk. I was the one who made the decision to stop trading. And that I did rely on Jim Blair. (Hillary Clinton quoted in Osborne, 1997, pp. 134–135)

She spoke of financial difficulties as evidence that the Clintons were not the high rollers the media spin on the story indicated and also to indicate that the president, "just like the rest of you," had money troubles too:

It's a little bit odd that in my twenty years of law practice and involvement in so many activities, you know, I'm getting grilled over what I did, which amounted to about an hour of work over each week over fifteen months, and it was by no means important or significant to me at the time. We've been through this now for four years, and it started off as one thing, and every time a particular set of charges are disproved and questions answered, the ground shifts.... My husband and I ... don't own a house, we own half of the house that Mother lives in, in order to help support her. He has his 1968 Mustang, I have my 1986 Oldsmobile Cutlass. A recent magazine said that with our legal bills, we are bankrupt. So, if we had intended to trade on my position, I've done a very poor job of it. (Hillary Clinton quoted in Osborne, 1997, pp. 131–132).

On April 22, 1994, Hillary Clinton held a press conference to answer questions about Whitewater, Vince Foster's death, and her commodities trading. This was the first full-scale news conference by any First Lady. The major television networks broke into their afternoon programming for live coverage of the "pink press conference." According to the *Washington Post*'s Bob Woodward (1999), Mrs. Clinton walked into the state dining room of the White House "wearing a pink sweater and long black skirt. Her hair was carefully combed back, exposing her ears and large round earrings. She sat down in a wooden armchair by the fireplace and folded her hands in her lap. A large portrait of Abraham Lincoln hung in the background" (p. 252).

Surrounded by ferns and flowers, the First Lady "deftly fended off dozens of hostile inquiries," arguing there was "really no evidence" of special treatment on the trades (Gould, 1996b, p. 644). For example, in response to a question about whether the Clintons should have been more aware of the Whitewater investment debts and loans, she said, "Well, shoulda, coulda, woulda, we didn't" (quoted in Woodward, 1999, p. 253).

Press reaction was mixed, with some suggesting the First Lady had "sold out" her true character. Leslie Bennetts wrote in *Vanity Fair* that "Hillary the Warrior had metamorphosed into Hillary the Submissive" just as the "proud Hillary Rodham" had once been transformed into "Mrs. Hillary Clinton" (quoted in Flaherty and Flaherty, 1996, p. 210). However, the *San Francisco Examiner* labeled the conference a "virtuoso performance," and "Pretty in Pink" was how many in the media framed their stories. Gwen Ifil wrote in the *New York Times*: "Defending her friends and telling stories about her parents and daughter, the First Lady turned what could have been a bruising tell-all about the Whitewater inquiry into a fire-side chat" (quoted in Flaherty and Flaherty, 1996, p. 209).

WEBSTER HUBBELL

In Kurtz's (1998) view, no other story illustrates the gulf between the Clinton administration and journalists than that surrounding Webster Hubbell, another member of Hillary Clinton's Rose Law Firm who joined the Clinton administration when he was appointed associate attorney general and avoided Senate confirmation hearings, which would have revealed his overbilling of the law firm. However, he accepted the position and was "easily confirmed before the overbilling matter surfaced" (p. 311). By the spring of 1997, however, Hubbell was the nexus of the Whitewater and fundraising scandals. There were different versions of who had helped him after he was forced to leave the Justice Department in 1994 and who had known about it. From President Clinton on down, White House staffers were defensive when reporters queried them about Hubbell's employment before he went to prison for eighteen months.

Lanny Davis, Mike McCurry, and John Podesta and their White House colleagues perceived his story as one of personal disgrace rather than public scandal. In their eyes, the media were searching for a conspiracy that did not exist. Hubbell made a fatal error of cheating his law firm partners out of a half-million dollars. A few friends had tried to help him out after he was forced out of the Justice Department by setting up some work in consulting.

Some journalists perceived the situation completely differently. Hubbell was a friend of the Clintons and Hillary Rodham Clinton's former law partner, and no doubt he was privy to insider information about Whitewater. He was under criminal investigation but still being paid hundreds of thousands of dollars for minimal work by companies connected to the First Couple. That the White House refused to talk about Hubbell seemed a tacit admission of an attempt to hide that his silence on Whitewater was being bought by the Clinton administration (Kurtz, 1998).

Many in the White House, including the president's friend Vernon Jordan, had aided Hubbell. However, there was a strategy in releasing information. Lanny Davis was sensitive to the fact that certain reporters had made heavy investments in the Hubbell investigation and that if he let information out to all the media, these reporters would lose their "equity" in the story. If that happened, any trust he had built with these journalists would disappear. It was agreed that the White House would tip off the newspapers that were "way ahead" in the Hubbell investigation, giving them a chance to break the story first. Unfortunately, the White House "leaked like a sieve," and the story broke before the key Hubbell reporters and network correspondents could have a substantial lead in breaking it to the public. President Clinton was advised to respond that the Hubbell supporters acted "just out of human compassion" and genuine concern for the man. The conspiracists in the media would not ease up. The *New Republic*'s Michael Kelly said that Clinton and his friends "had worked together to pay hush money to Webb Hubbell, and Hubbell had indeed hushed up" (quoted in Kurtz, 1998, p. 183). The *New York Times* and *Washington Post* fanned the Webster Hubbell scandal by printing as many as a half-dozen stories a day (p. 186).

Reporters Jeff Gerth and Steve Labaton reported that two of Clinton's confidants, including attorney David Kendall, had known that Hubbell potentially faced criminal charges when he resigned. But the president had gone out on a "rhetorical limb," insisting that "no one had any idea" about "the nature of the allegations" and "everybody thought this was some sort of billing dispute with his law firm." Kurtz (1998) writes that this was "an engraved invitation to reporters to prove otherwise" (p. 195). President Clinton occasionally "went too far" in his denials and was not as sensitive as McCurry to the way words might hang one up. McCurry played semantic games for a reason—to avoid media entrapment—but the president often responded with broader statements emphasizing his feelings, forgetting that transcripts of his views could be scrutinized by "prosecutorial journalists determined to find discrepancies" (p. 195).

McCurry believed the Clintons were sympathetic to someone facing press allegations because both felt they had been unfairly treated by the media. That Webster Hubbell turned out to be "a crook" and had lied to both, in McCurry's view, did not mean the president and First Lady were part of a conspiracy (Kurtz, 1998). McCurry responded to Gerth by splitting hairs, saying that "the full nature and seriousness of allegations against Mr. Hubbell were not fully known." Gerth considered McCurry's response "magnificently deflective and meaningless" (quoted in Kurtz, 1998, p. 195).

In December 1994 Hubbell pleaded guilty to felonies of income tax evasion and mail fraud and was sentenced to twenty-one months in prison. David Watkins was forced to resign after his use of a White House helicopter to travel to golf courses became public knowledge, and Bill Dale, who had run the travel office, was acquitted of all charges. Bill Kennedy, under continuing fire for failing to pay taxes for his family's nanny, resigned and returned to Arkansas and the Rose Law Firm. In August 1995, Jim and Susan McDougal were indicted for conspiracy, mail fraud, bank fraud, and making or causing false statements to a financial institution. Both initially entered pleas of not guilty. However, soon after the trial, McDougal began cooperating with prosecutors in an effort to reduce his sentence, suggesting that Webster Hubbell may have done the legal work on Castle Grande for which Hillary Clinton billed Madison. This would explain why she knew so little about Castle Grande but also raises other questions about her billing practices.

PAULA JONES AND TROOPERGATE

In December 1993, the tabloid *American Spectator* and then the *Los Angeles Times* reported on Arkansas state troopers' charges of Bill Clinton's infidelity and his alleged offer of federal jobs to two of the troopers in order to buy their silence. The troopers, then Governor Clinton's bodyguards and drivers, told the *American Spectator*'s David Brock that they had tracked down the spurned mistress of one of Clinton's Republican opponents and tried to bribe her into unmasking the father of her "illegitimate" child (Lyons, 1996, p. 24). The story went on for eleven thousand words about everything from oral sex in pickup trucks with department store clerks to the dropping of the gubernatorial pants before a state employee identified only as "Paula." Her last name turned out to be "Jones." Soon she was holding press conferences and, in February 1994, Paula Corbin Jones, a former employee of a state agency in Arkansas, accused President Clinton of sexual harassment during a Little Rock hotel room encounter (Reeves, 1996, p. 100).

Much of the piece was based on rumor and supposition, and Clinton's staff had hoped that the mainstream press might not pick up. Media coverage was widely varied on the day of Jones's original press conference, and many news outlets initially gave little attention to the story. CBS, NBC, and CNN ignored her accusations. President Clinton called the accusations "outrageous," and the credibility of the troopers was called into question by the revelation, reported soon after the *American Spectator* story, that they had lied in a 1990 auto insurance case (quoted in Sabato and Lichter, 1994). Still, by Christmas week, the First Lady was "cleaning up after Bill one more time" and accused the troopers of obtaining "trash for cash" and engaging in a "political vendetta" (quoted in Brock, 1996, p. 399). About the initial story, Hillary Clinton said: "I find it not an accident that every time he [Bill Clinton] is on the verge of fulfilling his commitment to the American people and they are responding, out comes yet another round of these outrageous, terrible stories that people plant for political and financial reasons" (quoted in Flaherty and Flaherty, 1996, p. 208).

The media's attention to the story varied from outlet to outlet. The immediate response of many journalists to the troopers' allegations was that Bill Clinton's "messy personal life" while governor of Arkansas had no relevance to the presidency (Sabato and Lichter, 1994, p. 38). Some news organizations, such as *U.S. News and World Report,* generally ignored "Troopergate," while others focused on profiles of the troopers and others involved in the allegations, or through analyses of press coverage. At this point, the story spun out and appeared to be "basically dead within a single week" (Sabato and Lichter, 1994, p. 10).

By mid-1994 and for a brief time, it seemed that Hillary and Bill Clinton's strategy to put Whitewater—and scandal—behind them was working. From the vantage point of the White House, the crisis might have been expected to run its course. The events in Arkansas during the 1980s had been pored over by the national media, and not much had surfaced beyond the initial stories. The Clintons' approach to media-framed crisis—to brush it aside, promise full cooperation, then frustrate every inquiry—was put in place during the campaign and seemed to solidify as they occupied the White House.

However, in May 1994, Paula Jones's lawyers, financed in part by the conservative Legal Affairs Council, had followed through on their threat and filed a $700,000 federal lawsuit against the president, claiming sexual harassment and a violation of her civil rights (Sabato and Lichter, 1994), the first such lawsuit against a sitting president. The complaint alleged a "deprivation and conspiracy to deprive Plaintiff of her federally protected right" and "intentional infliction of emotional distress, and for defamation." She initially filed her lawsuit because Brock's *American Spectator* article said she claimed to have been "dazzled" by Governor Clinton's romantic style and volunteered to be his mistress. She later claimed that Bill Clinton's advances were unwanted (Lyons, 1996). The filing of the suit generated much publicity, particularly from news outlets that had been reluctant to carry the story when Jones had surfaced months earlier. The complaint provided a graphic description of what Jones alleged had transpired between herself and Bill Clinton. Through his lawyer, Robert Bennett, the president denied the claims and asserted immunity from prosecution. The case was soon embroiled in procedural issue, and an appeals court ruled that Jones's suit could proceed while the president was in office. Delay, however, was a White House strategy, and challenges to the appeal meant that Jones's claims would still be pending during the 1996 presidential campaign.

It was not until a May 1994 *Washington Post* story, published the day after Mr. Clinton hired Robert Bennett to address Jones's lawsuit, that the national media became interested. For example, there were televised interviews with Jones on ABC's *Prime Time Live* with Sam Donaldson and CNN with Judy Woodruff (Sabato and Lichter, 1994). Reeves (1996) reports that the *Los Angeles Times* soon wrote four thousand "better-documented" words on the same troopers, and the "cops from Little Rock were on television within hours" (pp. 100–101). CNN considered the troopers' stories unverifiable but nevertheless covered the story, passing on only what they could prove, "which in the end was almost nothing." Bill Clinton had made a long-distance call from Virginia to a Little Rock woman at an "unusual hour." She told reporters he was talking her through a personal crisis (Lyons, 1996). All three networks cancelled interviews with Hillary Clinton because of White House orders that she could not be asked about Troopergate (Brock, 1996).

Early in 1997, Bill Clinton's popularity rating was at 60 percent, as high as it had been since he first assumed the presidency. Administration scandal had been replaced on the front pages by Newt Gingrich's admission that he had misled the House Ethics Committee over his handling of a tax-exempt college course. But when *Newsweek* put Paula Jones on its cover in January, the Clinton presidency crisis again became front-page news. The story, based on a previous piece in *American Lawyer*, said that Jones's charge that Clinton had exposed himself to her in a Little Rock hotel room in 1991 was far stronger than previously believed and that Jones had been unfairly dismissed by the media. In addition, the Supreme Court was set to hear arguments on President Clinton's effort to delay Jones's lawsuit until after he left office. In Kurtz's (1998) opinion, "constitutional issues—and oral sex—were at stake" (p. 94). The case had been successfully stalled by the

Clintons until after the 1996 election, but was now emerging as a fully developed scandal at the very beginning of their second stint as First Couple.

On June 1, 1997, while President Clinton was in Paris with Boris Yeltsin and other world leaders to sign the NATO expansion agreement, Clinton press secretary Mike McCurry was paged by the White House press office about the Supreme Court and Paula Jones. The case had not been a high-priority one for the administration. McCurry called Washington and was told that the Court had unanimously agreed that a sitting president was not immune to lawsuits over personal behavior and the three-year-old Jones's lawsuit could go forward. Rahm Emanuel called the president's lawyer, Robert Bennett, and asked him to handle all public comment about the case. Bennett conferred with Clinton after the Yeltsin meeting. The decision was a "disappointment," but the earlier strategy of delaying the story until after the 1996 election had been successful. Their next strategy was to work for an out-of-court and relatively low-media profile settlement.

The Paula Jones ruling led on all the networks, erasing the NATO agreement as top story. Rita Braver reported that White House officials were "shocked" and "trying to put an optimistic spin" on the events. McCurry had not released anything "official" to confirm the reports in the media, but realized that the president needed to deal with the story. Emanuel opted, for the moment, to "keep this away from the president personally" (quoted in Kurtz, 1998, p. 210). The front-page coverage continued with the *New York Times*'s headlining "Sense of Siege Deepens" and *USA Today*'s running a picture of Paula Jones with the headline: "Sex Trial Possible in Clinton Term." Kurtz (1998) believes that the president at this juncture was providing the country with tabloid entertainment, and reporters were relishing the chance to get down in the gutter while pretending to be interested mainly in the lofty goals of constitutional principles.

The tawdriness of the Paula Jones lawsuit was kept alive in the press as the case moved toward a scheduled trial date in the spring of 1998. Bob Bennett talked about the president's penis on *Face the Nation*, declaring Clinton a "normal man" in terms of "size, shape, direction"(Kurtz, 1998, p. 278). On talk radio and in Internet gossip columns, people were again debating "whether Clinton had dropped his pants in the presence of a subordinate in Little Rock's Excelsior Hotel and suggested she kiss part of his anatomy" (Kurtz, 1998, p. 210). Maureen Dowd wrote of "those rumors about that bald eagle tattoo," and Don Imus observed that everyone was sitting around "discussing the president's dick" (quoted in Kurtz, 1998, p. 210).

The next day at President Clinton's international press conference in the Hague, the Dutch protocol chief recognized only foreign reporters, who asked about the Marshall Plan and future aid to Europe. McCurry told the president that the American media needed some comment and suggested an impromptu outside news conference. The president agreed and informally told reporters that he was concerned about the ruling's effect on "future presidents" but would not go beyond that (quoted in Kurtz, 1998, p. 211).

Some White House aides believed that the Paula Jones scandal would not hurt President Clinton's image because people had already judged him and, despite media emphasis on his flaws, had reelected him (Kurtz, 1998). Bob Bennett, though, was deluged with interview requests from shows such as *Meet the Press*, *Face the Nation*, and *This Week*. He agreed to do them all, but made no commitments in case the story faded by week's end, so that he would not give it new life by going on television. On the other hand, if Jones's lawyers were on the shows, he would counter them.

Newsweek featured Jones on its cover and accused Bennett of threatening on national television to ruin Jones's reputation by bringing up her sexual history. Jones's lawyers were making an issue of her alleged pristine reputation and threatening to depose a long line of women who had slept with Bill Clinton. Privately, Clinton did not want to settle and insisted that Jones was lying and a tool of the right wing, but Bob Bennett had taken the case and turned it into a public relations disaster (Kurtz, 1998). He launched a media counteroffensive, saying to the *New York Times, Washington Post, Washington Times*, NBC, AP, Wolf Blitzer, Charlie Rose, and Ted Koppel that there was no desire to dig into Jones's sexual background. In so doing, he kept a story the administration wanted to go away before the media for another ten days.

Rahm Emanuel opted to change the media focus by highlighting Chelsea Clinton's high school graduation from Sidwell Friends School. McCurry had previously told the press that the ceremony would remain closed, in keeping with school tradition. However, the president was speaking at the commencement, and pictures of the president as a proud father of a graduating seventeen-year-old daughter would remind Americans that Bill and Hillary Clinton had raised a remarkable daughter. Although both Clintons vetoed the idea of opening the graduation ceremony to the media, the president did agree to write an upbeat front-page story for *USA Today* that led off with the president's recalling how he had hugged Chelsea after she got her diploma. Emanuel avoided similar contacts with the *New York Times* or *Washington Post* for fear of their spinning the piece as an effort to divert attention from Paula Jones. However, even the *USA Today* piece referenced infidelity, Paula Jones, and Whitewater as a counterpoint to his success as a parent (Kurtz, 1998).

THE FUNDRAISING SCANDAL

Media frustration climaxed in the final weeks of the 1996 campaign when allegations surfaced that foreign money had been funneled to the Clinton camp, and the White House seemed unable or unwilling to provide answers. On February 12, 1997, the lead story in the *Washington Post* was Bob Woodward's article detailing how the Justice Department had uncovered evidence that representatives of the People's Republic of China had tried to direct foreign contributions to the Democrats before the 1996 election. The Chinese embassy was used for the planning. The story did not say who was involved, what contributions were directed, how much money was involved, or when the event allegedly happened, but Woodward's name was enough to make the story fly. To counter, the White House put Lanny Davis on the talk show circuit, whose sole "mission" was to clean up after the fundraising scandals.

Kurtz (1998) argues that the DNC fundraising scandal was "nothing less than the selling of the presidency" (p. 51), which involved an alleged conspiracy by Bill Clinton and Al Gore to use high office to solicit money from foreign operatives, Asian American donors, and others, possibly in exchange for political favors. Major donors were rewarded with social gatherings at which they could lobby the president on favorite issues. Others brought business partners to meet the president. Some foreign companies without U.S. operations wrote campaign checks or laundered the money through employees and relatives. Those raising $10,000 to $25,000 were invited to large dinners with the president; contributions of $50,000 to $100,000 produced more intimate dinners or coffee with Clinton; and those who gave more than $500,000 got to fly on *Air Force One*, play a round of golf with the president, or stay overnight at the White House.

Press secretary Mike McCurry, assumed scandal control before the election and bore the brunt of hostile press inquiries, along with special counsel Lanny Davis. McCurry had to manage the administration's "Charlie Trie problem." Jack Quinn, White House counsel, and deputy chief of staff Evelyn Lieberman visited McCurry to brief him about the trouble at the president's legal defense fund, the trust set up to raise money for Clinton's bills in the Whitewater case and the sexual harassment suit by Paula Jones. The trust had dealings with Yah Lin "Charlie" Trie, a Taiwan-born businessman whom Clinton had known while frequenting Trie's restaurant in Little Rock. During the heat of the 1996 presidential campaign, Trie contributed $640,000 to the fund. However, the checks were suspect: some came from foreigners, some from people who seemed unable to afford the $1,000 donation, and some bore similar handwriting. All the money was returned. McCurry was informed by Michael Cardozo, the fund's executive director, that Hillary Clinton and Harold Ickes, the other deputy chief of staff, had been briefed about the situation earlier. No one at the legal defense fund had told the DNC about Trie's attempt to contribute money to the defense trust fund. Trie, his relatives, and his company had given the Democrats $210,000 over the previous three years, and Clinton had appointed Trie to a U.S.-Pacific trade commission less than a month after he delivered the improper checks to the defense fund. In addition, Trie had visited the White House twenty-three times.

Quinn and Lieberman queried McCurry about whether to make the "Trie" problem public. The defense fund did not have to file its next disclosure report for months. Would it be better to wait? Because NBC was already investigating Asian American contributions to the defense fund, McCurry believed they had to "bite the bullet," and on December 16, 1996, Michael Cardozo briefed reporters on Trie and the $640,000. The "press went wild"; McCurry "got hammered" and responded, "It appears that an old friend of the president tried to lend some assistance to a president and a First Lady who have a great deal of legal debt accumulated. That's the fact. The appearance is someone else's judgment to make" (Kurtz, 1998, p. 64).

The press pounding continued for days. From McCurry's standpoint, the story had turned into yet another feeding frenzy and blatant advocacy journalism. The media had collectively decided that what happened in 1996 evidenced that the campaign finance system was broken and needed to be fixed. Every story added to the pressure for reform, and every column and editorial "had to denounce the cash-crazed nature of the Clinton fundraising effort" (Kurtz, 1998, p. 68). McCurry ultimately followed what Kurtz (1998) labels a "rope-a-dope" strategy: taking the punches without swinging back, letting the reporters vent their frustrations by beating up on him in November so that by the time Congress weighed in after the January 1997 inauguration, "this would be considered old news" (p. 68).

A major strategy was insisting that Bill Clinton and Al Gore had done nothing out of the ordinary with Chinese businesspeople or in renting out the Lincoln Bedroom. They believed the public was tuning it all out—that most viewed the fundraising as typical "Beltway follies," and government could continue in a scandal-charged atmosphere while the journalists seemed equally determined to make their readers and viewers care. In Kurtz's (1998) words, for the Clinton administration, "neutralizing the media had become ground zero in the struggle for supremacy, and the spin would clearly be as important as the substance" (p. xxvi).

The year-long investigation into the Clinton campaign's fundraising abuses and influence-peddling charges built to a crescendo in the fall of

1997. The Justice Department expanded its investigation into questionable calls by Vice President Al Gore, as well as a probe of President Clinton's efforts to raise campaign cash in 1996. The charges that the administration had improperly raised millions of dollars by selling access to the president reached a critical mass when the *New York Times* headlined the new developments as its lead story.

Doris Matsui, Clinton's deputy director of public liaison and the highest-ranking Asian American in the White House, "felt that [White House attorney] Lanny Davis was hanging her out to dry" (Kurtz, p. 58). Tim Weiner, a *New York Times* investigative reporter, called Davis with the information that his paper had DNC documents laying out an election year plan to raise $7 million from Asian Americans and to reward big donors by inviting them to White House events with Clinton. One memo indicated that Matsui had helped devise the strategy. The story was competitive, since the memo was among the three thousand pages of documents from the files of John Huang, a former DNC fundraiser, that had recently been fed to the press. Weiner told Davis that the *Times* was going with the story as the right-hand lead of the next day's paper, "the spot reserved for wars and assassinations and landmark legislation" (Kurtz, 1998, p. 58).

The suffocating circumstances hit home when Hillary Clinton held her first issue briefing in early 1997 on "microcredit" loans for small-scale businesses. This was the first time she had sat for a formal session with reporters since the "pink press conference" of 1994 when she had fielded questions about Whitewater for seventy-two minutes. Journalists were told in advance they could ask any question. However, each "politely stuck" to questions about micro-credit, allowing Hillary Clinton to set the agenda. Finally Jill Dougherty of CNN said, "Mrs. Clinton, I really hate to bring up front-burner issues, but duty calls," and then she questioned the First Lady about her role in compiling a White House database of political supporters and whether the contents were used for political purposes by the Democratic National Committee. The First Lady "finessed" the question and a follow-up by Ann Blackman of *Time,* and the session was over. The *New York Times*'s James Bennett wrote in his story about the session that a reporter had "apologetically" raised the database issue. He got an angry letter from a reader asking why reporters were apologizing for raising issues that the White House didn't want to talk about. According to Kurtz (1998) Bennett realized the reader was right; "they had all fallen into that trap" (p. 41).

Despite White House efforts to dissuade her, Rita Braver kept researching the fundraising scandal. After the story broke, she discovered that a former White House aide who was raising money for the Democrats overseas may have been entertaining clients in the White House dining room, an unusual privilege for a Democratic fundraiser. She kept calling Clinton's press office, but as her deadline passed, officials insisted she didn't have the facts. The next morning Braver saw her story in the *Wall Street Journal*. Press secretary Mike McCurry called her later to apologize and said that the *Journal* had called with more information than Braver did, so the White House felt compelled to confirm the story. In truth, McCurry preferred to have the story come out in print rather than on the CBS Evening News. In his view, television was "hyperventilated," accusatory and, particularly regarding negative stories, less likely to provide details of the administration's perspective. At least in a newspaper story, there would be space for the Clinton side rather than a television report that "flashed by in a minute-twenty." Correspondent personalities also influenced McCurry's choice of media outlets for administration stories. For example, he considered Brit Hume, despite his openly more conservative personal views, to be more even-handed than Rita Braver, whom McCurry considered "more prosecutorial, more likely to slam the White House" (Kurtz, 1998, pp. 43–44).

Media coverage was enacted with an "arms-race mentality" and with a constant pressure not to get beaten on the "biggest story" in town. There was internal conflict over the strategy of disclosure from what Kurtz (1998) describes as the "Hezbollah wing" the White House—"hard-liners" such as Bruce Lindsey and the counsel's office and Hillary Clinton—who "never wanted to surrender a document without a fight" (p. 135). Podesta believed each set of documents should be examined separately but also realized they were waging a public relations war and was not sure the White House had enough time to review the documents adequately to answer the media questions that would come from their release. It was decided to let the Republicans release the material.

Ickes's attorney, Robert Bennett, who was also representing Clinton in the Paula Jones case, agreed to provide copies of the "Lincoln Bedroom" documents to the White House. Some of the material was "explosive": handwritten notes from the president that read "ready to start overnights right away" and "get other names at 100,000 or more, 50,000 or more." The president had approved a Democratic party plan to "energize" donors by rewarding them with overnight stays, coffees, golf outings, and morning jogs with him (Kurtz, 1998). The White House decided to reverse its decision and released the material to the press, after which the "scandal immediately went fever pitch" (Kurtz, 1998, p. 138).

The fundraising scandal became a proxy for reporters convinced of Clinton's "essential slipperiness" (Kurtz, 1998, p. 138). Questions of presidential character had been asked since 1992 about infidelity, the draft, marijuana, Whitewater, and Paula Jones. Many journalists believed the president could not be trusted to provide the truth. The "Lincoln Bedroom" notes provided hard evidence to support their beliefs. The presidential staff still insisted the coffees were not fundraisers, although the memos said they were. And overnight guests were "friends" and "supporters," although some were unknown to the Clintons. In Kurtz's opinion (1998), the spin had become surreal.

The press continued to headline the scandal. When it was calculated that 958 overnight guests had contributed more than $10 million to Clinton and the Democratic party, Tom Brokaw called the Lincoln Bedroom "the most expensive bed and breakfast in North America," and Wolf Blitzer reported that "the president blundered badly" (quoted in Kurtz, 1998, p. 140). At a senior staff meeting that included Clinton, strategies were discussed to discover how a scheduled presidential news conference with Chilean president Eduardo Frei could be recast into a defense of the Democrats' fundraising and the president's reputation. Questions from the media would not be about admitting Chile to NAFTA. According to Kurtz (1998) a perceptual gap appeared between Clinton and his staff regarding how to address the crisis. The president wanted to "counterpunch," while others advised that a low-key, scripted, nonemotional response was warranted. The last strategy was followed, and the president responded calmly to the questions, most of which were about the scandal. Still, the "media mob was in full battle regalia and charging at full speed" (Kurtz, 1998, p. 141), and they began targeting Hillary Rodham Clinton.

The First Lady had previously stated she knew nothing about the use of the official White House database being used for political ends—that "the design of it, the use of it, that was for other people to figure out." House Republicans released to the press a 1994 memo that referenced sharing the database information with the Democratic National Committee "for political purposes." She had written at the top: "This sounds promising. Please advise. HRC" (quoted in Kurtz 1998, p. 142). Substantive work of the presidency was sidebarred, and although polls still reflected a high public approval rating, it appeared that no journalist was defending the president. *Newsweek*'s Jonathan Alter called Clinton a "greedy fool," and the *Washington Post*'s Richard Cohen complained that "not since Richard Nixon's 1972 campaign has so much money been raised so cynically" (quoted in Kurtz, 1998, p. 142).

Publicly, the White House continued to insist that the decision not to make the papers public was only a logistical matter. But Dan Burton's House Oversight Committee continued to feed the Ickes papers to other news outlets. The CBS Evening News did the story with Rita Braver saying that the material "absolutely shatters the illusion the president has been trying to create that this was just an informal process"; the *New York Daily News* said the president had personally reviewed the memos, and the *Washington Post* revealed that Clinton, Gore, and the First Lady as well were asked by Ickes to make fundraising calls. Not until days later did the White House release Ickes's papers, producing more front-page stories about the Clintons' "servicing" of donors (Kurtz, 1998, p. 174).

In April 1997, the Democratic National Committee released ten thousand pages of documents related to fundraising and John Huang. Mike McCurry decided on that day to put out the long-promised report on fifty-six donors and fundraisers who got free shuttle service aboard *Air Force One* and the one fundraiser, Vernon Jordan, who stayed overnight at Camp David. The avalanche approach worked, and the details got lost in the dust. The DNC papers included an embarrassing memo urging Clinton to consider sixty top fundraisers for federal jobs; about half had been hired. But that revelation, and the *Air Force One* guest list, did not appear on any front pages. In media terms, the Senate fundraising hearings were a "total bust"—little drama, less news, almost no live television coverage. CNN, MSNBC, PBS, and C-SPAN had all but ignored the proceedings. The hearings were not on the front page of the *Washington Post,* and Peter Jennings led off with a new ABC poll that put Clinton's popularity at 64 percent, the highest of his presidency, before reporting on the hearings. The president was in Spain, meeting with the NATO allies.

Although network correspondents worked to keep it alive, the fundraising scandal slowed after six months; the basic outlines of the story were well known, and a "fatigue factor" had set in (Kurtz, 1998, p. 189). Reporters realized the public was no longer as hungry for scandal as before, and they were not spinning as rapidly or for as long. The number of scandal reports on network news declined by more than two-thirds. Still, not everyone was ready to modify their stance and regarded White House press releases about various conferences and proposals as lightweight and symptomatic of "second-term drift." Alison Mitchell wrote that the Clinton agenda was "minimalist," and *USA Today*'s Susan Page said that the fundraising scandal was freezing everything from ambassadorial appointments to arms sales to Indonesia because "the counsel's office and the press office increasingly was preoccupied with damage control" (quoted in Kurtz, 1998, p. 190). However, in the end, the White House had been able to "compartmentalize the scandal," with the result that most Americans had made a judgment that the cash and favor seeking were "politics as usual." The president's approval rating was still close to 60 percent.

THE MONICA LEWINSKY SCANDAL

On May 28, 1997, in a 9–0 ruling, the U.S. Supreme Court summarily rejected President Clinton's claim of immunity from civil litigation while in office. The Paula Jones case could proceed. Jones's attorneys could begin deposing witnesses under oath, and the case could go to trial while Clinton was president. In early 1998, a scandal erupted that, according to *Washington Post* reporter Michael Isikoff (1999), "turned American politics on its head." "In those days," according to Isikoff, "there was much talk that he wouldn't survive" (p. viii).

The allegations that President Bill Clinton had sexual relations with Monica Lewinsky and then lied about it under oath, first published in the nation's newspapers on the morning of January 21, 1998, "indicate the intimate role of the news media in public affairs." According to Sparrow (1999), a series of key decisions by editors, publishers, and news executives was necessary for the Lewinsky story to break. It almost never came into public view. *Newsweek* killed reporter Michael Isikoff's story about the president and the twenty-one-year-old female intern, but Matt Drudge, an Internet gossip columnist, put the story—including that *Newsweek* refused its publication—on his Web page. Only then did *Newsweek* put the story out on America Online, followed the next day by the *Washington Post* and the *Los Angeles Times* and, shortly after, most of America's media. Prior to this story, the major news organizations had generally ignored Drudge's stories. Drudge himself admits he is only "about eighty percent accurate" (quoted in Sparrow, 1999, p. xii).

The story was so prevalent that it overshadowed essentially all other major news of early 1998, including the policy initiatives contained in the State of the Union speech and the budget initiatives for fiscal 1999; discussion of the specific objectives that would be achieved by threatened U.S. military strikes against Iraq; the content and conditions of hundreds of billions of international monetary fund dollars being channeled to the Indonesian, Korean, and Thai economies; talks with Yassir Arafat and Benjamin Netanyahu on the peaceful resolution of the controversial Israeli settlements on the West Bank; and Pope John Paul II's visit to Cuba.

The Lewinsky story played out through the deliberate use of the news media by the staff and lawyers from Kenneth Starr's investigatory team, as well as the Clinton White House and the news media, which printed or publicized leaks by all of the political players. These included the independent prosecutor; the president and his staff and wife; Lewinsky's attorney, William Ginsburg; her friend and confidante Linda Tripp; and New York literary agent Lucianne Goldberg (Sparrow, 1999). Networks devoted more airtime to the Lewinsky scandal in one week than they gave to "all the Clinton scandals, from Gennifer Flowers to campaign fundraising abuses, combined." This one was "different" and could "spell the end of the Clinton Presidency" (Kurtz, 1998, p. xiii).

Isikoff heard of the allegations during conversations with Linda Tripp to learn more about Kathleen Willey's alleged sexual liaisons with Bill Clinton—as part of an attempt to document additional incidents of sexual harassment to corroborate Jones's claims in support of her lawsuit against the president. Tripp told, in considerable detail, of the alleged ongoing affair between Lewinsky and the president (Isikoff, 1999). Isikoff did not pursue the story at the time since whatever occurred between Clinton and Lewinsky seemed consensual and so fell outside the lawsuit. He learned that Tripp, fitted with a body mike by Ken Starr's office, had taped further conversations in which Lewinsky accused Clinton and his friend Vernon Jordan of urging her to lie about their affair in her deposition in the Jones case. Tripp, a former White House aide who had befriended Monica Lewinsky when both were moved to the Pentagon, and unhappy when Bob Bennett responded to her account by publicly questioning her credibility, decided to tape secretly her conversations with Lewinsky to convince Isikoff of the affair. Tripp told the reporter about the tapes during a meeting with her literary agent, Lucianne Goldberg, and offered to play the tapes. Isikoff declined to listen because he was afraid of becoming involved in a potentially illegal taping process. Starr was apparently running an undercover sting against the president of the United States. With his deadline approaching, Isikoff agreed to listen to one of the tapes (Kurtz, 1998).

On January 17, *Newsweek*'s editors opted not to run the story. Starr had asked them to hold off, and they also had questions about Lewinsky's credibility. Isikoff lobbied hard for publication, saying it was not the magazine's job to help Starr. For the second time in six months, the reporter was shadowed by gossip columnist Matt Drudge, who had learned of the Isikoff piece within hours and posted some of the details on his Internet site. Rumors grew that during his own deposition, the president had denied having sex with Lewinsky.

However, after the Supreme Court ruling prompted more media scrutiny, Isikoff investigated further for *Newsweek*. Although three women, including Willey, had been presented as potential interviewees, the magazine targeted Lewinsky, in part because "that Clinton was carrying on with a young woman barely half his age . . . had the potential to be explosive" (Isikoff, 1999, p. 142). By August 1997, Isikoff writes that he began to believe President Clinton's "serial indiscretions" really did matter because they "continued well into his tenure in the White House" and reflected the president's "brutal willingness to deceive the public." The "endless drip of scandals" in the Clinton White House, from Whitewater to Hillary Clinton's billing records, had "infected" Bill Clinton's entire presidency (p. 168). The Jones lawsuit, in Isikoff's view, was the test of "how far [the president] and his coterie of loyal aides would go to make sure" that "that which is embarrassing (or worse) was to be concealed" (p. 171). On December 23, President Clinton answered the interrogatories that Jones's lawyers had sent him in October—questions he had been court-ordered to answer. In response to the questions asking that he identify all state or federal employees with whom he had sexual relations between 1986 and 1996, Clinton's answer, signed "'under penalty of perjury' and filed with the court in Little Rock," was "none" (Isikoff, 1999, p. 255).

By January 1998, a campaign was in gear to present Linda Tripp's tape and allegations that Bill Clinton and his staff were coaching Monica Lewinsky to lie to Whitewater independent counsel Kenneth Starr. *Newsweek* and Michael Isikoff wanted to hear Tripp's tapes of conversations with Lewinsky in order to assess the latter's credibility. President Clinton was preparing for his deposition in the case of *Jones v. Clinton*, including a review of all the women about whom the Jones lawyers would be asking. The true identity of the "Jane Does"—including "Jane Doe #6," Monica Lewinsky—had been deleted from all public filings to protect their privacy. Lewinsky had signed an affidavit the previous week saying she had never had a sexual relationship with the President (Isikoff, 1999).

After Clinton took the oath and "some early skirmishing," the issue of questions about sexual relations—"the core of the case"—came to the forefront. Had Bill Clinton "done to others what he did to Jones"? Jones's attorneys agreed on a definition of sexual relations "most directly relevant to the allegations of their client," which included the focus of the case: oral sex. Clinton testified that he had never had "sexual relations" with Monica Lewinsky. By this time, Kenneth Starr had launched a criminal investigation into Bill Clinton's efforts to conceal his relationship with Monica Lewinsky and his recruitment of Vernon Jordan to help her find a job. In addition, *Newsweek* learned that Starr's prosecutors had conducted a "sting" of Lewinsky while she was talking with Linda Tripp and produced tapes that seemed to support Tripp's allegations that Lewinsky had had a sexual relationship with President Clinton. It was at this point that talk of Bill Clinton's having committed an "impeachable offense" began in earnest in the media (Isikoff, 1999). While *Newsweek*'s Isikoff argued that it was "as much a Ken Starr story as it is a Clinton story" and that "what Starr is doing here is extraordinary . . . potentially a bombshell," others at the newsmagazine argued, "People are going to look at this as a sex story . . .

about Clinton having sex with a young woman" (p. 329). A debate ensued on whether to publish the "Lewinsky story." Isikoff was "convinced" that his editors "were going to blow an enormous exclusive" (p. 334). One argument was that Starr's was a "pretty dipshit investigation," and he was now "trying to nail [Clinton] on sex"; since the story was not about "a terrorist or something," it would not matter if *Newsweek* "blew the investigation." The other argument focused on whether the issues were "hard enough" journalistically and if "we've got this right." Advocating the former argument, Isikoff (1999) remembers wondering, "What is going through [*Newsweek*'s editors'] mind" since "scoops are what it's all about. It's what we strive for every week. It's what you pay me for" (p. 335).

President Clinton's deposition ended with his denial that he had ever met Paula Jones as well as a denial of sexual relations with the other "Jane Does," including Monica Lewinsky. He did, however, after referring to the definition of sexual relations that had been "agreed upon," admit to sexual relations with Gennifer Flowers, a reversal of his 1992 denial and conclusive evidence that "established Clinton as a liar on matters relating to his relations with women" (p. 336).

The following day, the tabloid *Drudge Report* detailed not only that the president of the United States had had a sexual affair with a White House intern but that, to reporter Michael Isikoff's dismay, *Newsweek* had killed "his" story. The *Report* also reminded its readers that "ironically" Isikoff had left the *Washington Post* years earlier after its editors had refused to publish "even a portion of his meticulously researched investigative report that was to break Paula Jones" (pp. 339–340). The *Washington Post*'s Sue Schmidt, the "hard-driving Whitewater reporter," had "the goods" on the supposed affair. Her colleague Peter Baker was calling the White House for comment. Press secretary McCurry left a message for Davis, a go-between for attorney Bob Bennett, about Clinton's meeting the next day with Prime Minister Benjamin Netanyahu. "But Middle East diplomacy was about to be wiped off the media radar screen" (Kurtz, 1998, p. 291).

By January 20, Sue Schmidt's *Post* story on Monica Lewinsky was on the newstands, followed by reports on ABC radio and in the *Los Angeles Times*. The White House's Paul Begala did not know about the story until he read the *Post* the next morning. Lanny Davis felt he couldn't do much with the press until he had more facts. When reporters came into the press secretary's office, McCurry said Clinton was "outraged" by the charges and had "never had any improper relationship with this woman" (quoted in Kurtz, 1998, p. 293).

Most reporters automatically assumed that Clinton was lying—that he had been having an affair with Lewinsky and was trying to hide it. They had been "through too many bimbo eruptions, heard too many of Clinton's hedged denials" (Kurtz, 1998, p. 293). When the president sat for a previously scheduled interview with PBS's Jim Lehrer and said, "There is no sexual relationship," Begala was deluged with questions about why Clinton used the present tense, implying the president was "leaving open the possibility of a past affair" with the former intern (Kurtz, 1998, p. 293). Clinton's advisers and staff rallied. In an interview with E. J. Dionne, Ron Brownstein, and other columnists, Al Gore said he believed his friend. Hillary Clinton, reprising the role of loyal wife from 1992, did a round of radio interviews in which she dismissed the charges as false. Madeleine Albright and three other cabinet secretaries emerged on the White House driveway to express their faith in President Clinton.

The White House's initial attempt at rhetorical management of the Lewinsky crisis was a failure. Isikoff and other reporters unearthed more allegations that undercut the defense of President Clinton: Lewinsky had sent packages to the president through his personal secretary, Betty Currie. He had sent gifts, including a book of poems, and his voice was supposedly on Lewinsky's answering machine. She said they had had phone sex and that Clinton argued that oral sex was not adultery. Lewinsky also was said to have a dress stained with his semen and talked about becoming "assistant to the president for blow jobs" (quoted in Kurtz, 1998, p. 294).

The *Post* also reported that Clinton's deposition with Jones's attorneys included an admission of an affair with Gennifer Flowers, meaning that the very first thing most Americans had learned about Bill Clinton—his 1992 denial of having sex with Flowers—was a lie (Kurtz, 1998). The president's public relations team believed that Clinton needed to speak to the country immediately. Republicans were openly debating the possibility of impeachment or resignation, and even "longtime loyalists" such as George Stephanopoulos were suggesting that Clinton "might have to go" (Kurtz, 1998, p. 294). Some Clinton aides wanted the president to do an interview with a few reporters or a single journalist, but others, including Hillary Clinton—whose "vote was crucial in such personal crises"—believed he should say nothing until they had more information. Because they were in the midst of a criminal probe, Clinton was relying solely on attorneys such as Bill Bennett, who did not want him to complicate matters on which he had already provided a sworn deposition (Kurtz, 1998).

The White House spin strategy included suggestions to the press that Monica Lewinsky was flirtatious, obsessed with Clinton, and emotionally unstable. In addition, Linda Tripp's tape might have been doctored, and why was Ken Starr, initially appointed to investigate Arkansas vacation property, wiring one person to entrap another into admitting a sexual relationship with President Clinton? Attorney Bennett told reporters, "Mr. Starr seems hellbent on getting President Clinton" and said he was disappointed that the *Washington Post,* "one of the preeminent newspapers in the country, is becoming a tabloid paper" (quoted in Kurtz, 1998, p. 295).

The velocity of the story was incredible. Four days after the scandal broke, Wolf Blitzer was reporting that some of Clinton's closest advisers thought he had had sex with Lewinsky and were considering calling for his resignation (Kurtz, 1998). CNN replayed a videotape of Clinton's hugging Lewinsky at a postelection rally, "like it was some kind of porn flick" and journalists "grumbled privately about the intense, seemingly relentless pressure to match each new allegation that appeared somewhere else, or at least to regurgitate the charge" (Kurtz, 1998, pp. 295–296).

Charges were rampant. Deborah Orin reported in the *New York Post* that the president told Lewinsky he'd had sex with "hundreds" of women, while ABC reported that Starr was tracking Secret Service agents and White House staffers who had seen "an intimate encounter" between Clinton and Lewinsky. The *Washington Times*, in a story appearing only hours after her lawyer had made the deal, said Lewinsky offered to tell Starr in exchange for immunity that she had had an affair with Clinton. The White House was "furious" over what they considered leaks from Starr's office. Literally minutes after he subpoenaed some White House aide, a reporter would call to ask about it. Leaking in a criminal investigation was against the law, but the reporters seemed never to make an issue of Starr's behavior because they were "all scrounging for the next illicit tidbit" (Kurtz, 1998, p. 296). When White House staffer Begala tried to focus journalists on Starr's tactics, one reporter replied, "You will never get me to write a story decrying leaks. I live off leaks" (quoted in Kurtz, 1998, p. 296).

Clinton surrogates were sent to talk shows to ask Americans to "wait for the facts," including Ann Lewis on *Fox News Sunday*, Begala on *This Week,* Rahm Emanuel on *Face the Nation,* and James Carville on *Meet the Press* (Kurtz, 1998, p. 297). Emanuel said of the scandal:

I feel like I'm in a Greek tragedy. He's [Clinton] at 62 percent, one of the highest ratings of any president in this century. The economy is humming. The world is dancing to his tune. *U.S. News* just had a cover story on what Clintonism means. All that we've worked for, it's all there. And then you get a body blow and every accomplishment, policy and political, is hurt by this distraction. (quoted in Kurtz, 1998, p. 298)

The president made it clear that he did not want to stay silent. His advisers worked a compromise with his attorneys: he would make a forceful public denial but would not say anything new.

Hillary Clinton had long served as a back channel for advisers trying to influence the president's decisions, and she shifted into what one aide called her "battle mode." Ann Lewis, who was close to the First Lady, held a strategy session with Hillary Clinton and decided it was time to "publicly emerge as the president's chief defender," which she did, appearing on the *Today* show six days into the crisis. Prior to the First Lady's January 27, 1997, interview, the around-the-clock press mediation had been entirely about the scandal: what Clinton had done, whether he could survive, with virtually no one defending him. Hillary Clinton challenged reporters and the public on national television to pay attention to a different story: "This vast right-wing conspiracy that has been conspiring against my husband since the day he announced for President" (quoted in Tumulty and Gibbs, 1999). In response to interviewer Matt Lauer's question about the nature of Bill Clinton's relationship with Monica Lewinsky, she argued that Ken Starr was a "politically motivated prosecutor," part of a group of "malicious" and "evil-minded" people, and she referred to the media "feeding frenzy," which had become part of a plot against the Clinton White House (quoted in Kurtz, 1998, p. 298). She continued:

The important thing now is to stand as firmly as I can and say that, you know the president has denied these allegations on all counts, unequivocally. And we'll see how this plays out. . . . Bill and I have been accused of everything, including murder, by some of the very same people who are behind these allegations. So from my perspective, this is part of a continuing political campaign against my husband. . . . We get a politically motivated prosecutor who is allied with the right-wing opponents of my husband, who has literally spent four years looking at every telephone call we've made, every check we've ever written, scratching for dirt, intimidating witnesses, doing everything possible to try to make some accusation against my husband. . . . It's an entire operation. (p. 395)

When asked if she thought Bill Clinton would admit, again, to causing pain in their marriage and if the president had committed adultery in the White House and lied about it, should he resign, the First Lady replied that the American people should "certainly be concerned about it" and "if all that were proven true, I think that would be a very serious offense," but "that is not going to be proven true" (p. 393). Woodward (1999) considers the *Today* interview one of Mrs. Clinton's strongest. Not only had it indicated that "if she had settled accounts with her husband, why should anyone else dwell on it," but also "had managed to refocus media attention on Starr," who responded shortly after with his own press release labeling her suggestions that his office was part of a conspiracy as "nonsense" (p. 396). Although Ken Starr dismissed Hillary Clinton's accusations as nonsense, she had recast the debate.

The scandal continued to gain momentum. During an interview with a Los Angeles radio station, Dick Morris suggested that the president's behavior might be understandable if one would "assume that some of the allegations about Hillary sometimes not necessarily being into regular sex with men might be true." When a *Washington Post* reporter called McCurry to ask about the comment, the press secretary inquired whether the paper was serious about publishing Morris's speculative comments. Although the *Post* ultimately decided against the story, it was reported the next day in the *Los Angeles Times*, the *New York Post,* and Maureen Dowd's *New York Times* column (Kurtz, 1998, pp. 299–300).

The public reaction was more restrained than the media's. Fifty-seven percent of those questioned in a *Washington Post* poll said they believed that Clinton had had a sexual relationship with Lewinsky. Although they considered the denials to be lies, 59 percent said they wanted the president to remain in office, even if he had been having extramarital sex in the White House. Impeachment was favored only if Clinton had lied under oath about the affair. According to Kurtz (1998) the issue for most Americans was trust, not sex.

Still, Americans were devouring every detail of the scandal, following the media agenda. In Kurtz's (1998) view:

The Monica Lewinsky mess was a gripping train wreck of a story, racing down the tracks of real-time television, the seeming self-destruction of a president who only days earlier had been riding so high. It was almost comic. . . . Richard Nixon had been driven from office for burglarizing and spying on his opponents: Clinton faced political annihilation for failing to keep his zipper zipped. (p. 300)

Even the "most sympathetic" columnists decried the president's alleged behavior. *New York Times* reporter Tom Friedman called Clinton a "reckless idiot," while the *Times*'s Jeff Gerth and Steve Labaton reported that Clinton had met privately with Lewinsky in the White House shortly after Christmas, just before she denied the affair in an affidavit submitted to Paula Jones's attorneys. Linda Tripp said she had been with Lewinsky during a late-night call from the president and that she had seen the gifts they exchanged. Lewinsky claimed that Clinton had counseled her to explain her White House visits by saying she was visiting his secretary, Betty Currie, and that he suggested she leave town to avoid the deposition.

Yet to come was Lewinsky's potential testimony to Ken Starr as well as possible accounts of sexual episodes from other women and the Paula Jones trial itself. The *Washington Post*, which had initially played down the Kathleen Willey story that McCurry had tried to contain, gave her account page one headlines. The Clinton staff as well as the president and Mrs. Clinton continued what Kurtz (1998) called their "hunker-down strategy" and refused to comment on further questions about Lewinsky (p. 301). The administration decided public anger was subsiding, and they could ride out the storm. If many Americans thought Clinton was lying, he was still far more popular than his media critics wanted him to be.

Kurtz (1998) argues that this "digging in" reveals the "limits of spin." The strategy of feeding lines to the press, "browbeating" some reporters, and courting others might contain scandal damage so that bad news would be back-page news. Each time the Clinton administration did so, by shifting explanations and manufacturing or leaking information to redirect the public's focus, it paid the price of creating a more and more callous media (p. 302).

After the Lewinsky scandal broke, "rapprochement" between Hillary and Bill Clinton "took awhile." "The estrangement was not only between Bill Clinton and his wife but between the president and his most trusted adviser" (Franks, 1999, p. 170). On December 19, 1998, Hillary Rodham Clinton broke weeks of public silence and addressed reporters on the White House lawn. She said she thought the "vast majority of Americans share my approval and pride in the job that the President's been doing" and that "we in our country ought to practice reconciliation, and we ought to bring our country together." She concluded by mentioning social security, pensions, and the environment, about which she and the president were both concerned (quoted in Woodward, 1999). By the end of 1998, a majority of the public had come to agree with the First Lady about Ken Starr—"their fear of unaccountable government agents more intense than their distaste for even a lecherous, lying president" (Tumulty and Gibbs, 1999).

As the scandal festered and moved toward a trial in the Senate in January 1999, Hillary Clinton emerged as "the person fighting most fiercely in defense of the president." She had helped compile the case against Richard Nixon, the only other twentieth-century president to face impeachment, and now she was explaining to Congress with "legalistic dispassion why her husband's actions, while deplorable, were not impeachable." Congressional representative Nita Lowey said that Hillary Clinton "was very effective and certainly won him the support of the Democratic caucus" (quoted in Franks, 1999, p. 171).

IMPEACHMENT

In Ken Starr's view, with Monica Lewinsky and Bill Clinton on record before the grand jury, their firsthand testimony that there had been sex and possibly an obstruction of justice could serve as grounds for impeachment. August 31, 1998, was set as the date for the impeachment referral to Congress. The First Lady issued a public statement through her press secretary that she "believes in the President and her love for him is compassionate and steadfast, and she's very uncomfortable with her personal life being made public." Woodward (1999) notes that by this time, the media were playing the "Hillary story" second only to the details of her husband's intimate behavior with Lewinsky. "By the morning talk shows, Washington had gone crazy," and "there it was": impeachment. Isikoff (1999) recalls Sam Donaldson's statements from the White House lawn on *Good Morning America*: "If the president of the United States asked this young woman to lie under oath . . . that's a federal felony, that's a crime. And if sufficient evidence exists to really prove that, well, clearly an impeachment investigation will begin on Capitol Hill of a very serious nature" (p. 345).

After a PBS interview with Jim Lehrer, during which the president said there "is no improper relationship" with Monica Lewinsky, those in the White House press room went wild:

The White House press corps—and all the other journalists and politicos who had followed the man for years, who had watched his word games and his zigzags, his all-too-clever evasions and denials that sounded like one thing and turned out to be another—all knew right away: This thing was real. It was the Bill Clinton who didn't inhale. The Bill Clinton who forgot his draft notice. The president was not now, as we spoke, having an improper relationship. (Isikoff, 1999, p. 347)

While polls indicated that the public would be willing to "forgive Clinton the adultery," the numbers against him moved up if the president had lied and encouraged Monica Lewinsky to lie as well. A majority believed the president should be "removed from office" if he committed perjury and obstruction of justice. Isikoff (1999) notes that former Clinton consultant Dick Morris's recollection of Bill Clinton's realization that "we'll just have to win, then" and decision to "get those numbers up" as the chief strategy for managing the "Lewinsky affair, the most stunning political scandal in a quarter century" (pp. 347–349). And a chief crisis management strategist, as she had been for years, was First Lady Hillary Rodham Clinton.

While some may have viewed Mrs. Clinton's determination to remain in the political as well as marital relationship with Bill Clinton as hypocritical and flawed, others saw their marriage as no different from most others. Brock (1996) suggests that because of this perception, the Clintons survived. Americans had seen "in them the warts and blemishes that everybody has," and, after all, "we try to do good, yet we fail; we are all imperfect and need help; we all rely on spouses or lovers—this is only unsettling in politics" (Brock, 1996, p. 422). Such thinking might explain why attempts to make Hillary's and Bill Clinton's character flaws a political issue so often failed. And it may also explain why they survived such a crisis-ridden presidency. "Instead of bringing opprobrium on the Clintons," attacks on their characters made them "seem more human and approachable" (p. 422), and so acceptable. This was perhaps most evident during the final impeachment "supercrisis" of their copresidency. In September 1998 the First Lady "came out to bat publicly" when she introduced the president at a Democratic fundraiser:

None of what has been done in the last five-and-a-half years to put our country on the right track . . . could have been done without the leadership of one particular person. Day after day I've seen his determination—his unrelenting determination to do what is best for America and for the children who will inherit our country. I am proud of what he gives our country and all of us every day by his commitment. And I'm proud to introduce my husband and our president, Bill Clinton. (quoted in "Hillary Clinton" 1998)

In Isikoff's (1999) view, Kenneth Starr used the "awesome powers" of the prosecutor in ways that were "flawed from the start." For example, to "catch" the president in lies, Starr's team had compelled Monica Lewinsky's mother as well as Secret Service agents to testify before the grand jury. Lewinsky was asked the "most intimate questions" about where she was touched on what parts of her body. Although the president had "toyed" with a federal law enforcement agency, abused the "solemn powers" of his office, and invoked executive privilege for the "cheap purpose" of concealing his misconduct, there was concern over the justice of Starr's probe. His decision to support Newt Gingrich's call to release the report arguing the grounds for Clinton's impeachment, sexual details intact, was another of the special prosecutor's many bad calls. A backlash to what was perceived as a Republican-initiated unleashing of pornography and an unmitigated invasion of the First Lady's privacy developed so that "just when the public tide had seemed to be turning against Clinton, it began to ebb back the other way—and never stopped" (Isikoff, 1999, p. 353).

On October 8, 1998, the House voted 258 to 176 to hold an open-ended inquiry into the president's conduct. The November elections resulted in the GOP's stunning loss of five seats and the resignation of Newt Gingrich. The Republicans on the Judiciary Committee held brief hearings without calling any witnesses to the events in question, including Monica Lewinsky. On December 19, 1998, by a near party-line vote, the House voted two articles of impeachment of the president—one for perjury before the grand jury about his relationship with Lewinsky and another for obstruction of justice in the Jones lawsuit. President Clinton spoke at a Democratic National fund-raising dinner on January 15, 1999, which was also attended by the First Lady:

I don't even know how to talk about what I believe Hillary has meant to the success of our endeavors. She's been on every continent. She's gone to places most people in her position don't go.... And just a thousand other things.... And she has done it under circumstances I think are probably more difficult than anyone who has ever done it before. I love her for it, but our country should love her for it as well. It's been remarkable. (quoted in Woodward, 1999, p. 504)

On February 13, 1999, President William Jefferson Clinton was acquitted by the U.S. Senate. Neither of the two articles commanded a majority.

Chapter Eight

The Rhetorical Evolution of Hillary Rodham Clinton

> My relationships and my commitment to those relationships are the most important part of my life. I came to Arkansas because I loved Bill Clinton. He was a defeated politician when I married him. (Hillary Clinton quoted in Osborne, 1997, p. 18)

The United States is a media-dominated society. Both journalists and politicians realize that political events that get media attention frequently land on the political agenda. Politicians have a major advantage in controlling the content of journalistic coverage because they have an almost monopolistic hold over the "commodity the journalist needs the most—the political story itself." For example, in 1985 President Reagan visited a cemetery in Bitberg, Germany, that held the remains of Nazi storm troopers. Many journalists reported his visit as a mistake from which he would not politically recover, but Reagan "came right back," changing the topic of journalistic, and, thus public, talk by proposing an overhaul of the national income tax. The resulting growing discussion dwarfed the "Bitberg scandal," which soon became a nonissue (Press and Verburg, 1988, pp. 66–67). In short, a political actor's agenda-setting skill aids in deflecting criticism and directing the flow of electorate discourse. The progression of Hillary Rodham Clinton from political spouse to First Lady to presidential surrogate and savior is grounded in the theory and practice of that knowledge.

FIRST LADY OF ARKANSAS

Bill Clinton tended to go off "half-cocked" about the press and began blaming them for his setbacks in the fall of 1980 when the voters of Arkansas made him the youngest ex-governor in America (Kurtz, 1998, p. 69). During the 1980 reelection campaign for governor, his candidacy experienced problems. One source of voter resentment, according to Gould (1996b), was Arkansas First Lady Hillary Rodham's refusal to take Bill Clinton's name as her own. Though she did her best to skirt the issue by introducing herself as "Hillary—Governor Clinton's wife," some said that her decision not to take her husband's name cost him crucial support in the 1980 Arkansas race for governor, which he lost by less than 2 percent of the vote. Her politically risky decision to keep her birth name as the wife of a politician in a conservative southern state underscored the fact that she had independent interests to which she clung and which her husband supported. Her refusal to change her name to help Bill Clinton win reelection was perceived as evidence that she "wasn't that in touch" with the political climate and lacked an "innate feel for the Arkansas electorate" (Brock, 1996, p. 132). Clinton's loss was "a devastating experience for both of the Clintons" (p. 636).

According to Brock (1996) Hillary Rodham Clinton was "always willing to retrench tactically in the face of adversity." She has a history going back to the 1974 congressional campaign of fine-tuning and focusing her husband's political messages. After his 1980 defeat in the governor's race, she assumed responsibility for the political rehabilitation of Bill Clinton. For example, she encouraged an apology to voters for several of his unpopular "liberal" initiatives during his term as Arkansas governor. When Bill Clinton backed out of a 1981 seminar at the University of Arkansas analyzing the election returns, Hillary Rodham appeared with the newly elected governor, Frank White, and admitted how her husband's campaign had failed to pay attention to the voters of Arkansas. In a "candid analysis" that was well received by the Arkansas press, she admitted to making mistakes and not listening to "the people" (p. 136).

Hillary Clinton became her husband's watchdog, policy adviser, and problem solver, in addition to playing the roles of wife, mother, and family breadwinner. As she "picked up the pieces of Bill's career" they morphed into a symbiotic "cocandidacy" relationship that "would take them all the way to the White House" (Brock, 1996, p. 138). By the time of the early 1982 announcement of Bill Clinton's gubernatorial candidacy, Hillary Clinton and consultant Dick Morris planned televison ads to kick off the campaign that would ultimately return Clinton to the Arkansas governor's mansion. One spot portrayed the former governor as tough on crime. Hillary Clinton had wanted an apology for the first term included. And although he refused to use the word *apology*, he did "look soulfully into the camera, and say 'I learned that you can't lead without listening'" (Brock, 1996, p. 141).

Hillary Rodham became a major influence in the political comeback of her husband in 1981 and 1982. To appease her critics and protect him from their anger, she opted to become known as Hillary Clinton as he prepared to announce his reelection and also softened her image by being seen by the public in her role as mother, something she had avoided exploiting in the 1980 reelection campaign.

Surrendering to convention and seeming to subordinate her career to her husband's, the local press began to spin positively about both Mr. and Mrs. Bill Clinton. Hillary Clinton learned to become a behind-the-scenes operative during this campaign. She could be "deployed" as an effective weapon to combat her husband's critics, who "quickly found that they couldn't counter-punch a lady." Former Arkansas governor Frank White recalled a speech Hillary Clinton delivered at a parade: "She jumped all over me, said I wasn't being truthful about her husband and his record. This was a new thing in Arkansas politics. She comes in, lays waste to the opponents, and you know it's kind of difficult to get up there and let a woman have it" (quoted in Brock, 1996, p. 154).

This confrontation revealed an adeptness at turning what had been a liability—her reputation as a strong feminist—into an asset. During the first term of Bill Clinton's governorship, the image of Hillary Rodham as too ambitious and aggressive hurt his political goals. However, as Mrs. Bill Clinton, she could successfully participate in his political career. She used the Arkansas mores favoring traditionalism, over which she had previously stumbled, to combat press and public criticism (Brock, 1996). She was still outspoken and independent, but she had now become a "real wife"—a Mrs.—and so such behavior was not only accepted, it was applauded and it helped Bill Clinton become elected to a second term as governor of Arkansas. Mrs. Clinton also hired a fashion consultant to retool her personal image and "learned how to practice the politics of friendship and personality that was so much a part of the Arkansas environment" (Gould, 1996b, p. 637). Bill Clinton won the 1982 election and, after their third campaign effort and her image make-over, returned with his wife to serve again as Arkansas' First Couple.

After regaining the governor's office in 1982, Clinton came to view the press as a necessary evil and made himself extraordinarily accessible to the state capitol reporters, who generally responded in kind. However, he would often become testy when challenged at news conferences, and, according to Kurtz (1998), on a slow day, reporters might even pursue an aggressive line of questioning, figuring the governor might blow up and give them their story for the day (Kurtz, 1998).

By late 1989, after her husband's decision not to run in 1987, Hillary Clinton joined with him in looking toward the 1992 presidential campaign. She also joined with Dick Morris to remake her husband into an "electable southern centrist" (Brock, 1996, p. 234). In early 1990, *Newsweek*'s Eleanor Clift picked Clinton as one of the three rising stars of the new Democratic party, along with Virginia governor Doug Wilder and Senator Al Gore of Tennessee. However, as Clinton's star was ascending nationally, his standing in Arkansas plummeted. He faced a tough 1990 primary, and there was concern that if he ran for governor and lost, he would have no chance at ever becoming a presidential candidate.

At this point, some urged him to give up the governorship and run for president as the head of the Democratic Leadership Council, a group founded in 1985 to work for the election of moderate Democrats. However, this would have meant loss of the state party and fundraising apparatus. It was then that the Clintons considered the possibility of Hillary Rodham's running for governor of Arkansas in order to hold on to resources for a national race. According to Brock (1996), both of them were considering the idea only as a way to help him become elected president of the United States rather than to bolster her independent career. The Clintons were joined by others who thought Hillary Rodham might have a better chance at winning the Arkansas governorship. Columnist Paul Greenberg referred to them as the "Governors Clinton," while others spoke of how Bill Clinton had "overmarried' and that he was the "second-best politician in his family; the second-best speaker; the second-strongest personality" (quoted in Brock, 1996, p. 235).

However, because of discouraging polls, Bill—rather than Hillary—Clinton declared for reelection by saying he would not seek the presidency in 1992. He faced a strong challenge from Democrat Tom McRae, who headed the Winthrop Rockefeller Foundation, which had criticized Hillary Clinton's education reform package as well as other aspects of Clinton's record. Since she served on the foundation's board, she was familiar with its work. On a day when he knew Bill Clinton would be out of the state, McRae planned a mock debate to attack Clinton's record. At the beginning of the news conference, he unveiled a cartoon depicting a nude Clinton, his hands over his crotch, with the tag line: "The Emperor Has No Clothes." Hillary Rodham had anticipated McRae and relied on what Brock (1996) identifies as the same tactics she used to "knock over" Frank White in two prior governor's races. From the audience, she "suddenly shouted 'Get off it, Tom'" and then quoted from Rockefeller Foundation reports that had praised the same aspects of Bill Clinton's record that McRae was condemning. She continued: "I went through all your reports because I've really been disappointed in you as a candidate and I've been really disappointed in you as a person, Tom." McRae later said he felt "unfairly ambushed, and unable to respond sharply because of Hillary's status and gender" and because 'I wasn't running against her" (quoted in Brock, 1996, pp. 235–237). The counterattack was not successful; Hillary Clinton was reported to have overstepped "her" line and exposed the "true nature of the co-candidacy" of the Clintons. One reporter for the *Arkansas Democrat* wrote that the incident showed that Bill Clinton lacked "fire in the belly" and "steel in the spine" and accused him of sending his wife "'to do his dirty work for him" (quoted in Brock, 1996, p. 236). Still, Bill Clinton managed to win the primary, albeit with the narrowest lead since his 1982 comeback, and won reelection for his third term as governor of Arkansas.

FIRST LADY OF THE UNITED STATES

Clinching the Nomination and Changing the Image

Shortly before the October 1991 announcement of his presidential candidacy, Bill and Hillary Clinton appeared at Washington's Sperling Breakfast, named for its host, former *Christian Science Monitor* Washington bureau chief Godfrey Sperling. According to Brock (1996) these sessions were attended by "hotshot political reporters" for whom "Clinton's zipper problem was as much an open secret as Gary Hart's has been." The Clintons "carefully orchestrated" the event to give them an opportunity to dispel rumors about their private life. He spoke of their mutual love and how the relationship had not been "perfect" but that they would be together in the future, presidency or not, and concluded, "If she would run, I would gladly withdraw" (quoted in Germond and Witcover, 1994, pp. 169–170). Hillary Clinton's appearance was described as "unusual" by the *Boston Globe* and proved she would stand by her husband in the event of revelations of his extramarital affairs. In addition, her presence sent the message that it was safe to support Clinton because he would not be another Gary Hart, whose wife, Lee, had appeared "less than fully supportive" in the wake of stories about her husband's infidelity (p. 246). Had Bill Clinton appeared alone, perceptions of his marriage—and by implication his character—would not have "packed nearly the punch of the united front" (p. 252).

As Bill Clinton emerged as the leader for the Democratic presidential nomination, the press focused more keenly on Hillary Rodham Clinton, particularly her appearance, her statements, and her personal business affairs. For example, reporters discussed Mrs. Clinton's headbands in detail, until she stopped wearing them entirely (Flaherty and Flaherty, 1996, p. 168). Although Clinton was the front-runner, consultants advised him that while questions about morality matter, there were more pressing issues linked to perceptions of how "presidential" he might be. A top echelon met in April 1992, which included Clinton media consultant Frank Greer, chief strategist James Carville, and polling expert Stan Greenberg. Primary concerns included that the public felt Bill Clinton was "not real"; "for himself, not the people"; could not stand up to special interests; could not be "the candidate of change"; had ideas that were easily "discounted"; and was "privileged like the Kennedys." In addition, the "book" on Hillary Clinton was not good. She was perceived as a career woman who did not care for homemaking; outspoken, obstinate, " very intelligent, very opinionated, very sure of herself," and "overwhelmingly obsessed with power and career." In addition, Mrs. Clinton was considered "cold, harsh, defiant," with an attitude toward her husband that was "distant at best and glacial at worst." There seemed "very little softness or femininity about her." She was "all business, in charge"—the "opposite of Barbara Bush," capable of shooting "barbs that could eviscerate." In addition, the Clinton advisory team determined she was identified by the public as a woman who was "short-tempered . . . unaffectionate, and certainly did not suffer fools lightly" (King, 1996, pp. 160–161).

Their advice was for the Clintons to be "perceived as more husband and wife," which meant "in American terms" that there should be more "lovey-dovey photo opportunities." In addition: "Bill Clinton should come across as high-minded, aggressive, oriented to middle-class, a youthful agent of change who could stand up to special-interest groups. Hillary should come across as a serious-minded but fun-to-be-with woman, a person dedicated to her family as well as to her professional goals" (p. 161). King (1996) suggests that the basic goal was to replace the distorted images with more accurate ones that would be more appealing to the voters. For example, Bill Clinton's "untrustworthiness—the worst aspect of all," could be replaced by a presentation of the candidate as "a human being who struggled, pulled his weight, showed strength of character and fought for change" (p. 161).

And since Hillary Clinton, in particular, contributed to a "remarkably distorted" view of their marriage and family, both needed to talk more about their own family, including daughter Chelsea, as well as their affection for each other. She had to "look less as if she were in the race for herself, less as if she were strictly 'going for the power,' and less like a wife intent on 'running the [whole] show'" (King, 1996, p. 162). A detailed memo produced by Clinton's media advisory team and spelling out specific image-retooling suggestions reached both Clintons soon after it was drafted. They both followed its basic suggestions, and "soon the force of the memo began to manifest itself in their images" (King, 1996, p. 162). By July 1992, a *USA Today*–CNN Gallup Poll showed that 45 percent of the voters had a favorable opinion of Hillary Clinton. This was considerably up from the 36 percent rate in April, just before the interim report came out and the Clintons began reframing their images (King, 1996): "It was obvious to insiders that Hillary was having direct influence on the selection of those who would surround her husband at the White House. It was also obvious that she had almost as much say as he did. . . . However, only once in a while did her power become visible to the public eye" (p. 182).

Once the nomination was locked up, Hillary Clinton began another transformation, repeating a pattern from the 1982 Arkansas campaign, where the "tough," "aggressive," and "power hungry" woman emerged as a "kinder, gentler" wife, complete with physical makeover (Flaherty and Flaherty, 1996, p. 166). The "new" Hillary was on display, and the media were happy to facilitate her reintroduction to the voters (Flaherty and Flaherty, 1996). Although she adopted a lower public profile after Bill Clinton's 1992 nomination, Hillary Rodham Clinton's influence behind the scenes remained a powerful force (Flaherty and Flaherty, 1996).

After Bill Clinton received the Democratic nomination, the Republicans stepped up their criticism of his wife. Before the Republican convention, newspapers reported Republican charges that Mrs. Clinton had "likened marriage and the family to slavery" and had referred to the family as a "dependency relationship that deprives people of their rights" (quoted in Gould, 1996b, p. 640). At the convention, Patrick Buchanan told the delegates that she practiced "radical feminism" and believed "that twenty-year olds should have the right to sue their parents" and "has compared marriage and the family as institutions to slavery—and life on an Indian reservation" (quoted in Gould, 1996b, p. 640).

The strategy of attacking Mrs. Clinton backfired because voters who disliked her were inclined to support the Bush-Quayle ticket anyway and the undecideds, particularly women, reacted negatively to the attacks. She proved herself an adroit and effective politician who quickly recovered from mistakes made on the national stage. Hillary Clinton may have taken a page from her husband's campaign manual and "comeback kid" success during Campaign '92 as she enacted her role. In an almost literal sense, she became perceived by the American people as a part of—if not, in the end, the embodiment of—her husband's character. By cutting her losses and executing the "right" public gestures to remedy whatever the media or her critics spun into mistakes, Hillary Clinton "built up an abundant reservoir of goodwill with the voters on which she would draw when she became First Lady" (Gould, 1996b, p. 641).

Even after the election, the Clintons remained vigilant in attending to public perception and media framing of their respective roles. "Bill Clinton was all visibility; Hillary was still all invisibility," in part because the Clinton staff was not sure of the electorate's evaluation of Mrs. Clinton or her role as "probably the most influential of the transition group" into the new presidency. In her first days in the White House, she captured the national media who envisioned her a superwoman—wife, mother, lawyer, moral exemplar. There was even talk of her succeeding Bill Clinton in office (Flaherty and Flaherty, 1996).

After the Election

After the 1994 failure of the Clinton administration's health care program, she remained more or less out of the public eye, reemerging in a "slow and carefully orchestrated" appearance as "Traditional First Lady" (Flaherty and Flaherty, 1996, p. 210). The backlash plan and her role in it encouraged Mrs. Clinton to enact a lower-profile public persona as the 1994 congressional elections drew near. By this time, criticism of the First Lady had crossed the accepted boundaries of political attacks on the wife of a president. For example, Gould (1996b) recalls the burning of her effigy at a pro-tobacco rally in Kentucky in August 1994. During a speech delivered at the University of Arkansas in Fayetteville, she commented on her critics:

Stand up against the easy answers, the stereotypes, the labels. You know the kind of thing I'm talking about: If you're under twenty-five, you're an apathetic generation X-er. If you're over forty, you're a self-indulgent baby boomer. If you're a liberal, you're a bleeding heart. If you're a conservative, you have no heart. If you're a Democratic president from Arkansas, you're accused of being all of the above. And if you're the wife of a Democratic president from Arkansas, you have to worry about your hair a lot. (Hillary Clinton quoted in Osborne, 1997, p. 84)

Until 1980, when Bill Clinton had been defeated in his reelection bid for Arkansas governor, the Clintons had been a two-career family, and Hillary Rodham had paid little attention to his political career. After the defeat that year, Hillary Clinton took control and shepherded her husband's career until 1994, when her health care reform proposal was defeated in Congress and the Democrats lost midterm elections. At that point, in November 1994, she was damaged goods because "as the family lawyer and investor she had screwed up Whitewater, and then . . . health care reform." Bill Clinton's re-election was not guaranteed, and so he "in effect, fired her or she fired herself" (Woodward, 1999, p. 34). The Democratic congressional losses essentially guaranteed a heating up of the Whitewater issue as well as defensiveness on the part of the Clinton administration for the remaining years of the president's term. By this time, Mrs. Clinton was publicly less visible and began to model herself on more traditional, albeit activist, First Ladies such as Lady Bird Johnson and Rosalynn Carter: she would be an advocate for specific causes rather than adviser for presidential policy. In the aftermath of the failed health care reform initiative and the devastating midterm election for Democrats in December 1994, Hillary Rodham Clinton retooled her public persona to that of spokesperson for the welfare of women and children, a long-time personal interest. She also "vanished" from the West Wing and sent her chief of staff at the time, Maggie Williams, to meetings. The First Lady became the covert campaigner, keeping the national media off her plane as she stumped from city to city. Save for her star turn at the Democratic convention, Hillary Rodham Clinton "hovered below radar" (Gibbs and Duffy, 1996).

Gould (1996b) comments on the diversity of the judgments about Hillary Clinton's skill as a political figure and the nature of her influence on the Clinton presidency at this time. Some journalists gave her credit for intelligence and analysis skills, while others contrasted her husband's "intuitive mastery" of political matters with her "tendency to hold grudges" yet occupy the moral high ground. And while her remarks occasionally required "tactical retreats," by January 1995, she was still a "formidable presence" in the White House (p. 647).

She traveled extensively in campaigning for international human and women's rights. At this point Hillary Clinton presented a softer side when she began writing a newspaper column that combined advocacy of issue positions with stories of life in the White House. Her column, "Talking It Over," channeled her views directly to Americans, something only Eleanor Roosevelt had previously attempted. It debuted in over 150 newspapers. In addition, Hillary Clinton wrote a book on parenting, *It Takes a Village: And Other Lessons Children Teach Us*. By September 1995, after presenting a ringing endorsement of women's rights at the United Nations Conference on Women in Beijing, she was becoming "immensely popular" abroad, and her domestic popularity was increasing as well. In October, she traveled to South America for still more meetings and speeches on the role of women in developing nations.

The tacit influence of Hillary Clinton on her husband was evident during the State of the Union message on January 24, 1995. The eighty-minute address was a surprise to almost everyone. Only three hours before the television lights went on, White House chief of staff Leon Panneta had told selected reporters that the speech would be forty minutes long and the greatest emphasis would be on programs to discourage teenage pregnancy. He did not know that the president and Hillary Rodham Clinton worked alone together to add forty more minutes of material, which eliminated the pregnancy section. According to Reeves, the last-minute changes should "not have been a shock in the Clinton White House, where every one of the thousand staff members seemed to have the power to say 'No' but only two people, the president and his wife, had the power to say 'Yes'" (1996, p. 12). Reeves also recalled that Hillary Clinton influenced her husband's decision to go "south on his 'lift and strike'" policy in the early days of the civil war in Bosnia and that "it was not the first time nor the last that a Clinton decision made downstairs was reversed when he went upstairs" (p. 92).

Her staff announced that the First Lady would concentrate on expanding opportunities for women and children. In March 1995, she addressed conferences on women's issues in New York and Copenhagen and wrote several articles on issues relating to children and women as well. She also traveled with her daughter, Chelsea, on a twelve-day tour of Asia. One newspaper story at the time headlined "Hillary Clinton a Traditional First Lady Now" and predicted that the First Lady "doubtless will have to continue to walk a fine line between pretending she wields no influence and being seen as too powerful" (quoted in Gould, 1996b, p. 647). Brock (1996) considers Hillary Rodham Clinton to be either a "'soft' revolutionary" or an "'establishment' radical" whose politics have been colored by the religious moralism of the Christian left but who also clearly recognizes the political advantages of emphasizing conservative cultural themes, as evidenced in the post-1994 repositioning of Bill Clinton as a "centrist conservative" as well as in her book *It Takes a Village* (p. 413). Hillary Clinton, in this view, has been "nothing if not up-front" about what she stands for, but the "mainstream press" failed in reporting on her "real views" as well as in explaining the extent to which the First Lady was the "ideological engine" driving the Clintons' co-candidacy" (p. 414) and, eventually, their "copresidency."

By the time of the January 1996 publication of *It Takes a Village*, undertaken "to promote the First Lady's image as a strong advocate for children and keep a high profile on a safe issue," Whitewater and Travelgate were beginning to emerge as the mediated scandals of choice. In addition, both the press and Senate investigating committee "jumped on" these "crises" and Hillary Clinton was subpoenaed to appear before a grand jury in connection with the Madison Guaranty case. According to a January 1996 *USA Today* poll, she received her lowest favorable rating ever, at 43 percent (cited in Burrell, 1997, p. 12), while only 25 percent of a national sample thought she was telling the truth about Whitewater and most of the American public thought she was lying about her role in the Travelgate firings (p. 33). Due in part to backlash against "her" health care plan and other crises linked to the Clinton White House, most notably Whitewater, the Republicans had gained control of both houses of Congress for the first time in decades. By May 1995, the Senate voted ninety-six to three to convene hearings into Whitewater and related issues. They began in the summer of 1995 and intensified into 1996. At first the hearings attracted little public interest and cursory media coverage. However, as evidence appeared that seemed to contradict public assertions from the Clinton White House, the story began to evolve. President Clinton claimed executive privilege and attorney-client privilege, but, by late 1995 he still had approval ratings of above 50 percent. However, after the missing billing records appeared and the First Lady was called before the grand jury investigating Whitewater—the first time a First Lady had been subpoenaed in a criminal investigation—the Clintons' popularity spiraled down (Stewart, 1996).

By the 1996 Democratic National Convention, Dick Morris (who resigned from the campaign because of his involvement with a prostitute) had been brought back to the Clinton camp to refashion the president as a centrist conservative, while Hillary Clinton "went under cover, writing a fluffy syndicated column" and "staying out of the policy loop." Brock (1996) suggests the strategy worked in 1982 and worked as well in 1996. During her speech at the convention, the First Lady paid tribute to her husband and their marriage, assuming the same traditional persona that had served both of the Clintons so well during other crucial moments in their political life together: her initial *60 Minutes* appearance; the delivery of a tray of cookies after "Troopergate"; referencing "a romantic midnight swim" with her husband and "floating the idea of having another child" just prior to the 1996 election kick-off.

Whatever happens in what she calls her "zone of privacy," Richard Reeves observed in 1996 that Mrs. Clinton is the final adviser to the president—what Robert Kennedy was to his brother, the "last loyalist, the only one with no other political agenda than the rise of Bill Clinton" (p. 92). Prior to the 1996 election, Hillary Clinton moved into even more of a self-imposed isolation while she was portrayed as a broomstick-riding witch in the *American Spectator* and called a crook on talk radio throughout the country (Kurtz, 1998, p. 89). Essentially anything she said was news, particularly at the beginning of her husband's second term as president.

Would she be the policy activist of the first two years when she headed up the failed health care reform program? Would she be the more traditional First Lady of 1995 and 1996, downplaying her political influence? Would Whitewater cause her to maintain a low profile, or would Clinton's victory encourage her activism?

In a November 1996 interview, when asked, "What will your role be in the next four years?" she focused on welfare reform and said to *Newsweek*'s Martha Brant: "I want to travel around and talk to people about what is happening on the ground. I intend to speak out about it and write about it. If there's a formal role, this is how I see it" (quoted in Kurtz, 1996, p. 79).

Time's Ann Blackman interpreted these words to mean that Hillary Clinton wanted a formal role in welfare policy and wrote her story, "Reinventing Hillary," accordingly, which resulted in the White House's "going haywire over the story." The phrase *formal role* became a kind of "secret code," which signaled to the reporter a return to "behind-the-scenes power" and conjured up visions of the "health care debacle" (Kurtz, 1998, p. 80). By the time Mike McCurry, traveling with the president, arrived to brief the White House press, interest centered on the words *formal role*. McCurry told the reporters, "I'm not aware the president plans to ask her to take a 'formal role' in any area" but that she was, along with others, expected to help implement welfare reform. Still, one reporter asked, "So why is she saying she wants a formal role if there are no plans for her to have a formal role?" and "Could you explain what's going on here? It seems like you're backtracking." After further exchanges about McCurry's "sensitivity over the word 'role'" occurred in the press, rumors began to circulate that the president was unhappy with his press secretary for seeming to undercut Hillary Clinton. Kurtz (1998) says that although McCurry's strategy made sense at the time—to diffuse more rumors that the First Lady was still trying to wield power—some thought McCurry's framing of her comments made it look as if the White House was attempting to curb Hillary Clinton. Despite his efforts to spin otherwise, the story continued to "ricochet around the globe" (Kurtz, 1998, p. 81).

By 1996, it was clear that anytime Hillary Rodham Clinton said anything, she was buying herself a front-page story (Kurtz, 1998). Brock (1996) notes a "uniformly negative" perception of Hillary Clinton in the media by the end of her husband's first term of office. For example the *New York Times*'s William Safire called her a "congenital liar," and his colleague Maureen Dowd labeled her "Mommie Dearest." Other comparisons were to Leona Helmsley, Ma Barker, Eva Braun, and Louise Farrakhan. Newt Gingrich's mother said on a nationally broadcast news show that her son considered the First Lady a "bitch," and *U.S. News* cited one of Bill

Clinton's aides who called Mrs. Clinton a "dragon lady" and "the house SOB." That the First Lady might go to jail became a stock punch line of talk show host David Letterman. And radio host Don Imus aired a derisive adaptation of "The Lady Is a Tramp," a double parody in which a Rush Limbaugh character sang: "She goes to state dinners with her lesbian friends; makes big investments with high dividends / Forgets to pay taxes but then makes amends / That's why the first lady is a tramp" (quoted in Brock, 1996, pp. v–vi). Several books written at the time (1996) by authors of different political backgrounds all reached negative conclusions about the First Lady. FBI agent Gary Aldrich wrote of "Queen Hillary" as a "deranged, power-mad emasculator"; historian Roger Morris envisioned a cynical, ruthless member of a corporate oligarchy in *Partners in Crime;* and James B. Stewart's *Blood Sport* concluded that Hillary Clinton was a cheat (quoted in Brock, 1996, pp. vi–vii). That the First Lady's discourse was essentially a guarantee of front-page news coverage became an element in her management of the scandals in the Clinton administrations. These mediated images of Hillary Clinton, created from eager and incessant press coverage of her activities, became useful as rhetorical tactics for managing the crises during her husband's presidency.

Early in 1997, with new media interest in her role and Marsha Berry as a new chief spokesperson, Mrs. Clinton tentatively began abandoning her defensive posture toward the press (Kurtz, 1998). By the beginning of her husband's second term, the White House press staff wanted to "launder the news—to scrub it of dark scandal stains, remove unsightly splotches of controversy, erase greasy dabs of contradictions, and present it to the country crisp and sparkling white. The underlying garment was the same, but it was often unrecognizable" (Kurtz, 1998, pp. xiv–xx). Their challenge was to "change the subject" but to do so without the benefit of any dramatic presidential action like fighting a war, battling a recession, or tackling some national crisis. When the White House team broke through, they secured column inches and airtime for proposals on national education standards or seat-belt enforcement or funding for mammograms rather than world or national security issues. "At stake in this competing cacophony . . . was nothing less than the success of the second term, since history had demonstrated that a reelected president was at the peak of his power in the first year after his victory, when the echoes of his mandate were loudest and his impending lame-duck status least apparent" (Kurtz, 1998, p. xx). Mrs. Clinton's rhetorical presence was inextricably linked to the success of her husband's second administration, not the least of which was that it survived impeachment.

A MEDIA-SAVVY FIRST LADY

Contemporary politicians no longer passively accept everything the media serves its consumers. Like journalists, elected officials, as well as their staffs and surrogates, have, often out of necessity, evolved into calculating and careful critics of essentially everything in the print and electronic media (Press and Verburg, 1988). And like the press, politicians play for the audience, aggressively seeking favorable attention by spinning positive tales of their activities for a national audience. The first goal of politicians is to be noticed in a flattering context. In creating a positive image, political staffs stress the aspects of an elected official's character or personality to which voters may seem to respond positively. For example, Ronald Reagan, reporters were informed, worked as a lifeguard during summers in high school and cut eighteen notches in a stick for the people he saved; Gerald Ford was an All-American center at the University of Michigan, while John Kennedy and George Bush were both World War II heroes (Press and Verburg, 1988, p. 108). Certainly one symbol of President Clinton's official character was his First Lady, who became both image creator and creation during her husband's presidency.

Alger (1996) discusses the narrative device of condensational symbols, as exemplified by the flag of a nation. Although only a multicolored piece of cloth, "the meanings and emotions it condenses are strong and deep." The White House and Oval Office are condensational symbols that carry associations with "great" presidents and "great" events of the past. Words like *liberty* and *free enterprise*, with their associated ideas and emotions, also act as condensational symbols in America. *Family* is a word symbol, and faithfulness to it has high symbolic meaning as "Democratic candidates for president Gary Hart and Bill Clinton discovered the hard way." Most American politicians go to great lengths to have the tangible symbols of their spouses and other family members visible with them in campaign literature, ads and in front of TV cameras. The discursive maturation of Hillary Rodham Clinton is evidenced by her intentional service as a condensational symbol for her husband. One observer wrote at the end of Bill Clinton's first term as president that Hillary Clinton "now seems to exist almost completely in the realm of cultural mythology as a figure upon whom allies and enemies alike can project their hopes and their fears, their expectations and their disappointments" (Brock, 1996, p. vii).

This partnership carried the Clintons through over two decades of tough political tests to the White House. And while there have been other powerful couples in American politics, the Clintons were different because of the "extraordinary extent" to which Bill Clinton relied on Hillary Clinton as a condensational symbol to "balance his shortcomings and to guide his political career" (Brock, 1996, p. viii). She rhetorically positioned herself to become the flag around which President Clinton could rally. The president and his staff, as well as Mrs. Clinton herself, rhetorically morphed the First Lady into the "good wife" and a "person of integrity" who epitomized "grace under fire." She then became a focal and grounding point for developing a coherent rhetorical vision of the Clinton presidency, which included the creation of Bill Clinton as a "good husband," a "good father," and, ultimately, a "good president."

Her rhetorical skills merged with media savvy and resulted in a permanent "crisis-discursive mode" grounded in her visual and verbal narratives. In 1998, Kurtz wondered how a president so aggressively investigated on so many fronts could remain so popular with the American people. In his fifth year in office, Bill Clinton's approval ratings were almost as strong as Ronald Reagan's at the peak of his popularity. It was suggested that Clinton's performance was a media strategy of seducing, misleading, and intimidating the press: "No day went by without the president and his staff generating favorable headlines and deflecting damaging ones, to project their preferred image on the vast screen of the media establishment" (Kurtz, 1998, p. xvii). By this time, the First Lady realized she needed to work with the press because of their power over whether the Clinton administration's messages would even be received by the public. Reporters also controlled the channels through which the Clintons' political power could be extended. As a result, she developed a decidedly assertive attitude toward the media and its management: "We've had to deal with a lot of dirt and negative advertising: We've learned our lesson about how you stand up, answer your critics" (Hillary Clinton quoted in Osborne, 1997, p. 20).

Mrs. Clinton was particularly skilled in the use of television as a mediating channel, with its "infotainment" dimension and tendency to favor "style over substance" and "image over issue." This may have accounted for media events such as the carefully orchestrated "pink press conference" as well as the numerous occasions when she appeared before the camera with her husband, without publicly wavering in her literal and symbolic "stand-by-the-president-my-husband" stance.

Alger (1996) suggests that Americans favor television images and someone who uses them well more than someone who does not. They do not find televison necessarily the most trustworthy source of news but consider it the most believable. The perception of what is happening on the screen, due to the apparent reality of the moving pictures and sound, produces a believability that is not generated as strongly by the print media (Alger, 1996, p. 80). The Clintons' framing on television became a major criterion for the public's assessment of their worthiness to remain in office. Accordingly, television also became an important channel through which Hillary Clinton mediated the message she wanted the electorate to believe regarding Bill Clinton. Given the limited knowledge and the information costs that are the case with most people, the visual content of news film and other political communications on television plays a significant role in the images they develop of candidates and other political figures—images that are important elements in the public's evaluations of those figures and in their votes and other political responses (Alger, 1996, p. 81).

Mrs. Clinton's stories essentially always came back to mediated variations on the argumentative theme that Bill Clinton is a man of character—and so a good president—because "I am telling you and I know." Details became less important than her long-standing and publicly unwavering dedication. In early January 1998, the president and Mrs. Clinton, wearing bathing suits, strolled on a secluded beach that had been sealed off by the Secret Service. A French press photographer "secretly" took photos of the Clintons embracing, which appeared the next day in papers all over the United States. Isikoff (1999) suggests that although the White House officially complained about the invasion of the First Couple's privacy, the event may have been orchestrated by the Clintons to deflect from the Paula Jones lawsuit and "upcoming deposition of the president" (p. 264). The "why do you 'support' such a president/husband?" was trumped by the, "Well, you *are* still there ... even after *this*" perspective. Who better to provide characterological coherence, particularly within a rhetorical-political environment of perpetual ethos-shattering scandal (Alger, 1996) for William Jefferson Clinton than his wife and partner, Hillary Rodham Clinton?

The First Lady became her own media event and maintained—through counterframing of negative images and rhetorical construction and mediation of positive—an ultimately unimpeachable ethos for both herself and her husband—despite some occasionally cool moments with the political press. By the end of 1997, Hillary Clinton's relationship with the press was on occasion strained, and journalists were put off by her "prickly persona" and the "grating behavior of her closest aides" (Kurtz, 1998, p. 284). At one point she told her daughter Chelsea that one day "before it was over they'll attack me, they'll attack you, they'll attack your cat, they'll attack your goldfish" (Hillary Clinton quoted in Osborne, 1997, p. 72). When the *New York Times* requested an interview for the First Lady's fiftieth birthday, press secretary Mike McCurry warned she didn't "want to be laid out on a couch and psychoanalyzed." When *Time* reporter Karen Tumulty was able to question Hillary Clinton directly during a fall 1997 visit to Panama, she found the First Lady totally unwilling to answer anything "remotely personal" and was provided with responses such as, "I don't know what to make of that question" or "I don't view my life that way." In addition, questions had to be submitted in writing to staffer Marsha Berry so the First Lady could decide which could be used for on-the-record responses (quoted in Kurtz, 1998). The First Lady provided what Press and Verburg (1988) call "little dramas as political entertainment" (p. 115), which drew public attention from the president and kept the media's eyes—and so the public's as well—off "something else." According to Templin (1999) Hillary Clinton evolved into an ongoing story that extended for years as a series of media events focusing on the First Lady and related themes such as cookie baking, cattle futures, Whitewater, and the travel office dismissals.

Such events—as a First Lady in a striking "ensemble" remaining composed and devoted to a "philandering husband" as well as "innocent" of any wrongdoing herself—played off media competitiveness and took advantage of the appeal that good visuals have to national reporters. In this way, Hillary Clinton was able to deflect major negative criticism about herself as First Lady when "crises" such as Whitewater and the commodities trading issue threatened her ethos. Once these scandals were discursively managed, she was in place to both represent and reflect her embattled husband by mediating his character through her own.

FIRST LADY AS SURROGATE

Sabato (1991) contends that political actors' surrogates, particularly spouses, may—with varying degrees of success—best execute counteroffensives to the "feeding frenzies" resulting from press-initiated and pack journalist–mediated megascandal stories. This is particularly the case when an official's fidelity is under attack, as when Lee Hart and Marilyn Quayle stood by their husbands. From the outset, the Clintons knew damage control would be crucial to the 1992 presidential campaign and that Hillary Rodham would have to oversee it personally (Brock, 1996). Who better to defend a husband against allegations of infidelity than the alleged "victim"—his spouse? A quintessential example of spousal intervention as a strategy of presidential crisis and scandal management is Hillary Rodham Clinton's rhetorical mediation of the scandals in her husband's administrations.

Politicians may successfully defend their behavior and policies directly to the press if done so in a carefully managed way. Press and Verburg (1988) report that Ronald Reagan's typical response to criticism was "lighthearted and not defensive, folksy but tough and determined, and usually appealed for unity and decency." However, for Bill Clinton, with a history of tension between himself and the media beginning during his tenure as governor of Arkansas, such a crisis management technique was often not expedient, a reality that expedited the First Lady's rhetorical surrogacy. "Surrogating" became one of Hillary Rodham Clinton's successful and frequently used discursive strategies for managing the scandals during her husband's presidency. Brock (1996) alludes to the surrogated nature of the Clintons' political partnership, in place since the beginning of their personal and political lives together: "Bill is the messenger; Hillary is the author of the message" (p. 261).

Because she was not the president, but knew him best, Hillary Clinton evolved into Bill Clinton's foremost and most visible representative, stand-in, spokesperson, and, ultimately, copresident. Nelson (1993) suggests that in 1992, even if some doubted Bill Clinton's fitness for the presidency, the Flowers episode and Hillary Clinton's mediation of it increased her status, and some began to wonder "if perhaps the wrong Clinton was running for President (p. 45). Throughout the spring of 1992, the press acknowledged the Clintons' cocandidacy. *Time* headlined a story about the Clintons "Partner as Much as Wife"; *Newsweek* referenced Hillary Clinton as an "accomplished professional" who had "perhaps as much claim as her husband to a place in public life"; the *Chicago Tribune* wrote of her as "maybe the candidate's top asset"; and the *Houston Chronicle* headlined a story, "Hillary Clinton's Composure Carries Campaign Through Fire" (quoted in Brock, 1996, p. 261).

A *Time*/CNN poll asked respondents if Hillary Clinton "has what it takes to be President of the United States," and Bill Clinton began answering questions about whether he might appoint his wife to a cabinet post ("I wouldn't rule it out") and said he would ask her to study and recommend solutions to problems in areas such as education, child care, and health. He also spoke about the "cocandidacy" with his wife, saying that if he was elected president, it would be "an unprecedented partnership, far more than Franklin Roosevelt and Eleanor," and he announced the campaign slogan, "Buy one, get one free," to which Hillary Clinton added, "If you vote for my husband, you get me. It's a two-for-one, blue-plate special" (quoted in Brock, 1996, p. 261).

In Davis's (1996) view, presidents have a distinct advantage over other news makers because of their possession of both power and information. However, depending on the issue or event, other actors—who "emerge when a vacuum exists" because of the president's inability to set or control the agenda—may be in greater demand. Also, the president may be overshadowed if others are seen as having more information or expertise about a hot news story than the president. Certainly by the time of his impeachment, Bill Clinton had lost much of his power to control the agenda regarding the scandal. This situation opened the door wider to Hillary Clinton, not only to act as a surrogate for her husband but also because her role as wife of a president who was being impeached as a result of behavior connected to adultery made her a hot news story.

Candidates and other political actors may assume an above-politics posture because others are overtly campaigning for them while "they stay home being nonpolitical." For example, in 1972, Richard Nixon depended on the campaign tours of forty-nine surrogates, including members of his family, while he stayed in the White House during most of his campaign against George McGovern. Nixon was "so intent" on presenting the "illusion" of a "hardworking, nonpolitical statesman" that he rarely took a political trip or made a speech in his own behalf. Surrogacy also was prominent in Gerald Ford's 1976 presidential campaign, during which "for weeks on end" he did not leave the White House to campaign for his reelection but depended on his family, cabinet, and others while he remained at the White House acting "presidential" (Trent and Friedenberg, 1995, p. 77).

Ideally, surrogates should be competent public speakers and have some "clearly identifiable connection" to the candidate. They should also address why the candidate or politician is not present rather than trying to hide the fact and should "not hesitate to remind the audience that they are not the candidate" (p. 171). Benefits of surrogates include that, in some instances, a surrogate may be more credible for certain audiences than the candidate or government official. In addition, surrogates also have the liberty to address issues and say things the candidate or official may not wish to say. For example, in 1992 well-known public officials of Hispanic origin, such as the former Democratic mayor of San Antonio, Henry Cisneros, and Republican Secretary of the Interior Manuel Lujan, were often used by Bill Clinton and George Bush to address predominantly Hispanic audiences. Also in 1992, Bush surrogate Mary Matalin, deputy campaign manager and political director for the Bush-Quayle campaign, gave speeches and interviews suggesting that Bill Clinton was a drug user and draft dodger. And Clinton surrogate congressional representative Maxine Walters, not the candidate, called George Bush a "racist." Because surrogates are "not the candidate," they are able to make remarks that may not be "politically expedient" for the actual candidate or political actor to make (Trent and Friedenberg, 1995, p. 172).

At times President Clinton did not control his temper in public when aggressively interviewed by the media or asked questions he believed unfair. Kurtz (1998) notes how the president lashed out at ABC's Brit Hume for suggesting that politics had influenced the selection of Supreme Court justice Ruth Bader Ginsburg. And Clinton removed his microphone and abruptly ended an interview in Prague when NBC's Jim Miklaszewski asked questions about Whitewater instead of about the president's European trip. The president particularly disliked the *New York Times* for the intensity of its Whitewater coverage (p. 76). He also became frustrated by reporters' emphasis on their own agendas rather than those of his administration. In a 1993 interview with *Rolling Stone*, the president complained about not getting "one damn bit of credit" from "the knee-jerk liberal press" (quoted in Kurtz, 1998, p. 74). Clinton would keep "whining in public" about the press, which "prompted more stories about his struggling presidency" (Kurtz, 1998, p. 74). In 1994, he criticized CBS's Bill Plante and the *Washington Times*'s Paul Bedard for pressing him about the firing of the White House travel office staff. Although he later apologized, Bill Clinton's "disdain for journalists was palpable." He once said, "The press runs the government" and "likes to destroy people" (quoted in Kurtz, 1998, p. 75). His animosity toward the press was also reinforced by what Clinton considered scandal-focused media treatment of his wife (Kurtz, 1998).

During a prebriefing before President Clinton met the press with Mexico leader Ernesto Zedillo in Mexico City in 1997, one staff member mentioned a front-page story in the *Washington Times* by the paper's top Whitewater investigator, Jerry Seper. The reporter had discovered some previously sealed court records in which Ken Starr called Hillary Clinton a "central figure" in the probe and accused her of changing sworn testimony. The president gave his suggested answer, becoming defensive. Kurtz (1998) writes that one of the unspoken reasons for prebriefs was to give the president a chance to vent anger so he would not fly off the handle during televised press conferences. After he vented, his aides would coach the president to "take the emotion out of his response, to strip it to its factual essentials" (p. 197).

In Reeves's (1996) view, Republican "tough guys" ultimately learned what the press had known since Hillary and Bill Clinton initially entered politics: beating up Bill Clinton is something like punching a pillow. When things look bad, he "gives himself over to handlers"—staff members who "try to get him out of rooms or towns before he says too much, too soon" (pp. 104–105). Principal among these handlers are surrogates. Surrogacy, or letting another "do the talking," is a crisis management option for politicians wary of "getting into more trouble" through misstatement, lying, ignorance of details, or loss of temper.

There were several surrogates in the Clinton White House, including press secretary Mike McCurry and deputy communications director Ann Lewis. When the *News Hour* with Jim Lehrer asked for a Clinton spokesperson to address the DNC fundraising scandal, the White House sent Lewis—a woman with an almost grandmotherly ethos. With gray hair, old-fashioned glasses, a string of pearls, and a smile, she "looked like everyone's favorite fifth-grade teacher" and could sound "sweet and reasonable" regardless of whatever message she was spinning (Kurtz, 1998, p. 143). Lewis, with thirty years of experience as a Democratic activist and Clinton's 1996 campaign communications director, was adept at television performing. Before becoming an official staff member, she had gone on the talk show circuit defending Hillary Clinton when Whitewater first became an issue. Lewis was "on" always and never wavered in public regarding support for the president and refused to frame politics as sports but as issues about lives. When cornered by a reporter, Lewis would "just smile sweetly and recite her script in a tone that made it sound like she was correcting your homework" (Kurtz, 1998, p. 145).

Another successful Clinton surrogate and damage controller was John Podesta, staff secretary during Bill Clinton's first administration. According to Kurtz (1998) Podesta depended on a "pain management" metaphor for crisis management: the White House could tolerate only a certain amount of pain at any given time. Bad stories had to be "bled" off the front page and evening news. One negative story might be a headache, but a series of damaging pieces was akin to chemotherapy. Unless the cell count was rebuilt, the patient would die. Medicine would eventually help, but only after strength had returned (p. 145). Podesta gathered documents, fielded reporters' inquiries during the early days of Whitewater, and helped Hillary Clinton prepare for her "pink press conference." He also internally investigated Travelgate, testified before a grand jury, and disclosed that the Clinton's owed back taxes on their 1980 return. He was also, as well as a full-disclosure advocate, a rhetorically strong attorney who, when criticized by the *Washington Post*'s Richard Cohen, replied, "I have to publicly eat my mistakes. I hope you acknowledge yours" (quoted in Kurtz, 1998, p. 145).

One of the most important and successful surrogates for Bill Clinton was his First Lady, who had herself benefited from others' surrogacy on her behalf. Clinton's second administration was staffed by many who had grown up considering Richard Nixon a criminal brought down by right-minded investigators and journalists. Hillary Clinton had been an attorney for the House Judiciary Committee that had brought the articles of impeachment. Kurtz (1998) points out the irony of how, two decades later, the First Lady and the president were forced into many of the same defensive tactics Nixon's team used in response to the investigative machinery that was in part Hillary Rodham Clinton's and "Watergate's greatest legacy" (p. 285). Like Nixon, Clinton and his surrogates invoked attorney-client privilege; dragged their feet on subpoenas; blamed a hostile press for many of their problems; refused to answer questions or provided only partial or, on occasion, misleading replies; and attacked the special prosecutor who was investigating them. In addition, they failed to turn over embarrassing tapes; complained that Congress was unfairly exploiting the scandal for partisan gain; denied accusations of hush money; argued that everyone did what they were accused of doing; said most Americans just did not care about the scandal; and relied on junkets abroad to deflect public and media attention (Kurtz, 1998, pp. 285–286).

A savvy president's surrogate, such as the First Lady, can turn the media-politics relationship to her advantage by providing an attractive, upbeat, positive, television-friendly, and generally spinnable tale for the press. Cater (1956) referred to reporters' becoming part of the political process as "government by publicity." Publicity seeking and governing often complement and reinforce each other in the United States. Media strategies become increasingly useful means for political actors to pursue governance and become an increasing focus of their attention and activities (Cook, 1998). When policy requires the agreement of others, media strategies have become more useful for persuading others to act as face-to-face communication becomes more difficult with the growth of government. By appealing to the media, one can attempt to indicate one's preferences, respond to ongoing events, and attempt to persuade en masse about the "correctness of one's stance" (Cook, 1998, p. 125).

The presidency is particularly representative of this symbiosis. The presidency is personified by one individual who becomes a "recognizable protagonist, whose tribulations and triumphs" provide continuing material for news. The assumption that an American president is the leader of the free world also influences reporters who gravitate toward presidents and their activities as news items. Conversely, presidents enable reporters by rhetorical presentations, staging news events dramatically and colorfully (Cook, 1998). It follows that a president's power in Washington is partially dependent on a favorable evaluation from the public because Congress and other policymakers will be less likely to challenge a president who is popular (Miller and Krosnick, 1997, p. 271). Therefore, the president's chances of being re-elected and/or carrying out an agenda are in part determined by popularity, which itself is in part determined by whether the press mediates a favorable image of the president.

This media advantage may well extend to surrogates of the president, including Bill Clinton's "copresident," the First Lady. Hillary Clinton's challenge in countering deleterious press coverage of her husband's scandals was to reframe the negative pictures of Bill Clinton placed in America's mind by the media. By the time of the Lewinsky scandal, Hillary Clinton had become adept at rhetorically positioning herself as a major player in government by publicity, whereby she—rather than her husband—became The Story. Her most important task then became not only maintaining media attention on herself at least as much as on her husband, but also sustaining that attention in a positive manner.

In short, Mrs. Clinton's chief rhetorical strategy for managing the scandals in Bill Clinton's administrations was to take advantage of the press by joining with them in creating good stories about herself and her role as First Lady, wife, mother, and woman that were more interesting to—and so more attended to by—the press, and therefore the public, than were the narratives about her husband. Particularly after 1996 and the megascandals such as Paula Jones began to headline press coverage, the First Lady began identifying Bill Clinton by his status as her spouse rather than that of "The President" (Clinton, 1997b). Frequently her stories would detail events or statements or actions directly connected with the president, as when she paraphrased, "my husband," who "often says [the United States is an] indispensable nation," during a 1997 commencement address the First Lady delivered at Ohio University (Clinton, 1997a). She may have taken a page from her husband's campaign manual and "comeback kid" success during Campaign '92 as she enacted her role as First Lady and chief surrogate for President William Jefferson Clinton during each scandal drama of his administration. In an almost literal sense, she became perceived by the American people as a part of—if not, in the end, the embodiment of—her husband's character. McGrory (1998) describes Hillary Clinton as the "perfect surrogate" who "brought White House glamour to the provinces without any of the president's scandal baggage." In the earlier scandals, she had "only" to continue the effort until the next "occurrence" took precedent over whatever negative story was spinning about the Clinton administration, whether or not it included her directly. The Lewinsky scandal was different only by degree, in that if Hillary Clinton's story had not been more appealing than that of her husband, the Clinton administration, and all that entails, would have ended in impeachment.

The Clintons were probably also aware of the public's ambivalence about their copresidency, recalling Sally Quinn's advice that "if a First Lady is running the White House, nobody ought to know about it but her husband" (quoted in Brock, 1996, p. 383). King (1996) comments on speculation about "whether Hillary or Bill was the managing partner of the Clintons" and quotes Arkansas Education Association president Sidney Johnson, who "always considered Bill and Hillary as one working unit" (p. 186). However, as in Arkansas in the 1980s, Hillary and Bill Clinton learned that much of the American public was not ready to accept a feminist First Lady in a "two-for-one" political partnership with her husband.

Throughout the late winter and early spring of 1992, Hillary Clinton's public ratings began to slip. When an April 1992 Gallup Poll asked whether voters approved of her taking a "major position" in the Clinton administration, 67 percent said no. More people also rated her unfavorably than favorably. In a *Time*/CNN poll, among those who said their presidential vote would be affected by their views of Hillary Rodham Clinton, almost twice as many respondents said they would vote against Bill Clinton as for him based on their opinion of his wife (cited in Brock, 1996, p. 263). In Brock's (1996) view, the unprecedented copresidency offer, as well as the "assertive and strong-minded" woman that Hillary Rodham Clinton appeared to be, threw many Americans off base (p. 263).

Still, their partnership became the primary rhetorical strategy throughout the Clintons' terms as First Couple. The co-presidency empowered Hillary Clinton to deflect attention away from her husband to herself and pull particularly negative media attention—and the public eye as well—to herself. The *New York Times*'s Karl Meyer editorialized about Hillary Clinton's enactment of First Lady:

Her more formal role is less a radical break than a logical evolution of earlier developments in a society where women are seen as partners and coworkers, not simply homemakers. Moving her office to the West Wing formalized that change in status. The argument that she was not elected is only half true, since she was clearly as much a running mate as Al Gore. Did anyone doubt that she would play a policy role? Need anyone really mind? (quoted in King, 1996, p. 194)

Hillary Clinton relied on priming—the ability of the news media to determine for the public what issue or accomplishment or occurrence in an administration becomes a standard by which to judge a president—to make herself the issue and thus the standard by which, most significantly during the impeachment proceedings, Americans judged President Clinton. Furthermore, the First Lady saw to it that images caught by the press were framed in the most positive manner she could construct. This tactic was taken advantage of in October 1998, when Democrats were faced with a problem they identified as "the clutter": President Clinton himself was useless to them as a campaigner and only the First Lady remained as "the one politician in the country who would not be interrupted with questions about the scandal." Tumulty and Gibbs (1999) describe what happened in "the miraculous month of October":

While her husband made peace in the Middle East, the markets rebounded and John Glenn lifted off, Hillary barnstormed the country. Voters heard her on their car radios when they left work in the morning and on their answering machines when they came home. The last week of the campaign saw her hitting nine states, with two stops each in Florida and New York.

The results of this First Lady's surrogacy during Campaign '98 included Tom Vilsack's "surprise win" that made him the first Democrat to be elected Iowa's governor in thirty years. By covering some issues and ignoring others, Mrs. Clinton used her First Surrogate status in a variety of situations, enacted through several strategies, to polarize press coverage rhetorically into a framing mode of either praising or blaming the First Lady. Either way, she was successful in discursively deflecting media attention from her husband.

Chapter Nine

Rhetorical Strategies of Hillary Rodham Clinton

I'm a Rorschach test. (Hillary Clinton quoted in Osborne, 1997, p. 80)

The White House works to create an image of the president that supports that office's policy objectives and creates a reservoir of political capital or popular support as well. The First Family has been used to demonstrate a president's compassion and home life. Traditional First Lady involvement with noncontroversial causes such as Barbara Bush's work on adult illiteracy aids the image of the president as a concerned individual. The Clintons' First Family broke with tradition, particularly in the case of Hillary Rodham Clinton, who adopted policy roles, headed a task force on health care reform, testified before congressional committees, and directly lobbied members of Congress. Davis (1996) suggests that Mrs. Clinton's enactment of the First Lady's political role was a gamble because "a spouse so much in the forefront on public policy does not serve the traditional role of 'softening the presidential image'" and may become a lightning rod for critics, thus creating problems for her husband's administration (p. 222). Benz (1996) argues that Hillary Clinton was one of the most "hotly debated" subjects in the 1992 presidential campaign. The media focused on the "battle of insults, images, and 'values' that she symbolized." A 1996 *Time* report commented that the First Lady as "the human being on whom the Commander in Chief most relies is, incredibly, at or near the center of Whitewater, the Travel Office purge, the health-care task force lawsuit and, because of its tangential link to Travelgate, the FBI file scandal." The article concluded that the First Lady was "at once Bill Clinton's best asset and his worst liability" (Gibbs and Duffy, 1996).

THE SCAPEGOATING STRATEGY

At the 1992 Republican National Convention, attacks against Hillary Clinton reached a fever pitch when she was derided as a "radical feminist," "antifamily," and too influential in her husband's career. In addition, her role—one of the most "charged issues in the 'cultural war' declared by the Republicans"—was created in great part by the media (Benz, 1996, pp. 112–113). At the beginning of the convention, an opening speech unleashed a "scathing denunciation" of the Clintons. RNC chair Rich Bond criticized Bill Clinton for taking advice from "a wife" who compared "marriage and the family to slavery." His was a continuation of the Republicans' "family values" theme struck earlier in Dan Quayle's remarks about the sit-com *Murphy Brown*. Bond continued by referencing Bill Clinton as "Slick Willie" and Hillary Clinton as "that champion of the family who believes kids should be able to sue their parents rather than help with the chores as they are asked to do," playing off an article she had written about children and the law (quoted in King, 1996, p. 175). Pat Buchanan continued the theme when he said that "Hillary believes that twelve-year olds should have the right to sue their parents, and Hillary has compared marriage and the family as institutions to slavery—and life on an Indian reservation" and labeled her actions "radical feminism" (quoted in King, 1996, p. 175).

The Republican attacks on Mrs. Clinton did not rejuvenate the Bush campaign by blaming her for the Democrats'—as well as her husband's—flaws. Conversely, polls began showing that a majority of working women were defending her and were offended by the RNC, and they began deserting the Republican ticket in greater numbers than men, going over to the Democrats (King, 1996, p. 176). By Election Day 1992, the negatives of the Clintons had largely been erased or replaced, and Bill Clinton was elected president of the United States. Hence, the "lightning rod" effect is not always negative, particularly if the negative "energy"—or publicity in the case of the presidency—is deflected from the president to someone else. This scapegoating function was useful to Hillary Rodham Clinton, and she used it. By the end of Bill Clinton's first term of office, his wife's credibility, reputation, and political effectiveness "all but ruined," the president remained "strangely . . . unscathed by the scandalous revelations" and was favored to win reelection. Polls revealed her negatives had "soared to new heights," with "almost half the public considering Hillary Rodham Clinton to be a liar, while his had risen in almost direct proportion." Both Bob Dole and George Bush attacked the First Lady at the 1996 Republican convention, while a *New York Times* story suggested that the Clinton White House was spinning attacks on the First Lady to the president's advantage (Brock, 1996, p. viii).

Burke (1969a) in *A Grammar of Motives* describes the scapegoat as "'charismatic,' a vicar" and

> profoundly consubstantial with those who, looking upon it as a chosen vessel, would ritualistically cleanse themselves by loading the burden of their own iniquities upon it. Thus the scapegoat represents the principle of division in that its persecutors would alienate from themselves to it their own uncleanlinesses. . . . In representing *their* iniquities, it performs the role of vicarious atonement (that is, unification, or merger, granted to those who have alienated their iniquities upon it, and so may be purified though its suffering). (p. 406)

Therefore, scapegoating involves "an original state of merger" in which two "bodies" are united, "a principle of division" in which the shared elements are "ritualistically alienated," and a "new principle of merger . . . in the unification of those whose purified identity is defined in dialectical opposition to the sacrificial offering" (p. 406). Criminals, for example, serve as scapegoats in a society that "purifies itself" via "moral indignation" through condemning them (p. 408).

There is precedent in the modern presidency for scapegoating. Sabato (1991) suggests that while voter concern about vice-presidential candidate Dan Quayle might have cost George Bush enough votes to deny the GOP ticket a popular vote landslide, Quayle may have nonetheless helped George Bush by serving as a conduit for Democratic and press criticism. Bush's campaign manager, Lee Atwater, believed that if the Republican's opponents had spent as much time "trying to develop some real issues instead of going on a rabbit chase after Dan Quayle, they might have drawn blood" and defeated Bush in the 1988 presidential election (quoted in Sabato, 1991, p. 206).

The news media also may have been spooked by the expressions of public hostility generated by their incessant criticism of Dan Quayle, which may have aided the Republicans later. For example, after Quayle's "mechanical, remarkably poor performance" in the October vice-presidential debate in Omaha—"indelibly remembered" because of Democrat Lloyd Bentsen's "You're no Jack Kennedy" remark—television news commentators "tumbled over one another to declare Quayle's showing a fine one" (Boot, 1989).

The negative framing of Hillary Clinton as the "bad cop" in the Clinton political team began during the bitter political campaign of Republican Frank White in his comeback attempt during the 1986 Arkansas gubernatorial race. White opted to run the campaign against Hillary rather than Bill Clinton, who was perceived as invulnerable to political attack because of his wife's successful education reform act. Pundits generally admitted that White could not beat Bill Clinton so, according to Darrell Glascock, White's campaign consultant, "the theory behind the [anti-Hillary Clinton] campaign was to finally expose what everybody on the inside already knew was going on in Arkansas for years." Glascock claims he was the first to use the term "Billary" in 1986, as a "joke" on his home answering machine which gained national attention after "it got in the papers and then everybody started calling to hear the message"(quoted in Brock, 1996, p. 185).

When White's pledge to reexamine Hillary Clinton's education standards failed, he began to look at her legal practice and the Clintons' finances. White first argued that when he was governor, his wife was "a fulltime First Lady" who had not held a paying job. Commercials followed, including one that chronicled the list of the Arkansas Development Financial Authority bond deals during Bill Clinton's term of office as governor in which his wife's law firm was either the bond attorney or the attorney for the issuer. White was trying to demonstrate to the people of Arkansas that the firm had some link with every bond deal since ADFA was founded and then posed the question of why, followed by "a shot of the Rose firm and the words, "This is where Hillary Clinton works," an image of the governor's mansion, and the statement, "This is where Hillary Clinton lives. Power corrupts. Absolute power corrupts absolutely" (cited in Brock, 1996, p. 185). In truth, Rose did not have a piece of every bond issue; it was counsel on six of twenty. And while Rose's state bond work did increase after Hillary Clinton joined the firm, this coincided with a major increase in overall bond activity in the state during the period. The ad also "grossly" inflated the dollar amount of her earnings from the bond business, claiming that Hillary Clinton made $500,000, or about three times what the entire firm took in from seven years of business. Hillary Clinton delivered a detailed rebuttal in which she also challenged White to disclose his own returns and reveal earnings from his state business while employed in an investment firm, which he refused to do (Brock, 1996).

Particularly in the earlier crises such as the failed health care plan, Hillary Clinton deflected media attention from the president through scapegoating and the enactment of the good cop–bad cop routine. In her analysis of political cartoons, Templin (1999) suggests that Hillary Clinton was a "convenient symbol for much that conservatives loathe." As such, the

First Lady acted as a "site" for discussion of what family values were not about as well as a "stick to beat feminism and to scapegoat feminism for various ills of the modern world" (p. 32). Brock (1996) considers the Clintons' copresidency crisis management mode a major scandal management technique. Hillary Clinton's political role mandated that since her husband did not have "a Haldeman" to play "bad cop"—as had Richard Nixon—"the task might fall to Hillary." A pattern developed whereby President Clinton "distanced himself" from the "brewing scandal" by leaving the details to his wife. In so doing he escaped responsibility for many of the crises. Part of the tactic was for the First Lady to become "stigmatized and scapegoated" (p. 373), which took the heat away from her husband, the president. For example, as "the Clinton in charge of damage control" during Whitewater as well as Travelgate, it was clear that any obstruction of justice charge would target the First Lady and, in Brock's (1996) view, prove that the "ultimate meaning of 'two-for-one' might well be that one pays for the crimes of two" (p. 411).

THE FATIGUE FACTOR STRATEGY

That Hillary Clinton, as well as other surrogates and staffers in her husband's administration, held on and stayed the course throughout various scandals in the Clinton presidency may also have been a basic crisis management tactic. Kurtz (1998) speaks of the "fatigue factor" setting in when the media realize the public is no longer as hungry for scandal as before and so spin neither as rapidly nor as long as "before" (p. 186). The public dulls to repeated scandal mongering and tunes out allegations as "just another form of politics." Clinton adviser Paul Begala and others in the Clinton camp acted on the premise that most Americans didn't care about a president's "sexual peccadilloes" or other media-fanned scandals and that the old journalistic rules—that you didn't report that "someone was drunk or gay or a skirt-chaser unless it affected his public performance"—made sense (Kurtz, 1998, p. 247). According to this view, most scandals played to the electorate only as long as they were played up by the press. And even then, eventually most Americans would probably become bored by the constant reiteration of the same story, albeit with different headlines and in different outlets. The First Lady employed this tactic when she strategically enacted her "stand-by-my-man" persona throughout essentially all of the scandals. Whether she was wife, mother, First Lady, or "wronged woman," Hillary Clinton's public character was buttressed by her unwavering support of Bill Clinton, during and after each media frenzy.

For example, her Whitewater management strategy included running out the clock. By early fall 1996, Bill Clinton was on his way to reelection (Brock, 1996). And even if another crisis was impending, each lull before the next scandal created rhetorical spaces that she and other surrogates, as well as the president, could fill up with their own stories. When the DNC scandal eased, albeit temporarily, because of the fatigue factor, Clinton press secretary Mike McCurry began advising President Clinton to make announcements and proposals "as fast as his staff could churn them out." McCurry would then selectively leak them. He would give the wires and radio reporters material to use after midnight, saying the president would do a certain thing that day. When President Clinton planned to ask the Federal Communications Commission to crack down on televised liquor ads, the story was leaked to the *New York Times*. When he moved to force states to tighten seat belt enforcement, the story was passed to an AP reporter. When the president opted to require the federal bureaucracy to hire 10,000 welfare recipients, the advance word broke on the *Washington Post*'s front page. Clinton was cracking down on foreign sweatshops, expanding family leave, wiring schools for the Internet, and banning chemical weapons. Kurtz (1998) writes that "even when he hadn't decided what to do, his musings became news." The White House was turning itself into C-SPAN; "plain old talk," if packaged properly, "could pass for news" (p. 190).

The technique of dismissing damaging stories relating to the Democratic National Committee's fundraising as "old news" was highly effective. Mike McCurry downplayed a *New York Times* front-page article, based on a leaked White House memo, by stating that President Clinton had personally requested a list of potential contributors to call in an effort to raise $1 million in early 1990. Despite media focus on the scandal, other events in the country contributed to Americans' downplaying of such pieces. The Dow was past 8000, and the deficit was dropping. The Senate hearings were moving on to interrogate Haley Barbour about a Hong Kong benefactor, and the president had the upper hand in the debate with Republicans over how much tax relief should go to middle-class families. In addition, Republican in-house fighting was increasing as Speaker Newt Gingrich was caught in an aborted coup to remove him from power. In late July, Clinton and the Republicans reached agreement on tax cuts, a balanced budget, and an entitlement program that extended health coverage to uninsured children.

The first solid evidence in the Senate hearings that Charlie Trie, Clinton's friend and Little Rock restaurateur, bypassed campaign laws was overshadowed in the media by reporters' focus on IRA eligibility, college tax credits, and capital gains reductions. The *Washington Post* ran the Trie story in the top left-hand column, but filled much of the other five columns with three separate stories about the budget deal. *USA Today* didn't give front-page space to the story. And while the "big papers were running outraged editorials demanding campaign finance reform," no one else seemed to care (Kurtz, 1998, p. 241). President Clinton's communication staff had successfully ensured that his was the loudest voice in Washington.

Taking advantage of the fatigue factor allowed Hillary Clinton to frame herself as a woman of character, if not courage, and simultaneously rely on that ethos to fill up the space temporarily emptied of scandal stories with her own mediated realities of Bill Clinton and his presidency. For example, the networks were in full force at a White House conference on early childhood development; *Newsweek* published a special issue on the topic, including an article by Hillary Clinton. Networks "fell in love" with First Lady–endorsed volunteerism during a summit in Philadelphia, which included Colin Powell, George Bush, Jimmy Carter, Gerald Ford, and Oprah Winfrey. *Newsweek* and *Time* gave it top billing.

For all the journalistic indignation over the fundraising scandal, the story never caught on with the American people because they "already knew the script" and "knew the system was corrupt and awash in too much money." The people did not care to sort out all the players in the scandal, from China and Indonesia, because they concluded that the Democrats and the Republicans were going to "pound each other about fundraising abuses without cleaning up the cesspool that spawned such conduct" (Kurtz, 1998, p. 287). So Americans lost interest in scandals, and the president was able to garner their attention because he and his surrogates had remained focused on what he had been elected to do.

The press had taken on the Clintons and badly lost. The media portrayal of the president as a dishonest, cash-obsessed, sex-crazed opportunist was trumped by the White House depiction of Clinton as a proud, hard-working, unfairly criticized man who overcame the odds on behalf of the average American. In Kurtz's (1998) view, the "grave scandals" that darkened the first portrayal were barely visible in the official version. The administration's framing of their version of scandal and crises stories was bolstered by Hillary Clinton's continued use of herself as a source of grounding from which Americans could assess and evaluate her husband's presidency.

By 1997, the White House had learned to coexist with what was generally perceived as a hostile press corps. The Clintons had trumped the press by defusing the media's agenda and turned the national conversation away from their issues—which included the fundraising, Whitewater, and Paula Jones scandals—and toward the president's own: balancing the budget, expanding NATO, raising school standards, and fighting Internet smut and teenage smoking (Kurtz, 1998, p. 288). Although scandal spinning has existed in all administrations, it reached critical mass during Bill Clinton's. Much as presidents have had to "meet press imperatives" such as appreciating news values and the operation of the "news business" in order to acquire press coverage and a forum for influencing public opinion (Davis, 1996, p. 55), so too did Hillary Clinton in order to mediate her husband's scandals. The First Lady needed to address these scandal-based reports with stories that would, if not eclipse the press's version of events, at least shadow them. And even then, she was rhetorically constrained by the reality of journalism: news makers, even First Ladies, lack direct control over the news product. Reporters and editors still always had the last cut, could determine the final frame.

Media Aversion to Sex

A mitigating factor may have favored the First Lady's discursive handling of many of the crises during her husband's presidency. A major point that distinguishes sex scandals in particular, such as Troopergate and Paula Jones, from similar scandals such as those involving Clarence Thomas and Bob Packwood is that the target of the allegations during the Clinton administration was the president of the United States. Most American journalists are essentially uneasy with sex stories to begin with, an aversion that is magnified when the subject of scrutiny is the president. When Troopergate first broke, R. W. Apple, Jr., the Washington bureau chief of the *New York Times*, said he was "not interested in Bill Clinton's sex life as governor of Arkansas" and that for the "readers who are interested in that, there are lots of publications they can turn to to slake their thirst." Scott Pelly of CBS remembered that after his interviews with the troopers, "we just felt ... it didn't rise to the level of something that we wanted to put on the 'Evening News.'" And *Newsweek*'s Eleanor Clift said she thought it was about the Clintons' "private life" and said that if Bill Clinton "had affairs, if they've resolved it between themselves, what business is it of ours?" (quoted in Sabato and Lichter, 1994, pp. 37–38).

The media's unease about covering the president's personal life made reporters particularly apprehensive about the sex scandals. Elements in each story "gave them the easy excuses they needed to ignore or downplay the allegations" and so produced "an easy exit strategy for an unsettled press." Some of these factors included that the stories were old news, that the Clintons had a troubled marriage, and that he might not have been a faithful husband were already "out there and processed" by voters who had "digested" the facts by "electing him president anyway." Some political journalists may have considered the issue "resolved" with the Gennifer Flowers "frenzy" in January 1992 and the First Couple's subsequent *60 Minutes,* appearance, where he acknowledged causing pain in his marriage (Sabato and Lichter, 1994, pp. 41–42).

The American political press's reluctance to topple a presidency, particularly because of something related to the president's most intimate behavior—committing perjury before a grand jury and so, perhaps most important, "lying to the American people" about sex—may have inadvertently programmed many in the mainstream or elite press to be more inclined to respond positively to Hillary Clinton's framing of her husband's impeachment. Had the First Lady not been so successful in reframing his impeachable behavior, William Jefferson Clinton might very well have been the first American president removed from office.

"Performative" Language

One discursive tactic that Hillary Clinton employed included the use of performative language. In the most direct use of the news media in governing, publicity is policy in and of itself. Rhetoric, in Cook's (1998) view, substitutes for action and functions as "performative" language, where the "action" is in making the utterance. The epitome of performative language in political news is the noon briefing of the State Department, where the United States is placed on record as condemning, congratulating, doubting, agreeing, warning, and even not commenting. Elsewhere in government, officials engage in the performative: presidents order, legislators proclaim, judges rule. By making statements in public and encouraging their use in the news, officials both enact policy and alert larger audiences to these actions, presumably so that the latter may take this new information into account in planning what to do next.

Performatives are useful for both official and reporter. Reporters can incorporate politicians' performatives in their stories because their use enables the production of a story without the time-consuming fact checking. A defining characteristic of the performative is that it cannot be said to be either true or false; one may doubt whether people who say "I'm sorry" are really sorry or not, but "one cannot doubt that they have apologized" (pp. 123).

Officials, when "doing something with words," may accomplish that something quickly and directly in a way that otherwise may evade them. Performatives are accessible to officials who are also structurally advantaged through their control over the correct setting and timing of such utterances. Although performatives cannot be true or false, they must be spoken by particular people in particular places, or else they may lose their effectiveness. Cook (1998) recalls how, after President Reagan was shot and wounded in 1981, Secretary of State Alexander Haig probably alarmed his audience and undermined his authority by declaring in the White House press room that he was "in charge in this White House" (p. 125). Generally officials are provided with the trappings of office—the White House Oval Office, the well of the Senate, the state department briefing room, the Supreme Court's high bench—which endow them with the authority to make words into authoritative policy actions.

First Ladies certainly may use performatives, with an authority derived from their legal status as wives of U.S. presidents, if nothing else. And Hillary Rodham Clinton became adept at "doing something with words" by using her status as a rhetorical springboard, from which she launched many of her discursive crisis management strategies such as her enactment of surrogacy.

Subtextual Themes

Hillary Clinton used her knowledge of media subtexts about the Clinton administration, acquired during her tenure as First Lady, to realize the rhetorical world within which she had to function. In addition, she drew on elements of her own subtext to influence, if not reframe, the vision of the impeachment story created by the political press. With regard to Bill Clinton, the press focused on three basic and ongoing story lines or subtexts. The first was that the president did not ever fully level with people and that "on some level . . . was incapable of it." The second idea that drove coverage about Clinton was that he was "different ideologically . . . more liberal" than what he had once claimed. The third subtext was that he would "compromise too easily on virtually anything." These subtextual themes licensed the media to add even more spin to stories any time the president's action "did not live up to his rhetoric" since they seemed to feed into "a larger issue about the president" (p. 28). For example, a subtext of "Bill Clinton as a president of weak character" was mediated by the press to create a sort of self-fulfilling press prophecy, which primed the electorate to "expect" Clinton to behave as a person with an impaired character. An additional Clinton subtext in place as the Jones/Lewinsky/impeachment scandals evolved had been established when the "draft" episode first made news in December 1991, resulting in a mediated expectation that Clinton "was then, is now and would remain" unable to tell the truth.

Media suspicions about Bill Clinton were fueled by memories of an interview that the *Washington Post*'s Dan Balz had with Clinton about his draft history in December 1991. Michael Isikoff, one of the first mainstream journalists to break the Paula Jones story in 1994, comments on the Clinton-linked subtext that existed for many reporters at the time:

> With much of the national press corps, certainly with reporters like me and my colleagues at the *Post*, he had a history—and that history unquestionably influenced how I approached the story. . . . Many of my colleagues harbored profound doubts—about his glibness, about his lack of political spine and, most important, about his tendency to fudge the truth and even flat-out lie, especially when it came to inconvenient questions about his past. (1999, pp. 25–26)

By the fall of 1996, "the idea that turning over some new rock would bring the entire Clinton presidency tumbling down" was "deeply ingrained in the psychology of the Washington press corps" (p. 102).

Initially, many of the subtexts within which Hillary Clinton personally operated were also harsh, if not negative. Benz (1996) notes that the press mediated Hillary Clinton's "cookie baking" remarks as "gaffes" and "mistakes," which "helped ensure they were perceived that way" and resulted in 'cookies' becoming a major framing symbol and context for Hillary Clinton. The "cookie obsession" worked to keep the issue of women's roles as homemakers foremost in the public's mind. Whether the campaigns were projecting Hillary Clinton as "superwife" or complaining she was not domestic enough, "the cookie was the symbol of Hillary Clinton's fitness as a woman" and framed the debate about her in "terms preferred by Republicans." As a result, many substantive issues pertinent to the Clintons, ranging from her work on education reform to alleged conflicts of interest, were "simply not explored" (p. 114), eclipsed by the mediated "cookie baking" subtext. In 1992, while there were "only a couple of dozen articles" mentioning Whitewater or Madison Guaranty, there were "hundreds mentioning Hillary Clinton's 'cookies' remark" (Cohen and Solomon, 1996, p. 139).

The copresidency subtext was another through which the media initially criticized Mrs. Clinton. Ultimately it produced a useful role for the First Lady, one that she never abdicated, just enacted differently depending on the constraints of the rhetorical environment in which she found herself. The day after Bill Clinton's November 1992 presidential victory, the German Green party ran a banner headline in its journal announcing that "Hillary's husband" had just won the U.S. presidency. This "decentering" of the chief executive so that his wife became "First First Person" symbolized what Williams (1993) warned was "impending Gender Trouble" in the United States sparked by Hillary Rodham Clinton's "demonized" First Ladyship: "The questions being asked now are just better-modulated versions of Daniel Wattenberg's summary in . . . [the] *American Spectator* entitled 'Boy Clinton's Big Mama' and subtitled 'The Lady Macbeth of Little Rock'" (p.35).

Ultimately the First Lady played to and within personal subtexts that were positive—for example, as a woman of integrity—to counter the mediated vision of her husband. The dominant subtext surrounding Bill Clinton—that of an almost pathological liar and adulterer—was the rhetorical milieu within which Hillary moved as she framed her own versions of the scandals and crises surrounding her husband and his presidency. The media's priming effect correlates the attention the press gives an issue and that issue's salience in judging political actors. Hillary Clinton used thematic frames—such as arguing that Bill Clinton's intimate behavior is private because there is a difference between public and private behavior—to combat subtexts created via the episodic framing of Bill Clinton as a morally weak man and therefore "inevitably" an adulterer and liar.

The Clintons may also have been able to take advantage of Americans' distrust of the media as crass mercenaries who chased Princess Diana to her death and were thus no longer the "ink-stained heroes of an earlier era." Kurtz (1998) concludes that the Clinton presidency ultimately survived because it fit the tabloid times: the press had "gorged itself on the Lincoln Bedroom tawdriness, the coffees with rich rogues and scoundrels, the seemingly endless womanizing charges, and the impenetrable Arkansas land dealing," none of which mortally wounded Bill Clinton and most of which ultimately ran their course.

The public does play a role in determining how the target of a scandal frenzy fares. Therefore, if Hillary Clinton could get her story out, or at least rework some of the subtextual fabric of the stories surrounding the First Couple and the presidency, she might engender a sympathetic public. A large number of Americans were ambivalent about considering sexual misconduct an ethical problem for the Clintons and many, including some reporters, were uncomfortable with investigations into the intimate lives of Bill and Hillary Clinton. Lying was generally considered problematic. However, the lie in which the president was caught mandated revelations about his sex life, so the major scandal, as framed by the media for the electorate, was that he had been deceptive about a private rather than a public issue. Therefore, the negatives generated by the sex scandal–based stories may have been less severe than the press or critics of the Clintons might have expected.

An additional primary Clinton subtext—as constructed by the First Lady—was one in which the president was envisioned as a private citizen, pursued by a relentless press and "other enemies" who forced him into a lie to protect a most intimate part of any one's life: sexual behavior. Hillary

Clinton participated in this vision, both as the wife "wronged" by her husband and, more important, as a covictim of the press and "other enemies" as well. This mediated image, successfully framed and scripted, helped to force the political press to turn away from calling for Bill Clinton's impeachment conviction. The First Lady took advantage of the tendency for frenzies to pyramid, so that whatever happened in the Clintons' mediated pasts also played into their mediated futures. For example, the president had lied before and had long been rumored a womanizer. However, the public also knew that Hillary Clinton had stood with her husband then, as well as now, information that became as much a part of the rhetorical subtext surrounding her husband as that he was an adulterer. She had, years before, framed her role in their relationship as a devoted wife and mother as well as a surrogate for Bill Clinton.

Contemporary politicians should neither flee from nor ignore whatever serious charges are made about or against them in the press. Sabato (1991) argues that "in the modern age of negative attack politics, to make no defense when charges fly is a ticket to political oblivion." Questions cannot be brushed off and will be "raised continuously until credible answers are given." The "most rational, logical solution for candidates" is to "try to prepare for conceivable eventualities, especially when they have some hint of a future crisis" (pp. 238–239).

Accordingly, a wise politician or surrogate is "always acutely aware of the press' subtext" about that individual and "wary of taking actions that confirm the undesirable elements of it." For example, Gary Hart ignored the warnings and "recklessly validated his own womanizing subtext" with Donna Rice in 1987. Hillary Clinton's prominent role in previous crises—her public, albeit tacit, support in the face of a "womanizing" husband as well as her participation as an equal partner in marriage, parenting, the presidency, and perhaps even scandal—was well known. This public knowledge empowered the First Lady to mediate and redirect the final pack journalism–framed superfrenzy that was spinning toward the first successful impeachment of a U.S. president. In Kurtz's (1998) view, the battle was not between the "good guys and the bad guys" but rather between two morally ambiguous forces, and Bill Clinton proved to have more firepower than anyone in the media. Hillary Clinton's rhetorical staying power contributed to that firepower.

THE BEAT-THEM-AT-THEIR-OWN-GAME STRATEGY

Politicians use media to "know" just as public does. Senators and representatives have relied on the news for understanding Congress and the activities of individual members as far back as 1960 (Cook, 1998, p. 126). Ultimately, much of politics comes down to public policy, the polity's responses to what are considered public problems. Policies are usually aimed at solving, or at least alleviating, public problems and consist mainly of governmental decisions and actions such as enacting laws, issuing regulations, allocating funds, and undertaking military action. Governmental responses may also be symbolic, in that they do not "materially change" a situation but indicate "concern about and attention to it." Decisions not to take action about a problem may also be a "species of public policy" (Paletz, 1998, p. 218). Governments make most public policies, which in the American system are achieved at a national level by decisions reached by the presidency, the executive departments, regulatory agencies, Congress, and the courts. The impeachment trial of President Bill Clinton would certainly belong in the arena of public policy.

Policymakers also respond to public opinion as reported in the press, and decisions made by government institutions, including Congress, have been strongly related to public opinion (Jacobs and Shapiro, 1994). The president—and presidential surrogate—who attracts and maintains favorable press coverage enjoys a high level of public popularity; the higher the popularity, the more chance that Congress might defer to the president. On the other hand, the more controversial the message is emanating from the White House, the less likely is the president to enjoy legislative success. As a result, political actors vie for public approval and engage in "going public" style of governing (Iyengar, 1997c).

Public opinion is therefore crucial in setting the congressional agenda. Congress is more likely to pay attention—by holding legislative hearings—to issues highlighted by the news media. This is not because congressional leaders suspect that newsworthiness is a good barometer of the substantive importance of the issue but because the public is concerned about the issue. While much policymaking continues existing policy, changes and innovations do occur. One cause is partisan conflict between Democrats and Republicans. Other causes include deliberation and discourse and the ideas and arguments that emerge from each. Central to any policy change is issue definition and control over policy agenda. This is achieved in part by a mobilization of new voices that exploit opportunities to define issues, motivate the public, and gain access to policymakers. What these voices have to say is reinforced or undermined by media content, so "public officials and those trying to influence them strive to advance their policy perspectives and preferences through the media" (Paletz, 1998, pp. 219–220).

In Davis's (1996) view, "the news media are not merely a mirror reflecting society; their role is more closely akin to that of a prism, which gathers light, bends it slightly, and focuses it" (p. 132). Journalists serving as news gatherers are one major participant in the "struggle over the shaping of the news." The second major participant is the group of "news makers—the elected officials, bureaucrats, staff" who seek to influence news and are "deemed newsworthy, or potentially so, by news gatherers" (Davis, 1996, p. 136). Political actors must therefore strive to influence rather than control the news-gathering process, meeting the press on its own grounds, always seeking to "coordinate political moves with expectations of media performance." In addition, they are in competition with other political actors "also seeking access through the media's gates." Ultimately, news makers, like news gatherers, participate in the news-gathering process in order to influence the news coverage of themselves or their concerns. The success of their participation is measured by whether they receive press coverage, which itself depends on the political actor's skill in making the news.

As a result, news makers such as Hillary Rodham Clinton must manipulate the press to achieve the coverage they desire. Methods of manipulation include providing a flow of news, controlling access by the press, and "utilizing to their advantage the journalists' values of news" (Davis, 1996, p. 138). News makers may also stage events that are timely and dramatic, possess good visuals, and feature a star personality. In addition, conflict and uniqueness may be useful, as long as they do not reflect negatively on the news makers. In the early scandals, Hillary Clinton functioned rhetorically as a scapegoat to deflect attention away from her husband's role in the crises. In later scandals, particularly the impeachment, theirs was a role reversal of sorts, except that she became the star personality, and the impeachment—in terms of both conflict and uniqueness—reflected in a positive light both the traditional "stand-by-my-man" as well as "co-president" First Lady persona.

Hillary Clinton also rhetorically facilitated other political actors'—such as Congress during the impeachment trial—discovery of the "truth" regarding it and other scandals in her husband's presidency. She did this by constructing an image that she framed, and was in turn reframed by the press without substantial revision, of herself as an individual (her First Lady persona) and as the best evidence that her husband was a "good" president (her surrogate persona). Miller and Krosnick (1997) argue that competence and character, particularly in terms of integrity, influence the public's judgment of the president. If the primed issues are scandals, the latter is particularly influenced by press-mediated issues (p. 262).

The First Lady became a political actor who realized her version of a story, such as the "accident" of Bill Clinton's perhaps impeachable behavior with Monica Lewinsky, "needed" to make the papers and nightly news so that it would, in both the public's and other political actors' perceptions, become the dominant version of what was going on. The First Lady thus called attention to herself as a person of power and so caused the media to want to "cover her even more," which afforded her even more power and so made her even more desirable as a source of stories about which the media could spin. Rosenstiel (1994) believes the key to political communication is "understanding which media are right for which message and time" (pp. 2–3). Successful political actors also comprehend their own strengths and weaknesses, expanding the former and downplaying the latter. In addition, the mainstream/elite/"old media" in particular are crucial as the primary mediating lens for "telling Americans the president's business" (p. 45).

Political actors rarely call attention to an issue merely for the sake of doing so; instead, they stress issues that hold together their coalition and fragment the opposition. They also strategically define a dispute through terms that, if accepted, would almost automatically guarantee their success. Much political debate is not only about what issues should be on the agenda but also what those issues are really all about and what the sides of the issue are. Such debate frequently occurs behind the scenes and emerges into the open when an accident breaks the standard routines of officials and reporters.

For example, Cook (1998) asks, "How should we have conceptualized the oil spill in 1989 caused by the Exxon Valdez, and how should we respond with appropriate policy responses?" Was it a case of bad navigation by a drunken captain (in which case the courts can take care of it by punishing the infractor, and legislatures can increase penalties for navigating under the influence)? Or was it the consequence of the use of fragile single-hull vessels (in which case the flow of oil can proceed, but with the introduction of double-hull ships)? Or was it simply the inevitable risk of overconsumption of petroleum (in which case, rigorous conservation would have to be imposed)? Although all sides would see such an incident as something to be avoided, the public chooses different policies depending on how they understand the oil spill and its causes. The ability to have an account become the "perceived reality," the ability to create public events, thus becomes a "crucial dimension of power" (p. 127). In other words, the savvy use of publicity can influence policymaking. By packaging a story in such a way that its benefits are unchallenged and seemingly undeniable—even though benefits may be unclear or problematic—potential opposition to a political actor's policy or course of action may be diffused and attention diverted away from other alternatives. Calling attention to one's stand on issues and policy also calls attention to oneself. Cook (1998) notes the House press secretaries he surveyed in 1984 made few distinctions between using the news media to build a national constituency for an issue and to become a nationally recognized spokesperson on that issue." When one is covered as "in a position to know," a reputation can grow that will enhance one's stature, which can be "reinvested in further news opportunities" (p. 128).

Cook (1998) argues that it is not farfetched to suggest that the American news media construct a conception of what any political institution is and does, from which audiences construct their understanding of that institution, including of the individuals within it. The publicity provided by the news media assists public officials and politicians in two ways. First, the public tends to perceive those issues discussed in the news as more salient, and citizens are more likely to judge politicians by their stances on those issues, whether or not the news is linked to those officials. Second, even if public opinion is not generated, politicians respond differently to more salient issues. And issues are generally considered more important when they are presented in the *New York Times*. Increasing the visibility of a particular issue enhances the odds that political actors will do something about it in a way that is responsive to public attention.

Nimmo and Combs (1990) contend that mass-mediated politics has made politicians celebrities in their own right. This celebrity status may shift, so that "a hero can become a villain or fool at any time if popular perceptions shift." In addition, for political celebrities enacting a moral drama, such as the Clintons who began their tenure as First Couple promising an ethical administration, "failure to lead an exemplary life that projects high ethical and moral standards can be devastating." Therefore, "celebrity status becomes a prerequisite for attaining political powers in a mass mediated society" (p. 94). In addition, "winning and holding political power" requires celebrity status, which is mediated by a "fickle" press that may "withdraw it as quickly as they grant it." As a result, maintaining celebrity status requires "celebrity management ... orchestrating times, settings, and events to enhance the personal celebrity of a political leader *first*, governing second" (p. 103). The public scrutiny that accompanies political celebrity may result in an image tarnished through adverse publicity such as the press mediation of Ted Kennedy's Chappaquiddick affair and John Kennedy's alleged womanizing during his presidency.

Chappaquiddick cast doubt on Ted Kennedy's right to inherit the Camelot legacy, so he played to the image of a good husband, father, and family man. However, by the mid-1970s, the troubled marriage of Joan (a "nice girl" with "public sympathy," who was just "unable to cope with the tough and worldly Kennedys") and Ted was tabloid fodder (p. 98). Negative gossip generated by Joan Kennedy's revelations of her alcoholism and separation from her husband produced negative gossip, which "haunted the presidential candidacy" of Ted Kennedy in 1980. Still, she joined her husband on the campaign. *People* magazine reported her "gallant defense" against the womanizing rumors as "Joan's most skillful acting job since she made TV commercials for Coca-Cola and Revlon twenty years ago" ("Joan Kennedy," 1979). By June 1980, although the campaign had failed, Joan Kennedy, "once frail and pitiful," was labeled "the 'bravest Kennedy'" (Birmingham, 1980) and had become the "heroine of a mass-mediated soap opera with definite political consequences":

The popular expectation that political celebrities be good husbands made Ted a villain. If she was transformed in the rhetorical vision of women's magazines from a victim to a brave and independent new person, he was recast as lacking in character. ... If his wife was the personal victim, he was the political victim. ... His failure to supply a romantic *denouement* of "living happily ever after" in keeping with the expectation of popular royalty relegated him to playing on the stage of the U.S. Senate, not in the great theater of the Oval Office and Camelot. (Nimmo and Combs, 1990, pp. 99–100)

Similar circumstances facilitated Colorado senator Gary Hart's failed presidential bid. The Democratic front-runner in April 1987, Hart withdrew the following month after the *Miami Herald* suggested he had been unfaithful to his wife, Lee, with another woman, Donna Rice. Hart withdrew under increased tabloid examination and speculation of his alleged adultery. Like Joan Kennedy, Lee Hart publicly supported her husband, despite the fact that the media "reveled" in framing her as the wronged wife; she campaigned with him and remained at her husband's side when he reentered the race in December 1987. However, his campaign never gained momentum, and Hart withdrew permanently, indicating he wanted to spend more time with his family. Nimmo and Combs (1990) suggest that, like Ted Kennedy, Gary Hart never learned the lesson that popular fantasies of marital fidelity are a "prerequisite to [political] princedom" and that "fame, not infamy, carried a celebrity to the presidency" (p. 101).

Joan Kennedy, Lee Hart, and Hillary Clinton all had husbands accused of adultery, and all three "stood by their men," but only Bill Clinton politically survived both in his quest for the presidency and, later, during his enactment of that presidency. Of the three women, Mrs. Clinton's management of her political celebrity was the most rhetorically skillful. She mediated right back at the press with her own image; she stood by her husband as a partner First Lady, strong and ethical enough for them both. Unlike Mrs. Kennedy and Mrs. Hart, Hillary Rodham Clinton was no victim of a philandering husband. Her own celebrity carried the day when that of Bill Clinton could not. Pope (1998) contends that Hillary Clinton had "something to preserve" unlike other wronged political spouses: a partner status as well as a persona as a strong role model for many Americans at precisely the time her husband was not.

Who controls the frame is able to decide its contents, thereby influencing those who see or hear it. By framing herself as the most important story and calling media attention to herself, Hillary Clinton forced the Clintons' critics, including other political actors such as Ken Starr and Congress, to see that who she was and what she said and did was as significant as what her husband was doing. In this way, she controlled at least a portion of the media's agenda, which further empowered the First Lady as an agent of influence, particularly during the impeachment crisis. This might also have influenced the public to be not so focused on what happened with Bill Clinton personally since his wife seemed, at least as filtered through the news about her, to be acting as if "it's okay." Mrs. Clinton, for example, rarely addressed a crisis directly or at great length. If she did, she usually retreated to one of her stock strategies, such as maintaining the Clintons' truthfulness or arguing from common ground. In addition, she deflected some of the criticism against her husband by simply appearing on television and in other media without ever really seeming to waver in her support. This read to the public: "If his wife can 'stand him/by him' particularly during times as bad as these," then "where do 'we get off' saying that we are going to give up on him?" Ken Starr and other foes, following Cook's (1998) argument, were then forced to pay attention to Hillary Clinton's media status. This in turn may have influenced not only public opinion, but that of editors and Congress as well. More positive spin may have resulted in a press that realized its viewers and readers were responding well to good tales about the Clintons. More such stories might generate more readers, more viewers, and more revenues. And some in Congress may have paid attention to the media meta-framing of Hillary Clinton's agenda as a sign of which direction the electorate was leaning in its perception of Bill and Hillary Clinton. This may have influenced their behavior in political decisions, including whether to convict Bill Clinton in his impeachment trial.

Media attention is a major determinant of which issues will be paid attention to by the public and Congress. In addition, different media as well as different political personas tend to focus on the same issues because they track each other's stories. Journalists read each other's work, and congressional aides generate and try to shape media coverage. This interaction guarantees that shifts in attention by one set of actors are likely to be quickly followed by the others as well. The media help link all the other actors by serving as the principal channel through which individuals can keep track of others, as well as what is considered the "public mood" (Baumgartner et al., 1997, p. 350). In addition, media attention often precedes congressional attention, which feeds back to cause yet more media attention. Once begun, attention to an issue increases by a self-reinforcing mechanism. The more successful that proponents or opponents of an issue are in generating news coverage, the more likely that there will be congressional energy expended on the issue. And the more congressional energy expended, the more media coverage there will be of that energy.

The media do help to create situations that make increased government attention almost unavoidable (Baumgartner et al., 1997). The news may mend or extend divisions among political actors, frame issues in diverse ways, and give voice to some government officials while silencing others. It may play a crucial role in endorsing or rejecting policy initiatives, particularly when the government appears divided. However, some political actors are also sophisticated and, on occasion, successful in using the media for their particular ends (Sparrow, 1999).

It is likely that the media attention generally given Hillary Clinton as the scandals increased in intensity during her husband's two administrations influenced the outcomes of those scandals. She used the media to advance her agenda, honing her discursive skills as the scandals ebbed and waned during the two Clinton administrations. She also took advantage of the media's "voice-giving" ability by being sure that her presence became "heard" and "seen" more—and became more effective—as each new crisis presented. Ultimately, her response to the impeachment scandal was to manage the press rhetorically better than the Republicans so that her take on the situation dominated the press spinning and framing. The First Lady was able to appease the owners, producers, and advertisers of the news—because they still had "their story" of two opposing sides to sell papers and airtime—while maneuvering the media to produce narratives more favorable to her husband. When she was part of the scandal, as in Travelgate and Whitewater, as well as the failed health care plan, she strategically removed herself from the center of media attention. By "laying low," she was no longer a flashpoint off of which reporters could spin. When the First Lady emerged publicly after these scandals, it was as a seemingly retooled Hillary Clinton who no longer exhibited the negatives—such as thinking she was part of the presidency or being too much a feminist. She altered the lens through which the media, and so the public, and by extension, other political actors and institutions, defined the First Lady.

As the presidency continued and the final big scandal coalesced into "Sexgate," Hillary Clinton emerged as the most talented and successful rhetorical actor in her husband's administration. The stories told by reporters about the issues connected to the impeachment proceedings would contribute to the stories believed by the public and Congress about Bill Clinton as a president who should or should not be impeached. Hillary Clinton ultimately rhetorically positioned herself—by playing the media's game better than the media—so that tales of "Hillary the Good" rather than "Bill the Bad" became The Story about Bill Clinton's impeachment. The public and the press volleyed back and forth, embellishing their versions based on what the other was saying, so that ultimately the main theme of the "impeach Bill Clinton" issue to which Congress had to attend was acquittal. Accordingly, Congress's decision to proceed with the impeachment, yet not find President Clinton guilty, was directly connected to media framing of the issue. This framing was in part shaped by Hillary Clinton's rhetorical efforts to prime the media with an image of the First Lady as a steadfast wife, intelligent person, and good mother. The public mood and public mind during the impeachment was dominated not by the president as an adulterous liar but by a discursively structured, unimpeachable image of the First Lady. It was an image the media conveyed, the public liked, and to which Congress paid attention. Bill Clinton was acquitted.

ADDITIONAL STRATEGIES

The Common Ground Strategy

During interviews while campaigning in 1992, Hillary Clinton was asked general questions about whether she thought marital fidelity was an appropriate concern for voters. At one point, she commented on how the Clintons' marriage was like "anyone else's":

From my perspective, our marriage is a strong marriage. We love each other. We support each other, and we have had a lot of strong and important experiences together that have meant a lot to us. In any marriage, there are issues that come up between two people who are married—issues that I think are their business. . . . It is very important to me that what I care about most in this world—which is my family, what we mean to each other, and what we've done together—have some realm of protection from public life. (quoted in King, 1996, p. 136)

She also initially disarmed critics during the congressional hearings on health by introducing herself as "a mother, a wife, a daughter, a sister and a woman" (Brock, 1996, p. 330), thereby identifying with essentially all women in America. The First Lady used the common ground of familial obligation in response to questions about her own efforts to make a profit in Whitewater and commodity trading, despite her criticisms of the 1980s as the "decade of greed" during a 1994 interview: "I was raised to believe that every person had an obligation to take care of themselves and their family" and "I don't think you'll ever find anything that my husband or I said that in any way condemns the importance of making good investments and saving or that in any way undermines what is the heart and soul of the American economy, which is risk-taking and investing in the future." She continued:

What I think we were saying is that like anything else, that can be taken to excess—when companies are leveraged into debt, when loans are not repaid, when pension funds are raided. You know, all of the things that marked the excess of the 1980s are things which we spoke out against. I think it's a pretty long stretch to say that the decisions that we made to try to create some financial security for our family and make some investments come anything near there.... We obviously wanted enough financial security to send our daughter to college and put money away for our old age and help our parents when we could. (quoted in Woodward, 1999, p. 253)

In late January 1992, at a Democratic National Committee roast in Washington, D.C., for party chair Ron Brown, television host Larry King began his monologue, "It's ten o-clock, Hillary; where is Bill Clinton?" Her response was that her husband was with "the other woman in his life, his daughter Chelsea" at a father-daughter dance in Arkansas (quoted in Brock, 1996, p. 258). She continued to identify with the electorate as "family oriented" by working in references to her husband and daughter when given the opportunity. At a 1992 speech at La Salle University, the First Lady spoke of "being a full-time advocate for children's issues in the White House" and added that "the most important thing in my life right now is my daughter Chelsea." Later in the same year, she said, "Work in the home is very important," and in an interview with David Frost, she downplayed her husband's tendency to compare the Clintons to Eleanor and Franklin Roosevelt as "very nice hyperbole." At a Wellesley commencement, she spoke of how a young woman might choose to be "a corporate executive or a rocket scientist or you may stay home and raise your children." She also said that children could be cared for "by making policy or making cookies" and demonstrated her ability to use a sewing machine at an International Ladies Garment Workers Union Convention (quoted in Brock, 1996, p. 267). A photo of her having tea with Tipper Gore at the Waldorf accompanied a July 1992 *New York Times* article in which she said "My friends say my recipe is more Democratic because I use vegetable shortening instead of butter. I am an old-fashioned patriot. I cry at the Fourth of July when kids put crepe paper on their bicycle wheels, so this is, like, just incredible—it's so extraordinary to me" (quoted in Brock, 1996, p. 268).

Responding to this "every woman" ploy, the media began to spin in her favor. The *Los Angeles Times*'s Pat Morrison wrote of a "kinder, gentler Hillary Clinton" who was "but one more working mom juggling through hectic days" and a "new traditionalist, as down-home likable as she is intellectually admirable (quoted in Brock, 1996, p. 268).

The First Lady further demonstrated her skill at identification during a speech in early 1999 when she described her response to queries about how she could "stand politics":

Whenever someone asks me that, I pause for a minute and I say, "Well, you know, have you ever been a member of a family or a church or a synagogue or a civic organization or anything else where you had to work with people to make decisions by consensus, by majority vote, by working out the likes and dislikes of all the people who you were working with?" Because really politics—with a small "p"—is how in a democracy we get along with one another. And we make decisions that we think are in our best interest as well as the larger society's or a family's or a group's. (Clinton, 1999a).

The Apology Strategy

Apology—accompanying disclosure—and contrition, perceived as "an act of uncharacteristic humility—usually assists a pol in the effort to move beyond a problem" (Sabato, 1991, p. 241). It is a more effective tactic when coupled with "plausible efforts" to deflect full responsibility for the controversy, as when Michael Dukakis expressed sorrow for his "attack video" (on Joe Biden) but shifted blame to his staff (p. 241).

Apologias are speeches by candidates apologizing for some statement or behavior (Trent and Friedenberg, 1995). Generally the behavior or statement suggests such a substantial weakness in the political actor's character that it could prevent the politician from becoming elected. Such statements are relatively common because contemporary reporters target politicians' weaknesses and flaws as well as their private lives more than they did in the past. Candidates and other government officials also turn to apologia more because the press frames character as more important than in the past, which produces more scandals that must be rhetorically managed if a politician is to remain in public life. There may be several purposes for apologia rhetoric, including to explain the behavior or statement in a positive light, justify the behavior to minimize damage to image and character, or remove the topic from public discussion so that other issues may be discussed.

Trent and Friedenberg (1995) consider the Clintons' 1992 apologiatic response delivered on *60 Minutes* to the charges that Bill Clinton committed adultery with Gennifer Flowers the "best-known political apologia of recent years" (p. 200) and one that utilized the six strategies commonly employed by rhetors who produce such discourse. First, apologias are best delivered in settings where individuals other than the candidate seem in control. Viewers were no doubt aware that neither of the Clintons was in control of the situation as they responded to Steven Kroft, who appeared to control the interview. A second strategy is to deny the alleged facts or relationships responsible for the charges in the first place. While both Clintons suggested that Flowers's claim was false, there was no specific denial of "other infidelities."

"Bolstering strategies" are when the rhetor identifies with something the audience perceives favorably. Hillary Rodham Clinton—acting as the president's surrogate as much as his wife—asserted they had honestly informed Americans about her husband's inability to claim total fidelity in their marriage. In this way, she was attempting to bolster his case by claiming to display "candor and honesty" in addressing charges of infidelity, traits judged favorably by the viewing audience. Through this framing, the Clintons were able to focus audience attention on honesty rather than adultery.

Hillary Clinton's presence itself, as well as her "active defense" of her husband, may have served a bolstering function, suggesting the strength of their marriage. By presenting themselves as a married couple who has weathered relationship storms, Americans identified with the Clintons for their dedication to their relationship rather than abandonment of it. "Differentiation" occurs when facts or relationships are separated from a larger context within which an audience views that attribute. There is also a "role imbalance" attack, when political actors suggest the media have crossed the line between objective reporting into personal attacks, thereby exaggerating or falsely reporting charges against the politician.

During the *60 Minutes* interview, the Clintons strove to differentiate questions of infidelity from the context of Bill Clinton's fitness for office and to place it within the context of the right of privacy. If the public considered charges of Bill Clinton's infidelity more linked to the issue of a right to privacy rather than to presidential fitness, then the Clintons' role imbalance attacks on the press were relevant as they suggested that press coverage was a test of media objectivity. If reporters continued their "unbalanced adversarial attacks," then the public suffered as well. The transcendental strategy is a fifth apologia technique that the Clintons used when they motivated the public to think about the courage the First Couple had in appearing on national televison, their candor and honesty in leveling with Americans about their private lives, and the press's intrusion into the intimate details of their marriage.

The final apologiatic strategy Hillary and Bill Clinton used in their *60 Minutes* apologia was his tacit confession (he admitted to having caused "pain" in their marriage) of having extramarital affairs, if not with Gennifer Flowers, then with others unnamed. According to Trent and Friedenberg (1995), "Having so confessed, there was little more that the press could pursue on this story" (p. 204). The First Lady was sitting by her husband's side for the admission. That she remained by his side afterward was evidence that, at least as far as that part of the story was concerned, there was no story.

The Blaming Strategy

The First Lady implicitly suggested that Bill Clinton's adultery and "sexual misconduct" as well as lying were attributed not to a character deficit but to a press and GOP who would invade a family's privacy to the point that lying would be the only alternative left to protect that family. Hillary Clinton's unswerving defense of her husband during the early scandals only buttressed the "apologize-but-do-not-admit-guilt" strategy for managing the later crises in her husband's administration. If the political actor determines there is a way to "work the population" so it will feel a sympathy—if not empathy—for what "they" (the media) are doing to "us" (the politican and, by extension, any allies, including family), the momentum of the scandal may be slowed, if not halted. Sabato (1991) believes that in the case of Dan Quayle, the media frenzy was "checkmated by a real or pseudo vox populi frenzy" against reporters who were perceived as viciously harrassing the vice-presidential candiate. The *Washington Post*'s E. J. Dionne said that in the end, the "Bush people" were smart to "take advantage of the public's unhappiness with the press" (quoted in Sabato, 1991, p. 243). So too did Hillary Clinton take advantage of this innate dislike, which she coupled with the "innate attraction" of the American people for a "good wife and mother." She discursively morphed Bill Clinton from the media-framed adulterous and lying man to a beleaguered, all-too-human president and family man who resorted to lying as a desperate attempt to fend off a vicious, scandal-hungry, and invasive press.

Brock (1996) identified some of the strategies Hillary Clinton used during the 1993 health care reform initiative that became mainstays in her rhetorical arsenal. These included identifying an enemy and demonizing it to galvanize public support. In a September 1994 address, Mrs. Clinton noted that congressional "opponents" had "spent hundreds of millions of dollars to saturate the airwaves with negative advertisements" to combat the

Clinton health initiative. She asked that the audience of medical students remember that "when the Congress goes home and the pundits declare health care reform dead" to "just remember the millions of physicians and nurses, medical students and technicians who don't get to go home" (Clinton, 1994).

Even after her husband's admissions of infidelity, Hillary Clinton relied on the strategy of blaming the press for printing scandalous stories about Bill Clinton that were nothing less than propaganda for the president's opponents: "I find it not an accident that every time he is on the verge of fulfilling his commitment to the American people and they are responding ... out comes yet a new round of these outrageous, terrible stories that people plant for political and financial reasons" (Hillary Clinton quoted in Osborne, 1997, p. 51). She also attributed the collapse of the health care initiative to the focus on scandals in her husband's administration: "We thought we had a real window. I said to Bill after NAFTA passed [in the fall of 1993] and his ratings were so high, 'Well, I wonder what's in their arsenal now.' We soon found out. We had Troopergate. We had Whitewater as an issue. . . . We were under siege again" (quoted in Brock, 1996, p. 405).

A day after the 1992 *60 Minutes* broadcast, Gennifer Flowers appeared at a press conference with attorneys and employees of the tabloid *Star* to reveal tapes as evidence of her affair with Bill Clinton. King (1996) believes that Hillary Clinton actually "got the most mileage out of the story" (p. 149) when, during an interview shortly afterward with the *Daily Sentinel,* a Colorado newspaper, she suggested that the allegations against her husband were part of a Republican smear:

We now know that when Republicans first offered money to this woman to change her story, she held out, apparently negotiating with the media to change a story she had denied repeatedly. Part of the reason I feel so calm is that Bill and I are stronger today than when we got married. Bill and I will be fine, regardless of what happens. It's not easy running for president. You feel like you're standing in the middle of a firing range, and sometimes they come close to hitting you. (quoted in Nelson, 1993, p. 39)

A short time later, while on *Prime Time Live*, Hillary Clinton told Sam Donaldson that the Flowers story was "the daughter of Willie Horton," initiated by the Republican National Committee, Larry Nichols, and political foe and long-time Clinton critic Sheffield Nelson (quoted in Brock, 1996, p. 258).

King (1996) believes that by the time of the 1992 Sam Donaldson interview, the Gennifer Flowers scandal had "developed into a fight between two women for public support" so that the "crux of the matter," in Donaldson's framing of the issue, was "really Hillary" rather than Bill Clinton. Donaldson characterized Mrs. Clinton as her husband's "primary defensive shield" in deflecting charges of infidelity. She admitted having heard the tapes and read the transcripts. However, when asked if she heard her husband's voice on them, acting as "a skillful lawyer" who knew there was danger of raising doubts about a witness's integrity in an outright denial of admissions," she, the First Lady, "took the trained litigator's way out" and "rhetorically" (p. 149) stated:

I don't have any idea.... But he's talked to her.... I sat there in the kitchen one night when he returned a call to her.... Anybody who knows my husband knows that he bends over backwards to help people who are in trouble and is always willing to listen to their problems.... The first time he called her, I mean, we were in the kitchen together and he said, you know, "This woman thinks her life is over," and he felt sorry for her.... If somebody's willing to pay you $130,000 or $170,000, to say something and get your fifteen minutes of fame and you get your picture on the front page of every newspaper and you're some failed cabaret singer who doesn't even have much of a resumé to fall back on, and what's [more], she'd lied about—you know, that's the daughter of Willie Horton, as far as I'm concerned. It's the same kind of attempt to keep the real issues of this country out of the mainstream debate where they need to be. (quoted in King, 1996, pp. 149–150)

King (1996) identifies Hillary Clinton's discursive strategy for initially managing the Flowers scandal as that of casting doubt that such an affair even occurred. She managed to "turn the issue of Gennifer Flowers into an item on the opposition's dirty-tricks agenda" and in so doing "effectively removed herself from the limelight." Hillary Clinton was, in this sense, a "wronged woman" not because of her husband's infidelity but because of politicians in the opposing party. Her reframing of the story was that Bill Clinton needed no forgiving because he had done nothing. "The entire matter was simply the machinations of politicians trying to win an election" (p. 151).

Another example of this strategy was evident during a speech in early 1999 when Mrs. Clinton argued that "one of the untold stories about the 1994 elections and all the Democratic losses is that many Democratic members of Congress who were persuaded to vote for the Crime Bill and the Brady Bill lost their seats because of the incredible lobbying of the gun lobby against them when they were up for election" (Clinton, 1999a).

The Privacy Strategy

One of the First Lady's tactics for managing press inquiries into alleged infidelities of both herself and the president was to separate the Clintons' personal and political lives in order to counter media framing that merged the two: "I don't talk about it. I think my marriage is my marriage and my relationship with my husband is solely between us" (Hillary Clinton quoted in Osborne, 1997, p. 51). She also argued that the media can figure out if a person is "good" without scrutinizing that person's private life: "Maybe this time the candidate and the press will get it right. The public can learn enough to know whether a candidate is a decent person without having to pick you apart so much that there is nothing left at the end" (Hillary Clinton quoted in Osborne, 1997, p. 73). Commenting on what she considered invasive reporting on the cattle futures investments, she maintained, "I've always believed in a zone of privacy, and I told a friend the other day that I feel, after resisting for a long time, I've been rezoned" (Hillary Clinton quoted in Osborne, 1997, p. 136). In Nelson's (1993) view, "with that statement," Hillary Clinton saved her husband's campaign, if not his political life (p. 23). Marton (1999) argues that Hillary Clinton's 1998 reclamation of "a measure of privacy for herself after her husband's public admission of infidelity—not by pulling back like Mamie Eisenhower but by refusing to play by the prevailing rules of the confessional age" was a major achievement. She not only affirmed "her right to privacy, she focused on the issues, found her own voice and set her own boundaries." Furthermore, the nation seemed willing to abide by them, "a reaction without precedent in American history" (Marton, 1999).

The Strength Through Adversity Strategy

Woodward (1999) believes that Hillary Clinton's "scandal-managing role" included a "siege mentality" (p. 335) through which she managed crises up to and including the impeachment scandal. On occasion, the First Lady argued that the incessant media scrutiny of the Clintons' public and private lives had been a toughening experience, which served to help them continue to counter such efforts: "If we've proved nothing else, we've proved we are resilient. We know how to fight; we can take these people on" (Hillary Clinton quoted in Osborne, 1997, p. 59).

When asked in another interview, if fidelity had been a problem in her marriage Mrs. Clinton replied:

My marriage is my marriage and my relationship with my husband is solely between us.... We demand too much of our political people in terms of the way we expect them to live, the kinds of external, reactive life-styles we expect them to have. We have really collapsed the space in which public people can live, to the detriment of our overall politics. That's the way it is in this country. You lose not just privacy—you lose the opportunity to be a real person.... It depends on the candidate and the marriage. Any stressful undertaking can be made either better or worse by the relationship between the spouses. But if it's a supportive one, if people believe in each other, if they love each other, if they have a commitment to what each is trying to do, it makes life a lot easier than it is alone.... We've had to deal with a lot of dirt and negative advertising. We've learned our lesson about how you stand up, answer your critics, and then just counterpunch as hard as you can. (quoted in King, 1996, pp. 137–138)

During an address to the Washington Interfaith Network in May 1996, the First Lady alluded to the staying power of her own marriage when she spoke of how the "good faith" of even people who "still have differences" could bring "each other together." She continued by confessing, "There aren't two people who agree with each other on everything—just stay married long enough, you'll figure it out" (Clinton, 1996). When asked, during a 1997 interview immediately after the Lewinsky scandal broke, if her husband would admit to causing pain in their marriage, Mrs. Clinton said "absolutely not" and again suggested that while in their long marriage, they had endured much media-induced pain, they had also grown together:

We've been married for twenty-two years and I have learned a long time ago that the only people who count in any marriage are the two that are in it. We know everything there is to know about each other and we understand and accept and love each other. The great story here for anybody willing to find it and write about it and explain it is this vast right-wing conspiracy that has been conspiring against my husband since the day he announced for President. A few journalists have kind of caught on to it and explained it, but it has not yet been fully revealed to the American public.... In a bizarre sort of way this may do it. I don't know what it is about my husband that generates such hostility, but I have seen it for twenty-five years. (quoted in Woodward, 1999, p. 395)

The Fair Fight Strategy

An additional discursive strategy the First Lady used for countering media framing of the president and herself was to state her aversion to personal attacks and call for arguing issues instead:

I don't mind criticism, and I don't mind controversy, as long as people are criticizing what is being done or said instead of personally attacking each other. I think that's an unfortunate by-product of our politics today where, instead of engaging each other on the merits of an issue and searching for common ground, people stand back and hurl insults at each other. That's not a very useful way for us to work together. So let's be willing to work together instead of staking out ideological positions and engaging in personal attacks. And then the controversy is fair game. That's what a democracy thrives on. (Hillary Clinton quoted in Osborne, 1997, p. 77)

At one point early in her second stint as First Lady, Hillary Clinton said, "I am just not interested in spending my days falling into the trap that the fomentors of all this want us to—which is to become isolated and on the defensive and diverted" (quoted in Osborne, 1997, p. 140). She refused to play the "game" as framed by the media: to become defensive or aggressive or, simply, "un-nice." The agenda would be Hillary Clinton's to set. This stance came early in her tenure as First Lady, perhaps an adjustment of her rhetorical persona after the "dragon lady" moniker given her by reporters in the first administration primed Americans to expect the "worst" from Hillary Clinton. In addition, Hillary Clinton's "be nice" tactic was also employed before she and her husband had been in the fire of media allegations in the second administration.

The Martyr Strategy

Hillary Clinton relied on her persona as the "spouse under fire" to bolster her ethos as a woman of character and stamina. Nelson (1993) believes that the winning 1992 presidential campaign was forged by Hillary Rodham Clinton during the crucial weeks in New Hampshire earlier that year:

Had she even once expressed doubt about his honesty and character, Bill's bid for the presidency would have gone the way of Gary Hart's campaign after the Donna Rice scandal. No matter how strained things might have been privately, Hillary held firm publicly. During those long, dark days, she was a rock. In the snows of New England, Hillary stood by her man in a way that should have made Tammy Wynette proud. (p. 53)

Franks (1999) observes that as her husband was falling from grace, the First Lady was resurrected into what Hall (1998) described as a "wronged wife looking more than alright, the weakened woman who somehow seemed stronger." More popular as an "injured party than she ever was as an equal party," she hit the campaign trail and was credited with helping to save the senatorial campaigns of Chuck Schumer in New York and Barbara Boxer in California (Franks, 1999). As the political crises intensified, the public on occasion may have felt the media as well as "political enemies" had overdone their persecution of the Clintons. This may have convinced some in the electorate to "go easy" on the First Couple, particularly during the impeachment proceedings. At one point, described as "stoic before a husband's satyriasis" and "glamorous as triumphant victim withstanding adversity" (Fields, 1998), Mrs. Clinton admitted not being able to "imagine anything worse" than testifying before a grand jury [during the Whitewater investigation] "since you have no idea what the questions are" and continued: "These people think they can come out of left field, or more likely right field, and ask me anything. So, it's not going to be a very easy experience for anyone, but I will do whatever it takes" (Hillary Clinton quoted in Osborne, 1997, p. 142).

The Logic Strategy

The First Lady located much of her defense of the Clinton administration in a "logic" and reason frame through which she criticized and demeaned the media as foes of her husband's presidency. She spoke of the Whitewater furor as a "big-lie technique" and "conspiracy theory," which struck her as "kind of silly." If she had realized that the media were going to make such an issue out of a failed land investment, she "would have been more attentive and taken the whole press inquiry more seriously." Lesson learned, Hillary Clinton was "trying to do that now" and promised to "try to be more effective explaining what happened and answering questions" (quoted in Osborne, 1997, p. 142).

Her tactic for managing the grand jury appearance about the Whitewater records that "suddenly" appeared at the White House was to maintain her innocence, if not ignorance, in and of the matter: "This had been, for me, kind of a difficult time because I can't answer these questions. I don't know where they've been" as well as admitting she was "pleased that they were found because they confirm what I have been saying" (Hillary Clinton quoted in Osborne, 1997, p. 141).

The Honest and Humble Strategy

When a media crisis begins, complete and quick disclosure is usually the best policy. Any delay in responding should only be to check and gather facts. The legacy of Watergate and Chappaquiddick is that the best course of action for a scandal-ridden politician is to plan one's reaction to the inevitable by communicating relevant information. Addressing rather than denying the story may prevent a two-day piece from becoming a "weeks-long water torture frenzy" (Sabato, 1991, p. 240). For example, full disclosure helped to end "frenzies" such as Jimmy Carter's "Billygate," Geraldine Ferraro's finances, and Richard Nixon's secret fund.

On occasion, Hillary Clinton referenced misguided, if not well-intentioned, actions, as in her admission of her poor judgment during the formation of the failed health care plan:

There are many things I could have done differently and many things that perhaps would have been presented better. But I also believe that it is the most controversial subject in our political life. You know, if you look at Harry Truman, it just was very hard for him and it's hard for anybody who tries to approach it. So, yes, I know I made mistakes and I know there are better ways I could have done things. And if I were to go over it again, I would try to present it better. I don't know if we'd have a different outcome, but I certainly would try. (Hillary Clinton quoted in Osborne, 1997, pp. 166–167)

During the 1994 "pink Press conference," she admitted that "one of the reasons I wanted to do this" interview was to correct any impression she was trying to hide something and that "this is really a result of our inexperience in Washington" and a failure to "fully appreciate the need to answer questions from the media." The First Lady also promised reporters that she was "certainly going to try to be more sensitive to what you all need and what we need to give you" and indicated she felt confident that Whitewater and related issues should not become a "long-term issue in any way" (quoted in Woodward, 1999, p. 253).

During a 1997 speech to the Women's Leadership Forum, Mrs. Clinton spoke of how she wanted "to thank you, thank you for what you did together; thank you for what you did in your individual capacities" and of how she "honestly" believed the "kind of effort that so many of you made in gathering the energy and resources that were necessary to make the case about the kind of country we are working to build was critical to the outcome of the elections in 1996" (Clinton, 1997b).

Such public admissions, including the discursive transformation of her image into that of a "humble but fair" political actor, contributed to the "humanization" of Mrs. Clinton. After four hours of grand jury testimony in response to Kenneth Starr's January 1998 subpoena to testify about her role in Whitewater, Hillary Clinton spoke with reporters:

Well, you are all still here, I see. Glad to have the opportunity to tell the grand jury what I have been telling all of you: I do not know how the billing records came to be found where they were found, but I am pleased that they were found, because they confirm what I have been saying. (quoted in Woodward, 1999, p. 317)

Such an image played well for the rhetorical management of later scandals that involved the First Lady, such as Whitewater and Travelgate. In addition, her "human(e)ness" was an ethos booster when she acted as President Clinton's surrogate. She said in a 1999 interview after her husband had been acquitted in his impeachment trial:

I don't believe in denying things. I believe in working through it. Is he ashamed? Yes. Is he sorry? Yes. But does this negate everything he has done as a husband, a father, a president? And what is so amazing is that Bill has not been defeated by this. There has been enormous pain, enormous anger, but I have been with him half my life and he is a very, very good man. We just have a deep connection that transcends whatever happens. (quoted in Franks, 1999, p. 174)

A RHETORICAL INVENTION: HILLARY RODHAM CLINTON

Hillary Clinton has expanded the range of what the wife of a president can do in her role as a policy leader. Gould (1996d) believes that while subsequent First Ladies may draw back from such extensive involvement in substantial issues, others will build on the precedents she has developed. Once an innovation has occurred in the role of First Lady, it is not long before others in the White House use the example as a rationale for their course as the wife of the president. Muir and Benitez (1996) believe the First Lady serves as a "synecodochic representation of American woman" and argue that "given [Hillary] Clinton's strong sense of identity as a woman ... 'First Woman' seems much more appropriate in comparison to the more restrictive and 'appropriate' manner of behavior implicit in the current label for the president's wife" (p. 150). As professional women become First Ladies in the future, Hillary Rodham Clinton will probably be seen not as a dramatic departure from older norms but the first example of how the wife of the president mirrors social trends a decade or so after they have first been noticed (pp. xvii–xix).

Mrs. Clinton has been compared to her "political godmother" (Franks, 1999, p. 248) Eleanor Roosevelt, a First Lady who also had an unfaithful husband. However, while Franklin Roosevelt's adultery was kept quiet and his wife's "pain was private," Hillary Clinton was "subjected to the full glare of public scrutiny" (Franks, 1999, p. 168). According to Muir and Benitez (1996) just as a president establishes a sense of ethos with the public, so too does the First Lady. The expectations and responsibilities of First Lady are so diverse and focused on by the media that "a constant struggle exists to present a strong sense of oneself" as well as "balance this sense with an understanding of the various perceptions of being feminine" (p. 153). With a husband who narrowly avoided becoming the first president in the history of the United States to be removed from office, Mrs. Clinton, during her tenure as First Lady, has been "co-president and co-dependent, and in the time between the two roles her private life became a public space" (Franks, 1999, p. 168).

She was as much a political actor as Bill Clinton and did what needed to be done to preserve his presidency. The First Lady, for example, learned in 1982 that adding "Clinton" to her name helped her husband get reelected as governor. She learned a decade later that baking cookies and admitting she enjoyed sewing and being a mom—rather than corporate lawyering and admitting she enjoyed power and being political—enabled her husband to win the nomination and ultimately the presidency. During the early years, she may have been a source of "mini-scandal" to her husband as he moved up the political ladder. The initial reluctance to stop being known as Hillary Rodham and her refusal to heed critics' calls that she dress for success and be more traditional were impediments to his election goal. Both were cosmetic problems that were easily managed. Even the accusations that Clinton's health care program would not have failed had she not been at the helm were muted by falling back to a major tactic begun in Arkansas: becoming a traditional wife and First Lady. After such setbacks, she retreated to a behind-the-scenes place for the continuation of her private and political partnership with Bill Clinton. The fallback position was not necessarily the rhetorical strategy Hillary Rodham Clinton used for all of the crises in the Clinton administration, particularly those directly involving her, such as the S&L scandal, Travelgate, and even much of Whitewater. For these, she usually answered her critics directly. However, when the scandals involved her husband, particularly with regard to his relationships with other women, the "dutiful, but stalwart partner" image was revived.

She emulated Eleanor Roosevelt's First Ladyship by operating within the constraints of the role to enlarge that role and employed her First Lady ethos in two critical ways. Initially Hillary Clinton relied on the traditional "woman-behind-the-man" character to make the electorate more comfortable with her and, by extension, the president. In so doing, she reframed the Clintons' combined and singular ethos through the media and for the public, which influenced additional media spin in the Clintons' favor. This was particularly the case when an imbroglio was developing. Second, she relied on her ability to work within a system without being co-opted by that system to modify it.

Hillary Rodham Clinton came to the White House "representing a new era, a new generation, the age of the professional woman, the smart woman" with her own political power base, who "would not exercise influence behind the scenes and then sit gazing adoringly at her husband when he was on stage" (Burrell, 1997, p. 18). The notion of a First Lady's possessing political power is complex, involving issues about gender; the consideration of women in a role of major power grounded in a "private and deeply personal relationship—marriage—that has public implications"; and it is a "traditional symbol . . . an icon that has developed roles and images with great meaning for the public, that is being transformed." Finally, there is the issue of accountability: the First Lady has no formal government position, receives no pay and no congressional confirmation, and cannot be fired. Other advisers answer only to the president and may be dismissed. "Ultimately, the First Lady is held indirectly accountable through the job her husband does as President" (p. 23). If he has done a "good job," so has she, and vice versa. Hillary Rodham Clinton had greater opportunity for altering the separation of private and public spheres than had been afforded most of her predecessors because her private role became a "legitimate basis for public actions." This enactment of First Lady merged the private and public realms in a way that facilitated the public's acceptance of Mrs. Clinton as both an "admired person" and a political leader. In this way, the position of First Lady became a political tool not only to advance Hillary Clinton's personal agenda but to manipulate the electorate's perceptions of her persona and so of her husband's as well.

The role of journalists as cultural storytellers becomes especially important when crises erupt, accidents happen, and politicians lose control of political situations. At these times, the press interprets the significance of such events without the aid of planned press activities (Bennett, 1997). In addition, what voters learn and which cues they use to assess political actors depend on how much knowledge they already have about politics and the operation of the federal government. Voters with less knowledge about politics are prone to rely on judgments of personal character as a way of estimating political character or judging the issue positions of candidates. Popkin (1997) says that regardless of how much Bill Clinton talked about issues, it was still easier for many Americans to believe unflattering stories about his personal character than to become informed about his career or stand on issues. The more time he spent addressing personal issues, the more attention he focused on them. When scandals plague political actors, who are slow at or reluctant to or simply inept at handling the crises, the media are left to spin their own morality tales, more often than not in grand motif fashion with good guys and bad guys and very few shades of gray. Hillary Clinton took this script for scandal and performed as her husband's surrogate to replace stories told with themes negative to the First Couple with positively themed tales. Her best-selling stories thus far were those she began telling and dramatically enacting during the impeachment. Was the president of the United States immoral, depraved, and unworthy of the office? Or was he just another mortal human, who, like all of us, sometimes slips up or falls down badly? Perhaps he could still be our president and even a good man, because, after all, this smart, attractive, good mother/professional woman/dedicated wife has supported him unwaveringly throughout all of this.

The press initially told stories about Bill Clinton as the villain. His admissions, including that he lied to the American public, did not give reporters any good reasons to justify changing their story. However, Hillary Clinton did. The First Lady turned her husband's shortcomings, as evidenced by the scandals in his administration, into strengths by rhetorically recasting him as at least a good guy. By focusing press attention on herself as partner and creating an affirmative, strong, and engaging persona, Hillary Clinton successfully deflected, diminished, and/or recreated "bad" mediated realities of her husband and his administration. She then used the media's own strategies of spinning and framing to lure reporters into her camp, who then ultimately spun and framed her version of the stories.

In the beginning, the two offered themselves as a political team—the "two-for-one" duo from 1992. This backfired during the health care crisis when the First Lady was blamed for the failure of "her husband's plan." In that case, a scapegoating tactic produced negative framing of her but less hostile perceptions of him because, after all, she was in charge (even though he was the one who put her in charge). In later scandals such as "Travelgate" and Whitewater, the two-for-one deal, which had been the Clintons' political mantra since the Arkansas governor's races, held, and she again deflected criticism away from him to herself. Is so doing, Hillary Clinton eased, if not neutralized, the potential harm these crises could have done to the president or the presidency. Certainly it was bad enough that the First Lady was accused of conflicts of interest and lining her pockets in, if not illegal, then probably unethical ways. It would have been much more damaging, however, if the president had been the Clinton accused of inappropriate trading or indiscriminate firings. He may or may not have actually had something to do with these things, but in the press's view—and so in Americans' view—she was the villain.

In the later scandals, Hillary Clinton again proved the political equal to her husband and surrogate to the president, when she became the focus of the media as the president's "womanizing" morphed into "perjury," which morphed into "impeachable offenses." A sort of magical thinking occurred when the press began to frame Hillary Rodham Clinton as the litmus test for how her husband would fare during the impeachment trial. After her persona as "Hillary, loyal wife" emerged fully formed in August 1998, a *New York Times*/CBS News poll revealed 73 percent of Americans now approved of the First Lady (Wasserstein, 1998). By early February 1999, polls identified her as America's "most admired woman," and "the more humiliations" that were "heaped upon her, the more admired" she got ("Sunday Comment," 1999) and the less likely it seemed her husband would be convicted. In January 1999, Tumulty and Gibbs described the First Lady as in pursuit of "the private rescue of a marriage and the public rescue of the presidency." *Time* reporter Margaret Carlson wrote of this aspect of the Clintons' political relationship before the 1993 inauguration: "Perhaps Bill Clinton, rather than seeming weak by comparison with his wife, has proved that it takes a solid, secure man to marry a strong woman" (quoted in Brock, 1996, p. 289) who had revealed "not a muscle of public vulnerability" (Fields, 1998).

If the First Lady held true and stood by her man—as she apparently had over two decades of crisis and scandal—then, magically, he must be a good person. If she held the line, then Bill Clinton, whom the public rarely doubted was at least a competent president, would survive and even prosper because his wife, who had turned out to be a "real lady" with priorities set—husband and children first, career second—never wavered during their years as a political and marital team. Indeed, a May 1998 *U.S. News and World Report* poll indicated that 62 percent of Americans said they admired the way the First Lady "has stood by her man" (Walsh, 1998a). If Hillary Rodham Clinton, wife and partner and First Surrogate for William Jefferson Clinton, stood firm, the press, with their penchant for spinning human interest and highly emotional stories onto front pages and the six o'clock news, would tell her story. The public, consumers of agendas produced by the press, would attend to the story of "Bill and Hillary," just as they had since 1992, for better and worse. In this final crisis, it was—at least for President Clinton—definitely for the "better." And Congress, dependent on the votes of their constituents, would have to share in the rhetorical tale of Bill Clinton: spun by his wife, framed by the media, and participated in by the American people. Ultimately the First Lady maneuvered the media so that her voicings became the most credible of those heard talking about impeachment and enabled William Jefferson Clinton to avoid becoming the first American president convicted during an impeachment trial and evicted from office.

Her flexibility ultimately served the Clintons well throughout their public life as First Couple. From 1992 through 1999, the electorate continuously looked to Mrs. Clinton to determine how she framed her responses via the media to scandals in the Clinton presidency. The conversion in her rhetorical presentation of self as First Lady—from traditional to progressive—provided the discursive space within which Hillary Rodham Clinton maneuvered through these crises.

Conclusion

> At the end of the day, you have to be yourself, you have to say and stand for what you believe in, you have to be willing to get up and go ahead and take the slings and arrows and just try to persist through them, because it's apparently an inevitable part of our American democracy. (Hillary Clinton quoted in Osborne, 1997, pp. 103–104)

Political rhetoric is about storytelling—how journalists tell stories to citizens, how advocates tell stories to journalists to convey to citizens, and how "we tell stories to each other to try to make sense of what is happening to our families, neighbors, and people we do not know" (Bales, 1997, p. 401). Hillary Rodham Clinton was, by this accounting, a fine teller of stories. Historian Lewis L. Gould (1996b) reflected on her First Ladyship to that point: "Not since Eleanor Roosevelt has a First Lady been so demonized. If her husband wins a second term and creates an impressive record of accomplishment in office, Hillary Rodham Clinton will be correctly seen as one of the key elements in his success" (p. 648).

If Bill Clinton's impeachment acquittal is an unprecedented accomplishment for a twentieth-century American president, then the role Hillary Rodham Clinton played in that acquittal—as well as in rhetorically managing other crises in her husband's administrations—is without precedent for an American First Lady. The *Washington Post*'s Eleanor Clift wrote in 1994 that "the key to a First Lady's effectiveness is not whether people like you, but whether you can help the president" (quoted in Brock, 1996, p. 366). If this is a major criterion for assessing Hillary Clinton's tenure as president's wife, then hers has been remarkable in that her rhetorical intervention may well have saved her husband's presidency.

One of the reasons that Hillary Rodham Clinton was so successful in creating her own mediated image of her husband and his scandals may have been that, according to Richard Reeves (1996), the group that disliked Bill Clinton the most were white males. If this is the case, it may have been that white women as well as others were at least more willing to explore accepting the First Lady's vision. For example, many American women already identified with Mrs. Clinton before the scandals broke in full force. By the time of the impeachment trial, these women, if not entirely in favor of retaining Bill Clinton as president, were in favor of retaining his wife as First Lady. In addition, Hillary Clinton's credibility may have been so strong with many American women that when the choice became, "Who should we believe about the president?" her version of who Bill Clinton was and why he should remain president trumped any other channeled through the media. Images mediated symbolically—rather than direct experience—constitute the public's knowledge of politics and political actors. Therefore, many Americans were willing to accept Hillary Clinton's rhetorical packaging of and enactment as the president's wife. And because this construct made them feel "warm and fuzzy" about the First Lady who was "standing by her man" despite the "facts," they also "stood by their president," scandals or not.

Initially, the perceptions of the Clintons as the first First Couple produced by the 60s generation resulted in various framing responses ranging from their being targeted as examples of what "went wrong" with the nation to representatives of the "best of the baby boomers." *New York Times* media reporter Howard Kurtz wrote in 1998 that although it was unclear whether the Lewinsky scandal would force Bill Clinton from office or whether he would "manage yet again to hang on," the damage to his presidency would never be repaired because of Clinton's failed efforts to "rise above his slippery public image." Kurtz predicted that the last president of the twentieth century "would have his place in history, but it was not the one he had imagined" (p. 303).

That may well be true of the Clinton presidency, but for different reasons and in different ways. The power of political actors depends in great part on how the press opts to represent these individuals, through mediated strategies such as framing, priming, and agenda setting. Accordingly, how politicians and their surrogates are presented by and in the media is crucial. During Clinton's scandals, there was essentially an ongoing campaign to counterbalance rhetorically the weight of negatively framed stories about the presidency with stories and images provided by and from and about Hillary Rodham Clinton that the press could not dismiss or alter in significant ways. Reporters were constrained by the rhetorical strengths of Mrs. Clinton's images and so had to spin them positively. It is likely that the First Lady's "stand-by-my-man/I am a private person/good-mother-smart woman" discursive persona was simply one that could not be reconfigured by the press.

In 1996, former chief political correspondent for the *New York Times* Richard Reeves criticized Hillary Clinton for pretending to be a politician—as opposed to an engaged and energetic citizen—and chastised her as having " the political instincts of a stone" (1996, p. 96). Four years and a failed impeachment trial later, the words of these elite journalists ring not only hollow but possibly untrue as well. Hillary Rodham Clinton's rhetorical surrogacy facilitated the discursive rescue of her husband's presidency not only from the impeachment abyss but perhaps from an historical one as well.

Former presidential press secretary Marlin Fitzwater (1995) suggests that "every White House, every president, somehow becomes a metaphor for the times" (p. viii). The modern presidency has been described as a rhetorical presidency (Denton and Woodward, 1990; and Tullis, 1987) in that the president acts through the media as a public opinion leader (Tullis, 1987). The president determines goals and provides solutions for the nation's problems and realizes that because the media dramatize what presidents say—as opposed to what they *do*—image and personality will often be favored over substantive deliberation on issues (Trent and Friedenberg, 1995) so that "every act, word, or phrase" of a president "becomes calculated and measured for a response" (Denton and Woodward, 1990, p. 200).

Certainly Mrs. Clinton's rhetorical management of crises and scandals in her husband's administration could be understood according to the traditional—if not always openly acknowledged—role of First Lady as chief surrogate. However, there is also a strong argument that Hillary Rodham Clinton's enactment of the role is itself a metaphor for the times—the culmination of a transformation begun by Eleanor Roosevelt into a paradigmatic "rhetorical First Ladyship" and legacy for First Partners of the twenty-first century.

Bibliography

Adair, L. (1998, May 5). "Comfortable contradictions." *San Francisco Chronicle*, p. E10.
Alger, D. E. ((1996). *The media and politics* (2nd ed.). New York: Wadsworth.
Alter, J. (1993, Aug. 23). "Journalism as a blood sport." *Newsweek*, p. 33.
Alvarez, L. (1998, Aug. 12). "Hillary Clinton: Popular, and hardly in hiding." *New York Times*. Available at: http://search.nytimes.com/search/daily/b . . . e+8843+1+wAAA+Hillary%7ERodham%7EClinton.
Anderson, J. (1980, Nov. 30). "Why I tell secrets." *Parade*, p. 12.
Anthony, C.S. (1990–1991). *First ladies: The saga of the presidents' wives and their power, 1789–1961* (2 vols.). New York: Morrow.
———. (1996a). "Florence King Harding." In L. L. Gould (ed.), *American First Ladies: Their lives and their legacy*, (pp. 368–383). New York: Garland.
———. (1996b). "Patricia Nixon." In L. L. Gould, (ed.), *American First Ladies: Their lives and their legacy* (pp. 520–535). New York: Garland.
———. (1998). *Florence Harding: The First Lady, the Jazz age, and the death of America's most scandalous president.* New York: Morrow.
Auletta, K. (1997a). "Raiding the global village." In S. Iyengar & R. Reeves (eds.), *Do the media govern? Politicians, voters, and reporters in America* (pp. 82–89). Thousand Oaks, CA: Sage.
———. (1997b). "Three blind mice." In S. Iyengar & R. Reeves (eds.), *Do the media govern? Politicians, voters, and reporters in America* (pp. 77–81). Thousand Oaks, CA: Sage.
Bagdikian, B. H. (1997). "The U.S. media: Supermarket or assembly line?" In S. Iyengar & R. Reeves (eds.), *Do the media govern? Politicians, voters, and reporters in America* (pp. 66–76). Thousand Oaks, CA: Sage.

Baker, J. H. (1996). "Mary Todd Lincoln." In L. L. Gould (ed.), *American First Ladies: Their lives and their legacy* (pp. 174–190). New York: Garland.

Bales, S. N. (1997). "Talking back, Ernie Pyle style." In S. Iyengar & R. Reeves (eds.), *Do the media govern? Politicians, voters, and reporters in America* (pp. 401–408). Thousand Oaks, CA: Sage.

Barrett, L. I. (1987, June 22). "Orator for the next generation: Does Joe Biden talk too much?" *Time*, pp. 24–25.

Bartels, L. M. (1996, Sept.) *Politicians and the press: Who leads, who follows.* Paper presented at the Annual Meeting of the American Political Science Association, San Francisco.

Bates, S. (1989). *If no news, send rumors.* New York: St. Martin's.

Baumgartner, F. R., Jones, B. D., and Leech, B. (1997). "Media attention and congressional agendas." In S. Iyengar & R. Reeves (eds.), *Do the media govern? Politicians, voters, and reporters in America* (pp. 349–363). Thousand Oaks, CA: Sage.

Beasley, M.H. (1987). *Eleanor Roosevelt and the media.* Urbana: University of Illinois Press.

———. (1996). "Bess Truman." In L. L. Gould (ed.), *American First Ladies: Their lives and their legacy* (pp. 449–462). New York: Garland.

Begala, P. (1995, Oct.–Nov.). "It's the media, stupid." *George*, pp. 135–138.

Bennett, W. L. (1997). "Cracking the news code: Some rules that journalists live by." In S. Iyengar & R. Reeves (eds.), *Do the media govern? Politicians, voters, and reporters in America* (pp. 103–117). Thousand Oaks, CA: Sage.

Benz, D. (1996). "The media factor behind the 'Hillary factor.'" In J. Naureckas and J. Jackson (eds.), *The fair reader: An Extra! review of press and politics in the '90s* (pp. 112–115). Boulder, CO: Westview.

Benze Jr., J. G. (1996). "Nancy Reagan." In L. L. Gould (ed.), *American First Ladies: Their lives and their legacy* (pp. 583–607). New York: Garland.

Bernstein, C. (1992, June 8). "The idiot culture." *New Republic*, pp. 24–25.

Berry Jr., J. P. (1987). *John F. Kennedy and the media: The first television president.* Lanham, MD: University Press of America.

Birmingham, S. (1980, October). "The Kennedy women: America's seven wonders." *Harper's Bazaar*, p. 29.

Black, A. M. (1996). "Eleanor Roosevelt." In L. L. Gould (ed.), *American First Ladies: Their lives and their legacy* (pp. 422–448). New York: Garland.

Blair, C., and Houck, D. W. (1994). "Richard Nixon and the personalization of crisis." In A. Kiewe (ed.), *The modern presidency and crisis rhetoric* (pp. 91–118). Westport, CT: Praeger, 1994.

Blumenfeld, L. (1996, Apr. 8–14). "And one of them shall be first." *Washington Post National Weekly Edition*, pp. 6–7.

Boorstin, D. J. (1984) *The image.* New York: Atheneum.

Boot, W. (1989, Jan.–Feb.). "Campaign '88: TV overdoses on the inside dope. *Columbia Journalism Review, 27*, 23.

———. (1987, Mar.–Apr.). "Iranscam: When the cheering stopped." *Columbia Journalism Review, 25,* 25–30.
Branson, L. (1998, Sept. 9). "The first lady in waiting." *Scotsman* (Edinburgh), pp. 11–12.
Brant, M., and Thomas, E. (1996, Jan. 15). "First fighter." *Newsweek,* pp. 20–24.
Braver, R. (1997). "Show and tell: Reporters meet politicians on Larry King live." In S. Iyengar & R. Reeves (eds.), *Do the media govern? Politicians, voters and reporters in America* (pp. 33–39). Thousand Oaks, CA: Sage.
Brock, D. (1996). *The seduction of Hillary Rodham.* New York: Free Press.
Broder, D. (1987). *Behind the front page: A candid look at how the news is made.* New York: Simon & Schuster.
Bruck, C. (1994, May 30). "Hillary the pol." *New Yorker,* p. 91.
Burke, K. (1969a). *A grammar of motives.* Berkeley: University of California Press.
———. (1969b). *A rhetoric of motives.* Berkeley: University of California Press.
Burrell, B. (1997). *Public opinion, the First Ladyship, and Hillary Rodham Clinton.* New York: Garland.
Calhoun, C. W. (1996). "Caroline Scott Harrison." In L. L. Gould (ed.), *American First Ladies: Their lives and their legacy* (pp. 260–276). New York: Garland.
Cannon, C. M. (1993). "The story in the closet." *Forbes Media Critic,* 1:46.
Cappella, J. N., and Jamieson, K. N. (1997). *Spiral of cynicism: The press and the public good.* New York: Oxford University Press.
Caroli, B.B. (1995). *First ladies.* New York: Oxford.
———. (1996). "Jacqueline Kennedy." In L. L. Gould (ed.), *American First Ladies: Their lives and their legacy* (p. 476–495). New York: Garland.
———. (1998, Oct. 8). "From one first lady to another." *Newsday,* p. A57.
Cater, C. (1959). *The fourth branch of government.* Boston: Houghton Mifflin.
Ceaser, J. W., Thurow, G. E., Tulis, J.K., and Bessette, J.M. (1983). "The rise of the rhetorical presidency." In T. O. Windt & B. Ingold (eds.), *Essays in presidential rhetoric,* (pp. 3–22). Dubuque, IA: Kendall Hunt.
Cherwitz, R. A. (1980). "Masking inconsistency: The Tonkin Gulf crisis." *Communication Quarterly, 28,* 27–37.
Chiasson, Jr., L. (1995). Preface to *The press in times of crisis* (pp. ix-x). Westport, CT: Greenwood.
Ciabattari, J. (1998, Sep. 27). "Start the vote for a woman president." *Parade,* pp. 14–15.
Clinton, H. (1994, Sep. 29). "HRC remarks on national primary day care." *Speeches by the First Lady, the First Lady of the United States Web Page.* Available at: http//www.whitehouse.gov/ . . . /1994–09–29–first-lady-on-national-primary-day-care.tex.
———. (1995, Jan. 26). "Keynote address by First Lady Hillary Rodham Clinton at the dedication of Eleanor Roosevelt College, San Diego, California." *Speeches by the First Lady, the First Lady of the United States Web*

Page. Available at: http//www.whitehouse.gov/WH/EOP/First_Lady/html/generalspeeches/1995/1-26-95.html.

———. (1996, May 29). "Remarks by the First Lady to the Washington Interfaith Network." *Speeches by the First Lady, the First Lady of the United States Web Page.* Available at: http//www.whitehouse.gov/WH/EOP/First_Lady/html/generalspeeches/1996/inter.html.

———. (1997a, June 14). "First Lady Hillary Rodham Clinton: Commencement address for Ohio University." *Speeches by the First Lady: The First Lady of the United States Web Page.* Available at: http//www.whitehouse.gov/WP/EOP/First_Lady/html/generalspeeches/1997/ohiotr.html.

———. (1997b, Apr. 18). "Remarks by the First Lady to the Women's Leadership Forum." *Speeches by the First Lady, The First Lady of the United States Web Page.* Available at: http//www.whitehouse.gov/WP/EOP/First_Lady/html/generalspeeches/1997/wlf.html.

———. (1998, Dec. 4). "Remarks by First Lady Hillary Rodham Clinton: Eleanor Roosevelt Lectures." *Speeches by the First Lady, the First Lady of the United States Web Page.* Available at: http//www.whitehouse.gov/WP/EOP/First_Lady/html/generalspeeches/1998/19981204.html.

———. (1999a, Mar. 3). "Women's Leadership Forum Speech on Women and Politics. Remarks by First Lady Hillary Rodham Clinton." *Speeches by the First Lady, the First Lady of the United States Web Page.* Available at: http//www.whitehouse.gov/WP/EOP/First_Lady/html/generalspeeches/1999/19990303.html.

———. (1999, Mar. 4). "United Nations International Women's Day Speech on Women's Rights. Remarks by First Lady Hillary Rodham Clinton." *Speeches by the First Lady, the First Lady of the United States Web Page.* Available at: *http//www.whitehouse.gov/WP/EOP/First_Lady/html/generalspeeches/1999/19990304.ht ml.*

Cohen, R., Oliphant, T., Reeves, R., and Shogan, R. (1997). "Combat stories." In S. Iyengar & R. Reeves (eds.), *Do the media govern? Politicians, voters and reporters in America* (pp. 50–56). Thousand Oaks, CA: Sage.

Connolly, P. (1998, September 17). "First ladies share much in common." *Tennessean*, p. 1D.

Cook, T. (1998). *Governing with the news: The news media as a political institution.* Chicago: University of Chicago Press.

Cooper, M. (1989). *Analyzing public discourse.* Prospect Heights IL: Waveland.

Cordery, S. A. (1996). "Helen Herron Taft." In L. L. Gould (ed.), *American First Ladies: Their lives and their legacy* (pp. 321–339). New York: Garland.

Cottrell, D. M. (1996). "Lou Henry Hoover." In L. L. Gould (ed.), *American First Ladies: Their lives and their legacy* (pp. 409–421). New York: Garland.

Cronkite, W. (1998). "Reporting presidential campaigns: A journalist's view." In D. Graber, D. McQuail, and P. Norris (eds.), *The politics of news. The news of politics* (pp. 57–69). Washington, D.C.: CQ Press.

Crouse, T. (1972). *The boys on the bus*. New York: Ballantine.
Dahl, M. K., and Bennett, W. L. (1995, Sept.). *Media agency and the use of icons in the agenda-setting process*. Paper presented at the Annual Meeting of the American Political Science Association, Chicago.
Davis, L. (1994, Apr. 4). "The name of the rose: An Arkansas thriller." *New Republic*, p. 14.
Davis, R. (1996). *The press and American politics: The new mediator* (2nd ed.). Saddle River, NJ: Prentice Hall.
Denton, R. E., and Holloway, R. L. (Eds.). (1996). *The Clinton presidency: Images, issues, and communication strategies*. Westport, CT: Praeger.
———, and Woodward, G. (1990). *Political communication in America* (2nd ed.). New York: Praeger.
Devroy, A., and S. Schmidt. (1995, Dec. 20). "The mystery in Foster's office: Following suicide, what drove associates' actions?" *Washington Post*, p. A1.
Dowd, M. (1995a, Aug. 10). "The 2 Mrs. Clintons." *New York Times*, p. A19.
———. (1995, Oct. 19). "Return to gender." *New York Times*, p. A25.
Dumas, E. (1993). *The Clintons of Arkansas: An introduction by those who knew them best*. Fayetteville, AR: University of Arkansas Press.
Edelman, M. (1967). *The symbolic uses of politics*. Urbana: University of Illinois Press.
———. (1988). *Constructing the political spectacle*. Chicago: University of Chicago Press.
Edwards, G. C. (1983). *The public presidency: The pursuit of popular support*. New York: St. Martin's Press.
Emery, N. (1998, Mar. 28). "The first victim." Spectator (London), p. 15.
Entman, R. (1989). *Democracy without citizens*. New York: Oxford University Press.
———. (1993). "Framing: Toward clarification of a fractured paradigm." *Journal of Communication, 43*, 52–53.
"Excerpts of Mrs. Clinton interview." (1998, Jan. 27). *Washington Post*. Available at: http://www.washingtonpost.com/wp-srv/pol . . . ecial/Clinton/stories/excerpts012798.htm.
Feder, D. (1998, May 13). "Mrs. Clinton wants to run everything." *Boston Herald*, p. 27.
Feeney, Susan. (1998, Oct. 9). "First lady a hot ticket on the campaign trail." *Erie (PA) Daily Times*, pp. 1A, 12A.
Fenno, R. (1978). *Home style*. Boston: Little, Brown.
Fields, S. (1998, Nov. 30). "Hillary as the woman of the 90s." *Washington Times*, p. A19. Available at: http://proquest.umi.com/pqdweb?TS= . . . 3&Sid=6&Idx=4&Deli=1&RQY=309&Dtp=1.
Fisher, W. R. (1989). *Human communication as narration: Toward a philosophy of reason, value and action*. Columbia, SC: University of South Carolina Press.
Fitzwater, M. (1995). *Call the briefing! Bush and Reagan, Sam and Helen: A decade with presidents and the press*. New York: Random House.

Flaherty, P., and Flaherty, T. (1996). *The First Lady: A comprehensive view of Hillary Rodham Clinton*. Lafayette, LA: Vital Issues Press.

Fleming, S., and Gunther, M. (1987, Jan. 23). "Suicide photos pose dilemma for papers, TV." *Detroit News*.

Fournier, F. (1996, Mar. 26). "First lady's European tour gets off to emotional start." *Erie (PA) Daily Times*, pp. 1–2A.

Frankovic, K. A. (1998). "Public opinion and polling." In D. Graber, D. McQuail & P. Norris (eds.), *The politics of news: The news or politics (pp.150–170)*. Washington, DC: CQ Press.

Franks, L. (1999, Sept.). "The intimate Hillary." *Talk*, pp. 167–174, 248, 250.

Gans, H. J. (1979). *Deciding what's news: A study of CBS Evening News, NBC Nightly News, Newsweek and Time*. New York: Pantheon.

Germond, J., and Witcover, J. (1980, May 5). "The era of newspeak." *Detroit Free Press*.

———. (1994). *Mad as hell: Revolt at the ballot box 1992*. New York: Random House.

Gibbs, N., and Duffy, M. (1996, July 1). "Just heartbeats away." *Time*. Available at: http://cgi.pathfinder.com/time/moy/hillary.html.

Goffman, E. (1959). *The presentation of self in everyday life*. New York: Anchor Books.

Goodwin, D. K. (1987). *Covering the candidates: Role and the responsibilities of the press*. Reston, VA: American Press Institute.

Gould, L. L. (1996a). "Edith Bolling Wilson." In L. L. Gould (ed.), *American First Ladies: Their lives and their legacy* (pp. 355–367). New York: Garland.

———. (1996b). "Hillary Rodham Clinton." In L. L. Gould (ed.), *American First Ladies: Their lives and their legacy* (pp. 630–650). New York: Garland.

———. (1996c). "Lady Bird Johnson." In L. L. Gould (ed.), *American First Ladies: Their lives and their legacy* (pp. 496–519). New York: Garland.

———. (1996d). "The First Lady as symbol and institution." In L. L. Gould (ed.), *American First Ladies: Their lives and their legacy* (pp. xiii-xx). New York: Garland.

Graber, D., McQuail, D., and Norris, P. (1998). "Introduction: Political communication in a democracy." In D. Graber, D. McQuail, and P. Norris (eds.), *The politics of news: The news of politics* (pp. 1–16). Washington, D.C.: CQ Press.

Green, B. (1996, Feb. 26). "Hillary Clinton and the American way." *Erie (PA) Daily Times*, p. 5A.

Greenfield, J. (1997). "The business of television news." In S. Iyengar and R. Reeves (eds.), *Do the media govern? Politicians, voters and reporters in America* (pp. 90–98). Thousand Oaks, CA: Sage.

Grossman, M. B., and Kumar, M. J. (1979, Spring). "The White House and the news media: The phases of their relationship." *Political Science Quarterly*, pp. 37–53.

Gutin, M. (1996). "Barbara Bush." In L. L. Gould (ed.), *American First Ladies: Their lives and their legacy* (pp. 608–629). New York: Garland.
Hahn, D. (1998). *Political communication: Rhetoric, government, and citizens.* State College, PA: Strata.
Hall, M. (1998, Nov. 24). "A regal renaissance for First Lady." *USA Today*, p. 12A.
Hall, M., and Lee, J. (1998, Aug. 18). "Family goes on vacation with pain to bear." *USA Today*, p. 4A.
Hall, M., and Page, S. (1998, Aug. 19). "Nation may take cue from what First Lady does next." *USA Today*, pp. 1A, 2A.
Hallin, D. C. (1994). *We keep America on top of the world: Television journalism and the public sphere.* London: Routledge.
———. (1997). "Sound bite news." In S. Iyengar and R. Reeves (eds.), *Do the media govern? Politicians, voters, and reporters in America* (pp. 57–65). Thousand Oaks, CA: Sage.
Harbrecht, D. A. (1987, Mar. 30). "Is Joe Biden more than 'just a speech'?" *Business Week*, pp. 59–60.
Harris, J. F., and Devroy, A. (1996, Feb. 19–25). "In us we trust." *Washington Post National Weekly Edition*, pp. 6–7.
Hart, R. (1987). *The sound of leadership.* Chicago: University of Chicago Press.
Hay, M. P. (1996). "Julia Tyler." In L. L. Gould (ed.), *American First Ladies: Their lives and their legacy* (pp. 117–129). New York: Garland.
Henry, W. A. III, Bruns, R. and Ogden, C. (1983, Dec. 12). "Journalism under fire." *Time*, pp. 76–93.
Hess, S. (1981). *The Washington reporters.* Washington, D.C.: Brookings Institution.
"Hillary Clinton launches stern defence of husband—again." (1998, Sept. 11). *ITN World News* (Britain) Available at: wysiwyg://229/http://www.itn.co.uk/World/world19980911/091103w.htm.
Hoggart, S. (1994, Mar. 29). "The leader you paralyze isn't ours alone." *Star Tribune* (Twin Cities), p. 17A.
Hoogenboom. O. (1996). "Lucy Webb Hayes." In L. L. Gould (ed.), *American First Ladies: Their lives and their legacy* (pp. 216–229). New York: Garland.
Horn, M. (1998, Sept. 28). "Feminists don't know what to think." *U.S. News and World Report*, p. 35.
Hunt, A. (1996, Mar. 14). "The other vision problem." *Wall Street Journal*, p. 19.
Ifill, G. (1992, June 21). "For Clinton, attention grows, problems remain." *New York Times*, sec. 4, p. 1.
Ireland, D. (1996, Feb. 19). "Hot water: Whitewater investigations." *Nation*, p. 5.
"Is the attack back? TV news coverage of the Whitewater affair." (1994, Mar.–Apr.). *Media Monitor*, p. 3.
Isikoff, M. (1999). *Uncovering Clinton: A reporter's story.* New York: Crown.
Iyengar, S. (1997a). "Framing responsibility for political issues: The case of poverty." In S. Iyengar and R. Reeves (eds.), *Do the media govern? Politi-*

cians, voters, and reporters in America (pp. 276–282). Thousand Oaks, CA: Sage.

———. (1997b). "Overview to part III." In S. Iyengar and R. Reeves (eds.), *Do the media govern? Politicians, voters, and reporters in America* (pp. 143–148). Thousand Oaks, CA: Sage.

———. (1997c). "Overview to part IV." In S. Iyengar and R. Reeves (eds.), *Do the media govern? Politicians, voters, and reporters in America* (pp. 171–179). Thousand Oaks, CA: Sage.

———. (1997d). "Overview to part V." In S. Iyengar and R. Reeves (eds.), *Do the media govern? Politicians, voters, and reporters in America* (pp. 319–333). Thousand Oaks, CA: Sage.

Iyengar, S., and Kinder, D. R. (1987). *News that matters.* Chicago: University of Chicago Press.

Iyengar, S., and Simon, A. (1997). "News coverage of the Gulf crisis and public opinion." In S. Iyengar and R. Reeves (eds.), *Do the media govern? Politicians, voters, and reporters in America* (pp. 248–257). Thousand Oaks, CA: Sage.

Jacobs, L. R., and Shapiro, R. Y. (1994, Mar.). "Studying substantive democracy." *PS, 27,* 9–17.

James, C. (1999, July 12). "Stars indulge in fame game." *(Portland) Oregonian,* pp. C1, C3.

Jamieson, K. H. (1992). *Dirty politics.* New York: Oxford.

Jamieson, K. H., and Campbell, K. K. (1983). *The interplay of influence: Mass media and their publics in news, advertising, politics.* Belmont, CA: Wadsworth.

Jamieson, K. H., and Cappella, J. N. (1998). "The role of the press in the health care reform debate of 1993–1994." In D. Graber, D. McQuail, and P. Norris (eds.), *The politics of news; the news of politics* (pp. 110–131). Washington, D.C.: CQ Press.

"Joan Kennedy." (1979, Dec. 24). *People,* p. 51.

Judis, J. B. (1987, July–Aug.). "The Hart affair." *Columbia Journalism Review, 25,* 21–25.

Kates, J. (1998, Sept. 6). "A philandering president's wife searching for purpose with Mrs. Harding, a powerful first lady." *Plain Dealer,* p. 121.

Katz, J. (1992, Mar. 5). "Rock, rap and movies bring you the news." *Rolling Stone,* p. 35.

Kernell, S. (1993). *Going public* (2nd ed.). Washington, D.C.: CQ Press.

———. (1997)."The theory and practice of going public." In S. Iyengar and R. Reeves (eds.), *Do the media govern? Politicians, voters, and reporters in America* (pp. 323–333). Thousand Oaks, CA: Sage.

Kimball, P. (1994). *Downsizing the news: Network cutbacks in the nation's capital.* Washington, D.C.: Woodrow Wilson Center Press.

King, N. (1996). *The woman in the White House: The remarkable story of Hillary Rodham Clinton.* New York: Carol Publishing Group.

"Koppel covers for Limbaugh's rumor-mongering." (1996). In J. Naureckas and J. Jackson (eds.), *The fair reader: An Extra! review of press and politics in the '90s* (pp. 139–141). Boulder, CO: Westview.

Krauthammer, C. (1992, Jan. 31). "The press confronts its power." *Washington Post*, p. A19.

Kurtz, H. (1998). *Spin cycle*. New York: Free Press.

Kuypers, J. A. (1997). *Presidential crisis rhetoric and the press in the post–Cold War world*. Westport, CT: Praeger.

Lash, J. P. (1973). *Eleanor: The years alone*. New York: Signet.

Lavelle, M., and Barnes, J. E. (1998, Sept. 28). "Staring into the political abyss." *U.S. News and World Report*, pp. 16–20.

Leffler, J. J. (1996). "Ida Saxon McKinley." In L. L. Gould (ed.), *American First Ladies: Their lives and their legacy* (pp. 277–293). New York: Garland.

Lehrer, J. (1993, July 2). "Meanness in the media." *Boston Globe*, p. 15.

Lemert, J. B., Elliott, W. R., Rosenberg, W. L., and Bernstein, J. M. (1996). *The politics of disenchantment: Bush, Clinton, Perot and the press*. Cresskill, NJ: Hampton Press.

Leo, J. (1998, Sept. 28). "It's time for doomsday." *U.S. News and World Report*, p. 14.

Leonard, M. (1998, Sept. 25). "Feminists side with president." *Boston Globe*, p. A1.

Lichter, S. R., and Amundson, D. R. (1994). "Less news is worse news: Television news coverage of Congress, 1972–1992." In T. Mann and N. Ornstein (eds.), *Congress, the press, and the public*. Washington, D.C.: Brookings/American Enterprise Institute.

Lippmann, W. (1922). *Public opinion*. New York: Macmillan.

Lydon, C. (1992, May–June). "Sex, war and death: Covering Clinton became a test of character—for the press." *Columbia Journalism Review*, p. 58.

Lyons, G. (1996). *Fools for scandal: How the media invented Whitewater*. New York: Franklin Square Press.

Lyons, R. L. (1973, Oct. 17). "Rhodes seems certain to take Ford's place." *Washington Post*, p. A2.

Maher, M., and Chiasson, Jr., L. (1995). "The press and crisis: What have we learned?" In L. Chiasson, Jr. (ed.), *The press in times of crisis* (pp. 219–223). Westport CT: Greenwood.

Manheim, J. B. (1998). "The news shapers: Strategic communication as a third force in news making." In D. Graber, D. McQuail, and P. Norris (eds.), *The politics of news: The news of politics* (pp. 94–109). Washington, D.C.: CQ Press.

Maraniss, D. (1998, Feb. 1). "First Lady's energy, determination bind power partnership." *Washington Post*, p. A1.

Marcus, R. (1998, Aug. 24). "Standing by her man—again." *Washington Post National Weekly Edition*, p. 10.

Martin, S. T. (1998, Sept. 20). "Why stay? Because she's first lady." *St. Petersburg Times*, p. 2A.

Marton, K. (1999, Jan. 18). "The once and future Hillary." *Time*. Available: http://cgi.pathfinder.com/time/magazine/articles/0,3266,18299,00.html.p.36.

McCombs, M., and Estrada, G. (1997). "The news media and the pictures in our heads." In S. Iyengar and R. Reeves (eds.), *Do the media govern? Politicians, voters, and reporters in America* (pp. 237–247). Thousand Oaks, CA: Sage.

McGrory, M.(1998, Nov. 16). "Now starring: Hillary, the avenging angel." *Washington Post National Weekly*, p. 23.

McManus, J. H. (1994). *Market-driven journalism: Let the citizen beware?* Thousand Oaks, CA: Sage.

Means, M. (1995, Apr. 25). "Hillary legacy may be felt by future presidents' wives." *State Journal Register* (Springfield, IL), p. 6.

Meyrowitz, J. (1985). *No sense of place: The impact of television on social behavior*. New York: Oxford University Press.

Miller, J. M., and Krosnick, J. (1997). "Anatomy of news media priming." In S. Iyengar and R. Reeves (eds.), *Do the media govern? Politicians, voters, and reporters in America* (pp. 258–275). Thousand Oaks, CA: Sage.

Mitchell, F. D. (1998). *Harry S. Truman and the news media: Contentious relations, belated respect*. Columbia, MO: University of Missouri Press.

"More urge than surge." (1987, June 13). *Economist*, pp. 41–42.

Muir, J. K., and Benitez, L. M. (1996). "Redefining the role of the First Lady: The rhetorical style of Hillary Rodham Clinton." In R. E. Denton and R. L. Holloway (eds.), *The Clinton presidency: Images, issues and communication strategies* (pp. 139–158). Westport, CT: Praeger.

Nacos, B. L. (1990). *The press, presidents, and crises*. New York: Columbia University Press.

Naureckas, J., and Jackson, J. (1996). "Introduction: The media agenda." In J. Naureckas and J. Jackson (eds.), *The fair reader: An Extra! review of press and politics in the '90s* (pp. xv–xviii). Boulder, CO: Westview.

Neal, S. (1984). *Dark horse*. New York: Doubleday.

Nelson, R. (1993). *The Hillary factor*. New York: Gallen Publishing Group.

Neustadt, R. E. (1976). *Presidential power*. New York: Wiley.

Nimmo, D., and Combs, J. (1990). *Mediated political realities* (2nd ed.). White Plains, NY: Longman.

Noelle-Neumann, E. (1993). The spiral of silence (2nd ed.). Chicago: University of Chicago Press.

Norris, P. (1997). "Introduction: The rise of postmodern political communications?" In P. Norris (ed.), *Politics and the press: The news media and their influences* (pp. 1–17). Boulder, CO: Lynne Rienner Publishers.

Oliphant, T. (1992, June 7). "A challenge to journalism to get its act together." *Boston Globe*, p. 87.

Osborne, C. G. (ed.). (1997). *The unique voice of Hillary Rodham Clinton: A portrait in her own words*. New York: Avon.

Page, B. I. (1996). *Who deliberates? Mass media in modern democracy*. Chicago: University of Chicago Press.

Paletz, D. L. (1998). "The media and public policy." In D. Graber, D. McQuail, and P. Norris (eds.), *The politics of news; the news of politics* (pp.218–237). Washington, D.C.: CQ Press.

Patterson, T. E. (1980). *The mass media election*. New York: Praeger.

———. (1994, Spring). "Legitimate beef: The presidency and a carnivorous press." *Media Studies Journal*, p. 21.

———. (1998). "Political roles of the journalist." In D. Graber, D. McQuail, and P. Norris (eds.), *The politics of news; the news of politics* (pp. 17–32). Washington, D.C.: CQ Press.

Pertschuk, M. (1997). "Putting media effects research to work: Lessons for community groups who would be heard." In S. Iyengar and R. Reeves (eds.), *Do the media govern? Politicians, voters, and reporters in America* (pp. 391–400). Thousand Oaks, CA: Sage.

Peters, C. (1996, Apr.). "Tilting at windmills." *Washington Monthly*, p. 7.

Pierpoint, R. (1981). *At the White House: Assignment to six presidents*. New York: Putnam's.

Pious, R. (1979). *The American presidency*. New York: Basic Books.

"Politics and the media." (1992, Feb. 6–7). Conference report on the Mondale Policy Forum, Hubert H. Humphrey Institute of Public Affairs, University of Minnesota.

Pope, V. (1998, Sept. 28). "For love or loyalty?" *U.S. News and World Report*, pp. 25, 30–31, 34.

Popkin, S. L. (1997). "Voter learning in the 1992 presidential campaign." In S. Iyengar and R. Reeves (eds.), *Do the media govern? Politicians, voters, and reporters in America* (pp. 171–180). Thousand Oaks, CA: Sage.

Powers, W. (1996, March 12). "Time, engaging in 'blood sport.'" *Washington Post*, p. D7.

Press, C., and Verburg, K. (1988). *American politicians and journalists*. Glenview, IL: Scott, Foresman.

Pruden, W. (1998, Oct. 2). "The path to power for Hillary Rodham." *Washington Times*, p. A4.

Purdam, T. (1995, July 24). "The first lady's newest role: Newspaper columnist." *New York Times*, p. A10.

Quinn, S. (1992, Dec. 28). "Beware of Washington." *Newsweek*, p. 24.

Radcliffe, D. (1993). *Hillary Rodham Clinton: A First Lady for our time*. New York: Warner.

Reedy, G. E. (1970). *The twilight of the presidency*. New York: New American Library.

Reeves, R. (1983, Dec. 22). "Is the press out to get Ed Meese?" Universal Press Syndicate.

———. (1996). *Running in place: How Bill Clinton disappointed America*. Kansas City: Andrews and McMeel.
———. (1997a). "Overview to Part I." In S. Iyengar and R. Reeves (eds.), *Do the media govern? Politicians, voters, and reporters in America* (pp. 3–5). Thousand Oaks, CA: Sage.
———. (1997b). "The brave new world of media politics." In S. Iyengar and R. Reeves (eds.), *Do the media govern? Politicians, voters, and reporters in America* (pp. ix–xx). Thousand Oaks, CA: Sage.
———. (1997c). "The question of media bias." In S. Iyengar and R. Reeves (eds.), *Do the media govern? Politicians, voters, and reporters in America* (pp. 40–49). Thousand Oaks, CA: Sage.
Reno, R. (1996, Apr. 2). "Do we need pledge that Mrs. Dole will know her place?" *Buffalo News*, p. B3.
Richie, R., and Naureckas, J. (1996). "Lani Guinier: Quota queen or misquoted queen?" In J. Naureckas and J. Jackson (eds.), *The Fair reader: An* Extra! *review of press and politics in the '90s* (pp. 132–136). Boulder, CO: Westview.
Robinson, M., and Sheehan, M. (1983). *Over the wire and on TV: CBS and UPI in campaign 80*. New York: Russell Sage Foundation.
Rosen, J., and Taylor, P. (1992). *The new news and the old news*. New York: Twentieth Century Fund.
Rosenstiel, R. (1994). *The beat goes on: President Clinton's first year with the media*. New York: Twentieth Century Fund.
Rozell, M. J. (1996). *In contempt of Congress: Postwar press coverage on Capitol Hill*. Westport, CT: Praeger.
Sabato, L. J. (1991). *Feeding frenzy: How attack journalism has transformed American politics*. New York: Free Press.
———. (1998. Sept. 2). "Media frenzies in our time." *Washington Post*. Available at: http://www.washingtonpost.com/wp-s . . . /special/clinton/frenzy/frenzy.htm.
Sabato, L. J., and Lichter, S. R. (1994). *When should the watchdogs bark? Media coverage of the Clinton scandals*. Washington, D.C.: Center for Media and Public Affairs.
Sallee, S. (1996). "Ellen Axson Wilson." In L.L. Gould (ed.), *American First Ladies: Their lives and their legacy* (pp. 340–354). New York: Garland.
Schorr, D. (1997). "Who uses whom?" In S. Iyengar and R. Reeves (eds.), *Do the media govern? Politicians, voters, and reporters in America* (pp. 132–137). Thousand Oaks, CA: Sage.
Schwartz, A. (1992, Jan. 29). "Endless questions." *Washington Post*, p. A21.
Severn, S. (1996). "Frances Folsom Cleveland." In L.L. Gould (ed.), *American First Ladies: Their lives and their legacy* (pp. 243–259). New York: Garland.
Shales, T. (1980, Jan. 30). "Petty for Teddy." *Washington Post*, p. B11.
Shogren, E. (1998, Aug. 11). "First Lady works at being first in hearts." *Oregonian*, pp. A1, A6.

Sigal, L.V. (1973). *Reporters and officials*. Lexington, MA: D. C. Heath.
Simonton, D. K. (1996, Sept.). "Presidents' wives and First Ladies: On achieving eminence within a traditional gender role." *Sex Roles, 35*, 309–336.
Skiba, K. M. (1998, Sept. 13). "I just try to ignore it." *Milwaukee Journal Sentinel*, p. 18.
Smith, J. (1998, Sept. 25). "Are we ready to laugh at Jackie O? A new satirical play dares to send up Jacqueline Lee Bouvier Kennedy Onassis. Joan Smith asks if the same could be done for that other First Lady with a philandering husband, Hillary Clinton." *Guardian*, (Manchester), pp. T002–T004.
Smith, K. B. (1996). "Rosalynn Carter." In L. L. Gould (ed.), *American First Ladies: Their lives and their legacy* (pp. 556–607). New York: Garland.
Sobieraj, S. (1998, Sept. 11). "First Lady stands by her president." *Erie (PA) Daily Times*, p. 4A.
Sparrow, B. H. (1999). *Uncertain guardians: The news media as a political institution*. Baltimore: Johns Hopkins University Press.
Squires, J. (1993). *Read all about it!* New York: Times Books.
Stewart, J. B. (1996). *Blood sport: The president and his adversaries*. New York: Simon & Schuster.
"Sunday Comment: The next first lady profile: Hillary Clinton. Despite her humiliations, Mrs. Clinton is planning her most dramatic makeover." 1999, Feb. 21. *Daily Telegraph* (London), p. 35. Available at: http://proquest.umi.com/pqdweb?TS=919698 . . . 1&Fmt=3&Sid=3&Idx=1&Deli=1&RQT=309&Dtp=1.
"Tabloid prints new Bill Clinton infidelity allegations." (1992, Jan. 23). Transcript of *Nightline*.
Teasley, M. M. (1996). "Mamie Eisenhower." In L. L. Gould (ed.), *American First Ladies: Their lives and their legacy* (pp. 463–475). New York: Garland.
Templin, C. (1999, Jan.). "Hillary Clinton as threat to gender norms: Cartoon images of the First Lady." *Journal of Communication Inquiry, 23*, 20–36.
Terry, S. (1998, Sept. 23). "First Lady as mirror for America." *Christian Science Monitor*, p. 1.
Trent, J., and Friedenberg, R. V. (1995). *Political campaign communication* (3rd ed.). Westport, CT: Praeger.
Tullis, J. K. (1987). *The rhetorical presidency*. Princeton, NJ: Princeton University Press.
Tumulty, K., and Gibbs, N. (1999, Jan.). "Man of the Year 1998: The better half." *Time*. Available at: http://cgi.pathfinder.com/time/moy/hillary.html.
Underwood, D. (1998). "Market research and the audience for political news." In D. Graber, D. McQuail and P. Norris (eds.), *The politics of news: The news of politics* (pp. 171–192). Washington, D.C.: CQ Press.
Viles, P. (1993, Feb. 15). "Clinton carries on Saturday tradition." *Broadcasting*, p. 28.

Walsh, K. (1998a, May ll). "The survivalist: How does Hillary Clinton cope with the barrage of sex scandal charges? By launching a national campaign to make people be nicer." *U.S. News and World Report*. Available at: http://www.usnews.com/usnews/issue/980511/11hill.htm.

———. (1998b, Sept. 28). "Can she save him?" *U.S. News and World Report*, pp. 22–24.

Wasserstein, W. (1998, Aug. 25). "Hillary Clinton's muddled legacy." *New York Times*. Available at: http://www.froungpagemag.com/clinton/fem-hillary.htm.

Will, G. (1987, Mar. 1). "Tower report kind to slothful Reagan." *Washington Post Writer's Group*.

Williams, P. (1993, Jan. 26). "Bewitched: The demonization of Hillary Clinton." *Village Voice*, pp. 35–39.

Wills, G. (1997, Jan. 19.) "The Clinton principle." *New York Times*. Available at: http://www.searchnyx's.com/.

Windt, Jr., T. O. (1973). "The presidency and speeches on international crises: Repeating the rhetorical past." *Speaker and Gavel*, 2, 6–14.

Winett, L. (1997). "Advocate's guide to developing framing memos." In S. Iyengar and R. Reeves (eds.), *Do the media govern? Politicians, voters, and reporters in America* (pp. 420–427). Thousand Oaks, CA: Sage.

Winfield, B. A. (1994). *FDR and the news media*. New York: Columbia University Press.

Woodward, B. (1999). *Shadow: Five presidents and the legacy of Watergate*. New York: Simon & Schuster.

Worland, G. (1998, Sept. 4). "Scandals throughout presidential history." *Washington Post*. Available at: http://www.washingtonpost.com/wp- s . . . clinton/stories/scandalhistory.htm.

Young, N. B. (1996). "Eliza Johnson." In L. L. Gould (ed.), *American First Ladies: Their lives and their legacy* (pp. 191–201). New York: Garland.

Index

ABC, 47, 48, 56, 79, 80, 87, 160, 171, 207
Accuracy in Media, 47
Adams, Abigail, 6, 9, 22, 23, 120
Adams, John, 6, 11, 12, 23
"adversarial reporting," 61
Albright, Madeleine, 208
Aldrich, Gary, 229
Alter, Jonathan, 109, 202
Altman, Roger, 176
American Conservative Union, 115
American Council for Health Care Reform, 169
American Lawyer, 195
American Spectator, 47, 78, 80, 90, 193, 194, 195, 227
America's Most Wanted, 79
Anderson, Jack, 59
Anthony, Carl Sferrazza, 21, 130
AP (Associated Press), 32, 47, 60
Apple, R. W., Jr., 250
Arkansas Democrat-Gazette, 152, 221
Arkansas Development Financial Authority, 246

Arkansas state troopers. *See* Jones, Paula, and Troopergate
Arlington National Cemetery, burial plots, selling, 77
Arsenio Hall Show, 161
Association of American Physicians and Surgeons, 169
Atlantic Monthly, 66
Atlantic Monthly Press, 71
"attack journalism," 72
Atwater, Lee, 245

Baer, Don, 110, 117
Baird, Zoe, 157
Baker, Bobby, 84
Baker, Peter, 109, 207
Balz, Dan, 34, 160, 252
Barbour, Haley, 248
Barnes, Fred, 32, 78
Barone, Michael, 175
Bedard, Paul, 236
Beecher, Henry Ward, 123
Begala, Paul, 34, 58, 111, 207, 208, 209, 247
Bennet, James, 109, 112, 200
Bennett, Bill, 208

Bennett, Robert, 178, 195, 196, 197, 201, 207
Bennetts, Leslie, 191
Bentsen, Lloyd, 245
Bernstein, Carl, 37
Berry, Marsha, 229, 233
Biden, Joseph, 31, 90, 154
Blackman, Ann, 228
Blackman, James, 200
Blaine, James G., 96
Blair, James, 189, 190
Blauvelt Family Genealogy, 101–2
Blitzer, Wolf, 34, 76, 197, 202, 209
Blumenthal, Sidney, 111
Bond, Rich, 244
Bone, Robert L. "Red," 189
Bonnolly, Ceci, 34
Borders, Rebecca, 90
Boston Globe, 73, 221
Bowles, Erskine, 48, 111
Boxer, Barbara, 273
Bradlee, Ben, 51, 100, 102
Brant, Martha, 228
Braver, Rita, 81, 108, 112; fundraising scandal, 200, 201, 202; Paula Jones and Troopergate, 196; Whitewater, 177
Brinkley, David, 102
Britton, Nan, 97, 131, 132
Brock, David, 193
Broder, David, 82, 193
Brokaw, Tom, 60, 79, 108, 202
Brown, Floyd, 47
Brown, Jerry, 155, 162
Brownstein, Ron, 62, 117, 208
Brummet, John, 152
Bryant, William Jennings, 125
Buchanan, Patrick, 223, 224
Buffalo Evening Telegraph, 96
"bully pulpit," 95, 107
burial plots, selling. *See* Arlington National Cemetery, burial plots, selling
Burke, Kenneth, xiii
Burton, Dan, 202

Bush, Barbara (Pierce), xii, 8, 10, 13, 16, 17, 243; background, 22, 23; crisis management style, with George Bush, 147–48; role as First Lady, 4
Bush, George, 27, 30, 93, 154, 230, 245, 249; Hillary Clinton, criticism of, 245; crisis management style, with Barbara Bush, 147–48
Bush, George W., 148
Business Week, 31
Butz, Earl, 89

cable television, 53
Cammarata, Joseph, 76
Campbell (Exner), Judith, 101
Capital Cities/ABC, 66, 67
Caputo, Lisa, 113, 186
Cardozo, Michael, 199
Carlson, Margaret, 279
Caroli, Betty, 20, 21
Carson, Johnny, 161
Carter, Billy, 119
Carter, Eleanor Rosalynn (Smith), 13, 21, 170, 225; crisis management style, with Jimmy Carter, 145–46; role as First Lady, 4
Carter, Jimmy, 12, 27, 86, 119, 120, 154, 249, 274; crisis management style, with Rosalynn Carter, 145–46; and "Killer Rabbit," 32; *Playboy* interview, 154; press relations, 104–5
Carville, James, 163, 165, 222; health care reform, 169; Lewinsky scandal, 209; Whitewater, 178
Casey, Paula, 157
Castle Grande, 175, 180, 188, 193. *See also* Whitewater
Castro, Fidel, 101
Cateledge, Turner, 98
CBS, 47, 48, 56, 67, 71, 72, 75, 87; corporation holdings, 66; fundraising scandal, 201, 202; Paula Jones

and Troopergate, 194; Kathleen Willey, 76
Chancellor, William, 133
Chandler, Otis, 103
Chappaquiddick. *See* Kennedy, Edward, Chappaquiddick
Chicago Sun-Times, 156
Chicago Tribune, 71, 138, 139, 234
Christian Science Monitor, 221
Chung, Connie, 79
Cisneros, Henry, 235
Citizens United, 47
Cleveland, Frances (Folsom), xi, 1, 9, 23; crisis management style, with Grover Cleveland, 123–24
Cleveland, Grover, xi, 20, 23; crisis management style, with Frances Cleveland, 123–24; scandals, 96
Clift, Eleanor, 220, 250, 281
Clinton, Bill, 34, 56, 62, 72, 119; Hillary Clinton: as political partner with, 6, 14, 17, 18–19, as problem for, 152–55; draft scandal, 160–61; Gennifer Flowers scandal, 78, 161–62; fundraising scandal, 198–203; gays in military, 45–46; as Governor of Arkansas, 218, 219, 220; haircut on Air Force One, 108, 158; health care scandal, 168–72; "I didn't inhale," 155–56; impeachment, 213–15; and Paula Jones and Troopergate, 193–97; and Monica Lewinsky scandal, 19, 204–12; press relations, 107–8, 235–36; Franklin Roosevelt, compared to, 98; *60 Minutes* interview, 162–66; surrogates, use of, 236; Whitewater, 172–80; and Kathleen Willey, 77
Clinton, Chelsea, 197, 222, 226, 232, 264
Clinton, Hillary Rodham, 1, 5, 12–13; background, 22; Bill Clinton: as political partner with, 6, 14, 17, 18–19, as surrogate for, 233–41; as First Lady: changing image of, 225, as media-savvy, 230–33, role as, 21; and Vince Foster: intimate rumor, 91, suicide and Filegate, 185–89; "framing," in media, use of, 249–50, 254, 257, 261; health care reform, 11, 13; "performative" language, use of, 251–52; press criticism of, 14, 15, 16, 17, 18; "priming," in media, use of, 240–41, 225; public perception of, 4; Eleanor Roosevelt: compared to, 20, 21, 275, 276, "conversations with," 159; subtext, use of, 252–55; works: *It Takes a Village: and Other Lessons Children Teach Us,* 15, 225, 226, "Talking it Over" column, 225
Clinton, Hillary Rodham-crisis management: George Bush's mistress gaffe, 156; cattle futures trading, 189–91; "cookie" gaffe, 155; draft scandal, 160–61; Gennifer Flowers scandal, 161–62; fundraising scandal, 198–203; Lani Guinier nomination, 158–59; health care reform, 168–72; Webster Hubbel scandal, 191–93; impeachment, 213–15; Paula Jones and Troopergate, 193–97; Monica Lewinsky scandal, 204–12; Nannygate, 156–57; *Prime Time Live* interview, 166–67; *60 Minutes* interview, 162–66; throwing the lamp incident, 156; Travelgate, 181–85; West Wing office, 157–58; Whitewater, 172–80
Clinton Hillary Rodham-rhetoric: apology, 265–67; beat-them-at-their-own-game, 255–63; blaming, 267–69; common ground, 263–65; evolution of: as First Lady of Arkansas, 218–21, as First Lady of the United States, 221–29; fair fight, 271–72; fatigue

factor, 247–55; honest and humble, 273–75; invention, 275–80; logic, 273; martyr, 272–73; privacy, 270; scapegoating, 244–47; strength through diversity, 270–71
CNN, 47, 49, 51, 66, 72, 92, 153; burial plots, 77; Gennifer Flowers, 91; fundraising scandal, 203; Paula Jones and Troopergate, 194, 195; Monica Lewinsky scandal, 209
Cohen, Richard, 33, 109, 202, 237
Cole, Augusta, 131
Coolidge, Calvin, 69
Coolidge, Grace, 9–10, 22
Cornelius, Catherine, 182
Cornell, Douglas, 82
Cox, James, 134
"credence good," 42
Cronkite, Walter, 53, 60
Cross, Grace, 131
Crouse, Timothy, 61
C-SPAN, 115, 203
Current Affair, A, 73, 78, 79
Currie, Betty, 208, 211
Cutler, Lloyd, 187

Daily Sentinel, 268
Dale, Billy, 182, 183, 193
Dallas Morning News, 80
D'Amato, Alfonse, 91
Davis, Lanny, 92, 111, 115, 191, 192, 198, 200, 207
Deaver, Michael, 106, 117
"Deep Throat," 36
Democratic Leadership Council, 220
Democratic National Committee, 77, 248
Democratic Sentinel, 96
Dentzer, Susan, 117
Des Moines Register, 70
Dewey, Frances, 137
Dewey, Thomas, 137
Dickerson, Nancy, 103
Dickey, Helen, 91

Dionne, E.J., 31, 62, 109, 111, 117, 208, 267
"discursive symbols," 54, 55
Disney Company, holdings, 66, 67
Dole, Bob, 16, 111, 185; criticism of Hillary Clinton, 244–45
Dole, Elizabeth, 16, 17
Donaldson, Sam, 108, 166–67; Gennifer Flowers scandal, 268–69; impeachment, 213; Paula Jones and Troopergate, 195
Dornan, Robert, 40
Dougherty, Jill, 200
Douglas, Stephen, 120
Dow Jones Company, 66, 67
Dowd, Maureen, 77, 78, 109, 113, 196, 211, 228
Drudge, Matt, 76, 204, 205
Drudge Report, 74, 76, 207
Dukakis, Kitty, 147
Dukakis, Michael, 147, 154, 161, 265
Dwyer, R. Budd, 88

Eagleton, Thomas, 85, 90, 154
Economist, The, 31
Edelman, Marian Wright, 157
Edelman, Murray, 42
Eisendrath, Charles, 88
Eisenhower, Dwight D., xi, 23; crisis management style, with Mamie Eisenhower, 141–42; press relations, 96
Eisenhower, Geneva "Mamie" (Doud), xi, 8, 10, 19, 21, 23; crisis management style, with Dwight Eisenhower, 141–42; press criticism of, 14; role as First Lady, 3
Eisenhower, John, 141
electronic media. *See* cable television; Internet; radio; television
Emanuel, Rahm, 48, 49, 110, 117, 118; Paula Jones and Troopergate, 196, 197; Monica Lewinsky scandal, 209
Evans-Prichard, Ambrose, 91

Fabiana, Mark, 110, 115, 176
Face the Nation, 196, 209
Falwell, Jerry, 47
Farrakhan, Louis, 89
Federal Advisory Committee Act (FACA), 169, 170
"feeding frenzy," in media, 154
Ferraro, Geraldine, 31, 90, 119, 148, 154, 274
Filegate. *See* Clinton, Hillary Rodham, and Vince Foster, suicide and Filegate
Fillmore, Abigail, 11
Fillmore, Millard, 11
First Lady: ideal, 120; origin of term, 6; paradox, 8–9, 14; public perception of, 9; role, xvi, evolution of role, 1–4, 5, 8, 9, 12, 13, 21, 22
Fiske, Robert, 174, 175, 177
Fitzwater, Marlin, 283
Flowers, Gennifer, 17, 62, 73, 74, 78, 80, 90, 91, 161–62, 163, 164, 165, 178, 266, 268, 269
Ford, Betty, 4, 9, 22
Ford, Gerald, 31, 32, 86, 230, 249; press relations, 96, 104; surrogates, use of, 235
Foster, Vincent, 15, 74, 90; and Hillary Clinton: intimate rumor, 91, suicide aftermath, 185–89; and Travelgate, 181, 183; and Whitewater, 175, 177, 180
"fourth estate." *See* news media, as "fourth estate"
Fox News Sunday, 209
"framing," in news media, 27–31, 43, 45, 51, 152, 158, 224, 231; Hillary Clinton, use of, 249–50, 254, 257, 261; defined, 28; "subtextual," 31–33
Frantz, Doug, 40
Freneau, Phil, 58
Friedman, Tom, 211
Friendly, Fred, 61
Frost, David, 264

Fulbright, William, 160

Gannett, Frank, 45
Gannett Company, 67, 70
Garfield, James, xv
Garfield, Lucretia "Crete," xv, 12, 123
General Electric, 66
Gergen, David, 51, 110
Germond, Jack, 31, 84
Gerth, Jeff, 92, 109, 173, 178, 192, 211
Giancana, Sam, 101
Gingrich, Newt, 34, 111, 116, 195, 214, 215, 248
Ginsberg, William, 204
Ginsburg, Allen, 90
Ginsburg, Ruth Bader, 235
Glascock, Darrell, 246
Goldberg, Lucianne, 81, 204, 205
Good Housekeeping, 113, 135
Good Morning America, 147, 213
Gore, Al, 5, 26, 220; and fundraising scandal, 198, 199, 200; and Monica Lewinsky scandal, 208
Gore, Tipper, 22, 264
Gould, Lewis L., 281
Graham, Katherine, 102
Grant, Julia, 12, 123
Grant, Ulysses S., 12
Greenberg, Paul, 220
Greensberg, Stan, 222
Greensfield, Jeff, 89, 93
Greer, Frank, 222
Griffin, Merv, 79
Guinier, Lani, 158–59

Hagner, Isabelle "Belle," 1
Haig, Alexander, 252
Hale, David, 174, 175
Halprin, Maria, 123
Hamilton, Alexander, 83
Hard Copy, 78
Harding, Florence "Mabel" (Kling), xv, xvii, 12, 19, 22; crisis manage-

ment style, with Warren Harding, 130–34; press criticism of, 4
Harding, Warren G., xv, 12, 83, 96, 97; crisis management style, with Florence Harding, 130–34
Harris, John, 49, 109, 116
Harrison, Benjamin-Caroline Harrison, crisis management style, 124–25
Hart, Gary, 32, 33, 58, 86, 90, 93, 154, 161, 221, 230, 255, 260
Hart, Lee, 221, 233, 260
Hayes, Lucy Webb, 1, 14, 122–23
Hayes, Rutherford B., 122–23
health care reform, media influence on, 72
Health Care Security Act, 168
Hearst, William Randolph, 69, 83, 99
Helm, Edith, 10
Herman, George, 103, 142
Hermann, Margaret, 153
Heywood, Andrew, 153
Hickok, Lorena, 136
Holmes, Eugene, 160
Hoover, Herbert, 97, 134–35
Hoover, Lou (Henry), 134–35
Houston Chronicle, 234
Howe, Louis, 136
Hoyle, Rosa Cecilia, 131
Huang, John, 200, 203
Hubbell, Webster, 15, 48, 180, 191–93
Huber, Carolyn, 188
Hume, Brit, 31, 108, 201, 235
Hunt, Al, 174, 175

Ickes, Harold, 110, 199
Ifil, Gwen, 191
Imus, Don, 196, 229
Industrial Development Company (IDC), 180
"infotainment," 87
Inside Edition, 78
Inside Politics, 92
Insight magazine, 77

Internet, 56
Iran hostage crisis, 104, 105
Iran-contra scandal, 107
Irvine, Reed, 47
Isikoff, Michael, 76, 204, 205, 207, 208, 214, 252–53

Jackson, Andrew, 68, 83
Jackson, Jesse, 89, 154
Jefferson, Thomas, 11, 37, 83
Jennings, Peter, 59, 203
Johnson, Andrew, crisis management style, with Eliza Johnson,121–22
Johnson, Claudia Alta "Lady Bird" (Taylor), xv, 8, 12, 13, 19, 22, 23, 225; crisis management style, with Lyndon Johnson, 143–44; role as First Lady, 4
Johnson, Eliza (McCardle), 11; crisis management style, with Andrew Johnson,121–22
Johnson, Lyndon, xv, 12, 31, 60, 85, 86; crisis management style, with Lady Bird Johnson, 143–44; press relations, 96, 102–3
Jones, Paula, 20, 47, 76, 90, 180, 204, 207; and Troopergate, 47, 78, 193–97
Jordan, Vernon, 203, 205, 206
journalism, "junkyard," 85; "lapdog," 84; market-oriented, 72; "muckraking," 83; "yellow," 69, 83

Kansas City Star, 48
Kaus, Mickey, 169
KDKA, 40
Keillor, Garrison, 38
Kelly, Michael, 113, 192
Kemp, Jack, 154
Kendall, David, 192
Kennedy, Edward, 168, 260; Chappaquiddick, 85, 86, 259, 273
Kennedy, Jacqueline (Bouvier) (Onassis), xv, 4, 8, 19, 23; crisis management style, with John Ken-

nedy, 142–43; role as First Lady, 3, 10–11
Kennedy, Joan, 260
Kennedy, John F., xv, 16, 82, 84, 85, 86, 230; Bay of Pigs crisis, 101; crisis management style, with Jacqueline Kennedy, 142–43; press relations, 96, 101–2
Kennedy, William, 15, 180, 181, 193
Kiker, Douglas, 103
King, Larry, 52, 264
Kitt, Eartha, 143
Klein, Joe, 62, 109, 114, 152
Knight-Ridder, 67
Knoller, Mark, 34
Koppel, Ted, 58, 73, 197
Krauthammer, Charles, 81
Kroft, Steve, 163, 164, 266
Kurtz, Howard, 107, 282

Labaton, Steve, 178, 192, 211
Lamm, Richard, 89
Landon, Mrs. Alfred M., 137
Lane, Harriet, 13
Lardner, George, 33
Lauer, Matt, 210
Lawrence, Larry, 77, 78
Legal Affairs Council, 194
Lehane, Chris, 92
Lehrer, Jim, 208, 213, 236
Leno, Jay, 88
Letterman, David, 229
Lewinsky, Monica, 18, 19, 80, 119, 204–12, 229
Lewis, Ann, 111, 117, 209, 210, 236–37
Liddy, G. Gordon, 77
Lieberman, Evelyn, 198
Limbaugh, Rush, 40, 52, 74, 77, 186
Lincoln, Abraham, 68; crisis management style, with Mary Lincoln, 120–21
Lincoln, Mary (Todd), 1, 6, 11–12, 13, 22; crisis management style, with Abraham Lincoln, 120–21

Lindsey, Bruce, 110, 163, 201
Lippmann, Walter, 25, 27, 114
Long, Earl, 84
Los Angeles Times, 32, 39–40, 40, 46, 66, 71, 74, 78, 109; burial plots story, 77; Paula Jones and Troopergate, 193, 195; Monica Lewinsky scandal, 204, 207, 211
Lou Harris organization, 70
Lowey, Nita, 212
Luce, Clare Booth, 141
Luce, Henry, 45, 98, 99
Lujan, Manuel, 235
Lydon, Christopher, 73
Lyons, James, 173

MacArthur, Douglas, 100
Macmilan, Harold, 5
Madison, Dolley, 1, 6, 11, 13, 14
Madison Guaranty Savings and Loan, 173, 174, 176, 187, 188. *See also* Whitewater
magazines, influence of, 46–51. *See also* print media, nature of; *and names of specific magazines*
Marshal, Thomas Riley, 129
Mashek, John, 102
Matalin, Mary, 235
Matsui, Doris, 200
McAlary, Mike, 115
McCarthy, Joseph R., 60, 139, 140
McCormick, Colonel, 45
McCormick-Patterson newspapers, 99
McCurry, Mike, 56, 58, 90, 92, 108, 110, 111, 114, 115, 116, 228, 232, 248; burial plots story, 77; Hillary Clinton-Vince Foster, intimate rumor, 91; fundraising scandal, 198, 199, 201, 203; Webster Hubbel, 191, 193; Paula Jones and Troopergate, 196, 197; Monica Lewinsky scandal, 207, 211; as surrogate, 236; Whitewater, 178

McDougal, James, 172, 173, 179, 187, 193
McDougal, Susan, 172, 174, 180, 193
McKinley, Ida (Saxon), 123, 125–26
McKinley, William, 125–26
McLarty, Thomas "Mack," 110
McLaughlin, John, 175
McManus, John, 52, 56
McRae, Tom, 220, 221
Media. *See* news media; print media, nature of
"media technocrats," 107
Meese, Edwin III, 88–89
Meet the Press, 197, 209
Mercer, Lucy, 98, 135, 138
Metzenbaum, Howard, 169
Meyer, Karl, 240
Miami Herald, 33, 48, 57, 260
Miklaszewski, Jim, 108, 235–36
Mikva, Abner, 187
Miller, Alan, 92, 109
Mirabella, 113
Mitchell, Alison, 48, 49, 109, 203
Mitchell, George, 168
Mondale, Walter, 86, 119
Monroe, Elizabeth, 13
Morris, Dick, 110, 211, 213, 218, 220, 221, 227
Morris, Roger, 229
Morrison, Pat, 265
Moyers, Bill, 38
Moynihan, Patrick, 74
MSNBC, 49, 203
MTV, 54
"muckraking." *See* journalism, "muckraking"
Murdoch, Rupert, 79
Murphy Brown, 244
Murrow, Edward R., 69
Muskie, Edmund, 5, 154
Myers, Dee Dee, 110

NAFTA, 72
narrative, in media, as symbolic action, 25–30

Nation, The, 47, 175
National Enquirer, 52, 76, 91
National Gazette, 83
National Legal and Policy Center, 169
NBC, 45, 47, 48, 56, 66, 71, 72, 79, 87, 194
Nelson, Sheffield, 268
New Republic, 175
New York Daily News, 66, 91, 203
New York Post, 82, 91, 209
New York Sun, 68, 83
New York Times, 31, 46, 47, 48, 49, 52, 58, 62, 67, 74, 80, 81, 82, 109, 112, 232, 236, 245, 248, 250, 264; burial plots story, 77; cattle futures trading, 189, 191; Bill Clinton, comparing to Theodore Roosevelt, 116; First Lady, evolving role of, 5; fundraising scandal, 200; Webster Hubbel scandal, 192; importance of, 259; Paula Jones and Troopergate, 196, 197; Monica Lewinsky scandal, 81; Mary Lincoln, 121; Ed Meese, 89; New York Times Company, 66, 67; Travelgate, 184; Kathleen Willey, 77
New York Times Magazine, 113, 184
New York World, 40
New Yorker The 81, 109
Newfield, Jack, 175
news media, xi, 27, 28; as "fourth branch," 35; as "fourth estate," 33, 34, 39; "framing" in media: 27–31, 43, 45, 51, 152, 158, 224, 231, "subtextual framing," 31–33; as government institution, 33–40; power of, 43–46; "priming" in media, 27, 29, 254; public's reliance on, 40–43; relations with presidents, 37, 38; role in democracy, 41, 42; as scandal-driven, 80–93; sex, aversion to, 250–51. *See also* magazines; newspapers; radio;

television; *and under specific names*
Newsday, 71, 77, 82, 108, 158
newspapers, 46, 60; in colonial times, 68; influence of, 46–51; mass circulation, origins of, 40; "penny press": 40, 68, 69, origins of, 83; syndicates, 70; tabloids, 69, 73–80, 81. *See also* news media; print media, nature of; *and names of specific newspapers*
Newsweek, 66, 70, 75, 77, 80, 102, 113, 234, 249; cattle futures trading, 189; Hillary Clinton, and health care reform, 169; Gennifer Flowers, 162; Paula Jones and Troopergate, 195, 197; Jacqueline Kennedy, 143; lamp throwing incident, 156; Monica Lewinsky scandal, 204, 205, 206, 207
Nexis, 80
Nichols, Larry, 268
Nightline, 73, 77, 161, 179, 180
Nixon, Patricia Thelma Catherine (Ryan), xv, 4, 10; crisis management style, with Richard Nixon, 144–45
Nixon, Richard M., xv, 84, 85, 86, 119, 274; "Checker's speech," 144; crisis management style, with Pat Nixon, 144–45; press relations, 103–4; psychotherapist, consultation with, 103; surrogates, use of, 235
North, Oliver, 77
NPR (National Public Radio), 154
Nussbaum, Bernard, 15, 180, 181, 187

Odum, Reathel, 10
Oliphant, Thomas, 73, 74
Orin, Deborah, 209
Orwell, George, 104

Packwood, Bob, 250

Page, Susan, 48, 203
Panetta, Leon, 110, 226
Patrick, Deval, 159
Patterson, Martha Johnson, 122
PBS (Public Broadcasting System), 213
Peck, Mary Allen Hulbert, 21, 128
Pelly, Scott, 250
Pendleton, C.H., 123
Penn, Mark, 48
"penny press," 40, 68, 69; origins of, 83
People magazine, 260
Perdue, Sally, 91
Perot, Ross, 26, 27
Philadelphia Aurora, 59
Phillips, Carrie, 131
Pierpoint, John, 82
Pierpoint, Robert, 142
Pious, Robert, 61
Plante, Bill, 76, 236
Playboy, 32, 105
Podesta, John, 111, 191, 201, 237
Polk, James Knox, 23
Polk, Sarah, 11, 23
Powell, Adam Clayton Jr., 140, 141, 249
Powell, Colin, 249
Powell, Jody, 104
Prairie Home Companion, 38
"presentation symbols," 55
President's Task Force on National Health Care Reform, 169
press conferences, televised, origins, 100
Prime Time Live, 195, 268; interview with Hillary Clinton, 166–67
"priming," in media, 27, 254; defined, 29. *See also* news media
print media, nature of, 46, 49–51, 54, 55
Pulitzer, Joseph, 40, 69, 83

Quayle, Dan, 31, 81, 90, 154, 244, 245, 267

Quayle, Marilyn, 233
Quinn, Jack, 198
Quinn, Sally, 239

radio, development of, 40
Rather, Dan, 108
RCA, 71
Reagan, Nancy Anne Frances Robins (Davis), xvii, 10, 13–14, 22, 23; crisis management style, with Ronald Reagan, 146–47; role as First Lady, 4, 7, 12
Reagan, Ronald, 10, 12, 27, 32, 55, 119, 230; Bitberg scandal, 217; crisis management style, with Nancy Reagan, 146–47; criticism, response to, 233; press relations, 96, 105–7
Rebozo, Charles "Bebe," 103
Redbook, 113
Reedy, George, 107
Reeves, Richard, 5, 39, 52, 63, 89, 107, 111, 116, 152, 226, 227, 282, 283
Regan, Donald, 147
Rehm, Diane, 154
Rempel, Bill, 40
Reno, Janet, 157, 177
reporters, as mediators, 57–63
Republican National Committee, 268
Republican National Convention, 244
Resolution Trust Corporation, 173, 174, 180, 187. *See also* Whitewater
Reuters, 47
Rice, Donna, 32, 33, 58, 93, 154, 255, 260
Richards, Ann, 148
Robb, Charles, 79, 93
Roberts, Cokie, 34
Roberts, Steve, 34
Robertson, Pat, 47, 90, 93
Rolling Stone, 236
Roosevelt, Edith Kermit, 2, 120

Roosevelt, Eleanor, xv, xvii, 2, 8, 9, 10, 19, 170; Hillary Clinton, likeness to, 20, 21; crisis management style, with Franklin Roosevelt, 135–39; media, relations with, 3; press criticism of, 13; role as First Lady, 7; works: "My Day" column, 3, 137
Roosevelt, Franklin D., xv, 2, 21, 55, 82, 84, 275; crisis management style, with Eleanor Roosevelt, 135–39; press relations, 84, 96, 97–98
Roosevelt, Theodore, 2, 83, 95, 116, 126, 127
Rose, Charlie, 197
Rose Law Firm, 15, 180, 191, 193
Rowan, Carl, 34
Ruff, Charles, 178
Russert, Tim, 81

Safire, William, 109, 155, 175, 188, 228
"salience influence," 29
Salinger, Pierre, 100, 101
San Francisco Examiner, 191
"satisfice," 29–30
Scaife, Richard Mellon, 91
Schmidt, Susan, 92, 176, 178, 207
Schorr, Daniel, 103
Schumer, Charles, 273
Scott, Hazel, 141
Scott, Marsha, 90
Scripps-Howard newspapers, 99
Seattle Post-Intelligencer, 48
Seib, Charles, 88, 117
Seper, Jerry, 236
"sexual McCarthyism," 20
Shapiro, Walter, 32
Sheehy, Gail, 156, 165
Shipman, Claire, 179
Shogan, Bob, 32
Shribman, David, 117
Simpson, Glenn, 92, 109
Simpson, O. J., 43, 46, 72, 111

INDEX

Sinatra, Frank, 101
Sinclair, Upton, 83
60 Minutes, 17, 62, 73, 78, 161, 227, 251, 266, 267; interview with Clintons, 162–66
64 Thousand Dollar Question, 70
Sketch of the Life of Mrs. William McKinley, 126
Sklar, Kitty, xvii
Smith, Hedrick, 106
Solomon, John, 92
Sosnik, Doug, 111
Speakes, Larry, 105, 106
Sperling, Godfrey, 221
Sperling Breakfast, 221
St. Louis Post-Dispatch, 96
Stahl, Lesley, 108
Star tabloid, 73, 78, 91, 162, 163, 268
Starr, Blaze, 84
Starr, Kenneth, 19, 175, 177, 178, 182, 187, 261, 274; impeachment, 213, 214; Monica Lewinsky scandal, 204, 206, 208, 211, 212
Stephanopoulos, George, 110, 180, 208
Stephens, Jay, 180
Stewart, James B., 174, 229
Strobel, Warren, 92
"subtextual framing," in news media, 31–33
Summersby, Kay, 141, 142
Sunday Telegraph, 91
tabloid press, 73–80, 81

Taft, Helen "Nellie" (Herron), 2, 7, 12, 21, 123; crisis management style, with William Howard Taft, 126–27
Taft, William Howard, 12, 96; crisis management style, with Nellie Taft, 126–27
Tax Notes, 175
Taylor, Margaret, 13
Taylor, Paul, 93
Taylor, Zachary, 6

Teapot Dome scandal, 96, 97
television: development of, 40, 41, 53; as mediator, 51–57; nature of, 49–52, 53, 54, 55, 56; news: 28, origins, 69, 70; tabloid, 78, 79. *See also names of specific networks;* news media
terHorst, Jerald, 104
This Week, 197, 209
Thomas, Clarence, 46, 250
Thomas, Helen, 34
Thomas, Lowell, 69
Thomases, Susan, 157
Thomason, Harry, 161, 182, 183
Thomason, Linda Bloodworth, 161
Thomasson, Patsy, 186
Time, 4, 31, 45, 46, 66, 69, 75, 80, 113, 243, 249; Monica Lewinsky scandal, 81; political partnership of the Clintons, 23; Whitewater, 175
Time-Warner, 66, 67
Times-Mirror Company, 66
Today show, 210
Tonight Show, 161
Trie, Yah Lin "Charlie," 198, 199, 248
Tripp, Linda, 204, 205, 206, 208, 211
TRM, 182
Trohan, Walter, 139
Troopergate. *See* Jones, Paula, and Troopergate
Truman, Elizabeth Virginia "Bess" (Wallace), 3, 8, 9, 10, 22, 99; crisis management style, with Harry Truman, 139–41
Truman, Harry, 10, 96, 98–100, 274; crisis management style, with Bess Truman, 139–41
Tsongas, Paul, 155
Tucker, Jim Guy, 187
Tumulty, Karen, 232
Turner, Ted, 72
Turner Broadcasting, 66, 67
TV Guide, 113

310 INDEX

Twentieth Century Fox, 79
Tyler, Julia, 1, 11, 13, 14, 22
Tyson Foods, 189

U. S. News and World Report, 20, 66, 71, 113, 117, 194, 228
USA Today, 48, 49, 54, 70, 197; burial plots story, 77; fundraising scandal, 249; health care reform, 172; Paula Jones and Troopergate, 196, 197; Kathleen Willey story, 77

Vanity Fair, 113, 156, 191
Village Voice, 47
Vilsack, Tom, 241
Vlasta, Chris, 92
Vogue, 113

Wald, Patricia, 157
Wall Street Journal, 46, 66, 67, 70, 74, 80, 91, 92, 109; Hillary Clinton-Vince Foster, intimate rumor, 91; draft scandal, 160; fundraising scandal, 201; health care reform, 172
Wallace, Chris, 108
Wallace, Mike, 59
Walt Disney Company. *See* Disney Company
Walters, Maxine, 235
Wanamaker, John, 124, 125
Washington, George, 37, 58, 59
Washington, Martha, 4, 12, 13, 23
Washington Interfaith Network, 271
Washington Monthly, 174
Washington Post, 46, 47, 48, 49, 51, 62, 67, 74, 102, 113, 153, 248; burial plots story, 77; George Bush, 147; Mamie Eisenhower, 141; fundraising scandal, 198, 203, 248; haircut on Air Force One, 108, 158; health care reform, 172; Webster Hubbel scandal, 192; Paula Jones and Troopergate, 195, 197; Monica Lewinsky scandal, 204, 207, 208, 209, 211, 212; Eleanor Roosevelt, 139; Washington Post Company, 66, 103; Whitewater, 173, 174, 176, 177, 178, 180; Kathleen Willey story, 77; Edith Wilson, 128
Washington Times, 91, 197, 209
Watergate, 58, 273
Watkins, David, 90, 186, 188, 193
Watt, James, 89
Wattenberg, Daniel, 254
Weekly Reader, 71
Weiner, Tim, 200
Wellesley College, 264
Western Journalism Center, 91
Westinghouse, 67
WGN radio, 71
White, Frank, 218, 219, 220–21, 246
Whitewater, 14–15, 80, 171, 172–80
Whitewater Development Corporation, 172
Whitewater Senate Committee, 91
Wilder, Douglas, 220
Willey, Kathleen, 76, 77, 205
Williams, Brian, 108
Williams, Maggie, 113, 186, 225
Wilson, Edith Bolling (Galt), xv, 2, 4, 7, 12, 13; crisis management style, with Woodrow Wilson, 128–30
Wilson, Ellen "Louise" (Axson), 2, 10, 21; crisis management style, with Woodrow Wilson, 127–28
Wilson, Woodrow, xv, 2, 7, 12, 96; crisis management style: with Edith Wilson, 128–30, with Ellen Wilson, 127–28; and Mary Peck, 21
Winfrey, Oprah, 249
Winthrop Rockefeller Foundation, 220
Women's Leadership Forum, 274
Women's Wear Daily, 166
Wood, Kimba, 157
Woodruff, Judy, 108, 195

Woodward, Bob, 32, 37, 109, 177, 190, 198
Word Wide Travel, 182

Xerox, 71

"yellow journalism," 69, 83
Young Broadcasting, 67

Ziegler, Ron, 103
Zuckerman, Mortimer, 66

About the Author

COLLEEN ELIZABETH KELLEY is Assistant Professor of Speech Communication at Penn State Erie, The Behrend College. Professor Kelley is the coeditor (with Rod Troester) of *Peacemaking Through Communication* and has written various articles for learned journals.